The Problem of Democracy

The Problem of Democracy

America, the Middle East, and the Rise and Fall of an Idea

SHADI HAMID

OXFORD
UNIVERSITY PRESS

Oxford University Press is a department of the University of Oxford. It furthers
the University's objective of excellence in research, scholarship, and education
by publishing worldwide. Oxford is a registered trade mark of Oxford University
Press in the UK and certain other countries.

Published in the United States of America by Oxford University Press
198 Madison Avenue, New York, NY 10016, United States of America.

CIP data is on file at the Library of Congress

ISBN 978–0–19–757946–6

DOI: 10.1093/oso/9780197579466.001.0001

1 3 5 7 9 8 6 4 2

Printed by Sheridan Books, Inc., United States of America

Contents

Acknowledgments

I am a bit reticent to start with a cliché, but this really was a labor of love. And like any labor of love, there were moments when I wasn't sure if it would survive intact. But the fact that I am writing this, I suppose, is proof that it worked out in the end, although it is up to the reader to determine whether it worked out well.

It feels like a culmination. In one way or another, this book has been in the making for the entirety of my adult life. The themes and dilemmas discussed here are ones I have been wrestling with from when I was freshman in college in the days and months after September 11—and even earlier, although as a child I did not necessarily have the right words. But I had a feeling. Because my parents came from an authoritarian country, I was always attuned to the distinctiveness of democracy. I could not take it for granted. And I have tried my best not to take it for granted here. This book is my best attempt to marshal the various strands of my work from the past ten years and beyond into something suitably ambitious. I am not interested in tinkering around the margins, at least not anymore.

As is often the case, the book started one way and ended in another. That is part of what makes a project like this one exciting but also disorienting. One of the most thrilling things as a writer is to start a book not knowing how it will conclude. Until the very last moment, I did not know.

Considering the task at hand, I am more grateful than ever to those who encouraged me, believed in me, and helped make this book what it is. The Brookings Institution provided the ideal environment in which to read, research, to question myself, and to think about what I really wanted to do with this project. I am blessed to be part of an institution like Brookings that puts such a premium on ideas and letting them guide us, rather than the other way around. I am grateful to Suzanne Maloney, Michael O'Hanlon, and Natan Sachs for nurturing an environment that privileges long-form writing and serious, in-depth research. Each of them reviewed the full manuscript and generously offered extremely helpful suggestions for how to improve the book. With their characteristically thoughtful and sharp comments as a guide, the book became what I hoped it could be, and this, in turn, allowed me to let go in the end. It took some time, but I found a way to say what I wanted to say.

I am grateful to my research assistants who worked on the book over the course of these last couple years. In the beginning, and even before the beginning, Eliora Katz read early versions of the proposal and helped me refine the book's core arguments. As I dove into the writing, Israa Saber was a lifeline, and I am grateful for her guidance—and her ability to track anything and everything down in short order. Kevin Huggard reviewed the full manuscript and helped me reach the proverbial finish line, a line that I sometimes doubted I would reach.

I was blessed to be part of an intellectual community of friends and skeptics who constantly challenged me around core questions of democracy, pluralism, and American foreign policy. Some of these dear friends and sparring partners include Damir Marusic, Samuel Kimbriel, Christine Emba, Benjamin Haddad, Rachel Rizzo, Ani Chkhikvadze, Hannah Thoburn, Jamie Kirchick, John Hudson, Josh Glancy, Osita Nwavenu, Zack Beauchamp, and Ian Tuttle. Some of these unwieldly and fascinating debates took place within the Aspen Institute's Philosophy and Society "salons" in Washington, DC, a successful case of a book club becoming something more than a book club.

On all matters Middle East, Islamism, and democracy promotion, I am indebted to a group of brilliant scholars, teachers, and friends who influenced my research and writing in an endless number of ways. They include Peter Mandaville, John Voll, Michael Willis, Laurence Whitehead, Michael McFaul, Larry Diamond, Ovamir Anjum, Mustafa Akyol, Tarek Masoud, Nathan Brown, John Esposito, Michael Cook, Michelle Dunne, Tamara Wittes, Ken Pollack, Steven Brooke, Courtney Freer, Rashid Dar, Andrew March, Emad Shahin, Usaama al-Azami, Seth Anziska, Thomas Carothers, and Eugene Rogan.

And then, of course, there are so many people in Egypt, Jordan, Tunisia, and Turkey who were unfailingly generous with their time and attention that I cannot begin to list them all. Without them, this project simply would not have been possible. Tragically, many of my Egyptian interviewees are now either dead, in prison, or in exile. I pray and hope that they are not forgotten.

Many thanks are owed to Damir Marusic, Samuel Kimbriel, as well as David de Bruijn for kindly reviewing parts of the manuscript and offering extremely thoughtful comments. I am indebted to their wisdom and their willingness to push me on the theory of democratic minimalism that I outline in Chapter 2. Portions of Chapter 2 were first developed and presented for a workshop organized by the University of Pittsburgh's Center for Governance and Markets and George Mason's Institute for Humane Studies in May 2021. A hearty thanks to co-directors Jennifer Murtazashvili and Paul Dragos Aligica for their encouragement and inspiration.

I am especially grateful to Damir for being my co-conspirator in founding "Wisdom of Crowds," a podcast, newsletter, and debate platform focused on interrogating first principles—those deep assumptions that shape our most foundational beliefs and commitments. Week in and week out, Damir and I discussed, debated, and disagreed. It is through these conversations, unspooling over the course of years, that some of my more unorthodox ideas around the democratic idea coalesced into something (I hope) vaguely coherent.

On matters of religion and learning to live with deep difference, my friend and collaborator, the Evangelical theologian Matthew Kaemingk, was a constant source of inspiration. He introduced me to the work of a somewhat obscure Dutch pastor named Abraham Kuyper, whose insights on Christian pluralism informed Chapter 3 on "the problem of Islam."

Every writer needs a place to write regularly. Without this, either our ideas atrophy or we lose our ability to effectively translate thoughts into words. With this in mind, I want to thank Jeffrey Goldberg, Yoni Appelbaum, and Dante Ramos for giving me a home in The Atlantic to grow and extend myself as a writer. Many of the ideas in this book were developed and refined in the process of writing and researching various pieces for the magazine.

This book would have never happened without my editor at Oxford University Press, David McBride. He was incredibly patient and supportive every step of the way. I thank him for believing in this project. Thanks are also due to Alexcee Bechthold and the rest of the team at OUP who helped move the book through production. They, and so many others, made the impossible possible.

And, now, words are never enough for this part of it, but I will try. My parents found it somewhat confusing that I was working on another book (which, to be fair, is what I said in my last book). If you'll forgive another cliché, it really does make a difference when your parents have your back. Meanwhile, my brother Sherif has been one of my biggest supporters and has never hesitated to call me out when I say something I should not on Twitter. I love them more than anything in the world, and I really hope they like the book, after everything.

(And I hope you like it too.)

Introduction

During the Arab Spring, when I was living in the Middle East, I would come back to the United States and share my impressions with American audiences. The Middle East was confusing, even to those who lived there. I wanted to draw a contrast, because the contrast—at least then—seemed quite real.

Living there, I was struck by something that felt, quite literally, foreign. Perhaps that made sense. I was ultimately an outsider, as my Egyptian relatives often reminded me. I was born and raised in Pennsylvania, not Egypt. Egypt was the country of my parents, but was it *my* country? And if it wasn't my country, I wouldn't have to live with the consequences of my own ideas about democracy. They would—and they wanted nothing to do with it.

A new, democratic politics had emerged in a number of Arab countries, but the divisions seemed raw and existential in a way that intrigued as well as frightened me. A lot was at stake, and in retrospect we now know that too much was at stake. This had not been my experience with American politics, which was reassuring in its smallness. Americans had their differences, to be sure, but they appeared to agree on the fundamentals. There was both a founding moment and myth. There was a constitution, not quite sacred but close to it. Drawing on that shared history, we could pay tribute to a set of distinctly American ideals and ideas, even as we disagreed on their precise application. Because the country's foundations weren't in question, citizens were freed to debate policy—whether taxes, healthcare, or the deficit. It was possible to care deeply about things that weren't existential, and most things weren't.

Those times seem quaint, and it's remarkable just how quickly my country changed. I was reminded of this speed while recently re-reading a 2006 essay titled "Limits to Democracy," written by the late British philosopher Roger Scruton. The year 2006 *was* a different era. George W. Bush had propelled the question of democracy to the center of public debate, but it wasn't our democracy but theirs that we were debating. The blunders of Iraq were catching up with us, and the Bush administration insisted on covering or justifying those failures with the grandiose language of democracy.

The rudimentary coverage of Islam aside, Scruton's essay is useful in how it highlights the foundational challenge of democratic politics: how, or whether, to respect election outcomes that appear threatening to either us—ourselves, our families—or our nations. He contrasts America and the West with those pesky Muslim-majority countries that can never quite seem to get their act together. I did chuckle, in that gallows humor sort of way, when he says the following:

> The American norm . . . is wholly unlike that [of Islamic countries]. People vote Democrat and find themselves ruled by Republicans. And they accept this—unhappy, perhaps, but acknowledging a duty of obedience and a common loyalty that is far more important than any electoral differences of opinion.[1]

For Scruton, this ability or willingness to be unhappy but still obliging when one's adversary wins an election is "the precondition of democracy as we know it." In this sense, the other party is still merely an opponent, not an enemy.

According to this metric, today, the United States no longer meets this pre-requisite of democracy. The best glean on this is that, for now, a country such as ours can probably muddle through without this precondition being met. *Probably.*

The United States has certain advantages when it comes to containing the mutual antagonism of its two parties: strong institutions, democratic norms, and a long history of democratic practice. Longstanding, consolidated democracies rarely if ever break down. Decades or even just years ago, most observers would have said that the United States also enjoys the benefits of a democratic culture. In other words, Americans believe (or believed) in "small d" democracy. Culture can be overwhelming in its power, both mystical and mystifying—its judgments "so familiar that it exists like a voice in your head. And yet it is impossible to explain exactly how this happens."[2]

Despite their power, however, cultures can change as well as crumble. At the time of this book's writing, a growing number of Americans do not seem willing to respect democratic outcomes that go against their wishes. While this tendency is most pronounced among Republicans, it goes further and deeper. We can all feel it—that existential tenor of politics that fills us with both dread and foreboding, telling us that something isn't quite right.

Perhaps it is possible that we misunderstood what a democratic culture actually is in the first place. If a country can have a democratic culture in 2006 but then not have one in 2022, is it really a culture? Culture is sticky; it shouldn't be this easy to change in a mere matter of years. I don't believe that democracy is an aberration in human history, with an arc bending back toward authoritarianism. But I do believe we are moving toward a shared realization that existential politics is no longer, if it ever was, a Middle Eastern problem. It is a democratic problem. It is the problem of democracy.

This existential tenor is very much alive in countries as diverse as Poland, Hungary, Brazil, India, the Philippines, to cite only a few, and of course it has even spread to the world's oldest democracy, right here at home. For those of us who care about the the democratic, this is likely to be the fundamental question of politics for some time to come and maybe even the rest of our lives: How do we (as well as our opponents) respect democratic outcomes when the results threaten what we hold most dear? There isn't an answer, not an obvious one at least. Not all problems have solutions, and to think that they might may itself be the bigger problem. There is a certain kind of wisdom in the imperfection of otherwise great ideas, and democracy may be one of them.

1

Is Democracy Worth Supporting?

Can the overthrow of a democratically elected leader ever be justified? The case of Chile in 1973, after the socialist Salvador Allende came to power, is perhaps the prototypical example of a persistent American dilemma. As Henry Kissinger, perhaps the most influential—and controversial—foreign policy thinker of the twentieth century, memorably put it: "I don't see why we have to stand by and watch a country go Communist because of the irresponsibility of its own people."[1] Kissinger could say this with a characteristic mix of coldness and sly wit. In a sentence, he also happened to capture, rather starkly, a tension that would undermine American foreign policy and often render it incoherent.[2]

If Allende had won, would it have been "the end of the world" as one Latin America specialist at the State Department wondered?[3] Probably not. But there would have been a cost. This book is about that cost—the cost of democracy producing "bad" outcomes, and whether it is a cost Americans should be willing to bear.

More recently in the Middle East, the specter of anti-American Islamists coming to power in a democratic election only to cancel democracy—"one person, one vote, one time"—was a reminder that the tension was far from resolved. If democracy was about the right to make the wrong choice, why should America indulge in *other people's* wrong choices? Here, Kissinger once again saw things as he saw them in Chile. Referring to the rise of Islamist parties during the Arab Spring, Kissinger wrote that "the advocacy of elections may result in only one democratic exercise of them."[4] In other words, democracy might be nice, but it simply wasn't worth the trouble when its results were so uncertain and its participants so unreliable.

Islamist parties believe that Islam and Islamic law should play a central role in public life and organize politically around that goal. Naturally, then, they are likely to arouse suspicion. The fear of a democracy undone by Islamists has been as persistent as it is speculative. It is the fear of that which has not yet happened, which puts defenders of democracy in the uncomfortable position of either reassuring skeptics that Islamists will not win or that they will win but that they will be good, moderate, or otherwise acceptable. The more likely scenario is that they *might* win, but instead of ending democracy, they will do something rather more mundane: they will be *bad*, at least from the perspective of Western observers. Islamist parties will act against American interests or American values, or both.

One of the most persistent, vexing problems for America abroad, and particularly in the Middle East, is this "democratic dilemma": we want democracy in theory but not necessarily want its outcomes in practice. There are other, bigger problems, of course—nuclear warfare, irreversible climate change, and the end of the human race come to mind—but they are not dilemmas in quite the same way.

This democratic dilemma also happens to be a uniquely American one. Americans forget that very few countries insist on the promotion of democracy as a core component of their foreign policy, and fewer still have the power to do something about it. Because power and morality are inextricably linked in the American self-conception, the gap between interests and ideals is a question of identity as well as security. And no longer is this purely or even primarily a foreign policy problem. At home, a growing number of Americans are realizing that respecting democratic outcomes—when the ideological stakes are so high and when those outcomes appear personally threatening—is easier said than done. To look, then, at the democratic dilemma abroad is to consider a deeper set of questions around why we believe democracy is good as well as whether we think it is good for other nations and cultures.

To put the question more starkly: Is democracy worth it when it increasingly produces what seem to be destructive outcomes that put lives and livelihoods at risk? Why should mere democratic outcomes and elections take precedence over the other things we hold dear, such as liberalism, human rights, social justice, or racial equality?

This book proposes an ambitious and controversial reimagining of the ongoing debate and argues for "democratic minimalism" as a path to resolving America's democratic dilemma. In the seemingly eternal tension between democracy and liberalism, recognized by the ancient Greeks, the founders, and chroniclers like Alexis de Tocqueville alike, it may be time to prioritize one over the other, rather than acting as if the two are intertwined when increasingly they are not. As a matter of policy, what if there was a way to focus on democracy promotion, in the literal and narrower sense, rather than the promotion of both democracy *and* liberalism? There is an argument to be made for "liberalism promotion," but it is not the one I will make here. Instead, democratic minimalism would privilege democracy, with its emphasis on the preferences of majorities or pluralities through regular elections and the rotation of power, over liberalism, which prioritizes individual freedoms, personal autonomy, and social progressivism.

Deciding on such a course would alter America's basic foreign policy orientation, providing the beginnings of a grand strategy at a time when the United States seems unmoored and aimless abroad; it would transform bilateral relationships in the Middle East and our engagement with Muslim electorates more broadly; and it would help shift our own understanding of democracy at home, at a time when Americans are losing faith in American ideals. In addition, it would better preserve America's national interests—if not necessarily in the short term, then in the long run. Adopting a course as new and undoubtedly risky as this is no easy task, but there are compelling reasons—both moral and strategic—to attempt it. Over the course of this book, I will offer my own best attempt to persuade the reader of an admittedly unpopular position.

Why would something as controversial as this be a good idea, and why now? For starters, it would revive democracy promotion after being declared dead. But it would do so while taking into account a changing national mood and the limits of American power. Today, there is little appetite for the cultural and social engineering that was implicit (or explicit) in the liberal expansionist heyday of the 1990s and 2000s. Moreover, it would allow the United States to move away from the Middle East blunders of the past several presidents, each of whom, while radically different in temperament, ended up falling back on authoritarian regimes to diminishing returns. To put it as simply as possible: support for Arab authoritarian regimes undermines our interests over time, while violating the values we still claim to uphold. Of course, interests and values are intertwined in complex ways, so willfully undermining our own values ends up weakening U.S. leverage and credibility and allows regimes to disregard American exhortations as mere rhetoric, to be disregarded with the wink of an eye.

On a broader level, America's rising global preeminence from the early twentieth century into the twenty-first coincided with its commitment— partial and inconsistent as it no doubt was—to the spread of democracy abroad.[5] That one country was democratic and claimed that it was better *because* it was democratic had an important demonstration effect. The more the United States eclipsed the Soviet Union, the more pro-democracy forces

found themselves buoyed. The counterfactual is perhaps even more illustrative, and it is almost too self-evident to state: if the Soviet Union had
somehow beaten the United States—although it's never been made exactly
clear what this would mean—the so-called third wave of democratization
across Eastern Europe would not have happened.

The fact that American hypocrisy is so often brought up by critics of
U.S. foreign policy—including myself—is a testament to the fact that critics
believed that the United States was capable of being better and judged it accordingly. The charge of hypocrisy is only effective if the country in question
is good at least *some* of the time. Calling out the Soviet Union for similar
hypocrisies would have made little sense. No one, even (or particularly)
its most fervent supporters, expected Soviet leaders to respect democracy.
Instead, the goal was rather explicit—the establishment of the dictatorship
of the proletariat. It is true that Stalin's atrocities turned some against the
socialist project, but this had less to do with elections and popular representation and more to do with the difficulty that even true believers had in
stomaching mass killing on an epic scale.

The author Robert Kagan characterizes this somewhat differently, emphasizing the legacy of Enlightenment. "After World War II, because of America's
unrivaled power," he writes, "those Enlightenment principles suddenly
enjoyed a force behind them that they had never before possessed."[6] Which
Enlightenment principles might these have been? In Kagan's estimation, liberalism and democracy (as well as capitalism) went together. They did, in
fact, go together, but that is different than saying that they must at all times.

* * *

This might seem like an odd time to sing the praises of democracy, whether
at home or abroad, particularly as fears over democracy's staying power continue to grow, including in my own country, the United States. As the Dutch
historian David Van Reybrouk put it in his book *Against Elections*, "There is
something strange going on with democracy. Everyone seems to want it, but
no one believes in it any longer."[7]

Even if we did believe in it, haven't we already tried promoting it in the
Middle East and failed spectacularly? President George W. Bush's "Freedom
Agenda" is the most obvious example. The Freedom Agenda was certainly
bold and drew considerably from a controversial intellectual premise.
In many ways, it was a patriotic update of so-called blame America first
arguments associated with left-wing activists, which made it all the more

ironic coming from Bush and the neoconservatives. Their argument was also intuitive: in the absence of democracy and basic political rights, citizens are more likely to resort to violence because they lack peaceful, constructive means to express their grievances. Accordingly, the attacks on September 11 did not happen because they hated our freedom, but, rather, because the Middle East's stifling political environment bred anger, frustration, and, ultimately, violence.

However, the Bush administration's commitment to the Freedom Agenda didn't last. After a brief period of apparent democratic opening in 2004 and 2005, American officials backtracked after Islamist parties made significant electoral gains in Egypt, Lebanon, and Bahrain. In the Palestinian territories, the election of the militant group Hamas in 2006 became the new cautionary tale, much as Chile was during the Cold War.[8] While the Bush administration understood the importance of elections, perhaps to a fault, it incorrectly assumed they would produce "moderate" outcomes.[9] It is now the stuff of legend that National Security Advisor Condoleezza Rice's heart skipped a beat when she first heard the news of Hamas' victory while running on her treadmill at 5 in the morning.[10]

It is easy to poke fun at moments like this that grow in significance with the passing of time. We know Hamas won, but it could have been otherwise, couldn't it? There was a world in which the "moderates" of Fatah might have won instead, and those who believed in such a world would have been drawing on a considerable academic literature. The belief that participation and moderation went hand in hand also happened to be intuitive—even if it turned out to be wrong. As Bush's deputy national security advisor, Elliot Abrams, put it to me: "The assumption was that the average person is concerned about educating his or her children, making a living." In retrospect, he—like so many others—wondered how much good faith to extend to a fickle electorate:

> There's no question that some of the vote for Hamas was a protest vote against Fatah. But how much of it was that? And how much of it was the notion that Israel needs to be destroyed, and the only way to do that effectively is through violence? It's not zero. I mean, is it 5 percent? Is it 35 percent? Same thing in Egypt. When people vote for the Brotherhood, what are they voting for? And how many of them were actually, truly Islamists? Maybe we were much too optimistic in thinking, "You know, they're voting for good government. They're voting to end corruption."[11]

Most Americans, however, were not paying attention to the complex voting patterns of Palestinians or Egyptians. What they would have been aware of was a narrative of military supremacy and liberal ambitions, with the Bush administration attempting to aggressively spread its values and try its hand at social engineering in the form of "nation-building" projects in Iraq and Afghanistan.

Indeed, this has been the most persistent critique of America's post–Cold War foreign policy—that it has been led astray by an increasingly outdated vision of "liberal hegemony." Realist critics like John Mearsheimer and Stephen Walt[12] as well as younger scholars on the left like Stephen Wertheim[13] argue that these more expansive conceptions of liberal foreign policy aim to increase the prevalence of *liberal* democracies.[14] As this suggests, realists generally see liberal expansionism abroad as a natural extension of the universalist tendencies inherent in liberalism. If we accept the premise that liberalism is not neutral, then, like any ideological orientation, it will have trouble restricting its own application. It will want more for itself. On this they have a point.

The question is whether it is possible (or desirable) to limit the excesses of liberal hegemony while still retaining a pro-democracy posture abroad. If liberal dreams—a desire to remake the world in our image—have fueled American hubris, then these excesses can be mitigated by a conscious decision to put less emphasis on the *liberal* in the promotion of *liberal democracy*. What if, instead, we wished other countries to be "mere" democracies, emphasizing democracy as a system and means of governing and rotating power with no prejudice to substantive ideological outcomes? This would allow us to respect other countries' right to self-determination and self-government. It would limit our need to engage in social engineering in countries that American officials don't necessarily understand. It would also help resolve our "democratic dilemma"—particularly at a time when it seems that more and more electorates are deciding they would rather not be liberal.

The two core components of liberal democracy—liberalism and democracy—are diverging. For most of the modern era, the two concepts had gone hand in hand, at least in the West. The classical liberal tradition, emerging out of the Enlightenment after Europe exhausted itself with wars of belief, prioritizes non-negotiable personal freedoms and individual autonomy, eloquently captured in documents like the Bill of Rights. Meanwhile, democracy, while requiring some minimal protection of rights to allow for fair and meaningful competition, is more concerned with popular sovereignty,

popular will, and responsiveness to the voting public. In the suggestively titled *The People versus Democracy*, Yascha Mounk discusses the disjuncture:

> On the one hand, the preferences of the people are increasingly illib-
> eral: voters are growing impatient with independent institutions and less
> and less willing to tolerate the rights of ethnic and religious minorities. On
> the other hand, elites are taking hold of the political system and making it
> increasingly unresponsive: the powerful are less and less willing to cede to
> the views of the people.[15]

That democracy and liberalism can diverge is not a novel observation, but it
has become more obvious of late, not only in the might-be democracies of
the Middle East but also in actual democracies, old and new, such as Italy,
France, Hungary, Poland, Israel, India, and Brazil. In each of these countries,
illiberal right-wing parties have risen to power through democratic means.
Their commitment to individual freedoms and minority rights has been
questionable at best. At times, they have been actively hostile to the liberal
tradition.

The ascendance and hegemony of liberal democracy during the Cold War
and its seeming triumph after communism's fall made it easy to forget that
the story of politics is a story of a struggle between liberal and democratic
impulses, founded as they are on different conceptions of human needs and
wants. Whether the United States should emphasize liberal values—such as
the supremacy of the individual over the collective, gender equality, minority
rights, and sexual freedom—or electoral democracy hinges on perceptions
of what is, or should be, universal across time and place and what is not.
For the United States, such debates are inescapable. The country, after all, is
founded on a set of universal premises about rights and the sovereignty of
the individual (in theory if not necessarily in practice). If history has a progressive arc—in which good things go together and amplify each other—why
shouldn't they go together in the Middle East?

For its part, the realist tradition in international affairs tends to balk at
overwrought talk of universal values. For the good liberal, individual rights
and protections for minorities are sacrosanct, even if such protections run
afoul of the majority of voters. And if liberalism matters within borders, it
should also matter outside of them. Values are important in and of themselves, but they also help nations project soft power abroad. This soft power
may be amorphous, but this doesn't make it any less real. For the good realist,

anything that attracts the label "soft" carries less weight. In the place of values and arcs bending toward justice, a sense of the tragic is paramount. Because humans are fallible, neo-utopian notions of a more perfect world—and a global system where norms are enforceable—are inherently flawed.[16] Instead, anarchy defines the international realm. Power is the only true currency. Values may matter, but they are secondary, at best, or mere luxuries to be indulged in after the question of power is given due consideration.

For the purposes of transparency, I have been an outspoken critic of realism in its various iterations. While I am sympathetic to maintaining a developed sense of the tragic, I do not believe that further deemphasizing values in international affairs is the right response to a tragic world, particularly if it offers an easy pretext for excusing more tragedy. That said, realist arguments—however much I might disagree with their balance-of-power premises—need to be engaged with in good faith. Such arguments are gaining traction across the ideological spectrum. Two prior presidents, Donald Trump and Barack Obama, didn't share much in common, but they did share a skepticism about the possibilities of American power, particularly when it came to the stickiness of culture. To the surprise of some, President Obama recycled the controversial "ancient hatreds" thesis in his final State of the Union address,[17] while President Trump promoted his own vision of cultural sovereignty, declaring at the United Nations that "each of us today is the emissary of a distinct culture."[18]

I wish it were otherwise, but I represent the side that lost a great debate. Periodic conflagrations aside, Americans have lost interest in the Middle East. So, too, have American politicians. Obama was perhaps the perfect encapsulation of a particular kind of trajectory. Briefly, he allowed himself the possibility that the Arab Spring held the promise of better things. He was influenced, in these moments, by a younger generation of aides, who saw in the uprisings confirmation that the arc of history bends toward justice. Obama's optimism was real, but it was guarded, and feints of skepticism never quite disappeared. In time, his initial skepticism was validated. It was almost as if he had come to regret passion overtaking prudence, and so he overcorrected in the other direction. I asked senior officials who were in the room with Obama during key decisions how they perceived this change. One of them described it this way:

> What seems strange is . . . look at the way he talks about America, that we can perfect this model, which means that, at least in our context, he is an

optimist, given everything else. But when he looked at the Middle East, this notion of tribalism was probably the overriding perception that he had of the region. And he was saying, I'm going to give you guys running room to see if you can change it. But it became pretty clear in his mind, we couldn't. And when that became clear, his attitude was, I got better and bigger things to do. I don't need to be tied down by a region that won't change.[19]

As the Arab Spring turned dark, so, too, did Obama. He was known to privately joke, "All I need in the Middle East is a few smart autocrats."[20] He wondered why people in the Middle East couldn't just "be like the Scandinavians."[21] He said the region was "rooted in conflicts that date back millennia."[22] It bothered him that a growing number of Indonesian women were donning headscarves.[23] In his 2016 interview with *The Atlantic*'s Jeffrey Goldberg, Obama also puts the blame on Muslims for not being sufficiently peaceful. Muslims, he says, need to "undergo a vigorous discussion within their community about how Islam works as part of a peaceful, modern society." He speaks of a "reformation that would help people adapt their religious doctrines to modernity."[24] In remarks after a terrorist attack, he argued that it was "the responsibility of Muslims around the world to root out misguided ideas that lead to radicalization."[25] Taken together, these statements betray a particular kind of fatalism toward a people, a culture, a religion. Too many Muslims, it seemed, were intent on defying history's arc. As Goldberg notes, "One of the most destructive forces in the Middle East, Obama believes, is tribalism—a force no president can neutralize. Tribalism, made manifest in the reversion to sect, creed, clan, and village by the desperate citizens of failing states, is the source of much of the Muslim Middle East's problems."[26] Like so many others, Obama found himself frustrated by a region and its stubborn resistance to change.

* * *

Fatalism and resignation are understandable. An appropriate sense of the tragic is well and good. After twenty years of war in the Middle East and beyond, humility is the watchword, and it probably should be. But a well-earned modesty does not require deprioritizing democratic ideals. There is something odd about displacing much of the blame onto Arabs and Muslims, without discussing America's role in exacerbating and even fueling the region's conflicts. Despite everything, I do believe there is another way.

In the hope of addressing the skepticism around America's ability to shape outcomes abroad—and in the hope of reviving the democratic idea in foreign policy—I argue it is time to decouple U.S. support for democracy from U.S. support for liberalism. If this sounds odd, then it should. In fact, it is so odd that this is the first time the argument will be attempted in book form. I have put before myself a difficult and perhaps thankless task. By the time you have finished reading, you will be able to judge whether I have succeeded or failed.

Democracy versus Liberalism

A core premise of this book is that democracy and liberalism, though they cannot be separated entirely, can at least be distinguished in ways that are analytically useful. It is impossible to fashion an all-encompassing definition for everything liberalism has been, is, and will be. Most definitions, however, feature recurring themes and points of emphasis.

At the most basic level, liberalism is the ongoing project of carving out rights, with those rights deriving from a recognition of the dignity inherent to every human life. Since these rights are specific, they must be specified. John Rawls, arguably the most influential American philosopher of the twentieth century, describes liberalism "as a specification of certain basic rights, liberties, and opportunities."[27] By definition, these rights can only be specified with regard to individuals. As Francis Fukuyama notes, "The most fundamental principle enshrined in liberalism is one of tolerance: You do not have to agree with your fellow citizens about the most important things, but only that each individual should get to decide what those things are without interference from you or from the state."[28] Liberalism offers a particular answer to the question of human diversity. If people can't agree on the purpose of life itself, then politics should be emptied of ultimate ends and utopian projects.

If the unit of reference is the individual, it follows that particular importance would be attached to freedom of conscience, belief, and expression. The right to pursue happiness (or fulfillment) as one sees fit is sacrosanct, with the only real delimiting principle being one of harm to other individuals, since this would infringe on *their* own pursuit of happiness and fulfillment.

Liberalism is not synonymous with secularism, but it does imply a restricted role for religion in public life—although liberals have often disagreed among themselves on the degree of this constraint. For Rawls, believers did not have to give up their "comprehensive doctrines," but they would need to justify their policy preferences with resort to rationales that could be accepted by citizens who did not share the beliefs in question. This is what Rawls called "public reason." If there is pluralism, and there usually is, it must be a "reasonable pluralism."[29] But who decides what is reasonable in a pluralistic society animated by foundational disagreements?

The relative emphasis placed on individual freedom versus traditional norms and collective obligations is thus a central tension in liberal societies. For critics of liberalism, the preoccupation with the individual can only come at the expense of the collective. The collective has no legal, enforceable "rights"—or at least none that can supersede that of the individual. And this is where the tension between liberalism and democracy becomes palpable. They are concerned with different ends, and sometimes those ends will conflict.

There was a time when Americans could content themselves that liberalism and democracy went inseparable. In the Western experience, they usually were, to such an extent that "democracy" became shorthand for liberal democracy in popular usage. A cursory look at the opinion pages and various academic works is enough to illustrate how conflated the two notions have been. It wasn't always this way. For millennia, they were seen as "rival notions and not bedfellows."[30] Such tensions created a skepticism around the idea of democracy from the very start of the American experiment. As John Adams once wrote: "There never was a democracy yet that did not commit suicide."[31] Democracies are "as short in their lives as they have been violent in their deaths" is how James Madison, the father of the Constitution, put it.[32]

It might seem odd today, but the Founding Fathers of a country that came to be associated with democracy feared it, suffering from a sort of "political agoraphobia"—or fear of the man on the street.[33] Instead, they believed in the rule of the best—the well-heeled and the wise and those who possessed the gift of virtue. As Madison reasoned in the *Federalist Papers*: "The aim of every political constitution is or ought to be first to obtain for rulers, men who possess most wisdom to discern, and most virtue to pursue the common good of the society."[34] The Founders understood that constitutional liberalism, which was about constraining the will of voters, was not quite the same as "the rule of the demos, the citizen body: the right of all to decide what are matters of general concern."[35] Of course, the franchise, in America's formative years, was already restricted considerably. Blacks and women could not vote. The majority of white males couldn't either, due to property requirements and poll taxes. Modern democracy, even in its most minimal form, requires the right to vote for all citizens. By this standard, the United States was not a democracy and would not become one for some time.

In his book *The Future of Freedom,* published in 2003, Fareed Zakaria popularized the tension between liberalism and democracy, arguing that democratization was "directly related" to illiberalism.[36] A growing number of democracies were becoming illiberal, with majorities trampling on minority rights and empowered executives attacking civil liberties. For many, Zakaria's argument might have seemed confusing, and some of the confusion had to do with sequencing. In the American and European story, liberalism preceded democracy, allowing the latter to flourish. As the political scientists Richard Rose and Doh Chull Shin point out: "Countries in the first wave [of democracy], such as Britain and Sweden, initially became modern states, establishing the rule of law, institutions of civil society and horizontal accountability to aristocratic parliaments."[37] Only then did democratization—in the form of meaningful elections for executive power and gradual expansion of the franchise—take hold.

If liberalism and democracy were intertwined at home, it was only fair to assume that they would go together abroad. If liberal values derived from the dignity of the human person, it followed that they had universal applicability. This universalism—transcending culture, religion, and geography—made the liberal idea both inspiring and in line with America's self-conception. The only other "universalist" nation-state is France, but France, due to limits of location and power, has generally pursued a more traditional, interests-based foreign policy.[38] As the United States entered the twentieth century, it discovered that it had no such limitations. Or, as Teddy Roosevelt once put it: "Our chief usefulness to humanity rests on combining power with high purpose."[39]

For Americans, it was easy to forget just how unusual this was in the sweep of human history. Not just a country, we were a cause, and now that cause could be shared abroad, as American might and reach grew in the shadow of declining imperial powers. Because of its power, which would soon be unrivaled, an emboldened nation had the luxury to do what other countries couldn't. Of course, we didn't necessarily live up to our newly stated ideals. To pretend, however, was its own kind of privilege.

From the beginning, America's "higher purpose" was more closely associated with Enlightenment liberalism than popular democracy. We saw above what the Founders thought about the dangers of mass politics. This relative emphasis on individual freedom persisted. In the twentieth century, Franklin

D. Roosevelt emphasized the "four freedoms," while John F. Kennedy declared that "the 'magic power' on our side is the desire of every person to be free."[40] Democracy was part of the equation, to be sure, but it was not the primary thrust. And without liberalism tempering it, democracy could be a problem—and one best avoided in foreign societies and cultures that were not yet developed. In those places, liberal values and good moral character needed to be inculcated first, a theme that would figure prominently in America's colonial enterprise in the Philippines. President Woodrow Wilson, despite (or perhaps because of) his emphasis on freedom, shared such fears about the Filipino masses. "Only a long apprenticeship of obedience can secure them the precious possession" was how he put it.[41]

This is not to say that there is anything wrong with liberal values. There is much that is right. In the interest of being forthright about my own biases, I am a liberal myself, albeit the kind of liberal who is critical of what liberalism has become. My critics sometimes ask me if I would be comfortable living under a democratically elected Islamist government. My answer is a simple and emphatic "no." However, I am also well aware that my own liberalism is contingent—a product of the accident of birth and other unusual historical circumstances. I am a product of my own context, just as anyone else is a product of *their* own context. If my parents hadn't decided to immigrate to the United States and if I had had my formative cultural and political experiences in a religiously conservative environment, I would have been shaped by those experiences in turn.

Appreciating how individuals are malleable in the face of the force and stickiness of culture, I will try, over the course of this book, to suspend my preference for a liberalism that may be good or right but not necessarily universal. No one is a blank slate, of course, and even my decision to insulate my analysis from my ideological inclinations is itself a kind of ideological choice. There is the question of what should be—which is inherently subjective—and the question of what *can* be, perhaps also subjective but less so. In this latter respect, the spread of liberalism across the Middle East is unrealistic, to put it mildly. Although anything is possible, not everything is plausible. And liberalism, however attractive it may still be to many Americans, will be resisted in religiously conservative Muslim-majority countries.

Liberalism, as a value system as well as a set of premises about the primacy of reason and progress over revelation, speaks to foundational questions about the good life and the purposes of government. In this sense, it can't but clash with Islam—a religion that, in its various mainstream iterations, has jealously guarded its jurisdiction over such ultimate questions. This is not Islam as it "should" be, but Islam as it has been—nearly uninterrupted for the better part of fourteen centuries. As a set of ideological premises rather than a system of governing, liberalism requires liberals, and there simply aren't many of them in the Middle East. There may yet be, but as the allure of classical liberal ideas wanes in the very places where liberalism was born, it is difficult to imagine a scenario where a majority of Egyptians, Jordanians, or Algerians decide to become liberals, after having not been for so long.

Assessing the appeal, or lack thereof, of liberal ideas is critical. If democracy is part of a package that includes within it ontological premises about the nature of progress, human nature, and ultimate ends, then it is less likely to be accepted in societies where those premises are not shared. As the political theorist Joseph Kaminski puts it, Islam and liberalism "operate on fundamentally different baseline assumptions about the nature of reality itself."[42] With this in mind, it is better and more appropriate for Western observers and policymakers to focus on means rather than ends in their engagement with the Middle East. The ends of politics revolve around precisely those existential questions that cannot be answered by outsiders, however well-intentioned they may be. In practice, coming to terms with this reality means insisting on democracy promotion but also limiting its scope. This more limited approach is what I call "democratic minimalism." Supporting democracy abroad cannot be a project of ideological and cultural transformation, nor should it be America's job to refashion social and political institutions from the ground up.

At its core, the American conception of democracy is one of self-government—and that privileging of choice and agency which Americans insist on for themselves should be extended to other polities. Democracy as a system and a set of procedures—as a way of regulating politics without predetermining its outcomes—allows Arabs and Muslims to decide their own course and determine what values are most important to them. To try to compel people to become Western-style liberals is the mark of hubris—bound to be either ineffective, unrealistic, or both. After all, a liberalism not freely chosen is self-negating. In short, if democracy is a form of government, liberalism is a form of governing.[43] Putting it like this helps clarify the distinction between asking a country to be democratic and asking it to become liberal. The latter is more invasive—in both reality and perception—since it requires electorates to, in effect, repurpose their substantive ends and rethink their conception of what is just and good.

Liberals, for their part, might argue that theirs is the compromise solution, since it provides for a neutral public space in which individuals can freely express their beliefs and religious preferences. But the notion that liberalism is "neutral" can only be accepted within a liberal framework. Political liberalism, as expounded by Rawls in his numerous works, is based on the "veil of ignorance"—the notion that the founders of a new polity are free to construct their own society without any knowledge of their future position and without any distinctive set of preferences or values.[44] But as one of Rawls' most perceptive critics, Lenn Goodman, reminds us, "even neutrality, in Rawls's scheme, is not neutral. . . . Every one of Rawls's choosers is trapped in a liberal society." "They are not free," he goes on, "to construct a value system for themselves."[45]

What Is Democracy Good For?

Why might democracy be good if it doesn't produce liberal outcomes? Too often, democracy is seen as good insofar as it leads to other things we want, but the problem is that these things may be incidental rather than intrinsic to the democratic project. Among contemporary Muslim thinkers, the Turkish author Mustafa Akyol takes the position that liberty should be the ultimate political objective and that democracy is good for Muslim-majority countries to the extent that it helps preserve and extend liberty and freedom of belief and conscience.[46] Here, Akyol is speaking primarily to Muslim audiences, and his project is primarily about Islamic reform and how Muslims themselves relate to the ideas of freedom and reason. On those terms, this is a worthwhile, if daunting endeavor.

My goal in this book, however, is not to persuade Muslims to reinterpret various aspects of their tradition. I am seeking to answer a different set of questions and address different audiences. When it comes to American officials and politicians, for instance, they cannot—or at least should not—involve themselves in internal questions of Islamic belief and practice, in part because they are not equipped to do so but also because Islam itself is not the problem. Rather, the problem in the Middle East and various other Muslim-majority contexts is *the continued inability to accommodate competing conceptions of Islam's role in public life*. Interestingly, the rare former official who shares this interpretation is Condoleezza Rice, likely due to her formative experience with the thorny "democratic dilemmas" that arose during her tenure as both secretary of state and national security advisor to President George W. Bush. She writes, for example, that "religion and politics don't mix easily—but the exclusion of religious people from politics doesn't work either" and that "the region desperately needs an answer to [this] challenge."[47]

This failure to resolve foundational questions around the meaning of the nation-state and Islam's role in government contributes to violent conflict and the rise of brittle regimes that answer the question of deep difference by flattening it through force. Coercion might appear to provide stability but instead creates an ultimately untenable situation in which insecure autocrats respond disproportionately to even the mildest dissent. These regimes have no clear, reliable mechanism for the succession or transfer of power. They stand in perpetual fear of mass protests.

In this book, there is no "resolution" to the problem of religion and politics. The problem of deep difference over the role of Islam will remain, with neither side able to conclusively defeat the other. There will be Islamists and there will be secularists, with many shades in between. This is a reality that cannot be undone, and those who have tried have done so through escalating repression. Putting morality aside, the authoritarian option has not "worked" on even its own narrow terms. In Tunisia, Syria, and Libya, Islamist movements weren't merely repressed. They were eliminated outright, disappearing from public life for decades. Yet with the democratic openings of the Arab Spring, the groups in question—Ennahda in Tunisia and the Muslim Brotherhood in Syria and Libya—were able to quickly reemerge as powerful forces. They hadn't, in fact, been "eradicated," because they channeled broad ideological preferences that resonated widely. At the same time, however, *anti*-Islamist attitudes also enjoyed significant support. No one group could claim anything close to a monopoly on public opinion, because public opinion, by definition, was richly varied and multifaceted. There has long been a de facto pluralism in the Middle East, but it has only rarely been allowed to express itself peacefully.

A focus on democratic minimalism, therefore, starts to make sense as a way of regulating conflict and distributing power among competing ideological factions. In this sense, elections are the conduct of war through other means. In politics, there are friends and enemies. The question is how to accept this natural state of enmity while resisting the temptation to resolve it through violence. This is what even flawed and fragile democracies make possible. Democracy allows for the peaceful transfer of power, even (or particularly) in ideologically polarized contexts. As a set of mechanisms for conflict regulation, it contributes to long-term, if not short-term, stability—a difficult yet necessary trade-off that I will return to throughout this book. Democracy also offers predictability, since losers of elections have the chance to fight another day, as long as they are willing to fight peacefully. If, however, democracy is treated as merely a means to liberalism, this undermines the benefits mentioned above. If liberalism is the ultimate goal, then discarding democracy can be justified if it doesn't produce liberal outcomes (which it likely won't in Middle Eastern contexts, at least not at first).

Democracies, to put it simply, are helped by the fact that they are not dictatorships. Today, we hear constant laments over the incompetence and fecklessness of elected governments in addressing major crises. This understandable sentiment has been building in the few Arab nations that either are or were at least somewhat democratic.[48] In Iraq, Lebanon, and Tunisia, significant parts of the population long for strongmen as an antidote to ineffectiveness, gridlock, and endemic corruption. Authoritarian regimes, however, are only good at responding to crises when they're good, and when they are not—which is most of the time—there is no obvious way to correct course. Correcting errors is entirely dependent on the very people who made the blunders in the first place. There are no strong or autonomous power centers that can counter or even temper the decisions of the authoritarian executive. In dictatorships, then, there is a permanent structural uncertainty. If the dictator happens to be "benevolent," then such benevolence only persists while they remain in power. After the dictator is removed or dies, a radically different leader, in terms of skills and temperament, may emerge.

Democracies, meanwhile, are anything but glamorous, and they can appear aimless and even decadent. But at least they have the virtue—also a vulnerability—of often being better than they look. As the political theorist David Runciman argues, at any given moment, democracies appear chaotic, ineffective, slow, and inelegant. They tend to look more attractive only in retrospect with the passage of time.[49] In other words, democracies, however flawed, become more appealing in the future, slyly hiding their gifts. Interestingly, some of these insights around democracy's workmanlike features were grasped in the early twentieth century by Muslim reformers like the theologian Rashid Rida (d. 1935) who, despite (or due to) being Islamists, saw religious and political despotism as intertwined obstacles.[50] Operating in a context of colonial dominance, such thinkers may have feared Western cultural penetration, but they correctly understood that popular participation and parliaments, however flawed their association with liberal ideas, were the closest thing to a solution for preventing these twin despotisms.

With this in mind, American strategy in the Middle East has generally focused on the wrong thing. It has looked for ways to inject the Arab state, through technical assistance and economic support, into the lives of citizens. After all, from the perspective of U.S. officials, it is a good thing if Arab allies improve their performance on education, economic development, or government effectiveness. And as a preference, it seems sensible. This is the low-hanging fruit of bilateral relationships. Yet, the historical context of domineering, intrusive Arab states means that this type of assistance too often serves to strengthen autocratic elites, while empowering corrupt bureaucracies.[51] The United States, for wholly understandable reasons, has facilitated the very conditions that make despotism more likely.

The goal, from a democracy-first standpoint, would be quite different. The United States would seek to constrain and even *weaken* the Arab state in order to protect citizens and civil society from its excesses. From a policy perspective, this will likely be one of the more controversial arguments offered in these pages. I do not believe that the United States should provide significant economic or developmental assistance to authoritarian regimes, however friendly they may be, especially if they have not yet demonstrated a commitment to—or even just an interest in—political reform. To be clear, this call to limit foreign assistance also includes "good" things like helping Arab regimes provide better healthcare, education, and employment opportunities for their own citizens. The more authoritarian regimes receive support from the world's sole superpower, the more they are likely to be persuaded—or persuade themselves—that they are too big to fail. This is a classic moral hazard, insulating regimes from the consequences of their own failure.

The Middle East Exception

A "democracy-first" strategy might make sense in the abstract, but it makes particular sense in the Middle East—where ideological polarization has been unusually high. This is where the procedural aspects of democracy become, quite literally, a matter of life and death. The minimalist objectives of managing conflict might appear modest at first, but they are vital for a region that has seen more than its share of violent competition and military intervention in politics.

It may not be glamorous or fashionable, but preventing violence, channeling polarization into peaceful participation, and providing a basic check on despotism are what the region needs now and has long needed. It is certainly possible that democracy, however illiberal, might lead to the inculcation of liberal attitudes in due time. This is how many scholars of the region have tried to make the case to skeptical Western observers. As the Arab Spring was beginning to turn into something darker, Sheri Berman reminded readers that "stable liberal democracy usually emerges only at the end of long, often violent struggles, with many twists, turns, false starts, and detours."[52] However, this framing runs the risk of raising expectations too high—that there is a teleological story, that we all naturally incline toward liberalism, and that history is best conceived as having a final destination. Instead, democracy advocates should more readily acknowledge that democracy is no panacea. Even when it works well and long, democracy will at times undermine American interests. Its twists and turns may not lead to substantive outcomes Americans will be enthusiastic about. With as much sense of sobriety and sense of the tragic, it seems reasonable, then, to address any likely dissonance before it emerges, rather than after. Democracy is good for some things, less so for others, and we must make our assessments accordingly.

The other option, of course, is to *try* to stop caring too much about the Middle East, because it's simply not worth the anxiety it produces, particularly with the United States dispensing with its dependence on Middle Eastern oil. This view has gained traction in light of the Arab Spring's failures as well as our own consuming battles at home. Some of my colleagues have reluctantly come to this conclusion, and it is an entirely understandable one.[53] In an influential 2018 *Foreign Affairs* article, Mara Karlin and Tamara Wittes outlined a conscious downsizing of America's commitments in the region, acknowledging that while it "[would] be painful and ugly for the Middle East. . . [i]t's time for the United States to begin the difficult work of getting out of purgatory."[54]

Yet, the Middle East still matters—quite a lot, in fact. We don't need to go too far back to understand why. The seemingly endless chaos and conflict in the Middle East have repeatedly come back to haunt us, producing a refugee crisis that undermined American leadership, roiled Europe, and fueled the rise of far-right populism across Western democracies. Formerly tolerant European societies will have to contend with the consequences for decades to come, as millions either struggle to integrate amidst rising anti-Muslim sentiment or attempt to return to their home countries at considerable risk. As recently as the 2016 U.S. presidential election, Donald Trump propelled the threat of terrorism—and specifically Muslim terrorism—to the forefront of American political debate. What would come to be known as the Muslim ban was his signature proposal, drawing on the interrelated fears of immigration, terrorism, refugee runs, the foreignness of American Muslims, Muslim Brotherhood infiltration in U.S. government institutions, and the surreptitious introduction of sharia into the American legal system.[55]

It is possible to argue that the Middle East *shouldn't* matter. It is also possible to argue that it has mattered in the past but won't in the future. But these are normative and speculative arguments. Even if the Middle East, itself, does decline in importance—with the caveat that foreign policy analysts do not agree on what constitutes "importance"—it does not mean that others will agree.

If America's new, defining struggle features a confrontation with China, then presumably China's growing economic and diplomatic stature in the Middle East is a relevant consideration. A decade ago, Vali Nasr warned that "just as we pivot east, China is pivoting farther west."[56] In 2021, trade between China and the Gulf reached record highs.[57] At the time of writing, China is also making inroads in the region on sensitive military and security matters. That this is happening is no accident. As the *New York Times* reports, Gulf states are "increasingly looking to China not just to buy their oil, but to invest in their infrastructure and cooperate on technology and security, a trend that could accelerate as the United States pulls back."[58] The paradox of U.S. policy is that in trying to pivot away from the Middle East to confront China, America is undermining its ability to do exactly that.

This is the practical argument for staying engaged in the region—not despite China's rise but because of it. But there is also an ideological argument, one that demonstrates how moral and strategic interests can't help but be intertwined. From the start of his presidency, Joe Biden identified the struggle between democratic and authoritarian governments as the central challenge of both the present and future. As he put it in his first press conference as president: "It is clear, absolutely clear . . . that this is a battle between the utility of democracies in the 21st century and autocracies."[59] How might one fight such a battle for the supremacy of democracy over the alternatives while propping up some of the most repressive autocracies in the world, autocracies that happen to be in the Middle East?

My argument in this book is that the entire American paradigm, and not simply part of it, has been faulty in its starting premises, and so the resulting policies are built on a broken edifice. While rhetoric might suggest otherwise, this American paradigm—let's call it "stability first"—has not varied considerably from one administration to another. Instead, it has reflected a bipartisan consensus. In the postwar period, "stability" in the Middle East has been treated as the paramount concern, with Republican and Democratic presidents alike viewing friendly if unsavory autocrats as a means to that end. Pro-American autocrats, the thinking goes, can be counted on to further American interests. Young, fragile democracies, on the other hand, are wild cards: unpredictable, uncertain, and susceptible to the anti-American sentiments of their citizens.

"Stability" has long been the watchword, but it is worth putting it in scare quotes and questioning the easy resort to a word that can easily mislead. The stability provided by authoritarian regimes is illusory. If we look at developments in the Middle East over the past several decades, backing autocrats has not actually worked. It has contributed to the spread of terrorism, long-running insurgencies, the outbreak of civil war, and ill-considered military interventions that prolong those civil wars. Those are the more destructive outcomes, but there have also been more prosaic ones: for instance, a multiyear Gulf crisis in which two close U.S. allies (Saudi Arabia and the United Arab Emirates) blockaded another (Qatar). The focus on stability has counterintuitively created a situation where the countries the United States relies on most are brittle and erratic, led by a new crop of reckless authoritarians. In sum, can anyone really argue that the Middle East is more stable today than it was in 2010, 2000, 1990, or 1980? The stability argument, whatever else one wishes to say about it, fails on its own terms, which leads to a delicious if tragic irony: it is the very pursuit of stability as an end unto itself that fuels cycles of instability. In turn, American presidents see this instability and recoil from the region and dismiss it as hopelessly tribal and resistant to change—when it's their very policies that have fueled the instability they so lament.

That both Barack Obama and Donald Trump hoped to disengage from the Middle East only to find themselves enmeshed in various regional controversies says something about misplaced hopes. Disengaging from the Middle East is hard to do. Consider the oft repeated request to "do no harm" in response to a particular regional crisis. Deciding not to directly intervene against the regime of Bashar al-Assad in Syria, for example, was a conscious, deliberate choice, one with moral content and implication.

Whatever else one thinks of President Obama's decision, it was not neutral, in part because it couldn't be. This applies more broadly. The United States is already tipping the scales across the Middle East by backing authoritarian regimes. In these cases, deciding not to do anything in the name of constraint or humility is not a neutral posture. It effectively means staying the course— persisting in a position that is either counter to American values or America's long-term interests, or both. It also tends to mean outsourcing problems to autocratic allies in the region. We do less, but they do more. We are implicated in that, too, because they intervene under the cover of America's security umbrella, with their weapons systems and militaries supported and maintained by American largesse. In such contexts, to do no harm is to cause more harm. There is no innocent bystander option, for the simple reason that the United States is not a bystander and never has been, at least not in my lifetime.

The innocent bystander option becomes even less feasible in the context of great power competition. This makes it difficult to anticipate whether crises can be contained. Not only does the region draw in the United States, it draws in other outside powers as well. If Americans are willing to dismiss the strategic importance of the Middle East, it is unclear if other countries are quite so willing to do the same. Regional conflicts have been effectively internationalized, with China and Russia widening their ambitions. As perceptions of American weakness grow, a long list of actors will continue to press their advantage, both responding to and fueling ongoing conflict.

Illiberal Democracy and Ideological Competition

One criticism of democratic minimalism is that it runs the risk of devolving into "competitive authoritarianism," where "free elections are held but incumbents tilt the political playing field to their advantage."[60] However, for even the most minimalistic democracy to stay democratic, the opposition would need a fair enough playing field to have a real shot at defeating the incumbent. Citizens should always have recourse to change their minds in subsequent elections, and opposition parties should always have the opportunity to oppose and organize; otherwise, outcomes can no longer be trusted to reflect popular preferences. The right—and ability—to oppose the governing party require basic protections of freedom of speech, expression, and assembly. Without such protections, civil society and opposition groups would not be able to draw attention to government abuses and persuade voters to choose differently the next time around.[61] In practice, this requires establishing checks and balances through autonomous institutions, such as the judiciary, that can monitor and constrain abuses of executive power.

Democratic minimalism, then, is not a recipe for tyranny of the majority. A constitutional framework delineating limits on the will of majorities would still be in place. That framework may be more permissive than usual, allowing greater room for troubling majoritarian sentiments to be expressed, but it would still be a framework. It is also worth remembering that even in the most advanced liberal democracies, large enough majorities can undo constitutional protections through the amendment process. The real question is where—not whether—polities decide to draw red lines, and this, too, is ultimately a product of democratic deliberation.

When democracies produce illiberal outcomes, it is worth asking what *kind* of illiberalism is being expressed. If liberalism is about expanding individual freedom, illiberalism is about constraining it. Under this rather broad category, one can make a number of distinctions. Political illiberalism— limiting the ability of protesters to gather in public spaces or criminalizing speech against heads of state or militaries—is different than social, cultural, or religious illiberalism, which is about expressing a particular conception of the Good. The former is generally concerned with means, while the latter is concerned with ends. For example, laws restricting the right to consume alcohol, have an abortion, or insult prophets and divine texts are about ends, while a law that prohibits public gatherings of more than 100 people is about means. Presumably, citizens gather in public because they want to change policy, but the act of gathering itself has no inherent ideological content. Protesters can be socialists, liberals, leftists, or Islamists, each with significantly different visions for how society should be organized.

For those who wish to see democracy succeed, political rather than social illiberalism is obviously the bigger concern, since it undermines the fairness of electoral competition and makes it harder for opposition parties to, well, oppose. Examples abound. Venezuela's Hugo Chavez and Hungary's Viktor Orban are two populists whose illiberalism rapidly devolved into a desire to hold on to power and exert hegemony over their opponents. If "Chavez is the people," as billboards in Venezuela announced, then this said more about Chavez as a would-be dictator than about the content of the socialist utopia he promised.[62]

To be sure, such distinctions are messier in lived reality. Illiberal politicians may be so driven by ideological ambitions that they decide to crush opposition parties. But it is just as common for politicians to seek power for its own sake, without much in the way of deeply held beliefs or commitments. The temptation to maximize power is just about universal and not limited to explicitly ideological actors. The experience of the Middle East makes this clear enough. The region's motley crew of autocrats have not believed in anything as much as they believed in the indefinite perpetuation of their own power.

In particular, debates around gender equality and minority rights can straddle both political and sociocultural illiberalism, making them difficult to disentangle. Even here, though, some broad observations can be helpful. Any piece of legislation that removes from women or minorities the right to vote, even if passed through democratic means, would render that polity nondemocratic. There is no way to determine what majorities (or pluralities) actually want if large numbers of citizens are prohibited from making their preferences known at the ballot box. On the other hand, a law that limited female inheritance to half of that of a man's—as is common even in relatively "secular" Arab countries—would be an example of social illiberalism but *not* political illiberalism, since it would in no way restrict women's ability to organize, protest, and otherwise express their policy preferences in public life. This does not mean that such a law wouldn't be objectionable. It only means that, as a matter of definition, it wouldn't be a violation of political liberalism.

Accepting these premises would have major implications for U.S. democracy promotion abroad, which has elevated gender equality as a key pillar.[63] It would mean, for instance, that the United States would *not* withhold aid if a democratically elected parliament passed such legislation, however much we, as Americans, found cause for outrage that other cultures or societies might diverge from ours. One should, in theory, be able to do two things at once: to recognize that democracy, which is good, may produce outcomes that are not. Good things do not necessarily go together.

These dilemmas are difficult to discuss, in part because they relate to existential questions around the meaning and purpose of politics.

Most liberal theorists include minority rights and gender equality as well as some expectation of "reasonable" deliberation as part of political liberalism.[64] Of course, these are also *cultural*. They are also things that the United States has long cared about. In periods of overconfidence abroad, Americans could often act and speak as if first principles were resolved and no longer contested. But they *are* contested. The inability and unwillingness to acknowledge tensions between competing values fueled misplaced and unrealistic expectations about what the Middle East could become. When the Arab Spring began, Americans saw something they could relate to. This foreign world seemed less foreign. Finally, Arabs were catching up with history. The narrative was seductive: here were young, English-speaking liberals using Twitter and Facebook. All they wanted were the things we already had. As Obama once memorably said, "What I want is for the kids on the street to win and for the Google guy to become president," referring to former Google executive Wael Ghoneim, one of the early, young organizers of the protests.[65] This idealization of the Arab Spring in America's image laid the groundwork for the inevitable disillusionment that would follow.

Ideological gulfs were apparent in other ways. There was a time when it was possible to speak about the Middle East in isolation, as if the region's future could be determined in a vacuum. Today, the politics of the Middle East should be understood in the context of growing doubts about the future of liberalism and the "liberal order" that the United States helped fashion during the second half of the twentieth century. Increasingly, autocrats, hailing from different regions, cultures, and religious traditions, see themselves as fellow travelers, emboldened by what they see as America's growing insularity in the post-Trump era. With Western democracies facing uncertainty and internal turmoil, the Chinese model of vigorous, centralized growth—and its more palatable cousin, in Singapore—gains adherents. Americans, themselves, are losing faith in their purpose abroad, including whether they should even have one in the first place. In light of these challenges, the mere return to the status quo ante that many seem to pine for is remarkable mostly for its lack of imagination.

The End of the Bipartisan Consensus

At some point, if the United States keeps doing the same things and the outcomes continue to disappoint, then policymakers should be willing to try something new. To insist on staying the course and supporting brittle and reckless autocrats, despite a persistent record of failure, is, as the saying goes, the definition of insanity.

Of course, policy change—especially after a particular strategy, or lack thereof, has set in roots—is difficult. At times, it can seem hopeless. But this book cuts against the pessimistic grain and presents a minority and even contrarian view: it is particularly during and after times of crisis that previously unlikely and even unimaginable policies should be attempted. In this case, the claim that democracy promotion has already been tried is simply untrue. Successive presidents (with the notable exception of Donald Trump) *said* they would prioritize support for democracy in the Middle East, but none has come close to matching the rhetoric with reality. And even when they have, however briefly, their strategies have been dogged by the democratic dilemma that is the subject of this book.

Ironically, the Trump administration helped make this rethinking of U.S. policy possible. Whether intentionally or not, President Trump both shook and undermined the bipartisan foreign policy consensus. For the first time, at least in my adult life, there is real room for ideas that would have previously been dismissed as "radical" or wishful thinking, or both. The center hasn't held—and that's not necessarily a bad thing. Some commentators insisted that Trump was an aberration, and that once he left office, we could all go back to "normal."[66] But normal isn't good enough; in fact, it's not even good. If America's approach in the Middle East is fundamentally flawed, then tinkering around the margins will not do. The problem goes much deeper—and it gets to the heart of who we are as a nation and how we understand our place in the world.

A "Democracy-First" Strategy

This book will lay out the case for democracy in the Middle East, carefully considering counterarguments in good faith, and assessing costs and benefits for a new American strategy in the short, medium, and long term. Before discussing what the United States can do, however, we need to discuss what it *should* do. The first step, then, is to revive the idea of supporting democracy in the region. And it can only be revived by offering a resolution to the Islamist dilemma in particular and fears of Islam playing too large a political role in general. Such fears have been the enduring obstacle to believing that democracy in the Middle East is a worthwhile objective in the first place. A country cannot support something that it does not believe is good.

As for whether Washington can support democracy, after determining that it should, the answer to this is a resounding "yes," although reaching any real level of effectiveness requires a fundamental rethinking of interests, values, and trade-offs. It is not merely enough to decide to "do more" on democracy promotion. George W. Bush, Bill Clinton, and Barack Obama all said, at various points in their tenures, that they would take democracy in the Middle East seriously. But rhetorical flourishes, for all their sincerity, mattered little so long as the basic paradigm remained unchanged.

For democracy promotion efforts to bring tangible results, what is needed is a commitment—at the level of the president and his most senior aide— to exercise the full extent of U.S. leverage on Arab regimes, including our close allies. The kind of strong language that I use here may make Americans nervous. Indeed, a major obstacle to supporting democracy in the Middle East is a sense of futility shared by voters and politicians alike. After all, haven't we tried this before? (No, we haven't.) Can the United States shape democracy in countries whose culture and politics it doesn't really understand?[67] This sense of futility, however, is more tied to the perils of forever wars and nation building in Iraq and Afghanistan than it is to democracy promotion, which is a (comparatively) modest endeavor.

Sustaining high levels of pressure on not just autocrats but friendly autocrats hasn't been done before—and for understandable reasons. Doing so would necessitate absorbing short-term blowback and even retaliation. For the United States, it would mean, among other things, prioritizing long-term objectives over short-term interests—something that is notoriously difficult for American politicians, in part because it requires tabling the temptations of instant gratification.

The organizing principle in any "democracy-first" strategy is discouraging repression wherever possible, through either positive incentives or punitive measures. Counterintuitively, the United States should seek to put *greater* pressure on allies like Saudi Arabia than on adversaries like Iran. Considering that Washington has little credibility in the region when it comes to good intentions, concentrating American pressure on "friends"—rather than convenient targets like the Iranian regime—can demonstrate to skeptical audiences that being an ally is not enough, and that the United States is not cynically using democracy promotion to destabilize just those countries it doesn't like. Not to mention that the United States has limited leverage with the Iranian regime; it does, however, have considerable leverage with full-fledged dictatorships like Saudi Arabia and Egypt as well as "softer" authoritarian regimes like Morocco and Jordan.

Debates on how to deal with authoritarian allies are often marred by status quo bias; today, they seem durable, with little risk of major instability or mass protests. But this is precisely the problem with dictatorships: they seem stable—until they're not, and then it is too late, as we saw during the early days of the Arab Spring. On the first day of Egypt's protests on January 25,

2011, then Secretary of State Hillary Clinton said: "Our assessment is that the Egyptian regime is stable."[68] Two weeks later, the assessment would have been the opposite.

The durability of authoritarianism is deceiving, which means that policymakers must consciously correct for any status quo bias. Michael McFaul captures this confusing dynamic well when he says, "[T]he longer a democratic regime survives, the less likely it will collapse. . . . The longer an autocracy survives, the more likely it will collapse."[69] To the extent that autocracies survive, they do so through coercion. Even "popular" autocracies rely on repression, suggesting that they, too, realize the brittleness at their core.

With this autocratic impermanence in mind, it is worth thinking about how American officials might respond in the event of large-scale protests in strategically vital countries—countries that may seem stable for now and perhaps even for the foreseeable future. Imagine mass demonstrations, for instance, against the Saudi royal family in Riyadh. It is, of course, difficult to imagine. But if it happened, the United States would find itself in a bind. While Washington should not openly agitate for the overthrow of allies, it *should* unequivocally back the right of citizens to protest peacefully. It should make clear, in no uncertain terms, that the use of force against protesters would represent a severe breach in relationships with regional partners.

This is where the question of leverage and how to use it grows more important. What I propose in this book is the use of *maximal leverage*, which to my knowledge has never been exercised in any of the cases in question. I resist calling it the nuclear option, since this might make it sound more radical than it actually is. I am reminded of the satirical television program *Yes Minister* where an aide tells the minister that a particular policy will be "courageous," which causes the minister to panic. For the self-interested bureaucrat, courage is something to be avoided. I discuss the details in later chapters, but the general idea behind maximal leverage is to demonstrate to autocratic allies that the cost of an authoritarian turn exceeds the benefits. The goal, then, is to undo the perception of authoritarian allies that the United States will be the first to blink in a staring contest, so to speak. Authoritarian regimes want to survive above all else, so the only thing that can change their behavior is to affect their calculations about their own survival.

Saudi Arabia and Egypt are two of the more repressive regimes in an already repressive region.[70] Such levels of repression suggest an inherent weakness. If leaders felt that they were legitimate and that their citizens recognized this legitimacy, they would not need to overcompensate so dramatically. The insecurity that authoritarian regimes acutely perceive is why external backing is so vital. That they need us more than we need them is the source of America's leverage. But it has not been used. The question of what might be, and what might have been, remains tantalizingly unanswered.

For this book, I conducted extensive interviews with former U.S. officials, including some of Presidents Bush and Obama's top aides overseeing the Middle East. To ensure that I wasn't getting carried away with my own arguments, I raised with them the possibility of using maximal leverage and outlined various scenarios, such as removing security guarantees and effectively grounding the Saudi and Egyptian militaries. They confirmed that such proposals never came close to becoming policy. Some were intrigued but still skeptical. Several looked at me quizzically, as if the thought had never occurred to them.

To one former State Department official, I offered up a counterfactual history: What if President Obama had publicly announced that there would be a full, immediate suspension of *all* military assistance to Egypt, including spare parts and maintenance, if army leaders went ahead with their coup in that summer of 2013? It is one thing to convey something privately, where it can be easily dismissed or misinterpreted by the official on the receiving end. It is another thing to set clear standards for all to see, including media outlets, foreign governments, and international organizations. A look of amusement on his face, the former official responded that U.S. military leaders and the Department of Defense would resist and counsel Obama to take less drastic action. I then countered that Obama, as commander-in-chief, could insist that this was his final decision and demand that everyone follow suit, regardless of their own reservations. At this point, my interlocutor laughed out loud. It may have been my well-acted performance as President Obama in the White House Situation Room, but it also may have been the difficulty of imagining Obama taking such a strong stand in the face of spirited opposition. However improbable the prospect may have been, the fact remains that these options were never seriously considered. So when observers and former officials alike say that the United States *tried* to promote democracy in the Middle East and failed, they are missing an important part of the story.

A recurring theme in this book is that we discount the role of outside actors at our own peril. In studies of democratization, there has been a long-standing tendency to focus on the internal at the expense of the external. This began to change with the work of my doctoral advisor, Laurence Whitehead. In his book *International Dimensions of Democratization*, he noted that close to two-thirds of democracies existing in 1990 "owed their origins, at least in part, to deliberate acts of imposition of intervention from without."[71] As we will see, the role of external powers is even more notable in the Middle East. With the exception of Tunisia, all of the Arab Spring countries—in both their initial promise and their ultimate failure—found their fortunes tied to outside powers.

In March 2011, Saudi Arabia and the United Arab Emirates spearheaded a military intervention to quell the largest demonstrations in Bahrain's history. The intervention in Bahrain may have been dramatic, but it was not unique. At the time, no one would have known just to what extent Saudi Arabia and the United Arab Emirates would work at cross purposes with the United States in conflicts and confrontations spanning Egypt, Tunisia, Libya, Yemen, and Sudan. There would be a steady succession of incidents in foreign capitals where Saudi and Emirati diplomats, only days (or even hours) after their American counterparts had been there, told struggling autocrats to ignore the United States and follow through on their most repressive instincts.[72]

This can make sound as if the United States was a hapless observer, unsure of its footing and slow to move regardless. In many ways it was, but that it even found itself in such a position was no accident. This was the regional order that American policymakers had helped fashion over decades. Saudi Arabia and the United Arab Emirates lived in the shade of American security guarantees, their militaries built with U.S. equipment and training. The support they receive from the United States has only grown. In his defense of the Obama administration's foreign policy record, Derek Chollet, who served as a special assistant to the president and then assistant secretary of defense, notes that from 2007 to 2016, the Pentagon "approved arms sales worth more than $85 billion to the [Gulf] states, nearly as much as in the 15 years combined."[73]

How American Aid Enables Arab Repression

It might seem an accident that just as Saudi Arabia and the UAE were becoming more repressive at home and promoting repression abroad, they were attracting more, rather than less, American support. But I argue that this is a feature, not a bug, of U.S. policy in the Middle East. The largely

ignored case of Jordan offers perhaps the clearest illustration of this conflu-
ence of American aid and Arab repression, and it began long ago. For most
of the 1950s, U.S. assistance was minimal. Jordan had held reasonably free
elections. Then something changed. Suleyman al-Nabulsi, a socialist, was
the victor in the 1957 parliamentary elections. As prime minister, the ambitious Nabulsi clashed with King Hussein, then a young and weak monarch.
Hussein decided to move against the elected government. In the confrontation that followed, U.S. support increased almost immediately. Days after
Hussein declared martial law, he received a $10 million emergency grant
from the Eisenhower administration.[74] This doesn't sound like much, but at
the time it was a lifeline. The government was nearly bankrupt. As Sean Yom
recounts in his history of America's relationship with the Jordanian monarchy, from 1958 to 1967, the amount of U.S. aid—averaging $50 million a
year—exceeded Jordan's entire domestic revenue nine years out of ten.[75]

Those were different times, of course, an era of Cold War intrigue, impro-
vised CIA plots, and suitcases full of cash to anti-communist figureheads.
But the trend persisted well after the Soviet Union's fall. In 1989, Jordan held
its first free elections since Nabulsi's ouster. Islamists, along with nationalists
and leftists, dominated the polls, together claiming a slight majority and
electing Jordan's first (and last) Muslim Brotherhood speaker of parliament.
After the Gulf War, Hussein, now a much older monarch, found himself isolated and cash-strapped after refusing to back the U.S.-led coalition against
Saddam Hussein. The king was a survivor, and he decided, correctly it turned
out, to demonstrate his value by pursuing peace with Israel. But there was a
problem. Jordan was becoming democratic, and democracies tend to reflect
popular sentiment. In the case of Jordan, with its Palestinian majority, such
sentiment was firmly anti-Israel. A parliament controlled by Islamists and
nationalists would never ratify an accord with Israel. And so Hussein instituted a new electoral law that made it much more difficult for Islamists to
win. It worked. The 1993 elections produced a pliant parliament. Even after
signing the treaty, however, the king would need to keep the opposition from
weaponizing the treaty against him. The remainder of the 1990s saw an escalating crackdown—just as U.S. assistance was increasing in recognition of
King Hussein's role as peacemaker.

If not for American. support at key moments over more than five decades,
the Hashemite Kingdom wouldn't exist, at least not in its current form.
Jordan is less politically open today than at almost any point in the past thirty

years. In Chapter 4, I discuss the country's long, seemingly endless process of de-democratization, completely undoing past gains and setting the country back decades.

Why might aid have this effect? External assistance, from a superpower no less, empowers autocrats to seek the defeat of their opponents. Having outside patrons who are invested in your success is good for one's confidence. It makes compromise less necessary and therefore less appealing.[76] In the case of Jordan, King Hussein was more focused on a peace deal with Israel than his own country's democratization process. In fact, the latter undermined the former. And the peace process mattered because Israel mattered.

Israel and "Linkage Theory"

When the Arab Spring began, I was of the view that Israel didn't matter much anymore. Like so many others, I had turned against the so-called linkage theory, which asserts that the Arab–Israeli conflict must be resolved for the region to progress on other fronts.[77] As former Secretary of Defense Chuck Hagel once explained:

> The core of all challenges in the Middle East remains the underlying Arab-Israeli conflict. The failure to address this root cause will allow Hezbollah, Hamas, and other terrorists to continue to sustain popular Muslim and Arab support—a dynamic that continues to undermine America's standing in the region and the governments of Egypt, Jordan, Saudi Arabia, and others, whose support is critical for any Middle East resolution.[78]

Such a view held the Middle East hostage to the improbability of a final peace. The promise of the Arab uprisings—and the fact that they even happened in the first place—seemed to confirm the absurdity of focusing on Israel. Protesters may have cared about Israel, but they cared about their own governments more, and they could apparently topple them, with or without regional peace. If there was any doubt before, it seemed clear enough that the Israeli–Palestinian struggle was far from the central challenge for the Middle East.

We may have been wrong. In light of subsequent events, it may be time to bring Israel back into the conversation. The Arab Spring failed. More importantly, the United States was unable to alter its reliance on authoritarian regimes across the region. In every other part of the world, successive American administrations became at least somewhat better on democracy promotion, everywhere except here. As a senior aide to President Obama put it to me: "Democracy can bring into power organizations that are hostile to Israel and they're going to threaten Israel's security. I mean, otherwise, why would we care that much?"[79] This might be overstating things, but it gestures toward the truth. Both in the reality of the Middle East and in the American imagination of it, Israel plays a predominant role. In any rendering of U.S. interests in the region, Israel's security, along with other mainstays like access to oil and combating terrorism, is paramount.[80] The preoccupation with a peace process in the service of a two-state solution is derivative of this. Otherwise, except for the fact of Israel's role, the Arab–Israeli conflict would be comparable to other conflicts, important to be sure, particularly to the belligerents, but not overwhelmingly so.

If linkage theory is to be revived, the question is what to do about it. U.S. administrations, particularly the Clinton administration at the height of the Oslo Accords, believed in the formula of peace first, democracy (maybe) later. As Martin Indyk, one of the architects of Clinton's Middle East strategy, explained it to me:

> Our priority was making Arab-Israeli peace and we needed the regimes in the region to support our efforts. We were not going to complicate it by pushing a democracy agenda. That could come later. I could second guess myself now, but that was our view at the time because it looked like all the stars were aligned for a breakthrough to peace. It very much was a case of Middle East exceptionalism. Decidedly so. But it wasn't that we were in favor of autocrats and were against democracy. It was rather that peace was a heavy lift and we needed to devote our diplomatic energies to that. If we succeeded then a lot of other positive dynamics would be unleashed which would advance our democratic ideals in a more conducive environment. For example, Arab governments would no longer be able to use the Israel card to divert their populations from basic political reforms at home.[81]

If prioritizing peace over democracy was ever a sound approach, it isn't any longer—peace between the Israelis and Palestinians appears as unlikely as ever. Moreover, even if there was a final settlement, many in Palestine and the broader region would be unhappy with the terms, including those who might leverage such dissatisfaction into political gains. In other words, some conflicts can merely be managed; not all of them can be *resolved*. (Paradoxically, the desire to resolve the Israeli–Palestinian conflict has made resolving it less likely.)

The "peace first, democracy later" approach of the past can be turned on its head. If peace is improbable at best, then there is no reason to hold democracy hostage to it (unless you believe Israel's security so paramount that the risk of Arabs expressing their preferences through democratic means is too high a price to pay).

It is worth noting that Israeli leaders have their own views, and they aren't shy about sharing them. Israel, despite being the region's only established democracy, is a staunch opponent of democracy everywhere else in the region. Nearly all the Obama and Bush administration officials I spoke to, running the gamut from those skeptical of Israel's role to those who saw it deservedly as America's closest regional ally, recounted just how furious their Israeli interlocutors were with their perceived naivete over the prospect of Arab democracy. The Bush administration's Elliot Abrams described the tenor of disagreement: "It was mockery behind our backs. They'd say, 'You don't understand at all. You know nothing about Arabs. . . .'. Because their argument was, 'You will see who wins. The bad guys are gonna win. The Islamists are going to win victory after victory if you open these systems up.' "[82] Meanwhile, a member of the Obama White House put it this way: "The strongest lobbying I got for going easier on Sissi was from Israel." I asked him how much it mattered. "There's not one piece of it that matters," he replied.. "It's the drumbeat, it's the constant something you take into account. I don't know how it affected Obama, how it affected Kerry, how it affected others but you keep hearing it. It can't but have an impact."[83]

At least the executive branch is insulated—to some extent—from heeding allies, even close ones like Israel. The same can't be said for Congress. Much has been said about the role of pro-Israel lobbying groups like the American Israel Public Affairs Council (AIPAC) when it comes to advocacy in favor of Israel. (I am skeptical that this plays as much of a role as Israel's critics suggest. There are strong cultural and religious factors that go a long way in explaining American support for Israel, particularly among Republicans.[84]) What receives much less attention but deserves more is how Israeli officials and pro-Israel groups advocate for Israel's autocratic partners in the Arab world. As one foreign policy advisor to a U.S. senator told me, "[after the 2013 military coup] AIPAC was the best lobbyist for the Egyptian government you could ever imagine."[85]

If one has a narrow and short-term perspective of Israel's security, then it is true that Israel would probably have an easier time dealing with unaccountable autocrats or military leaders who can conduct foreign policy without domestic oversight. Democracies, as is their wont, are more unpredictable on matters that concern public opinion. But no one said democracy was easy (or if they did, they were wrong).

Soft Authoritarians

Two of the region's "soft authoritarian" regimes have signed peace deals with Israel, and there is linkage here, too. We have already discussed Jordan. Morocco, which gained independence from France in 1956, is another Arab monarchy that is authoritarian but not *too* authoritarian. Outright brutality is avoided. Parliament and political parties operate, albeit within clear limits. As far as monarchies go, Jordan and Morocco are corrupt but not as corrupt as some of their neighbors. They are perceived as "islands of stability" in an unstable neighborhood. Their reigning monarchs appear unusually progressive, certainly more progressive than their own people, particularly when it comes to women's rights and religious minorities.

In 2020, as part of the Trump administration–brokered "Abraham Accords," Morocco was able to further burnish its credentials as a force for moderation. Progressive monarchs who make peace with Israel and prioritize the protection of disadvantaged minorities and women— what's not to like? It's worth noting that if Morocco or Jordan were actual democracies, they would likely be less "moderate" on these metrics than they are now. This is why the true test of any purported reorientation of American strategy in the Middle East needs to address soft and not just hard authoritarians. This does not mean the United States should go out of its way to punish the Moroccan or Jordanian regimes or treat them as pariahs. But it does mean that the United States should do what it can to help reverse troubling trends of authoritarian retrenchment, including by tying existing and prospective assistance to substantive political reforms. Regardless of my preferences, the United States will have to deal with and support authoritarian regimes, but there is no reason for Washington to strengthen authoritarian regimes that are becoming *measurably more authoritarian over time.*

To return to the example of Jordan, why shouldn't the United States hold the monarchy to its own pledges? In 2007, King Abdullah told ABC News' Peter Jennings that he "absolutely" wanted Jordan to become a constitutional rather than an absolute monarchy, although he qualified this by saying his time horizon was "eventually."[86] How long is too long? In the absence of external pressure, Jordan—the world's second largest per capita recipient of U.S. foreign aid—will remain mired in an authoritarian holding pattern. This raises the question of whether authoritarian regimes can sustain their authoritarianism indefinitely. Even if the answer were "yes," is it America's responsibility to help sustain this authoritarian future until the end of time? Even for those more favorably disposed to soft authoritarianism, why not assist such autocrats in becoming softer still? Again, there is no neutral ground: if the United States is not using its leverage to encourage gradual reforms, by default it means that the United States prefers Jordan stay an absolute monarchy not just in the short run but in the long run as well. In practice, this puts American officials in the awkward position of helping autocrats become "better" autocrats or more effective autocrats. Of course, there is no need to imagine such a scenario. To the extent that the United States has a Jordan policy, this is what it currently is as well as what it has been.

To be sure, a hard-nosed approach to the region's soft authoritarians—or more obviously repressive ones in Egypt or Saudi Arabia—comes with risks. Real reform, however gradual, brings with it uncertainty about what comes after. In authoritarian contexts, democratic change becomes possible once citizens begin regaining their ability to imagine alternative possibilities.[87] Revolutions are born in these in-between states. A king who loses a little bit of power each year ends up losing a lot of it, and it is precisely during these moments of transition that citizens may find the courage to organize en masse. In other words, adopting such an approach may, in effect if not intent, undermine the very allies we have stood by for decades. For some, this will be a nonstarter. It is worth remembering, however, that persisting with the status quo comes with its own risks. That the Arab Spring happened should have confirmed this once and for all. Still, considering the inescapable fact that politics, like life, is about trade-offs, I will try to be as explicit as possible about the potential drawbacks of the path I am proposing. Readers can then judge whether or not it would be worth it.

* * *

As daunting as such a shift in American foreign policy might sound, I will argue that it is both plausible and necessary. Some of that argument draws on personal experience. I lived in the Middle East during the "first" (and largely forgotten) Arab spring of 2004–2005 as well as the Arab Spring of 2011–2013. I spent a large chunk of those years discussing and debating America's role with the very people who find themselves on the receiving end of both American power and American neglect. At the same time, I came to know many of the key figures in the Obama and Bush administrations who worked on the Middle East, and I have spent the past several years trying to understand what went wrong. That said, I am not a neutral observer nor will I pretend to be.

I remember the eighteen whirlwind days of protest in Egypt in January and February 2011, some of which I was in Cairo for. As an outsider granted a rare glimpse of revolution, I was trying my best to understand and observe. I was also hoping. What would come to be known as the Arab Spring had begun. I interviewed brave Egyptian activists. They cried to me on the phone, pleading for the United States to act. On muffled phone lines, they told me about the military planes buzzing above them, perhaps a sign of worse to come. They, quite literally, saw America as their last and only hope. Their hopes may have been misplaced, but there was something powerful about their belief in our moral authority despite the apparent absence of that morality over the intervening decades. In hindsight, perhaps it was a mistake to believe in us more than we believed in ourselves.

It is no accident that when Americans saw the images of young Egyptians camped in Tahrir Square demanding their freedom and willing to die for it, it became a sensation—the rare time when Middle East news became *our* news. For a moment, Americans, even those who hadn't thought much about the Middle East before, felt connected to what was happening more than 5,000 miles away. This was something that they knew, instinctively, deserved their recognition and support, even if they were wrong to assume it meant that Arabs would embrace American ideas.

For the United States, then, the moral element matters: what we, as Americans, do abroad shapes how we understand our own country and its founding ideals. Some of those founding narratives may be fictions, but fictions nonetheless serve a purpose. The historian Edmund Morgan once colorfully wrote that "the success of government thus requires the acceptance of fictions, requires the willing suspension of disbelief, requires us to believe that the emperor is clothed even though we can see that he is not."[88] As this book will show, foreign policy isn't just foreign; it is also about the forging of American national identity. A vision that elevates democracy abroad—and the dignity that comes from self-government—can remind Americans that the democratic values they believe in at home are also worth believing in and fighting for in an otherwise staid foreign policy arena.

For some time now, we haven't had an animating "mission" abroad, yet survey after survey shows that American voters respond positively to appeals around values, morality, and using American power and influence to support democratic ideals beyond their own borders. According to one 2018 poll, 71 percent of Americans "favor the U.S. government taking steps to support democracy and human rights in other countries." And by a 2-to-1 margin, Americans would "prefer to increase rather than decrease U.S. efforts to support democracy and human rights abroad."[89] Yet, there are fewer and fewer politicians on either side of the aisle who speak to these convictions. We have lost our sense of place in the world, and so foreign policy has become just another site for partisan skirmishes. But it does not have to stay that way.

The democratic idea is worth believing in even in those places that seem most inhospitable to it. But to believe in something is to understand what it means, and it is not clear that we do. Just as "democracy" has become an uncontested good, its actual meaning is as contested as ever. To promote something, presumably, we first need to understand what it entails in both theory and practice.

The Book

What follows is informed by hundreds of hours of interviews and informal conversations with activists, leaders, and politicians in Egypt, Jordan, Tunisia, and Turkey. To state what I hope is obvious, a book on how to think about the Middle East must be informed by those who live there. But a book on how the United States can begin to think differently about the region must also be informed by those officials and policymakers who have found themselves in positions of influence and responsibility from the inside.

I spoke to more than twenty-five senior officials in the White House, State Department, and Defense Department, many of whom were in the room with either the secretary of defense, secretary of state, or the president himself at key moments. I focused on the Obama administration, but I also conducted interviews with veterans of the George W. Bush, Clinton, and George H. W. Bush administrations. To get a better sense of domestic constraints on policymaking, I also spoke to the foreign policy advisors of several U.S. senators. I was surprised at the frankness of some of the conversations, and I will relay the insights as well as the objections of my interlocutors in the pages to follow. This is also the first book on the topic to draw from all the memoirs of the principal figures of Obama's foreign policy, several of which have only been published recently.

I take a chronological and thematic approach. Chapter 2 outlines my theory of "democratic minimalism" at greater length, with a focus on how the democratic idea has been conceptualized and reconceptualized according to time and place. Chapter 3 addresses the role of Islam and how Muslim-majority societies, contrary to popular belief, are well suited to democracy if not necessarily in practice then in theory. The "problem" of Islam is, at least in part, a problem of liberalism—the fear, often unstated or implicit, that the more democracy there is, the less liberalism there will be. In Chapter 4, I turn my attention to largely forgotten democratic openings in Egypt, Jordan, and Algeria in the late 1980s and explore why they were closed. This is also where I lay out in detail the potentially controversial argument that Israel's role in the region—and the American desire to forge Arab–Israeli peace—undermines prospects for Arab democracy. Chapter 5 discusses the strained relationship between the United States and Egypt's first democratically elected government—one that happened to be led by an Islamist party. I consider whether the Obama administration gave the military what amounted to a green light to stage a coup, assessing the final few days that changed the region forever. In Chapter 6, I explore various explanations for American discomfort with religion-inspired movements in the Middle East. Is it about culture or interests or some combination of the two? How one answers this question affects how one views the trade-offs involved. Chapter 7 considers the extent to which the United States can influence the internal politics of foreign countries. How much does the United States actually matter? Here, I make the case that outside powers can be decisive in tipping the balance toward or away from democracy. In Chapter 8, I lay out in detail what we can reasonably expect Islamist parties to do if they remain in power for a significant period of time. We know that Islamists are illiberal, but what does that illiberalism entail in practice? Finally, I end the book with two shorter and perhaps unusual chapters on "power" and "hypocrisy," two things that are inescapable in discussions of the democratic idea. These chapters are more reflective, introducing a note of ambivalence that might appear to contrast—and even contradict—the rest of the book. At some fundamental level, arguably like American policy itself, I am torn.

2

Democratic Minimalism in
Theory and Practice

In old and aspiring democracies alike, the word "democracy" has managed an unlikely feat: it still offers the prospect of a panacea but tends to deliver profound disappointment in voters' lived experience. Democracy has become increasingly ill-defined, a problem that has far-reaching implications both at home and abroad. For progressives, the presumption is that democracy leads—or should lead—to "good" outcomes, and if it doesn't, then this is evidence of a democratic deficit. This ideologization of democracy weakens support for democratic ideals because it associates a system of government with a particular conception of the Good. In foreign policy, the tendency to instrumentalize democracy becomes even more pronounced, as we will see.

In this chapter, I will advance a more limited conception of democracy, which I call "democratic minimalism." This "de-instrumentalized" version of the democratic idea proposes to see democracy as an end unto itself rather than a means to other ends. In making this case, I separate the basic functions of democracy from the liberal ends with which they are so often associated. I also explore the question of whether a democracy must be effective to be successful. What would be "better"—an authoritarian regime that governed well and produced economic growth or a young, shambolic democracy consumed by polarization, protests, and gridlock? This is an important step in the broader argument, because one of the main obstacles to supporting democracy in the Middle East (or anywhere else for that matter) is the notion that democracy doesn't produce good outcomes. Which is at least partly true: democracy doesn't necessarily produce good outcomes, nor should it. My goal here is to sever a democracy's performance indicators from the question of whether democracy is worth supporting.

At their core, democracies offer one essential advantage: they allow for the peaceful alternation of power and the regulation of existential conflict. Existential politics is the heightened state in which political competition becomes anchored around identity rather than policy. The so-called who we are questions take precedence over "what works" and what government can do. With existential politics becoming a near-universal phenomenon in recent decades, even in advanced democracies, being able to regulate it without resort to large-scale violence is no small thing.

Definitionally, "democratic minimalism" shares something in common with how democracy was originally conceived by earlier political scientists. Joseph Schumpeter defined democracy as "that institutional arrangement for arriving at political decisions in which individuals acquire the power to decide by means of a competitive struggle for the people's vote."[1] Democracy, in other words, is primarily about the means through which citizens select their leaders. This has also been referred to, often critically, as "electoral democracy," "procedural democracy," and "leadership democracy." This understanding of democracy became "canonical in postwar American political science."[2]

Joseph Schumpeter was born in 1883 and died in 1950. Like most men, he was a man of his time. Universal suffrage was not yet the norm. In the early twentieth century, when Schumpeter began making his name, the number of citizens who would have had any college education was limited even in the advanced industrialized economies, including in his home country of Austria. Elites without apology, Schumpeter and his contemporaries were inherently distrustful of mass politics, particularly as workers' parties expanded their share of the vote in democratic contests.[3] Accordingly, conceiving democracy in narrow terms served an important purpose: it helped preserve elite dominance and guarded against the rash unpredictability of unlettered voters. There was no belief, here, in the wisdom of crowds.

Moreover, Schumpeter was skeptical that individuals had much independent political will in the first place. Instead, they were shaped and manipulated by leaders, although Schumpeter saw this as a feature rather than a bug. In this sense, democracy was not participatory and wasn't meant to be. Here, the descriptive and the normative were conveniently intertwined. The people, in this story, did not have a general will, and if there was no general will, then there would be no "common good" for democracy to realize.[4] Schumpeter was adamant that democracy was merely a method and a means—he likened it to "a steam engine or a disinfectant"[5]—and not an end in itself. This was not quite the same as illiberal democracy or tyranny of the majority, at least not yet. (The latter, after all, is precisely what Schumpeter hoped to avoid, fearing that majorities, unmediated by their betters, might choose socialism.) It happened to be the case that those democracies that existed before or after World War I were all liberal by the standards of the time. In retrospect, this might be viewed as a historical accident, contingent on a particular sequence of events. In Europe, liberalism preceded democracy. Because of this, democracy was unlikely to produce illiberal outcomes since political and intellectual elites had already embraced liberal ideas coming out of the Enlightenment. One of the reasons that Enlightenment philosophers (and politicians) insisted on liberalism first while holding calls for universal suffrage at bay was their understanding, dating back to the ancient Greeks, of the tension between popular democracy and responsible government.

Eventually, the Schumpeterian approach fell out of favor. It was ethically neutral and nakedly instrumentalist. It prioritized elite decision making over citizens' participation and representation, two growing concerns for political theorists and political scientists during the third wave of democratization that inspired a new generation in the 1990s after the fall of the Soviet Union. The center of gravity for democratic theory would soon shift to the health of democracy, questions of justice and equality, and the gulf between voters and representatives and how to close it. "Direct democracy" came into vogue, with fantasies of town halls and caucuses where citizens could transform themselves into daily, enthused participants in the task of self-government.

If this was direct democracy, it was also a deeper democracy, invested with more meaning because, presumably, more people were participating. As democracy's stature grew, liberating millions from communist rule, it would have seemed odd to think of it as little more than a method—the political equivalent of a "disinfectant." The academic literature on "hybrid regimes," popularized by political scientists like Larry Diamond, Steven Levitsky, and Marc Plattner, took a dim view of democracy's minimalistic pedigree.[6] So much more was possible. It was a time of optimism. Democracy would change attitudes and shift cultures.

After history's end, democracy became as close to an uncontested good as it could have possibly been. The more democracy triumphed, the more it spread. The more it spread, naturally, the more kinds of democracies there ended up being. Many of these new, fragile democracies were in Latin America, Asia, and Eastern Europe, which meant that liberalism hadn't already established itself. These, then, would not necessarily be or become liberal democracies. As a result, democracy increasingly required adjectives for the purposes of clarity. Were these flawed and partial democracies good or bad, and what made them so? Where there had been relatively few illiberal democracies before—mostly in Latin America where they were known as *democradura*—the idea (and reality) of illiberal democracy, which might have otherwise been dismissed as an oxymoron, began to proliferate.[7] In theory as well as practice, democracy and liberalism were diverging. In the Middle East, the tensions between democracy and liberalism became increasingly apparent in the 1990s (Algeria), 2000s (Egypt, the Palestinian territories, among others), and 2010s (the Arab Spring). With the partial exception of Tunisia, these were either aborted democracies or autocracies that had ended democratization, so expectations of what an illiberal democracy might look like remained mired in speculation. In the rest of the world, however, popular democracy produced outcomes that could be assessed—and they turned earlier notions of elite-driven democracy upside down.

Contrary to what Joseph Schumpeter might have hoped, democracy was becoming more popular and, as a result, more populist. Whether they believed it or not, established parties were paying homage to "the people," even though it wasn't entirely clear who the people were. The "people," though, had their own ideas. In growing numbers, they voted for outsider, far-right, and far-left parties and politicians—the League in Italy, Syriza in Greece, Donald Trump in the United States, Jair Bolsanaro in Brazil, Rodrigo Duterte in the Philippines, and Narendra Modi in India. Even a relative insider and centrist like Emmanuel Macron could run in France as an anti-establishment candidate, fashioning his own party from scratch. In Western European democracies, many of the old center-left parties that had dominated politics for decades were collapsing. Elites, party leaders, and the technocrats they appointed were facing something of a revolt.

Ostensibly, this centrist establishment believed in a thick and substantive conception of democracy. They saw democracy as intertwined with liberalism at home and the "liberal order" abroad. Democracy, then, wasn't merely a method—or at least you would be hard-pressed to find a major politician in the United States or Western Europe who would reduce it to a mere set of procedures. But this made for an unlikely paradox: many of these politicians operated under the assumption that democracy was the best means to securing various other things that they held dear, whether it was economic growth, political consensus, rising living standards, technocratic expertise, individual autonomy, a new multiculturalism in the form of permissive immigration policies, or a supranational union that would minimize and even extinguish dark nationalisms. And for several decades, democracy produced precisely those things, so there was no need to separate the democratic idea into what it was and what it made possible. The two were one and the same. The contradictions, which had always been there, could remain dormant for a time.

When Democracy and Liberalism Diverge

There was a brief interlude of democratic optimism. These were the years of unstoppable economic growth, relative peace, and the expansion of ambitious collectives like the European Union (EU). The EU, as most unions tend to be, was wildly ambitious in theory if not necessarily in practice. There was a catch, though. It didn't last. Elections started producing troubling outcomes. This could only complicate the triumphalist story that led different concepts—*liberal democracy* and *democracy*—to be treated as interchangeable and synonymous. That they were diverging presented a new set of problems, marking a return to the old debate over democracy as a means or an end, which seemed to have been transcended through good fortune.

It was one thing for populists to be "illiberal democrats." After all, Hungary's Prime Minister Viktor Orban explicitly endorsed the phrase.[8] For our purposes, though, the more interesting development was that liberalism and democracy were also diverging in another direction—courtesy of the very people and parties that had championed thicker forms of democracy over the merely procedural. If democracy was no longer producing "good" outcomes—including things valued above and beyond democracy—then how could democracy retain its status as intrinsically good? Mirroring Schumpeter, democracy *was* (or had again become) a means to an end, but this time that end was liberalism, social justice, economic development, or responsible policymaking more broadly, instead of simple elite domination. Schumpeter was also wrong that elite domination would render the individual will irrelevant. Individuals had their own ideas, and the aggregate outcome of millions of those individuals voting their own way was a "popular will" that was at odds with the standard-bearers of traditional party politics.

Means-based arguments were returning, but now they were being wielded not by reactionaries but by "undemocratic liberals."[9] This had to do with the nature of the modern state in all of its bureaucratic glory, asserting itself through regulatory agencies, guardian judiciaries, and watchful central banks. The reach of technocratic policymaking had rendered large swaths of the policy process either unintelligible or inaccessible to a majority of voters.

At the same time, higher levels of education and the universal availability of information (false or otherwise) made citizens more aware of the things they were unaware of, and they weren't necessarily happy about it. As Yascha Mounk notes: "A vast share of the rules to which ordinary citizens are subject are now written, implemented, and sometimes even initiated by unelected officials. . . . The case for taking so many policy decisions out of democratic contestation may be perfectly sound. But even if it is, this does not change the fact that the people no longer have a real say in all these policy areas."[10]

If young and old democracies alike can produce dangerous outcomes (or altogether head-scratching ones) on a somewhat consistent basis, then it undermines the results-oriented argument for democracy. For classical liberals—if they prioritize liberalism over democracy when the two are in tension—democracy inevitably loses value if it produces illiberal outcomes. This, in other words, is the peril of equating liberal democracy, specifically, with democracy, broadly: it makes support for democracy contingent on things that are not intrinsic to it and invites skeptics to wonder whether other methods can better bring about whatever their ultimate good happens to be. This end can be liberalism, socialism, or, on the other end of the spectrum, something like Islamism or Catholic integralism.[11]

Counterintuitively, thickening the democratic idea—making it more substantive than procedural—had the effect of diluting the force of democracy, or at least democracy without adjectives. If democracy was intimately tied to liberalism (and, for a growing number of Americans, social progressivism and racial justice), then it contained the seeds of its own downfall. Democracy could only be good if it produced a growing list of *other* goods. And if democracy was good, as we long suspected it was, then it would naturally lead to those other goods, suggesting a tautology that conflated means with ends and ends with means.

Perhaps, on average, in the broader sweep of history, democracy *is* intimately tied to all of these other things, but in particular moments—and, in historical time, moments can last for decades—this is likely to be of little solace. Acknowledging these trade-offs is important, because it lowers expectations that have long been too high. In a criticism of John Stuart Mill's assertion that liberty was best equipped to nurture integrity and love of truth, the philosopher Isaiah Berlin observed, tucked in a footnote, that "this is but another illustration of the natural tendency of all but a very few thinkers to believe that all the things they hold good must be intimately connected, or at least compatible, with one another."[12]

This all matters because as democracy grows distant from other goods that we hold dearer, it loses its allure, and those who would otherwise consider themselves democrats lose faith. And they *are* losing faith. According to the 2011 World Values Survey, when Barack Obama rather than Donald Trump was president, 24 percent of American millennials were already saying that democracy was a "bad" or "very bad" way of governing the country.[13] Perhaps more strikingly, only 19 percent of American millennials said it was illegitimate for the military to "take over" when the government is failing. Interestingly, in the mid-1990s, it was the wealthy who were the most opposed to authoritarian rule. In the intervening decades, this was reversed, with the rich now "more likely than the poor to express approval for 'having the army rule.'"[14]

Are Democracies More Effective?

The question about Americans' support for a hypothetical military dictatorship might seem odd considering its unlikelihood, but the idea of a strongman "getting things done" makes sense for those who see democracies, even successful ones, as ineffective, inefficient, and consumed by gridlock. Tied to the metric of a government's effectiveness, or lack thereof, is the matter of "performance legitimacy" or "output legitimacy."[15] When it came to dwindling social protections and ballooning inequality after the 2008 financial crisis, it was difficult to give Western democracies high marks (unless you were comparing—and few were—what actually happened with what might have happened under various other worse-case scenarios). As a candidate, Donald Trump appeared on the scene and told his followers, "I alone can fix it," generally a nonsensical remark for a democracy that happened to have a fairly large and sprawling "administrative state."[16] This was the promise of would-be populists: they would take the complexity and messiness of normal politics and render it intelligible. They would fix and solve problems through sheer force of will, knocking heads if need be. This wasn't inherently authoritarian, but it did betray the authoritarian instinct that a leader, if sufficiently strong, could transcend the give and take that makes politics political.

The pandemic intensified the perception that democracies—despite (or due to) being democracies—were underperforming. The largest Western democracies, as well as some of the smallest like Belgium, were among the

world's leaders in per capita deaths from COVID-19.[17] It was only natural for a growing number of Americans and Europeans to doubt not only
their own politicians but their own political systems. If democracy was the
best form of government, shouldn't it also be the best form of government
during a pandemic? As Sheri Berman writes, in times of crisis, "the under-
lying strengths and weaknesses [of political systems] are laid bare." It is little
surprise, then, that President Joe Biden, almost immediately upon taking
office, defined the coming struggle as one between democracies and autocracies. He had in mind China, of course, which through its unbridled authoritarianism seemed able to snuff out the virus in short order, even if it
was the country's very authoritarianism that fueled the outbreak in the first
place.[18] In depicting the challenge, Biden fell back on the instrumentalist language of democratic effectiveness. In his first joint address to Congress, he
declared, "Autocrats think that democracy can't compete in the 21st century
with autocracies, because it takes too long to get consensus."[19] Further clari-
fying this remark to reporters, Biden said, "Think about it. You know, things
are moving so damn rapidly. Things are changing so rapidly in the world in
science and technology and a whole range of other issues that—the question
is: In a democracy that's such a genius as ours, can you get consensus in the
timeframe that can compete with autocracy?"[20] In his first press conference
as president, President Biden had also said: "It is clear, absolutely clear . . . that
this is a battle between the utility of democracies in the 21st century and
autocracies."[21] This was beginning to be a theme. The key metric, explicitly,
was utility.[22]

The emphasis on utility is a concession to authoritarianism. Autocracies
derive their legitimacy, if they have it, from delivering goods and services and
being effective—the "performance legitimacy" mentioned earlier. The other
option, popular legitimacy, is much more difficult for them to attain. Instead,
a bargain is struck. Subjects have to forgo their freedom, but at least they get
something in return.[23] Superior performance is certainly a good thing for
democracies, but democracy does not (or at least should not) rely on it. If superior performance occurs, it is a welcome by-product of democracy rather
than intrinsic to it. Biden's framing of the problem—and his proposed solution of demonstrating that democracies can be just as effective or efficient as
autocracies—betray a technocratic bias that regime types should be judged
based on whether or not they work. What might be termed "what works-
ism" provides us with a purely instrumental argument, and one that wades
into the democracy versus authoritarian contest on authoritarians' terms.

There was a time when democracies were better at producing consensus, particularly during the Cold War, when having a shared enemy helped Republicans and Democrats to minimize their differences on foreign policy. That time has passed. Moreover, the United States has grown increasingly diverse along ethnic as well as religious lines. It doesn't help that these differences are overlaid on a partisan divide, which effectively amplifies each of the divisions in question. In a two-party system with high levels of polarization, partisan balancing—where the party in opposition basically does the opposite of the party in power—becomes the norm. Consensus can happen, but it requires struggle (and if consensus is a struggle, it calls into question whether the consensus is real).

For their part, European democracies were thought to have an institutional advantage when it came to sustaining consensus, because they prioritized parliamentary over presidential rule. A long academic literature has testified to the inferiority of the latter.[24] Parliamentary systems with proportional representation have long seemed superior on a number of metrics. And they *are*. As the political theorist Ian Shapiro notes, however, this conclusion may require reassessment in light of recent developments. In the case of Germany, for instance, "the greater ability of proportional representation systems to deliver social protection seems, in hindsight, to have depended at least partly on the presence of left-of-center parties like Germany's Social Democrats that were frequently in government."[25] But the future success of such parties is far from guaranteed, even where they have been long been dominant. In the absence of strong centrist parties and grand coalitions, fragmentation and rapid turnover are something close to inevitable in parliamentary systems. Italy, for example, has been notorious for its ephemeral governments, numbering sixty-nine of them in seventy-six years at the time of writing.[26]

In short, consensus is made more difficult in the American system, and achieving consensus has become more challenging even in the "consensual" democracies of Western Europe. If consensus is difficult, and is growing more so, the instrumentalist argument for democracy struggles—and even fails—on its own terms. Roberto Foa and Yascha Mounk, in a pithy sentence, capture the paradox of making democracy both more and less than what it might otherwise be. "Even as democracy has come to be the only form of government widely viewed as legitimate," they write, "it has lost the trust of many citizens who no longer believe that democracy can deliver on their most pressing needs and preferences."[27]

The irony is that the more recent catch-all conceptions of democracy, as containing all good things, rely on minimalistic logic for maximalist ends. In contrast, democratic minimalism lowers the stakes. Democratic government does not need to secure all ends and all aims, because it can't but also because it shouldn't. Contra Schumpeter, the minimalistic conception of democracy offered here elevates democracy from a means to a perhaps modest but still powerful end.

There is a certain urgency to shifting the parameters of what democracy is and what it should be. In their illuminating book *Democracy for Realists*, the political scientists Christopher Achen and Larry Bartels underscore how democracy in practice diverges from the instrumentalist ideal whereby democracy leads to smarter, effective, and more consensus-driven politics. Instrumentalist arguments render democratic politics unimpressive, in other words, because they promise that which they cannot deliver. There aren't always policy solutions to policy problems, and even (or particularly) the best educated do not necessarily vote based on policy. Achen and Bartels' register of misplaced hopes is sobering: Citizens cannot accurately assess "changes in their own welfare"; voters "[adapt] their ideas to those of the presidential candidate they [favor]" and not the other way around; "ideology is more often an effect of partisanship than its cause," and apparently "most people make their party choices based on who they are rather than on what they think."[28] This might all sound depressing, but it doesn't have to be.

That we expect democracy to do everything at once—to "work" and work well—suggests a system of government becoming the victim of its own success. No longer content with democracy as such, our gaze extends to new horizons. The basics are easily forgotten, but the basics are increasingly important as would-be (or might-be) democracies remain ideologically polarized and as support for strongmen grows.

The Purposes of Democratic Minimalism

In this context, a focus on democratic minimalism begins making sense for securing the foundations of legitimate government, irrespective of any secondary outcomes or benefits. While this might sound like a somewhat vague purpose, there is a simpler way of putting it: democracies have the advantage of not being dictatorships, and this, by itself, renders them superior. Or as Robert Dahl put it, "Perhaps the most fundamental and persistent problem in politics is to avoid autocratic rule."[29] Of course, this is almost too obvious, which is perhaps one reason we have tended to forget it.

Democracy allows for the peaceful transfer of power, even (or particularly) in ideologically polarized contexts. It is a truism that democracy is more difficult in divided societies, but it is also true that democracy is more *necessary* in divided societies, precisely because citizens do not agree on ends. As a set of mechanisms for conflict regulation, democracy contributes to long-term, if not short-term, stability—a necessary if difficult trade-off. Democracy removes the unpredictability inherent in arbitrary rule. For the opponents of any given government, democracy offers predictability, since losers of elections have the chance to fight another day, as long as they are willing to fight peacefully.

One might argue that this, too, betrays an instrumentalist logic, but these benefits are not incidental to democracy. They are intrinsic to it as a system for governing. Beyond this, though, there are deeper reasons—having to do with its relationship to the human person—for viewing democracy as its own end. If man "is by nature a political animal," per Aristotle, and if God created man, it is possible to combine the propositions to say that man was *made* a political animal. Therefore, those who live under autocracies—those who have no access to politics or political participation—are being "forced to be less, in some sense, than God wanted them to be."[30]

Why might God have wanted them to be this way? The political theorist Josiah Ober argues that "the opportunity to associate in decision is a necessary part of human happiness and the capacity to associate in decision is constitutive of what it is to be human."[31] Living well in this way requires "the opportunity to exercise, freely and virtuously, the human capacities of reason and speech."[32] This human happiness is constricted in any political regime that blocks or punishes the right to associate with others. As Ober writes, "A benevolent dictator who satisfied all other conditions of justice harms her subjects by denying them opportunity to associate in the decisions by which their community is governed."[33] If liberty is conceived as nondomination, then a dictator, however "benevolent," is a contradiction in terms. There is no such thing as a benevolent dictator. Domination is intrinsic to dictatorial rule. And domination, by its very nature, prevents the development of individual agency and moral responsibility.

While God has generally figured prominently in movements of liberation and self-determination, belief in God is not necessary to reach the above conclusions. Aristotle's argument is that adults have an innate disposition to "rule and be ruled in turn."[34] Where this innateness originates from is secondary.

In modern contexts—where this innate sense of being human is diminished and the measurement of economic, technological, or scientific outcomes is elevated—such justifications for democracy have grown rarer. Reconceptualizing democracy as *a system and means of governing and rotating power with no prejudice to substantive ideological outcomes* allows us to move away from a preoccupation with democratic instrumentalism. Suspending judgment on ends while insisting on democratic means, regardless of the outcome, might seem like thin gruel if the goal is to unify divided societies. But what is needed is not necessarily unity. In polarized societies, unity is impractical. And, somewhat counterintuitively, unity hinges on an exclusionary premise, asking citizens to put aside their deepest convictions in the name of a greater good, a greater good that is determined by those who hold cultural or political authority. To ask someone to hide who they are in the name of a greater good, though, is to ask the impossible. We may be able to suppress our deepest commitments for a time, but not indefinitely.

3

The Problem of Islam

Unity and consensus are beyond reach when societies are polarized around foundational questions. And if unity and consensus are, in fact, either illusions or impossibilities, then this has far-reaching implications for the democratic idea. Democracy, to the extent that it seeks to aggregate the opinions and preferences of all citizens, will not—and cannot—produce consensus, if no such consensus already exists. Citizens cannot be expected to suppress or alter their deepest convictions about God and the Good.

When I was living in the Middle East during the Arab Spring, I was struck by something that felt foreign and unsettling. A new democratic politics had emerged in a number of countries, but the divisions seemed raw and existential in a way that intrigued as well as frightened me. It seemed like quite a lot was at stake, perhaps too much. This had not been my experience with American politics, which, at the time at least, was reassuring in its smallness. Americans had their differences, to be sure, but they appeared to agree on the fundamentals. Because the country's foundations weren't in question, citizens were freed to debate policy—whether taxes, healthcare, or the deficit. It was possible to care deeply about things that weren't existential, and most things weren't.

Of course, Americans would get a rude introduction to existential politics soon enough. But at the time, Middle Eastern countries—perhaps because they were also Muslim-majority societies—seemed unusually contentious. This was a revolutionary situation, and revolutions tend to be vehicles of excess and violence. But it was easy to forget that in the midst of the euphoria. I certainly remember forgetting it.

The founding moments of these new democracies were contested from the very start. Almost immediately, in those first few months of what would come to be known as the Arab Spring, the role of religion in public life and Islam's relationship to the state became the subject of intense disagreement. Despite underemployment, income inequality, and poverty being the most proximate concerns for ordinary citizens, they were rarely discussed, in part because there was little to discuss. Most parties mouthed the same banalities.

Candidates routinely promised more jobs, better wages, and campaigns to root out poverty, corruption, and any number of other social ills. If you wanted to distinguish yourself from the competition, discussing the economy was probably not going to rally the base. "Left" and "right" weren't the relevant categories, because a traditional left–right spectrum didn't reflect the primary cleavage in these societies, which revolved around religion, culture, and identity.[1]

In countries like Egypt and Tunisia, Islamist parties emerged as the strongest and the most electorally astute. In the case of the former, the predominance of a group like the Muslim Brotherhood wasn't much of a surprise. Banned but tolerated within limits, it had been Egypt's largest and best-organized opposition movement for decades. In Tunisia, however, the main Islamist party, Ennahda, hadn't just been repressed. It had been decimated, with no organizational presence for the near entirety of the 1990s and 2000s. Yet, it was able to rapidly reemerge in the matter of mere months. At least the Islamists of Tunisia were relatively mild, almost gratuitous in their eagerness to please.[2] The same couldn't quite be said for the rest of the region.

And so democratization did not, as many Western observers suspected and hoped, naturally propel liberals and liberalism, because liberalism had limited electoral appeal. During Egypt's brief democratic experiment, even liberal parties avoided the "liberal" label. As Mustafa al-Naggar, founder of the Justice Party, explained it to me, "We help people understand liberalism through behavior and example, through an understanding of citizenship."[3] At the same time, he said, "none of us are using the word 'liberalism' because for the Egyptian street 'liberalism' equals disbelief." The pervasiveness of religion and rhetorical support for sharia produced a skewed playing field, with Islamists enjoying a built-in advantage.

The Islamist dilemma was returning, just as it always did when there were democratic openings in the Arab world. The skeptics and naysayers could say that they were correct—that American hopes for democracy in the Middle East were as misplaced as they were naïve. Democracy was a problem because Islam was a problem. Too many citizens, for different reasons and to different degrees, wanted (or at least said they wanted) Islam to play a significant role in politics. If democracy was meant to channel and reflect popular sentiment—and if popular sentiment was inclined in the direction of whatever the opposite of progress was—then more democracy wasn't necessarily something to laud. It was almost enough to be angry at Islamists themselves, not necessarily for what they did but for the reactions they provoked in their opponents. If there weren't Islamists, there wouldn't be an Islamist dilemma. And if there wasn't Islam—or at least if Islam had been domesticated the way Christianity had in Western Europe—there wouldn't be an Islamist problem.

Taking Islam Seriously

Religion in general, but Islam in particular, has often been portrayed as an obstacle to promoting pluralism, tolerance, and various other good things. In an attempt to correct for this tendency to essentialize an entire faith and its adherents, various scholars have argued that religion doesn't matter as much as we think it does. What matters instead are those tangible things—politics, economics, temptations of power, and the distribution of resources. In this reading, religion is a mode and a means and a way of articulating grievances, but it is not the end. Islam itself—or, more precisely, Islam as it's refracted through the actions of Muslims—is not the prime mover. Even when faith is expressed with sincerity, believers may be under the grip of false consciousness, thinking that they are acting for religion's sake when, in fact, religion is providing a cover for deeper and rather less romantic impulses. This, then, is an argument for the primacy of the unsacred. Religion is both separate and secondary, shaped by ultimately secular forces. Or, so the thinking goes.

However understandable or well-intentioned, the reluctance to take Islam too seriously comes with its own drawbacks. It addresses the "problem" of Islam by basically eliding it or hoping that it will go away in due time. In so doing, it replicates the very problem it is ostensibly trying to address. If Islam—in the sense of both theological conviction and lived practice—is secondary in practical, political terms and is used and abused by cynical or otherwise oblivious actors, then there is little to do but to wait and hope that Islam will be saved by its own growing irrelevance.

We might wish it were otherwise, but religion isn't going anywhere in the Middle East. Some surveys—conducted after the failures of the Arab Spring and the rise and fall of the Islamic State, or ISIS—have pointed to a decline in religiosity. One widely cited 2019 Arab Barometer poll produced a flurry of headlines proclaiming, with barely concealed glee, that secularism was finally gaining ground across the region.[4] What they failed to note was that the number identifying as "not religious" had, in fact, only increased from 8 to 13 percent. The Middle East has been so disproportionately religious and religiously conservative that slight shifts are taken as harbingers of a secularizing period that never seems to come. Something was lost in translation as well, it turns out. In English, the category of "not religious" implies not being theologically Christian or Jewish. They are not religious insofar as they do not have a religion. These are the "nones." The common Arabic phrase for "not religious"—*lastu mutadayyin*—means something different in Muslim contexts. One could easily describe themselves as not being religious while still being a Muslim believer. In Islam, to be religious is often tied to ritual practice (more so than it would be in Christianity), so if someone says they are "not religious," they may simply mean that they are not particularly observant.

Such hopes for a secular future reflect a stubborn logic—that, over time, reason will *eventually, somehow* gain the upper hand against religious passions. In this story, reason and revelation are in perpetual tension, if not necessarily opposed outright. Instead of seeing the brief heyday of secular Arab nationalism in the 1950s and 60s as an aberration in the broader historical sweep, it sees the Islamic revival that followed as contingent and ephemeral. In 1974, the political scientist Tareq Ismael could write that "in recent years Islam has so declined in authority and vitality that it has become a mere instrument for state policy, although it is still active as a folk religion."[5] The decade in which Ismael was writing marked the beginning of an Islamic revival that would grow in strength, persisting in various iterations and to varying degrees of intensity until the present moment.

Few today would make an argument as bold as Ismael's, that Islam is doomed to irrelevance as a political force. But the notion of Islam as a kind of religious garb that covers truer sentiments is commonplace. This framing is not necessarily unique to Islam; it is used to describe and diminish right-wing evangelical movements that have been influential throughout American history.[6] These groups, the thinking goes, are not *really* about Christianity, so there is little reason to study or interpret them as genuinely Christian. However, due to low and declining levels of Christian observance in Western democracies, there are simply fewer of these movements to focus attention on or to be particularly worried about. By default, then, any skepticism around religion in public life, if not in intent then in effect, ends up being disproportionately concerned with Islam, since Islam—unlike Christianity—has retained an outsized role in public life both in Muslim-majority countries and among growing Muslim-minority populations in Europe.[7]

There's nothing intrinsically "bad" about an Islam that is public, unless, perhaps, one is a secularist who believes that all public manifestations of religion are, in principle, bad, whatever their specific content. Putting aside one's normative preferences, however, it should be relatively uncontroversial to say that Islam's prominent place in politics is and will be a reality for the foreseeable future. And if it is a reality, then it must be contended with. For their part, Muslim thinkers in various works of Islamic apologetics have highlighted Islam's political relevance as something to celebrate—and so, too, have some Christian thinkers, lamenting that Christianity unlike Islam has allowed itself to be defanged.[8] That Islam seems political and perhaps even *is* political is a feature, not a bug. But even this framing has its drawbacks, since it implies that "religion" and "politics" are discrete categories. For much of human history, and until quite recently, this would have struck believers of most if not all faiths as an odd proposition indeed.

Even if it were preferable, cordoning off religion—and in this case Islam— is impractical and unrealistic. What would it mean to promote the slow, gradual privatization of religion in the world's most religiously conservative societies? Even the region's more "secular" countries, such as Tunisia, Lebanon, and Turkey, retain extremely high levels of religious identification. In Tunisia, for example, 99 percent of respondents say God plays an "important role" in their life, while 97 percent say the same for prayer, according to a 2020 Pew survey.[9] (Tunisians may be falsifying their preferences to pollsters, but if people think they *should* be praying regardless of whether they actually are, that, too, tells us something about secularization or the lack thereof.) In the event that rapid and widespread secularization somehow occurs in the future, it could have the counterintuitive effect of *increasing* polarization. Generally accepted religious norms would become more contested. The gap between religious and less religious citizens would grow, since there would be more room for the latter to be overtly non- or even anti-religious.

The reality of religious diversity in the Middle East—and the regular bouts of religious conflict that result from an inability to peacefully process that reality—means that secular political frameworks are no longer best equipped to manage religious diversity. Secular frameworks start from the premise that public religiosity—particularly when it has political implications for rulers, which it usually does—is a problem to be solved. In theory, this invites coercion. In practice, it has. An insistence on secularism as the only legitimate framework for society and politics relies on a religious "Other." That Other is painted as illegitimate and a threat to order.

Despite carefully managed appearances, ostensibly secular Arab regimes are not, in fact, secular in the sense of separating religion from politics or separating mosque and state; the state is still intimately involved with the production and regulation of religious knowledge. But these regimes portray themselves to Western audiences as more secular than the alternative, and they seem secular insofar as they are anti-Islamist. In so doing, they are able to legitimize their repression, or to at least make it appear less bad than it might otherwise be. After all, it may be repression, but it's the sort of repression wielded in the name of the state, in the name of stability, and in the name of modernity and progress.

A strong, relatively "enlightened" state, however repressive, represented the best opportunity to secure the freedom and safety of the two groups that suffer—or are thought to suffer—under democratization: women and religious minorities. As the conservative writer Luna Simms argues: "We in the West suppose that democracy is some kind of cure for Islamist radicalism. We're foolish to think so. Every attempt at democracy, and every democratic-like government that has been set up in Muslim-majority countries, has inflicted great harm on its religious minorities."[10] Arab leaders and officials are well aware of the secular bias of Western interlocutors. If ordinary citizens were conservative and retrograde on things like gender equality and minority rights, then top-down, authoritarian leaders might be bad in theory, but perhaps, in a universe of necessary evils, they could be seen as an instrument of progress. If democracy was ultimately supposed to produce good outcomes, with electorates like these it clearly wouldn't. All the reason to be circumspect about the right of those citizens to vote in meaningful elections in the first place.

Morality aside, there was another presumption, namely that coercion and repression could kill an idea that enjoyed significant public support. Even at the height of the secular nationalist project, President Gamal Abdel Nasser, the lion of the Arabs and perhaps the most popular Arab leader of the modern era, failed to eradicate the Muslim Brotherhood despite his best efforts. Nasser did reach unrivaled dominance but only by employing extreme levels of repression against the Brotherhood and its organizational structures. In this sense, the preeminence of secular nationalism, however brief, was not the natural outcome of political and electoral competition.

What, then, is the "natural" state of the Middle East? There's no way to really determine this, of course, but there are probably a few intuitive propositions worth taking into account. The first is that coercion, by design, is meant to prevent individuals from doing what they otherwise might do. If brute force is wielded by authoritarian regimes to promote "unity" or the "nation," then that unity is, by definition, unnatural. National unity, here, reflects an artificial, imposed consensus. If the consensus was true and uncontrived, it would not require the application of force.

In the absence of coercion or when coercion decreases over time, citizens are able to act with less fear of sanction or persecution. What they do, in such circumstances, is a more accurate reflection of their needs and desires than what they might do under the threat of some exogenous force. Once the fear and terror of arbitrary repression are removed, a rich array of human beliefs and preferences quickly make themselves apparent. In the early months of the Arab Spring, autocrats were overthrown, and, almost immediately, hundreds of new parties and movements from across the ideological spectrum sprung up. It's not that these beliefs and preferences were not there before; it's that they weren't allowed to be expressed. It is easy to resort to cliché and speak of the indomitable human spirit. I certainly saw evidence of that spirit the day that Hosni Mubarak, Egypt's dictator of three long decades, fell from power. In the streets of Cairo, the celebrations were, in a very real sense, spontaneous. Of course, there was a dark side, too. No one was quite prepared for this outpouring of sentiment, which had been building for years, slowly and with some sense of foreboding. Ideological and religious diversity, in its unmediated state, can be overwhelming and chaotic. And without strong institutions, it can easily give way not to a pluralism of reciprocity and respect but rather to existential conflict. In a country like Egypt that had long seemed homogenous, it was striking to watch the emergence of opposed factions, each with its own strong identity and each feeling threatened by the other's growing presence. They were all Egyptians, of course, but it became apparent that this wasn't enough.

This freewheeling diversity, threatening as it was to the status quo, provoked its own vigorous, authoritarian reaction. This is the way of the modern Arab state. It seeks decisive victories that flatten difference, but this compulsion to constrain and control is evidence of a fatal paradigmatic flaw. The modern diversity of Arab societies—and, for that matter, increasingly diverse societies around the globe—cannot be undone. It can be suppressed, but only for a time. This suppression of difference is both the raison d'être and the false promise of authoritarianism, an authoritarianism that attempts to fashion unity by force, where none exists.

* * *

There was a time when a semblance of unity was possible. But it no longer is, for important reasons. This is why the ideological diversity of Arab societies is very much a modern condition. It is simply a reality now in a way that it wouldn't—and *couldn't*—have been in centuries prior. Before the advent of modernity, few if any Muslims questioned the idea of Islamic law. They may have disagreed vehemently with particular legal interpretations or how laws were implemented, but that the law had a divine source was not in question. Sharia, often misleadingly reduced to "Islamic law," wasn't simply a matter of rules and punishments. Not just a legal system, it was a moral architecture, a social order, and a source of legitimacy.[11] There was intellectual and philosophical diversity, to be sure—the infamous rift between the *mutazilites* and *asharis* comes to mind[12]—but it was within the bounds of the existing Islamic order. No movements of note were calling for an alternative to Islamic governance, even as they disagreed on what Islamic governance meant in practice. For the better part of fourteen centuries this was the way of things, until it all changed.

New Divides

If secularism failed to attract mass support in the Middle East, it succeeded in other ways. Even among those who resisted it tooth and nail, secularization reshaped Muslims' relationship to their religion, whether or not they realized it.

With the introduction of secular ideologies in the nineteenth century—including the somewhat novel idea that religion was better understood as a private affair—the place of Islam as a "hegemonic moral system" was irrevocably undermined.[13] This provoked a reaction: if Islam was no longer the natural order of things, it had to be reasserted. It was taken away, so it would have to be regained. And this marked the origin of what would come to be known as not Islam but Islam*ism*. In the broadest sense, Islamists are those who believe that Islamic law or Islamic values should play a central role in public life. They feel Islam has things to say about how politics should be conducted and how other people—not just themselves—should behave in both private and public. But this sentiment, by itself, is not enough to be or become an Islamist. As the Princeton historian Michael Cook writes, Islamists are "at pains to construe their politics out of their Islamic heritage."[14] One must, in other words, *decide* to act politically as an Islamist.[15]

In the pre-modern era, to think that Islam had something to say about law and politics and how individuals should act outside of their own homes would be entirely unremarkable. It went without saying, so it wasn't said. With the advent of secularism as both a challenge and a threat, Islam would, for the first time, become a political enterprise to be fashioned, developed, and advocated for. And it is no accident that Islamist groups speak quite explicitly of promoting *al-mashrou' al-Islami*, literally "the Islamic project." But what did it mean for a religion to be a project? Islamism is what it meant to mobilize Islam as a distinct political identity, one that could only exist with its (perceived) opposite. This was an Islam that was self-conscious and mannered, and this is what made it different from what had come before. This was a distinctly *modern* Islam. And this presented a paradox inherent to the Islamist project: in order to retrieve something that was lost—this supposedly pure, original Islam—it would be transformed into something new and unprecedented. Islamism wasn't so much a reaction to modernity but a product of it.

The insertion of Islamism into social and political life was both a response to polarization and an engine of it. Once the status of Islam and Islamic law was made subject to popular debate, it would always be contested. There was no way to undo what was done and return to a consensus that had slowly frayed, then shattered. Some of this had to do with the influence and intellectual dominance of Western democracies, each featuring some iteration of secularism. Inevitably, those ideas flowed into the Middle East through tourism, travel, and education (and, before that, colonialism) and were adopted by "secular" educated elites with various degrees of enthusiasm. New nation-states, which replaced sprawling multiethnic and multireligious empires, contained their own secularizing logics. It wasn't a coincidence that the rise of the modern bureaucratic state coincided with secularism's ascendance. The two were intertwined, and Islam found itself threatened by this accident of history. By the first half of the twentieth century, no other religion could still claim a privileged role in the formulation of public law and politics. Islam still did, but this, too, would change.

In an alternate universe where European colonialism never was, secularism would have still spread. One could even argue that, without the taint of Western coercion, these ideas would have been more appealing to Arabs and Muslims, and they could have been embraced without quite the same accusations of cultural and religious betrayal.[16] New ideas are appealing because they are new—they speak to the challenges of changing time and place.

Insofar as they spurred the West's political and economic innovation, secular and liberal ideals were successful from a practical standpoint if not necessarily a spiritual one. At the core of what the West would become was the nation-state. What made this idea of the state so distinctive is that it radically altered the sources of political legitimacy.

Under the Ottoman caliphate, membership and autonomy in the polity were based on one's religion, with Christians answering to local church leaders and Jews to the local rabbi.[17] After the fall of the Ottomans, however, to be a citizen was to become the citizen of a nation, irrespective of religion. It is difficult to overstate the implications of this shift in legal and political legitimacy. Take, for example, the issue of blasphemy. In the pre-modern era, blasphemy was considered an attack not just on religion but on the state as well, since the two were intertwined. Attacking the Prophet, questioning the Qur'an's divine authorship, or even renouncing Islam were treated as political rather than strictly theological acts, more or less equivalent to treason. "This mode of thinking about religion as a political and communal identity as opposed to a mere matter of conscience went unchallenged until the modern period," writes Jonathan Brown, a leading scholar of Islam.[18]

It is either blindingly obvious or controversial bordering on bigoted to say that Islam is incompatible with the nation-state. For precision's sake, it would be more accurate to say that Islam was not *designed* for the nation-state. The Qur'an, which Muslims consider not just the word of God but God's actual speech, with every word and letter divine, was revealed in an era when nation-states did not yet exist.[19] At the same time, the Prophet Mohamed and the first generation of Muslims were intimately concerned with governance, particularly after Mohamed and his followers emigrated to Medina, setting up something akin to a proto-state there. In the subsequent centuries, drawing on the Qur'an as well as prophetic sayings and actions known as *hadith*, a rich and layered corpus of Islamic jurisprudence and legal scholarship developed.

But the sharia, contrary to modern understandings of law, wasn't a compendium of legal codes to be found in one place. It also wasn't the sole or even primary purview of the state, as represented by the caliph or sultan. This was not radical at the time, but it is radical in retrospect. As Knut Vikør notes, "We see in the Islamic case that the law is drawn away from the state, personified by the sultan, and so presents in many ways an anomaly compared to the theoretical model of state power as the embodiment of state law."[20] Accordingly, the clerical and judicial classes enjoyed considerable independence and autonomy from executive authorities, helping make the sharia into the dynamic, living thing it was once.[21] This dynamism is what would make it anathema to newly independent Arab nations, which, taking their cue from rising European states, sought to centralize power and promulgate uniform legal codes. In the process, they divested the law of its ambiguities and flexibility. The state, particularly under the sway of authoritarian paternalists like Ataturk, Gamal Abdel Nasser in Egypt, and Habib Bourguiba in Tunisia, wished to remain powerful and become more powerful still. This meant asserting control over religious knowledge and religious production, subsuming the clerical class and religious scholarship under the shade of a bureaucratizing state.

There would be no recovering from this. The conflict between the state and Islam was won. To call it a conflict would be perhaps overstating matters, since "Islam"—a mere religion with no army to call its own—was no match. In their effort to make Islam safe for the nation-state, the region's strongmen helped make the question of Islam's role in politics and its relationship to the state a perpetual source of grievance. Islam had become a problem. And there wasn't a solution, at least not an obvious one.

Messy Pluralism Instead of Suppression

In hindsight, it was probably inevitable. We live in a world of nation-states. The idea of nation and state worked out better in non-Muslim countries, where there was less temptation to regulate religion because religion had become less resonant and therefore less threatening. But if Islam—as a faith, an inspiration, and a reminder that justice was something God asked men to uphold—remained unusually potent in the hearts and minds of Muslims, then young, insecure regimes couldn't afford to let it be. Islam was no longer, if it ever was, just a matter of faith; it was a question of national security and survival.

Nearly a century after the abolition of the last caliphate, Islam's relationship to the state and the state's relationship to Islam remain unresolved, a seemingly permanent source of conflict. The problem isn't Islam itself, then, but rather the failure to come to a consensus over the role it should play in public life. The solution, then, would be to somehow come to a consensus, but such a consensus is beyond reach, and any attempt to fashion one would be morally untenable, requiring ever escalating levels of repression. It would require repression because diversity and difference are—now, after everything that has happened—the natural state of the Middle East. Amoral cynicism is unlikely to be helpful in this regard; even if one had no moral qualms, a regime's suppression of Islam-related differences has little chance of "working." It has already been attempted repeatedly, by one strongman after another, in a wide variety of contexts. Moreover, it might provide the appearance of success in the near term—the more a regime suppresses dissent, the less noticeable the dissent, and the more popular and therefore "legitimate" a dictator might seem—but such appearances are difficult to sustain indefinitely. To the extent that ideologues can be killed but the ideas themselves cannot, repression is only likely to postpone the inevitable and come at a considerable moral and political cost. Some of the consequences are difficult to anticipate and may only make themselves apparent in the longer run.

The alternative to suppression is clear enough—and it involves fully accepting the fact of a messy pluralism, not only of ethnicities and sects but also of the less tangible ideological divides over Islam among believers. There was a time when most Islamists still held out hope that the tides of the twentieth century could be reversed, that secularists—or really anyone who challenged Islam's place in politics—could be marginalized or perhaps excluded altogether. As recently as the early 1990s, Muslim Brotherhood branches in Egypt and Jordan could still equate secularism with atheism, arguing that the latter disqualified them from political participation. In one pamphlet, Jordan's Muslim Brotherhood outlined its stance on political pluralism. "The nation," it said, "has reached a high level of awareness toward the role of [Islam in] its life [and] we view with disdain and disgust anyone who underestimates this fundamental aspect. We classify such people as outside the circle of the nation and we reject their belonging to it."[22] Meanwhile, in Egypt, the Brotherhood accused leftist parties of apostasy, or *ilhad*, for their opposition to sharia. "The philosophy of [the leftist party] Tagammu rests," said the Brotherhood leader Hamed Abu Nasr, "on a foundation of the denial of God and the idea that religion is the opiate of the people . . . and so it is impossible that the party will ever have a place among the Egyptian people."[23]

For their part, secular and liberal parties have an even longer record and history of insisting on the exclusion of Islamists.[24] Of course, this is not to say that all secularists take this position or that there is anything inherent to secularism that necessitates exclusion. My argument is narrower but perhaps also more tragic: as an empirical matter, significant numbers—and sometimes large majorities—of secular and liberal activists have opposed and continue to oppose Islamist participation, even to the point of backing military coups to undo democratic outcomes not to their liking. To the extent that either "side" wishes to exclude the other, they are operating under an illusion that the battle over Islam's role in public life can be resolved by eliminating their opponents.

Considering the reality of religious and ideological diversity, there simply aren't enough secularists for secularism to claim victory. An Islamist victory is similarly out of reach. While Islamist parties may represent a numerically larger—sometimes much larger—segment of the population, this does not mean that all or even most who vote for them would consider themselves Islamists. Many ordinary voters who aren't particularly politicized would fail to meet Cook's aforementioned definition of "Islamist." These voters may be many things, but it is unlikely that many of them are "at pains to construe their politics out of their Islamic heritage."

In short, there are Islamists, there are secularists, and many still who are neither. And it will always be this way, short of an act of God. Or, to put it differently, disagreements around the role of religion in public life will persist, in part because they should. The alternative is considerably worse. The only way such disagreements could disappear is by eradicating them through force. But even this wouldn't make the differences disappear so much as simply suppress them until a subsequent period of political opening.

That these disagreements over religion would solidify was inevitable. Once alternative means of political legitimation—in this case, Western secular ones—are introduced into the public and particularly elite imagination, they cannot be unremembered. In this sense, some developments, in politics as in life, are permanent, and they shape and constrain all possible futures. There is simply no way to fight back the palpable diversity of religious options and opinions available in modern societies. Education levels, which rapidly increased in the Middle East during the second half of the twentieth century, coupled with a growing awareness of how other people live, mean that individuals have choices in a way they hadn't previously. While the democratization of politics can be halted through repression, the democratization of religion, short of an outright totalitarian gambit, is more difficult to stop. Anyone with Internet access can wake up and go fatwa shopping.

Since we are modern, and this is all we know, it is difficult to grasp that most Muslims centuries ago would have had very limited access to religious resources. If they were in Anatolia, they wouldn't be aware of religious developments in Andalusia. They were part of a global *ummah* but one that was disjointed and diffuse. During the so-called golden ages of Islam, there were dueling philosophical approaches and often a greater openness to heterodox opinions, but these would have concerned only a rarified, lettered elite. Most Muslims could not read the Qur'an, and those who did would have accepted without question that it was not their role to interpret it. That would have been the job of the *ulama*, who, then unlike now, retained a visible and elevated role in everyday life and social and business interactions.[25] And unlike under modern states, these scholars and clerics had power because the legal system depended on them, particularly on the local level, when local autonomy was still possible.

A State of Diversity

It is one thing for citizens to cast their votes for Islamist parties, suggesting a general desire—perhaps visceral but certainly vague—for Islam to play a prominent role in politics. This, however, does not mean that those voters share any real sense of what exactly that role might entail in practice. Even among themselves, Muslim Brotherhood members don't agree on what applying Islamic law would actually mean, which is one reason that their vision of governance tends to stay rather abstract—sometimes maddeningly so, at least as far as their opponents are concerned. What defines Islamist movements isn't what they do, but rather who they are (or who they are not). They promise a basic orientation that privileges Islam, and that basic orientation can go a long way. "Islam is the solution" is the famous Brotherhood slogan, but the solution to what?

When it comes to Islam, secularists also disagree among themselves, divided between hardliners in former French colonies who believe religion has no place in politics (which, of course, is itself a political position) and those who believe religion has a public role but not to the extent Islamists do or not in the way Islamists do. What unites non-Islamist parties, then, isn't secularism per se, since many members and leaders of secular parties aren't secular in the Western sense and certainly not in the French sense.[26] Rather, what unites them is that they aren't Islamist. Across the region, haphazard coalitions of otherwise warring factions—from old-style Marxists to neoliberal businesspeople—have been formed solely on the basis of an inchoate anti-Islamism.

In short, these are societies that lack consensus and are unlikely to find it, nor should they try to. As the Dutch theologian and prime minister Abraham Kuyper once succinctly put it: "Theocracy is only possible when everyone voluntarily agrees with the theocracy but this is very rare."[27] He wrote this in the late nineteenth century, after the fact of diversity in the Netherlands, then a society at risk of civil war, became inescapable. There was a patchwork of secularists, humanists, liberals, and socialists, and none was in any position to defeat the other. The core premise, here, applies to all societies: theocracy is only possible if there are enough theocrats. Short of using force, an Islamist *regime*—as opposed to a government led by democratically elected Islamists—is only possible if there are enough Islamists, and there aren't. Similarly, secularism is only possible if there are enough secularists, and there aren't. Unity, however desirable in theory, is in direct conflict with diversity in practice.

Foundational divides over religion and identity cannot be transcended. These divides aren't artificial, manufactured, or temporary; they reflect legitimate differences beyond the scope of "normal" politics and rational deliberation. "On matters of economic policy and social expenditures you can always split the difference," the political scientist Dankwart Rustow once wrote.[28] How, though, do you split the difference on religion? But also: *Should* it be split even if it were possible? Some problems don't have resolutions, beyond resolving to live in a state of flux and uncertainty. Consensus in deeply divided societies is illusory, because "all forms of consensus are by necessity based on acts of exclusion," as the Belgian political theorist Chantal Mouffe writes.[29] Consensus is only possible when there is already a consensus, and there rarely is—and there certainly isn't in the countries in question.

To give up on misplaced hopes can be liberating. If consensus, unity, or strong centralized states (which are often perceived as a means to unity) are seen for what they are—vehicles for the suppression of difference—then we can start from a different set of premises and build a distinctive strategy on a new foundation. If divides over Islam and the state cannot be undone—and if one side cannot conclusively "win" and impose its preferences except through escalating force, and even then only temporarily—then pluralistic arrangements that allow for the peaceful transfer of power from one side to another are the only viable long-term option. The catch, if one wishes to see it that way, is that this pluralism will require, at least to some degree, the accommodation of conservative and even illiberal religious ideas. Secularism isn't the solution, and neither is Islam. From a secularist perspective, this indeterminacy—accepting that there is no final victory for secular or liberal rationalism—is the price that must be paid not just for democracy but for any stable, sustainable outcome in the Middle East. There is really no other way to deal with the "problem" of Islam.

Pro-democracy advocates tend to argue that democracy is well suited for all societies, its universal applicability the precise source of its strength. I would take the argument one step further. Democracy is particularly suited for deeply polarized societies, and most Middle Eastern countries can safely be described as such. Over the decades, authoritarianism has fueled that polarization through the use of state power to distort individual preferences, including on matters of conscience. Which brings us to a paradox: democracy might be especially vital for polarized societies, but the fact of polarization makes it harder to establish democracy in the first place.

This makes it seem daunting, and in many ways it is. Democracy is most difficult to promote where it hasn't already taken hold—and democracy is most necessary where it is most difficult to promote.

On Toleration

One of the more damaging aspects of modern authoritarianism is how it distorts religion in an attempt to control and limit religion's power. According to the Pew Research Center, eighty countries worldwide had "high" or "very high" levels of restriction on religion in 2018. Of the "very high" countries, 65 percent are classified as authoritarian. On the flip side, only 7 percent of countries with low government restrictions on religion are authoritarian.[30] Islam especially has suffered as a result. Often, skeptics of democracy have argued the inverse, that authoritarianism is made more likely by an intolerant Islam. Accordingly, religious tolerance should come first, rather than after. This is what authoritarians themselves have long insisted. Pointing to the instability that the Arab revolts wrought, they argued that this was not the time for democracy, political reform, or anything that might challenge the existing authorities. Political freedom and democracy were all luxuries that a neighborhood as dangerous as the Middle East simply couldn't countenance (whether this dangerousness was itself a product of decades of political repression was not necessarily addressed). Instead, these regimes prioritize *religious* reform instead of political reform and promote things like interfaith dialogues. In this way, religious reform can become a trojan horse for democracy.

The United Arab Emirates has emerged as a primary sponsor of such inter-faith summits, with a focus on mutual tolerance between Abrahamic faiths overlaid with a Sufi tenor. Meanwhile, in Morocco, which practices a softer, gentler authoritarianism, Sufi traditions—once associated with anti-colonial rebellions but today tending toward deference to political authority—figure prominently in Morocco's brand of quietist Islam. As Sarah Alaoui writes, "This quietism is necessary in a country where the king rules over both the secular and spiritual spheres, and heavily relies on Islam—and a purported lineage to the Prophet Mohamed—to legitimate his rule. This control of the religious sphere has only increased post–September 11."[31]

Such religious control raises a vital question: Can authoritarian regimes, which are by definition suspicious of dissent and free inquiry—the very bedrocks of religious freedom—truly be champions of religious liberty and pluralism? Arab governments appear to be saying that, "yes" they can, and there is no other way regardless. A related question is whether religious pluralism first can pave the way for political pluralism later. At least in the case of the modern Middle East, this second query brings an easier reply. If religion and politics are inextricably intertwined even under *anti-Islamist* governments, then to have freedom in one category but not the other is simply impossible. If certain religious interpretations are not strictly private but threats to the state—because threats to the state's monopoly over reli-gious production are threats to the state itself—then an authoritarian regime will only allow religious expression that does not threaten the state. As Vali Nasr notes: "States can easily dominate their subjects physically; but to effec-tively rule over them . . . they must also control their subjects ideologically—that is, control the cultural underpinnings of their sociopolitical outlook."[32] The level of authoritarian control over religion is made obvious by the fact that many Arab countries appear to have low levels of social hostilities re-lated to religion, which would indicate government reliance on repression to manage religious expression.[33] If a society that has long had religious divides somehow suddenly discovers religious harmony, then there is prob-ably good reason to be suspicious. In pluralistic societies where citizens disagree on fundamental questions and have the freedom to express those disagreements, religious harmony is not possible nor it is something to de-sire. Sometimes dissonance is better.

Why are autocrats so insistent on stifling even the mildest hints of dissent? This repressive instinct might seem largely cynical—and to some degree it is—but there are a deeper set of philosophical assumptions driving what might be called repression in the name of tolerance. One might even call it *liberal*, if we consider the history of Enlightenment proponents in Europe striking Faustian bargains to protect hard-won liberties from the too pious masses. As the political theorist Faheem Hussain notes, "Enlightenment philosophes were prepared to make a spoken or unspoken agreement with authoritarian interests, promising obedience and loyalty as long as core liberal values such as freedom of expression over private beliefs were maintained, at least those opinions that wouldn't trouble the security of the state." Hussain goes on: "As the philosophes did before them, Egyptian liberals find themselves within societies that have religious majorities who view liberal ideas as at best religiously problematic, or at worst foreign or infidel."[34]

For Jean-Jacques Rousseau, writing in the eighteenth century, the influences of the emerging liberal culture masked tyranny in rosier glasses. In *Discourse on the Sciences and the Arts*, he offers us a memorable statement: "The sciences, letters, and the arts . . . spread garlands of flowers over the iron chains which weigh men down . . . and make them love their slavery by turning them into what are called civilized people."[35] "Liberal repression" today might seem unreasonable—convenient excuses for the will to power and subjugation. But it draws on a widespread strain in political science that democracy, to be done well, requires a sequential, multistage approach. Before democracy can take hold, there must be a democratic *culture*. In the sequencing paradigm, the liberalization of old, traditional modes of thinking—reason over revelation, science over superstition, the individual over the collective—is a first step and a prerequisite, setting the foundation for everything that comes after. Hearts must be habituated to democratic ways, and this requires a change in mentality and attitude, rather than a change in political behavior.

It is never entirely clear how a democratic culture might emerge in an environment that discourages democratic behavior. The idea of mastering democracy under conditions of dictatorship is odd at best and absurd at worst, something more appropriate to a Kafkaesque novel. Authoritarian regimes, by definition, have a vested interest in *not* promoting democratic values among their own people. They have a vested interest in precluding cooperation and compromise between ideological factions. How exactly can a democratic culture come into being when the overriding incentives encourage distrust and prioritizing one's own survival over everything else?

Political compromise is not something one can simply read in a book and then believe in, and then one becomes a "democrat." Even if this were possible, such books—or any kind of education that encouraged critical thinking skills—would be a threat to any self-respecting autocracy. The incoherence of sequential approaches is that they presume that the very things that democracy produces must precede it. Another argument along these lines is that a strong, well-functioning state is a prerequisite for democratization; otherwise, chaos will result. These tropes are so ubiquitous that they often go unstated. They are the mood music of decades of American policy prioritizing the stateness of Arab states. This, too, is understandable: the United States, as a government, isn't equipped to do business with non-state entities, whether they be citizens, local councils, or civil society organizations. Naturally, the U.S. government will incline toward other governments, particularly those that appear strong, and strongmen happen to be proficient at promoting the impression of strength.

The character of the modernizing autocrat—a bold, if repressive, reformer who gets things done—will be familiar to Western audiences, since it appeals to the notion of progress without the attendant messiness of mass plebiscites and fickle electorates. There are a few cases of apparently "benevolent" autocrats, such as Singapore's Lee Kuan Yew, so it is not entirely a myth. But it's close. To believe that an autocrat, against the odds, might prove extraordinary belongs more in speculative fiction than it does in policymaking, particularly when it comes to the Middle East. With the arguable exception of Ataturk, the region has had no great modernizers. In deeply polarized contexts, an authoritarian leader has even less incentive than they might otherwise to allow institutions their autonomy or to take rule of law seriously. These are products of democracy, rather than prerequisites. When there are threats, and the Middle East tends to have an abundance of them, regime survival takes precedence over all else. And regime survival as a preoccupation is not conducive to good governance or rule of law or liberalization, since it invites paranoia, the concentration of power, and the fear of one's own citizens.

The very premise of sequentialism—of democratic values first, democracy later—betrays a suspicion of democracy, which is why it's not just mild-mannered academics who subscribe to it but also autocrats themselves. The unpredictability of democracy is what worries observers, and understandably so. But even the most well-ordered democratic transitions can't help but be risky. Democracies are *supposed* to produce uncertainty, since there is no way to be sure which parties will win ahead of time. That uncertainty provides autocrats with an easy justification for their refusal to democratize.

In 1993, former Egyptian President Hosni Mubarak observed that a democratic transition "needs generations" and "democracy should be on a gradual basis until the people understand and swallow each step and digest it."[36] To swallow each step and then digest it would presumably be a time-consuming process.

Uncertainty requires compromises from all sides. It also means that "tolerance" on its own is not enough. To tolerate suggests a temporary concession to an unfortunate reality. Toleration, according to an interpretation prevalent among early Enlightenment thinkers, is a means to an end. Tolerance and free expression allowed for a free marketplace of ideas, which, in turn, allowed for the "best" ideas to rise to the fore, to then be adopted by policymakers for the common good.[37] This ideal-type deliberative model seems easy to disprove empirically. We know that a free marketplace does not produce the best ideas, but the only reason we know this is because citizens do not agree on what the best ideas are in the first place. Modernity creates a paradox because it longs for sameness precisely as that sameness drifts out of reach. As the philosopher John Gray argues: "Ancient societies were more hospitable to differences than ours. This is partly because the idea of human equality was weak or absent. Modernity begins not with the recognition of difference but with a demand for uniformity."[38]

Much of modern political theory and moral philosophy developed in relatively homogenous Western states, which means that the fact of difference and what to do about it was, and remains, undertheorized. Political pluralism requires a conscious effort to "preserv[e] difference."[39] And if political and religious pluralism are intertwined, then a freer marketplace of ideas will not necessarily lead Muslims in a given country to become more "enlightened"— what liberals might prefer—or more conservative, which is what Islamists would prefer.

Is it possible that pluralism would at least make a greater number of Muslims aware of alternative Islamic interpretations and demonstrate to them a wider range of religious possibilities? Yes, and this is why Muslim liberals as well as Western policymakers who hold out hope for an "Islamic reformation"—something I myself do not believe in, in part because I believe it already happened[40]—should flip their preferred sequencing and start with democracy. Democratization is what will facilitate political pluralism, which, in turn, will allow, in due time, for some semblance of religious pluralism.

The link between political and religious pluralism, but with the political part coming first, has the virtue of being intuitive. As the Turkish author

Mustafa Akyol writes, potentially controversial religious ideas will only be introduced and contended with in "an atmosphere of free speech in which novel ideas can be discussed without persecution."[41] Similarly, the political theorist Nader Hashemi highlights the example of the late Islamic philosopher Fazlur Rahman, who fled Pakistan for the United States in the 1960s, soon landing at the University of Chicago. Over the subsequent decades, Rahman rose to prominence as a bold and heterodox advocate of Islamic reform. "It is not a coincidence," Hashemi remarks, "that Rahman developed his powerful and persuasive ethical reading of Islam in an open society where his academic freedom was protected. This allowed him to debate, explore, criticize, and rethink Islamic norms." In short: "An ethical and humanistic reinterpretation of Islam can only take place in a free and democratic society."[42]

In a free society, however, those who believe the opposite of what Fazlur Rahman believed in will also have their day, and this is the catch that makes pluralism as challenging as it is necessary. Let us consider a "liberal" autocracy that suppresses ultraconservative interpretations of Islam. To the extent that liberalism would appear dominant, it would be because of state coercion, not because society has actually become more liberal. Removing that unnatural limit of state intervention would allow ultraconservative interpretations of Islam to come to the fore, just as they would allow Rahman's more liberal interpretations. And, over time, those conservative interpretations could plausibly become widely read and accepted. A free marketplace of ideas is no guarantee that citizens will coalesce around the truth. In a society where there is no consensus around what constitutes a good idea or a bad one, the "bad" has just as much of a chance of winning out.

America, Islam, and Democracy

Needless to say, some of these discussions are speculative. How could they be otherwise, considering that so few democracies have existed in the region and fewer still have survived? They never had a chance. The tragedy of American policy in the Middle East is its circular nature—haunted by a tautology of its own making. Henry Kissinger once remarked that "the history of things that didn't happen has never been written."[43] The same could be said for the history that the modern Middle East might have had.

American policymakers have spoken of the Middle East as a region inhospitable to democracy, an inhospitality that makes promoting democracy there especially risky. Such an argument would be more persuasive if the United States were a hapless bystander, merely watching events unfold and wishing them to be different than they actually were. Let's grant the argument that the United States had limited room for maneuver during the Cold War and little choice but to indulge egregious regimes. Back then, if Arab allies threatened to move into the Soviet Union's orbit, their threats might have been at least somewhat credible. Yet, in the 1990s, after history had duly ended, Washington continued to obstruct democratization in the Middle East, including in the countries where it had the best chance of success. There was no longer any Soviet scapegoat, but there might as well have been.

For the first time, the United States was confronted with an Islamist dilemma when the Islamic Salvation Front found itself on the verge of an election victory in Algeria. By tacitly and then explicitly backing the 1992 military coup, the United States and European nations guaranteed that the dilemma would remain—entirely unresolved—over the subsequent decades. And so here we are today, engaged in many of the same debates and much of the same speculation about what would happen if Islamist parties came to power as we were three long decades ago.

There are various reasons why American officials remain reticent, and those reasons often have to do with "moderation"—or, more precisely, Islamists' seeming lack thereof. While I attempted to define the word in a more systematic way in my first book *Temptations of Power*, it remains a confusing concept, changing wildly according to who is assessing it.[44] Often, it means little more than "people we think aren't so bad." Almost always, because moderation is an inherently relative measure, it signals moderation relative to Western standards of secularism: liberalism, gender equality, and so forth. In many of their own countries, however, those who advocate for secularism or liberalism are not moderates and are generally considered to be outside the mainstream. In other words, in a socially conservative society, advocating for full gender equality (including, for example, on issues of inheritance) would be considered radical rather than moderate.

Somewhat confusingly, "moderate" is also used to describe regimes, parties, or individuals that are less anti-American, support Israel's right to exist as a Jewish state, or are sympathetic to Israel's security concerns.[45] A former Defense Department official described the mood in the Pentagon during the Muslim Brotherhood's brief rise to power:

> A lot of the folks on the military side were really just concerned about the practicalities of Suez Canal access and overflight rights as technical things that they relied on in order to enhance U.S. war-fighting capacity in the Middle East and saw it almost through a fairly narrow technical lens. They would also mention Camp David. I think, for some, the Camp David question was also a little bit more of a cultural litmus test. It was a way to determine whether these groups were sufficiently mainstream. In some cases, that Camp David question, support for peace with Israel question, was this sort of almost dual-use litmus test. On the one hand, if the Camp David accords are a linchpin of U.S. security in the region, there are technical reasons for making sure that they're okay with it. But my sense also was that this was part of an effort to place these groups on a spectrum of moderate to extremists as well.[46]

It is unclear what exactly support for better or closer relations with Israel has to do with moderation, unless moderation is determined relative to American preferences rather than, say, popular Egyptian or Jordanian preferences. Why exactly would Jordanians prioritize Israel's security concerns? They wouldn't, and they don't.[47]

The subtext of these worries, from the Algerian coup onward, is one of uncertainty—of not knowing what might happen before it happens. Democratization in Algeria would have been risky, and it is impossible to know exactly how it might have played out (although, in retrospect, it's hard to imagine *not* canceling elections leading to a civil war the way canceling elections, in fact, did). Algerian democratization would no doubt have been difficult from an American policy perspective. A contested democratic transition—one that would have likely involved intense polarization and threats of intervention from an army that saw itself as the guardian of the state—would have necessitated greater U.S. attention and engagement. American officials would have also had to think seriously about what to do if Islamist parties started gaining ground elsewhere in the region, including in countries much more strategically vital than Algeria.

Democracy does not necessarily produce good outcomes, but that is precisely the point: it shouldn't need to. To come to terms with this, however, entails rethinking why we believe democracy is good in the first place. Must democracy lead to "reasonable" or "rational" outcomes? The question of reasonableness relates to the role of religion in public life. Religion is associated with intensity, passion, and unverifiable truth claims. It is about the things that one feels deeply, perhaps more deeply than anything else. The philosopher Martha Nussbaum asks: "Should the fact that someone stands up and says 'I feel this way' count in discourse and public policy, especially if that person can't give any reasons for what has been said?"[48] Nussbaum's remark raises a number of questions. Why is the act of "feeling" inherently suspect? Who decides whether reasons are reasonable? In divided societies, where citizens have diametrically opposed understandings of what is right and just, reason itself cannot answer such a question; only power can.

When it comes to the Middle East, then, the "problem" of Islam is at least in part a problem of liberalism—the fear, often unstated or implicit, that the more democracy there is, the more religious passions will be unleashed beyond "reason." And the more such passions are unleashed, the less liberalism there will be. However, this lack of liberalism, by itself, isn't enough to invite such worries—at least from the perspective of policymakers. After all, Saudi Arabia had been one of the world's only theocracies for decades, yet that didn't impede Washington's desire to maintain close ties under both Democratic and Republican administrations. Since the founding of Saudi Arabia, this is the way it had always been, and it was left to the United States to deal with the world as it was. Moreover, Saudi leaders were able to demonstrate, over the course of decades, that the regime's Islamic and theocratic character did not prevent it from backing America's regional objectives.

In contrast, if the United States supported democratic reform in a given country and democratization led to the election of an Islamist government, then Washington would both feel itself responsible and be held responsible. Any resulting consequences, including short-term instability and the panic of allies, would be perceived as America's fault, rather than just the regular instability that the region produces "on its own." It is also a question of standards and expectations. It's one thing for autocracies to do things we don't approve of, but for a fledgling democracy—one viewed with anticipation and optimism—to produce illiberal, Islamist, or anti-American outcomes violates a sense of the way we think the world should be.

To the extent that the Middle East undermines a story of linear, gradual progress, it undermines the narrative arc of the democratic idea and why we think it's worth supporting. Most American policymakers, like most Americans, will be less enthusiastic about democratization abroad if democratization doesn't produce encouraging outcomes. Skeptics may make some combination of two related if distinct arguments: first, that it's not really democracy if it's not sufficiently liberal. Or, second, that it might be "democracy" but not the good kind. Phil Gordon, who served as President Obama's coordinator for the Middle East, captures these various concerns when he writes that "[the Arab world's] main opposition parties are not primarily liberals, who form a distinct minority in all its countries, but Islamists, nationalists, or minorities of one form or another who are no more committed to democracy or freedom or good relations with the United States than most of the current leaders."[49] Even if U.S. officials are aware of the tensions between liberalism and democracy, those aren't easily explained to a broader audience—or for that matter to the opposing party in Congress during a charged election campaign.

Why should we go out of our way to support Arab democracy if it undermines our belief in what democracy should do? Those American officials who would have used their political capital to push for a new pro-democracy strategy would, understandably, feel responsible for any negative outcomes. For most policymakers, unless they happened to have a distinct and somewhat unusual commitment to democracy promotion, these would seem like unnecessary risks. Few would criticize you for going along with the status quo, however much of a failure it happened to be. It is always easier to continue doing what has already (or always) been done. To alter that in any significant way requires overcoming considerable inertia and internal resistance. As Stephen Krasner, who was the State Department's director of policy planning under George W. Bush, put it: "One thing I saw in the bureaucracy is that you really get punished if you make a mistake. You don't necessarily get rewarded if you do things right."[50]

Foreign policy is difficult, a fact that those on the outside can try to appreciate but still never fully grasp. When I first talked to him about this book and what I was trying to do, the first thing Jeffrey Feltman, who had served as assistant secretary of state, told me was the following:

> What strikes me is how no one who wasn't inside the government at the time seems to understand what it was like to try to deal with all of these issues exploding at the same time. There simply wasn't the time available to consider as carefully as would have been ideal what the options were and what potential consequences faced us. . . . [M]y own workload and travel schedule exploded, meaning that, even as the issues became more urgent and critical, I had less and less time to consider what would be the best approach to take.[51]

Even if one could make a sustained case for a bold new strategy, there's no guarantee that it would work out in the end, in part because policymakers do not agree on what working out looks like. Any bold strategy is, by definition, risky. If it wasn't risky, then it wouldn't be bold. A young democracy, being young, will be racked by unpredictability. On the other hand, after decades of authoritarian rule in the region, authoritarianism has become predictable and therefore comforting in its own way. It's how nearly everyone pictures the region. Democracy advocates see the Middle East as tragically authoritarian and hope to change it, while autocrats and the millions who support them see dictatorship as a bulwark against chaos and the dangers of mass politics.

Young democracies tend to experience significant instability precisely because they propel uncertainty to the surface rather than suppress it. Meanwhile, institutions aren't yet strong enough to temper uncertainty by institutionalizing it, in other words making it more tolerable by making it more predictable. Fear of uncertainty is magnified in the Middle East since both American values and interests are at stake. Interests and values are difficult to disentangle, since the presumption is that liberals are more likely to be pro-American (or at least less anti-American), while religious conservatives, in addition to being illiberal, are more likely to express anti-American as well as anti-Israel attitudes. This may be true, but only up to a point. Anti-Americanism in the Middle East is widespread, cutting across ideological or political divides.

Democratic transitions, in short, are likely to bring about disappointment, not only for the people who live in the region but also for those trying to understand it from afar. The word "democracy," and how we react to hearing it, present a challenge. It is possible to think of democracy as universalist, rights-based, and as something quite wonderful. But democracy's wonder— if "wonder" is quite the right word—is to be found in its prosaic attachment to the mundane trials of everyday life and collective action. The political scientists Jack Knight and James Johnson highlight "the important role that democracy plays, not in achieving consensus or commonality, but rather in addressing the ongoing conflict that exists in modern society." They continue: "Significant beneficial consequences accrue to societies that rely on democratic arrangements to accommodate tensions that in any event do not lend themselves to any principled and lasting resolution."[52]

What this suggests is that a more minimalistic approach to democracy abroad is also a more practical one, allowing us to adjust expectations accordingly. For Western powers, shifting to an explicit focus on political pluralism first—and worrying about religious pluralism later—would have major implications. It would mean, among other things, politely removing themselves from certain kinds of questions. American officials are better off being agnostic when it comes to what Islam is or what it should be.

On the other hand, being a democracy itself and having promoted democracy successfully in other regions, the United States does have something to say about transitions from authoritarian rule. To say it, however, requires a realization that democracy will produce uncertainty and that it will take time for that uncertainty to become normalized. Democracy may not lead to Western-style liberalism. It may be better to assume that it won't. Instead, democratic minimalism does something simpler and more profound, even if it ends up being less inspiring: it addresses the "problem" of Islam by coming to terms with the inability to solve it.

4

Democratic Dilemmas

Egypt, Jordan, and Algeria

It didn't have to be this way. Contrary to popular perceptions, the Middle East was not always some hopeless, walled redoubt of authoritarianism. Reducing the region to this distorts a much more complex history. The tragedy of democratic promise followed by authoritarian retrenchment did not begin with the Arab Spring. Something like this had happened before. Which returns us to the circular nature of the dilemma, endlessly repeating itself in predictive, if not entirely predictable, patterns.

Long before the uprisings of 2011, the Middle East was becoming increasingly authoritarian just as the world was becoming less so. Oddly enough, this authoritarian turn coincided with the *expansion* of democracy elsewhere during the triumphalism of the post–Cold War period. This makes the region's democratic deficit all the more puzzling. Not only was the Arab world seemingly oblivious to the profound shifts happening all around it; the region was at cross purposes with a mood and with the world, as if running against history. Either this is an odd coincidence—or there was a reason behind what would turn out to be a historic divergence.

To understand the divergence, we must revisit the region's forgotten decade. If one was an Egyptian opposition activist in the 1980s, one could have been forgiven for being mildly optimistic about the future. Egyptian independence, in 1952, had come with a military coup refashioned as a revolution. Then, after decades of authoritarian rule, it finally seemed to be getting better.

Egypt registered its best ever Freedom House score in 1984.[1] Jordan was similar in some ways, and even more promising. It began opening up in the 1980s. Martial law formally ended in 1989, and later that year Jordan held free and fair elections for the first time in decades. Jordan garnered its highest Freedom House score in 1992.[2] That year, Jordan's rating was, right up until the Arab Spring, the best ever for an Arab country. These eras of (relative) optimism are largely forgotten today. They are worth remembering. These are years that point to a different set of possibilities.

* * *

In 1980, President Anwar el-Sadat, fresh off a seeming victory after signing the Camp David Accords with Israel, was gripped by paranoia. His fellow Egyptians did not seem particularly appreciative of his bold peacemaking. He had found himself feted in Western capitals as a good Arab and a great Egyptian, but his own people shared little of this enthusiasm. Facing growing opposition and dogged by growing resentment, Sadat launched a wide-ranging crackdown, jailing over a thousand political activists across the ideological spectrum. Soon after, on October 6, 1981, he was assassinated during a military parade celebrating Egypt's alleged victory over Israel in the 1973 war. Sadat assumed the officers approaching him were part of the parade and stood to salute them. They subsequently opened fire. Sadat died from two bullet wounds in the chest and one in the neck. Others were wounded or killed, but Hosni Mubarak, who would become Egypt's next president, escaped unscathed.[3]

Mubarak, defiantly conventional and uncharismatic, instituted a political thaw, hoping to earn the goodwill of a country that knew little of him, besides the fact that he happened to be Sadat's vice president. Shortly after Sadat's death, Mubarak invited opposition leaders to take part in a national dialogue on reform. This opening of political space led to an extended period of optimism, guarded as it may have been. The journalist Anthony McDermott wrote that "there was a sense of freedom on a scale which had not been felt for some years,"[4] while the political scientist Robert Springborg called the period of 1984–1986 "the golden age of the opposition press."[5] Meanwhile, the parliamentary elections of 1984 and 1987 were the freest Egypt had ever seen as an independent nation-state (although far from free and fair in absolute terms). Some were even prepared to use the term "transition to democracy."[6]

Jordan's transition seemed to hold even more potential. As in Egypt, the year 1984 proved to be an important marker. For the first time since martial law was instituted in 1967, reasonably free by-elections were held for eight vacated parliamentary seats. This was a dry run for landmark national elections five years later, to this day the freest in Jordan's history. In the 1989 elections, the Jordanian Muslim Brotherhood and non-affiliated Islamists won thirty-four of a total of eighty seats. Along with small leftist and nationalist parties, the opposition claimed a slight majority. Soon enough, Jordan would have its first (and last) Muslim Brotherhood speaker of parliament.

And in a largely forgotten episode, likely because it appears quite strange in retrospect, six Brotherhood members joined the government as cabinet ministers, another historic first that would not be repeated.

I was young then and have no memories of the politics of the time, but it must have been heady, to be blissfully unaware of the Middle East's subsequent dark turns. The great democracy activist and one of my teachers, Saad Eddin Ibrahim, proclaimed in 1989 that Egypt was "on the road of democracy."[7] Fifteen years later, he would find himself languishing in the notorious Tora prison, adopted home of Egypt's countless dissidents. In hindsight, Egypt's "democratic opening" was nothing of the sort. However, from the perspective of the actors involved, there was a sense at the time that something unprecedented was taking place.

If these democratic pressures were building from below and if the sense of something new and promising was widely shared by academics and activists alike, what exactly went wrong—and why did it go wrong in the 1990s of all decades? If anything, the immediate aftermath of the Cold War—and the apparent victory of liberal democracy over the communist alternative—should have helped bring about different outcomes in the Middle East, shattering the region's exceptionalism once and for all. But to argue "oughts" is to argue with history. Instead, I will make a more modest claim: that it *could* have been different, but it wasn't, and there are a number of reasons why. Importantly, for our purposes, some of those reasons have to do with the United States.

During the 1980s, the Middle East wasn't exceptional, so the starting premise of exceptionalism—that there was something unique about the region on the matter of democracy—would not have been accurate, at least not yet. Several Arab countries seemed to be experimenting with democratic reform. Talk of transitions was in the air. On the whole, Latin America and East Asia were more democratic, but not obviously so, with a majority of countries in both regions still under authoritarian rule. And, of course, the near entirety of Eastern Europe was under Soviet domination.

The United States, under the Reagan administration, had begun pressuring friendly dictators like Ferdinand Marcos in the Philippines and Augusto Pinochet in Chile to open up their political systems after decades of largely unwavering support. Opposition parties were emboldened. They could see, like everyone else, that the international environment was shifting in their favor. The more they took to the streets, the more sclerotic regimes might have wished to respond with brute force. But they no longer had American cover to do so.

In the Middle East, by contrast, democratic openings had little to do with the United States. If anything, these openings were the product not of American attention and involvement but rather its absence. In the 1980s, when the communist threat still loomed large and where Soviet proxies remained a force to reckon with in Central and South America, the United States wasn't paying close attention to the more subtle developments taking place within Arab society. In Egypt, after Sadat's assassination, Mubarak appeared to have struck the right notes, solidifying his rule after initial doubts. Egypt was slowly opening up and seemingly on its own terms. Perhaps most importantly, the Muslim Brotherhood wasn't a major concern. In the recollections of senior Reagan administration officials, the Brotherhood—or Islamist parties more generally—might as well have been nonexistent. The question of democracy promotion is raised repeatedly, but after searching in several such memoirs, I couldn't find any reference to democratization in the Middle East or even the thought that democracy in the region might be something worth thinking about in the first place.[8]

Oddly enough, for Arab nations, the 1980s marked the last decade in which the regional and international context would prove conducive to real political reform of any kind. It was when the United States started paying attention that things started to take a turn for the worse. This isn't to say that America caused de-democratization, but rather that it began to play a role that amplified the worst instincts of autocrats once they decided to roll back reforms and crack down on the opposition. The subsequent decade, the 1990s, would see the largest overall global rise in the number of democracies in history.[9] The Middle East, however, went in the opposite direction, earning the otherwise misleading label "exceptional."

The main reason autocrats undid democratic gains, however modest, and turned to repression was the rapid ascendance of Islamist parties, which they began to perceive as an existential threat. And, naturally, for any self-respecting autocrat, regime survival was what mattered in the end. In January 1992, the Algerian military moved to cancel the second round of elections after the Islamic Salvation Front (FIS) was within days of rising to power. This was a seminal moment for the region, but in the worst way possible. Algeria was an extreme case—it was the country that had gone farthest toward a full democratic transition. Then it became the country that saw the most vigorous return to military dictatorship. Though it was on a smaller, less dramatic scale, Egypt's and Jordan's authoritarian turns were also triggered by unprecedented gains by Islamists in the 1987 and 1989 elections, respectively. These two countries soon invited greater American interest—a product of the geographic misfortune of bordering Israel and being deemed "strategically vital." Islamist groups had risen to political prominence, becoming the leaders of the opposition. It would have been difficult to ignore them. Not only that, they were also the most vocal opponents of the Arab–Israeli peace process, which was just then coming into vogue. King Hussein in Jordan and President Mubarak in Egypt increasingly tied their futures to American support, and this meant demonstrating their usefulness on one of the Clinton administration's core priorities. The demise of the Soviet Union and unparalleled American dominance meant there could be no more hedging. King Hussein found this out the hard way after he chose the wrong side during the first Gulf War.

Islamists, Repression, and the Peace Process

Without fanfare and in the workmanlike fashion that would become their signature, the Egyptian and Jordanian Muslim Brotherhoods had prepared themselves for this moment, making the leap from minority group to mass movement. They were gradualists par excellence. Up until the mid-1980s, they had largely stayed away from partisan politics, opting instead to build local networks, providing much-needed social services and spreading their message to a public that knew little about them. They exuded deference to regime elites in an effort to reduce tensions over their growing public role. But a clash was inevitable when they surprised others, as well as themselves, with their considerable electoral success.

Most scholars of Egyptian politics agree that something fundamental changed in the early 1990s. As Hesham al-Awadi notes, the relationship between the regime and the Brotherhood "went through two distinctive phases, where the first, from 1981 to 1990, was a period of accommodation and tolerance, and the second, from 1990 to 2000, was a period of confrontation and repression."[10] Mona el-Ghobashy meanwhile points to 1992 as the turning point.[11]

The first clear sign of the Brotherhood's growing reach was its showing in the 1987 parliamentary elections, far from free or fair but still Egypt's most competitive elections up until that point. The Islamic Alliance, consisting of the Brotherhood and two smaller parties, won sixty seats, the most of any opposition grouping since Egypt became a republic in 1952. Thirty-six of those seats went to the Brotherhood, representing a more than fourfold increase from its previous total. Meanwhile, the elections handed Mubarak's National Democratic Party its worst-ever result. At only 69 percent of the vote, it was a comfortable victory still, but embarrassingly close in what was supposed to be a proper dictatorship.

The elections confirmed what had already become obvious just by looking at Egyptian society. It had been close to unheard of to see young, educated women covering their hair. By the early 1980s, it was ubiquitous. Educational attainment was increasing exponentially, with millions of Egyptians acquiring high school diplomas and university degrees for the first time. More education did not lead to greater secularization, as early social scientists may have expected. Islamism was not a movement of the most destitute, nor was it a particularly rural movement. It drew strength, instead, from a newly aspiring counter-elite of engineers, doctors, lawyers, and teachers. This was Egypt's new professional managerial class, a counter-elite of would-be technocrats.

The Muslim Brotherhood had become too powerful too quickly. While it avoided questioning Mubarak's legitimacy as president, it was increasingly asserting itself on foreign policy questions, one of the regime's points of greatest sensitivity. It opposed Egypt's participation in the Gulf War as well as the Madrid peace talks of 1991. Through the Doctors' Union, the Brotherhood organized a mass rally of as many as 20,000 participants against peace with Israel.[12] In September 1992, Brotherhood-affiliated candidates won a majority of seats on the board of the Lawyers Union—one of Egypt's last liberal strongholds—an event that provoked "shock and soul-searching among the nation's secular politicians and intellectuals."[13]

Egypt already had peace with Israel, though a rather cold one. But the peace treaty had always been unpopular, and Mubarak was well aware that Sadat's paranoia in his final years was due to the Camp David Accords and his resentment that Egyptians didn't appreciate the magnitude of what he had done. American and Israeli politicians saw him as a statesman and a hero, while at home he grew increasingly isolated. Despite (or perhaps due to) being one of America's closest partners in the region and one of only two Arab countries at peace with Israel, Egypt had long featured extremely high levels of anti-American and anti-Israel attitudes. This was where official policy was most at odds with popular sentiment. In a 2019–2020 poll conducted by the Arab Center for Research and Policy Studies, 85 percent of Egyptians surveyed said they opposed Egypt's diplomatic recognition of

Israel, despite the fact that the peace settlement between the two countries had already done just that decades ago.[14] Autocracies are somewhat insulated from public pressures but not completely so. It is difficult, after all, to rule by brute force alone, all sticks and no carrots. This requires a commitment to nearly unlimited repression. Most authoritarian regimes, however, rule through a mix of coercion and co-option, and Mubarak's Egypt was no different.

For Mubarak, limited electoral competition was useful for persuading opposition groups to work within the system rather than calling for revolution. It also provided a patina of legitimacy to an otherwise illegitimate regime and allowed some citizens to believe they had a voice even if they did not. But elections presented a problem, particularly when regime priorities diverged significantly from public attitudes. If popular sentiment was staunchly anti-Israel, then anti-Israel parties were likely to do better than pro-peace parties (except for the fact that there were scarcely opposition parties of note that could be described as pro-peace). And if Islamist parties were most effective at reflecting and mobilizing anti-Israel and anti-American sentiment, then they would gladly use their parliamentary presence to agitate against the regime's perceived betrayal of Arabs, Muslims, and the Palestinian cause.

Before the Madrid peace talks and the Oslo process, which would linger on for the remainder of the decade, anti-Israel demonstrations could be ignored as mostly harmless, and perhaps even as a constructive way to allow citizens to let off steam against someone other than their own government. Soon enough, however, it would become more and more difficult to separate the Mubarak regime from the Mubarak regime's pro-Western orientation, particularly when it was precisely such an orientation that guaranteed it American support.

Peace versus Democracy

Jordan's democratic experiment had its brief run between 1989 and 1992. It's not an accident that it happened, and was allowed to happen, before King Hussein made the fateful decision to finally cast his lot with the United States. It is difficult to recall it now. Jordan wasn't always a close American ally, and it certainly was not a reliable one. Once Hussein made his decision, as we will see, democratization became a liability, threatening to complicate what he hoped would be his core achievements: a peace treaty with Israel and enhanced regime security under American stewardship. The latter depended on the former. The problem of democracy—at least for Hussein (as well as his American backers)—was that it would, or even just that it *could*, produce outcomes contrary to both objectives. With the United States rising to unipolar dominance after the conclusion of the Cold War, there was no one to temper American hegemony in the region. Accordingly, there would be growing pressure to toe the line, particularly when Hussein found himself increasingly dependent on foreign assistance after the debacle of the Gulf War.

Saddam Hussein invaded Kuwait in August 1990. In response, a U.S.-led coalition launched its invasion of Iraq on January 17, 1991. Why would King Hussein, known for his savvy and keen instinct for survival, fail to pick the right side?[15] This was unfortunate timing. Those early months of 1991 were the high-water mark of Jordan's fledgling democratization process. Public opinion was, if not necessarily pro-Saddam, then at least very much opposed to the idea of an American war against Saddam.

Of course, Jordan was far from a full democracy, and the monarchy was still, in the end, absolute. Yet, Hussein was cautious, and over his long career of staving off otherwise expected demise, he came to think of himself as being connected to his people and cognizant of their hopes and fears. He saw himself as a kind of father to the Jordanian people with a responsibility to protect and care for this larger family.[16] There was also, of course, simple self-interest. One of the reasons Hussein initiated democratization in the first place was the unprecedented riots over austerity measures that took place in early 1989. The austerity measures were implemented in compliance with an International Monetary Fund (IMF) agreement meant to address Jordan's growing budget deficit. The subsequent price hikes in combination with an already struggling economy as a result of the aftermath of the oil crisis of 1979 led to the widespread social unrest.[17] The point of giving people a say was to provide an outlet for their anger. But, at the same time, the maxim couldn't help but be true, perhaps truer still in the Middle East: elections have consequences.

King Hussein, the Muslim Brotherhood, and the Pursuit of Peace

Jordan's 1989 elections were held at the peak of the new democratic euphoria—a day before the fall of the Berlin Wall and three days after half a million people gathered in the streets of East Germany. The end was near, and so was the beginning. When I was living in Amman, I spent dozens of hours combing through newspaper archives covering nearly every day of 1989. It often sounded like an alternate universe, and one that I couldn't quite recognize. The optimism, as it often is, may have been overstated. It was also undoubtedly real. During my time in Jordan, I conducted extensive interviews with opposition figures and activists from across the ideological spectrum. There is no accounting for nostalgia, but nearly all of them remembered this period as the high-water mark for what they wished and hoped Jordan might become. But the festival-like atmosphere of the 1989 campaign, coming after decades of martial law, was mostly anticipatory. Things would get complicated after the elections were actually held—and after the results told a story not to everyone's liking.

Like his counterparts in Egypt and Algeria, King Hussein underestimated the Islamist opposition and overestimated his control of the democratization process as well as his grasp of a changing national mood. His predictive powers also left something to be desired. As Mudar Badran, who was then chief of the Royal Court, recounted to me, Hussein predicted the Brotherhood would win only around ten seats. The king also felt that Badran's estimate of sixteen seats was "too much."[18] As it turned out, it was too little. The Brotherhood won twenty-two of the twenty-six seats it contested (out of eighty), a remarkable win at 85 percent. Badran, who stayed up all night with the king after the results were announced, recalls the tense discussions.[19] As he described it to me, several former ministers were urging Hussein to cancel the elections and dissolve parliament. The king, fearful of the domestic and international backlash, brushed their suggestions aside. But he was shaken.

The parliamentary elections of 1989 were the first that were freely contested since 1956, when the socialist Sulayman al-Nabulsi became the country's first (and, to this day, only) democratically elected prime minister. Hussein, then a young, inexperienced monarch, waited a year before forcing Nabulsi's resignation and bringing his country's earlier democratic experiment to a close. Back then, when Islamist groups were relatively marginal, it was the prospect of socialists winning elections that worried the Jordanian authorities most. For its part, the Brotherhood feared the socialists for their anti-religious orientation. After Hussein moved to arrest Nabulsi's supporters, the Brotherhood organized mass rallies in defense of the monarchy.[20] Brotherhood leaders would have likely thought it ludicrous that they might eventually find themselves in a situation resembling that of the ousted Nabulsi. Since its founding in 1945, Jordan's Muslim Brotherhood had enjoyed a cooperative if tense relationship with the monarchy. It had backed Hussein at critical moments, not only after the 1956 elections but also during the Jordanian civil war of 1970, also known as "Black September." The Brotherhood saw itself as the loyal opposition, and they were indeed loyal, refusing to challenge the legitimacy of the monarchy.

The question, then, is why the relationship, forged over decades, would fray irreparably. The answer is twofold, with one reason amplifying the other. First, Islamists were becoming (relatively) popular in part because they were Islamist, drawing on the support of an increasingly religious population. And in part because they were Islamist, their growing support challenged the monarchy's legitimacy, based as it was on both religious and historical claims. To be sure, the Muslim Brotherhood wasn't exactly loved, and polls generally showed a mixed picture.[21] But it had a significant and reliable base of support, low in absolute terms but much higher than every other political party. Dedicated cadres coupled with high levels of organizational discipline translated into a knack for getting out the vote, allowing the Brotherhood to seem more formidable than it actually was. Second, the Brotherhood was exceedingly vocal about a topic that was more sensitive in Jordan than in any other Arab country—the question of Palestine.

Unlike Egypt, Jordan had not yet signed a peace treaty with Israel, so while Mubarak was simply expected to support a regional peace process, Jordan was expected to be a direct party to a peace settlement. To further complicate matters, more than half of the country's citizens were of Palestinian origin. In my interviews with Jordanian political figures, the inconvenient realities of demography seemed a perpetual subtext, though it was generally frowned upon to speak about it too explicitly. I remember how my Jordanian friends would give me confused looks when I brought up Black September, the civil war that fell largely along Jordanian–Palestinian lines in 1970. The memory had been erased.

Majorities matter in all societies, but they matter more in countries contending with democracy. With democratization, formerly disenfranchised populations can expect to have a greater say in politics. They don't even need outright majorities to make their presence felt; they can represent pluralities or be well organized. Arguing *against* rapid democratization in fractious societies, various scholars, most notably Edward Mansfield and Jack Snyder, warn that political openings drive ideological confrontation at home and fuel the desire for foreign policy revisionism abroad.

Democratization, they write, "increase[s] the chance of involvement in international war in countries where government institutions are weak at the outset of the transition."[22] In short, because democracy empowers voters, it allows them to be in tune with their aggressive impulses and support aggressive policies. This is intuitive enough. If you're looking to mobilize voters, you have to mobilize them around *something*, and platitudes about jobs and fighting corruption are unlikely to do the trick. You need to distinguish yourself from the competition. This, one might say, is the very point of democracy—to give voice to the identities, preferences, and passions of voters, whatever they may be.

When it came to Jordan's foreign policy, having to accommodate public passions quickly became a problem. The Gulf War began in August 1990. Saddam had dutifully, if not always persuasively, nurtured his persona as the new Nasser, scourge of the imperialists and defender of the Palestinians. Considering Jordan's demographic makeup, this made joining the American invasion somewhat more complicated. At first, King Hussein tried to avoid getting dragged into the war, professing neutrality. But even this proved too controversial, arousing the ire of the opposition, particularly a secular left that saw Saddam as a bulwark against American imperialism. Meanwhile, Jordan's Islamists—who had opposed Saddam's invasion of Kuwait—saw the potential long-term presence of American troops on Arab land as a greater evil. This pushed them to make common cause with nationalists and even communists, who had long been anathema due to their presumed atheism. On August 19, 1990, there was the odd spectacle of Issa Madanat, head of the Jordanian Communist Party, announcing to the press that his party had forged a broad front with the Brotherhood to combat Western imperialism.[23]

Between Islamists, socialists, and nationalists of various stripes, the opposition could claim an absolute parliamentary majority from 1989 until 1993. It was during the early, promising days of the democratic transition that King Hussein felt the most pressure to meet popular demands. Indeed, in a largely forgotten episode, something quite unusual happened in Jordan around this time. It would not be repeated. After protracted negotiations, the Muslim Brotherhood joined the government of the aforementioned Mudar Badran, the confidante who had counseled the king to proceed with democratization, despite fears over Islamist gains. On New Year's Day, with the Gulf War as the backdrop, the Brotherhood accepted five cabinet positions, the ministries of religious affairs, education, health, justice, and social development.

It was already the country's largest grassroots movement. Now with the prestige of being in government, the Brotherhood organized anti-war protests and demonstrations across the country. It took advantage of rising anti-American sentiment, using the war to raise its profile. Despite the obvious international consequences of standing with his people and standing against the United States, King Hussein was boxed in by a challenging domestic environment.

Soon enough, in what turned out to be a massive miscalculation, the king jettisoned Jordan's neutrality and came out against the American invasion of Iraq. Weeks after the United States began its bombing campaign, and with pressure mounting at home, the king addressed the nation on February 6, 1991. He did not mince words. "The real purpose behind this destructive war . . . is to destroy Iraq and rearrange the area in a manner far more dangerous to our nation's present and future than the Sykes–Picot agreement," he solemnly declared. "The world has known cruel wars, but never one like this. . . . This war is a war against all Arabs and Muslims, not only against Iraq."[24] If such language seems odd, that's because it was. Today, Jordan has a reputation as one of America's staunchest allies, making it difficult to imagine a time when its monarch opposed in such stark language one of the most important U.S. foreign policy engagements of recent decades. It's true that King Hussein had his bouts of nationalism, and he certainly saw himself as a defender of the Palestinian cause. But there is no way to fully comprehend Hussein's behavior during this period without reference to the unusually intense domestic pressures of the period.

The democratization process that began in 1989 pushed the regime to more closely hew to public sentiments. As Markus Bouillon notes, "With mass demonstrations and volunteers signing up to fight for Iraq in Amman, acting in accord with public sentiment was the safest course of action. . . . [T]he longer the crisis endured, the closer King Hussein moved toward the position dictated by his people."[25] Hussein's popularity reached new highs. He found, however, that public sentiment would be of little help after Iraq's resounding defeat at the hands of the U.S. coalition. The monarchy was in an extremely vulnerable position. There was the matter of Jordan's deteriorating economic situation, aggravated by the war. Because of his support for Saddam, Hussein lost the backing of Saudi Arabia and Kuwait, Jordan's most generous donors. After the war, he pleaded for assistance, but his advances were rebuffed. Saudi Arabia and Kuwait, after all, had just faced an existential threat, and Jordan had betrayed them. Increasingly isolated and concerned (as always) with survival, an embattled king began crawling toward the Western orbit. The crawl soon became a sprint. And with the United States demonstrating its might in its first war as an uncontested superpower, it was clear what Jordan would have to do to get back in the good graces of the international community. After the Gulf War, the Bush administration's attention shifted to the Israeli–Palestinian conflict. And this is where King Hussein saw his opportunity. But there was a problem. Prime Minister Mudar Badran's government included five Brotherhood ministers, as well as two independent Islamists, none of whom were exactly fans of what would come to be known as the "peace process."

The Muslim Brotherhood in Jordan was even more anti-Israel than it was elsewhere in the region. Some of this had to do with the status of Jerusalem and the Al-Aqsa Mosque, Islam's third holiest site, which had been under Jordanian control until the 1967 war. Jordanians of Palestinian origin were especially attracted to the Brotherhood, because it was the only political force where divisions between indigenous Jordanians (East Bankers) and Palestinian Jordanians (West Bankers) became less relevant. The whole idea was that you were a Muslim before anything else. If you were committed to the Brotherhood's ideology and went through the onerous process of being and becoming a member, then you were a *Brother*. An additional factor that heightened the Jordanian Brotherhood's anti-Israel orientation—and an ongoing subject of controversy within the organization—was Hamas' influence. Until the 1990s, Hamas, effectively the Brotherhood's Palestinian analog, shared its headquarters with the Jordanian branch. Several of its leaders were based in Amman, before departing to Syria in 1999 under growing pressure. In practice, this meant that the Jordanian Brotherhood too often found its fortunes tied to that of Hamas, at a time when Hamas was looking to sabotage attempts to broker a peace settlement.[26]

King Hussein knew these things about the Brotherhood. If he wished to regain the confidence of the United States and the international community—at a time when Bush's "New World Order" seemed like the only one—he would need to thrust himself into peacemaking. This required removing domestic constraints, including the Badran–Brotherhood coalition government as well as a parliament dominated by Islamists and nationalists, all of whom despite their ideological differences agreed that Western hegemony was to be opposed and the Palestinian resistance supported. In a sign of things to come, King Hussein moved to replace the government with one more open to negotiations, even if—or, more precisely, *because*—it was less representative of public sentiment. This was no minor shift. The Brotherhood never again returned to government. It was the first and the last time.

If there was a trade-off between foreign policy goals and democratic re-form at home, then the king had to make his choice. "Only peace," writes Bouillon, would "fully [rehabilitate] Jordan in regional and international politics."[27] The Madrid talks weren't quite a success, but they paved the way for a flurry of peacemaking. By 1993, the Clinton administration had made it clear that a resolution to the Arab–Israeli conflict was its foremost regional priority, something that did not escape Hussein's notice.

Peace, as the king saw it, would remove a dangerous source of tension with Israel. Just as importantly, it would produce a "peace dividend" and revive the country's battered economy. The numbers certainly looked good. A World Bank report argued that a peace settlement could provide Jordan with con-siderable economic benefits, including the establishment of a regional free trade zone.[28] The pursuit of peace would be King Hussein's redemption. And once he understood this, it became the preoccupation—one might even say the obsession—of his final years.

Elected Parliaments as an Obstacle to Peace

In the second half of 1991, the king appointed a peace process government led by Taher al-Masri—interestingly enough, Jordan's first ever prime min-ister of Palestinian origin. But there was still the democratically elected par-liament, dominated by the Muslim Brotherhood, which could spell defeat for (and popular mobilization against) any peace initiative. The Islamist-led opposition led the charge against the prime minister's efforts. In anticipation of a no-confidence vote, Masri resigned in November 1991.

Already, it appeared that simultaneously pursuing peace and democ-racy would prove increasingly difficult, if not impossible. For Hussein, the Brotherhood was the greatest threat to what he hoped would be his legacy—at long last, a peace treaty with Israel that, in turn, would guarantee Jordan's stability after his passing. Fortunately, for the king, new parliamentary elections were scheduled for November 1993. And so Hussein decided to en-sure parliament would never be a problem again.

The year 1993 represents something of a turning point—it was the year that the tensions between the pursuit of peace and democracy came to a head. Jillian Schwedler notes that "the political liberalization initiated by King

Hussein in 1989 was halted by 1993, with key provisions steadily reversed,"[29] while Renate Dieterich calls the introduction of a new electoral system in 1993 "a decision which set in motion a rollback of the whole democratic process."[30] King Hussein unilaterally enacted the so-called one-person, one-vote electoral law (*sawt al-wahid*), the primary objective of which was to limit Islamist power at the polls. The external and the internal, in this case, were intimately linked. Hussein needed a pliant parliament to guarantee ratification of a future peace treaty with Israel.

"One vote" made it nearly impossible for the Brotherhood to reprise its previous success. The 1989 legislative elections had been conducted under a plurality bloc voting system where voters in a given district could cast a ballot for as many candidates as there were seats. For example, if a district had six seats, Jordanians could vote for up to six candidates, which benefited well-organized groups like the Brotherhood that could call on the commitment and discipline of their supporters. In turn, smaller leftist groups and Christian candidates sought alliances with the Brotherhood. Both sides benefited.[31] These dynamics would change considerably under the new law.

Brotherhood leaders whom I interviewed would consistently rail against the electoral law, saying, "it has no parallel anywhere else in the world" (*ma andu mithal fi al-alam*). As it turns out, they may have been exaggerating but not by much. The system the Jordanian regime constructed—known as single non-transferable vote (SNTV)[32]—was (and still is) exceedingly rare, with Afghanistan, Vanuatu, and post–Arab Spring Libya among the few countries that have used it in recent decades.[33] There is a reason why SNTV is still sometimes used in local elections but almost never nationally. As Democracy Reporting International notes: "A reason for the infrequent use of SNTV as an electoral system is that it is widely acknowledged to be specifically disadvantageous toward the development of political parties and because it tends to result in votes being cast for individual candidates or those who represent specific groups in a district rather than those who stand for political party platforms."[34]

Under Jordan's new "one-vote" legislation, in a district of six seats, each voter could cast a ballot for only one person rather than six. The negative effects of SNTV in the Jordanian context were compounded by the role of tribal loyalties. With only one vote, indigenous Jordanians were more likely to vote for a candidate from their tribe. Ideological or programmatic considerations become secondary to most voters, making it difficult for actual parties or movements with agendas to gain support. Perhaps more ominously, the

1993 law provided no criteria for apportionment or districting. Instead, the government was granted full discretion to determine the number and size of electoral districts, which led to gratuitous gerrymandering.[35] Generally, tribal regions, long the backbone of the regime, were overrepresented, while the urban areas of Amman and Zarqa, the predominantly Palestinian strongholds of the Muslim Brotherhood, had considerably less representation. Remarkably, some pro-regime regions were represented by as many as one parliamentarian per 5,700 constituents, with Brotherhood strongholds represented by as little as one parliamentarian per 52,000 people.[36]

Would the new election law be enough? It was a critical time for King Hussein. Elections—and any less than ideal results—could still prove an embarrassment and a liability. The Oslo Accords as well as the Jordan–Israel Agenda were signed on September 14, 1993, amidst rising public opposition. Hussein considered going as far as "postponing" the November elections, which points to his mindset at the time.[37] Everything else had been subsumed under the drive for peace and the stability the king hoped it would bring. The mood couldn't have been more different from what Hussein had declared four years prior, on the day of the landmark 1989 elections: "This day is one of the most distinguished days in our lives. It is the day when, after a long absence, the sons and daughters of Jordan are exercising their full right to participate in drawing a new picture for the future."[38]

In the end, "one vote" did precisely what it was supposed to do. Only sixteen of the thirty-five candidates from the Islamic Action Front (IAF), the Brotherhood's political party, won seats. Where the Brotherhood had won 85 percent of the seats it contested in 1989, the IAF win percentage was a mere 48 percent. Many incorrectly interpreted the result as evidence of Islamist decline. In reality, compared to 1989, the IAF's vote share actually increased slightly according to some estimates, which suggests that the electoral law accounted in large part for the drop in seats.[39] In any case, the conclusion was clear. The Brotherhood's dominance had been broken.

The 1993 electoral law was important both on its own terms and as a statement of intent on the part of the Jordanian regime. But it was just as important for what it would later enable, setting into motion a chain of related events. Fundamentally, "one vote" made future breaches of the democratic process possible. It produced an overwhelmingly pro-regime parliament that, in turn, proceeded to pass legislation that further undermined the democratic process.

In the short term, this gave King Hussein the freedom to pursue peace without having to worry aboutparliament causing trouble and vetoing any future treaty. The Brotherhood, meanwhile, was humbled by the results and found itself preoccupied by internal divisions over how to respond to the repressive turn that would define the rest of the decade. The Palestinian Authority was charting its own course, signing an economic protocol with Israel in April 1994, which put additional pressure on Jordan. Fearing he would be left behind, King Hussein frantically moved to conclude a peace agreement with Israel. On July 25, 1994, Jordan and Israel signed the Washington Declaration, moving the two countries one step closer to a formal peace.

The Israel–Jordan peace treaty was signed on October 26 and, in a fait accompli, parliament ratified it 55 to 23. The regime had succeeded in clearing the way for normalization with Israel. Fearing instability might derail peace, it had little tolerance for opposition in the months leading up to the treaty. A purge of Islamist teachers from the public school system had begun earlier in the year, while a month after signing the Washington Declaration, twenty-four imams were suspended from giving sermons.[40]

The peace treaty itself did not mark the end of the regime's intolerance for dissent. If that were the case, the argument that peace and democracy were inversely related would still be strong enough, but at least one could then argue that there was a limit, and that a country and a people had to simply bear the costs—temporarily—in the name of a separate peace. But this is not quite how it works, and it is certainly not how it worked in Jordan. After the treaty was signed, the need to keep opposition groups in line only increased. Peace with Israel never really ended. It was a process—and a prelude to a wholesale strategic alignment. In a matter of mere years, Jordan would go from rallying (or at least trying to rally) the Arab world against America's invasion of Iraq to becoming a loyal and devoted member of the region's pro-Western bloc.

For the monarchy, there were clear benefits. The king got much of what he wanted, namely debt relief of nearly a billion dollars, a tourism boom, increased military support, "major non-NATO ally" status, and a generous American aid package making Jordan the world's second-largest per capita recipient of U.S. foreign assistance.

This bargain, if one can call it that, represented a decisive shift in Jordan's domestic politics. Just three years prior, democracy—and the public responsiveness that resulted—necessitated moving closer to Saddam's Iraq just as the rest of the region was moving away. Now, something resembling the opposite was taking place. Moving closer to Israel (and the Clinton administration) necessitated halting, and even reversing, Jordan's democratization process. In effect, Jordan had claimed its place as a client state, one in which "institutions reflect the preferences of the external power" rather than "society's preferences."[41]

It would not be the last time that international demands would take precedence over democratization at home. For King Hussein, and later his son and successor King Abdullah, the lessons were clear enough. And in a sense Jordan never really recovered. The legacy of Hussein's decision to end his country's democratic "experiment" has withstood the test of time.

What Does Jordan's De-Democratization Tell Us about U.S. Policy?

Jordan is an important if understudied case study, because it offers something close to a natural experiment: What happens when a country that is democratizing ends up pursuing peace with Israel because it urgently needs American support? We can draw several conclusions. Regime-initiated democratization in countries with anti-Israel populations is not likely if regimes need to curry favor with the United States. This will often involve American pressure to pursue peace and diplomatic normalization with Israel. This, in turn, requires carefully managing, controlling, and constraining public opposition. In the process, the public—the very citizens on which a country ultimately depends—becomes not just a threat to the treaties themselves but also to regime security.

The problem is that the threat never really goes away. Once a regime becomes more dependent on American support and adopts unpopular geopolitical positions as a result, it never stops being vulnerable to public pressures. And the way authoritarian regimes, naturally, contend with the pressures of public sentiment is by limiting their expression.

Fortunately, or unfortunately depending on your perspective, not all Arab regimes depend on international largesse or American protection in the way that Jordan does. Perhaps a country that doesn't enjoy a close relationship with the United States would be immune to such pressures. Fortunately, but tragically, there is a case here, too.

In the Shadow of a Civil War

Islamist opposition parties across the region were treading carefully because of what had happened in Algeria. When "one vote" was introduced, the Jordanian Brotherhood was thrown into disarray. Should it boycott, or should it participate? The Brotherhood would stand a better chance of blocking the peace treaty from within parliament; and if King Hussein hoped to marginalize Islamists, a boycott would play right into the government's hands. Hussein's authoritarian reversal was also happening in the shadow of the Algerian civil war. So Jordan's increasingly embattled Islamists "wished to avoid [confronting] the authorities to the point of the breaking of bones," increasingly something it feared in light of developments in Algeria.[42] They also decided to contest relatively few seats, to avoid the "risk" of winning too many, although their worries were misplaced considering the difficulties the new election law posed. In any case, the Brotherhood was torn about playing a prominent political role of any kind now that Arab–Israeli peace was high on the agenda. The prospect of power, in a sense, was anathema—holding any executive authority would entail clashing over recognition of Israel. As the longtime Brotherhood leader Ishaq Farhan put it, "Our phobia is Algeria. This is what we want to avoid."[43]

The problem with the pursuit of peace is that peace wasn't only, or even primarily, a foreign policy issue. It was in a quite literal sense domestic policy, too, considering that this was a country where millions of citizens were Palestinian refugees or the children of refugees. Often, in limited democratic openings, regimes maintain control over "sovereignty" ministries, to ensure that weighty issues of defense and foreign affairs remain in the right, responsible hands. Education ministries, on the other hand, were seen as less important. After all, what could be more "domestic" than domestic education? But there was a problem here, too. During the short-lived Badran–Brotherhood government, for example, the Brotherhood's minister of education, Abdullah al-Akaileh, issued directives to schools warning of "Zionist" influence and calling on teachers to focus greater attention on the value of jihad.[44] Even having Islamists as faceless bureaucrats in education would prove to be a national security issue. Until 1993, there was a significant Brotherhood presence in the ministry of education.[45] In the 1970s and 80s, the monarchy had been content to outsource the running of the ministry to the Muslim Brotherhood. Ishaq Farhan became minister of education in 1970, until the 1990s one of the few times Islamists anywhere had joined the government. Before that, Farhan had been head of curriculum development for six years.

With the push for peace, however, this would all change. The government began purging ministries of Islamist influence. This made it increasingly difficult for Brotherhood members in the civil service to advance in the bureaucracy. For Jordanian officials, the goal was simple enough—nurturing a new generation attuned to the demands of peace with Israel. The educational aims of Islamists and the royal court were becoming irreconcilable. The Brotherhood no longer aspired to executive power, since any role in government would implicate the movement in normalizing Israel. Freed from potential responsibility, it could afford to be more confrontational. And the realm of education was a key area of contestation.

In its 1993 electoral program, the IAF called for a "[greater] focus on the Palestinian issue in curricula and in textbooks, since it is the central concern for Arabs and Muslims." This was innocuous enough. But when it said that educational policy should be redirected to "wage war against educational normalization with the Jewish enemy," it was directly challenging the monarchy's foreign policy prerogatives. Increasingly suspicious of the regime's pro-West realignment, the Brotherhood also warned against "importing foreign experts due to the danger of their influence [on Jordan's educational system]."[46]

The government's decision to limit Islamist influence in education and increase its reliance on Western advisors on curriculum development was a major loss for the Brotherhood. It was also evidence that the Jordanian regime was more than willing to marginalize Islamists well beyond the political arena. Because Islamists were the country's largest opposition force, marginalizing them inevitably meant limiting—and in effect ending—any process of democratization. This also had implications for the United States, and it is worth stating this as explicitly as possible: To the extent that the United States was pushing Arab regimes to make peace with Israel, it was *also* undermining prospects for democratization in the region.

For their part, Arab regimes understood that this was a—or even *the*—top U.S. priority, and that U.S. priorities were best indulged. This was the post-Cold War. American dominance, which would soon be taken for granted, was still something new. In the new world order, with America present at the creation, it would be critical to choose the right side, except that there were no right sides. There was only the United States, or so it seemed. Regimes across the region were embracing repressive policies over the course of the 1990s, a dark decade, only to be surpassed by the 2010s after the devastation of the Arab Spring. In this sense, turning toward the United States—and being provided a more reliable security umbrella—emboldened King Hussein to be more outwardly authoritarian, even though this may have otherwise gone against his more accommodationist instincts.

After Algeria—first the coup, then a civil war—Islamists would be viewed as existential threats. By and large, they still are today. If it could happen in Algeria, it could happen anywhere. Jordan was an important case, since it was the only country where the Brotherhood had operated legally for the entirety of its existence. Yet while the Brotherhood was never banned outright, it found itself increasingly restricted by the same monarchy it had once defended during the tumultuous episodes of the 1960s and 70s. At the same time, it's not quite fair to put the blame entirely on regimes. Oppositions and electorates have agency, too. And the Brotherhood in Jordan certainly had agency. In our conversations over the years, Brotherhood youth frustrated with their septuagenarian leaders would often use the metaphor of an elephant to describe the organization—big, bloated, clumsy, and slow to move. When the movement did decide to move, however, it was a force to be reckoned with. Getting there was difficult, though. These were cautious and careful organizations.

What did it mean to be haunted by Algeria? Algeria remained remote, and few were particularly familiar with the details. But the broad strokes were clear enough, and in my interviews with Islamist leaders in Egypt and Jordan, the word "Algeria" became something of a specter, both a lament for what was lost and a weapon to be wielded to make a simple point. It was evident what the mere mention of this country meant, and no further explanation was necessary: Islamists would not be allowed to govern, even—or particularly—if they came to power through democratic means.

Understanding Algeria

Because it was strategically remote, Algeria might have been the one place where the United States and other Western powers might have taken a calculated risk. It was one thing to fear democracy in Egypt and Jordan, which were—or at least seemed—vital to various foreign policy objectives. Where they were too important to fail, Algeria certainly wasn't.

But this lack of importance cut both ways. If the United States couldn't be expected to take bold risks when something, perhaps too much, was at stake, it also had little reason to expend the necessary time and attention when much less was at stake. To do something unusual—such as actually pushing for democratization in an Arab country—you had to care, and you had to be committed. This paradox would hobble the United States in the years and decades to come. The more important a country was, the less willing American officials were to experiment with new approaches. The less important a country was, the less engaged senior American officials would be, often delegating day-to-day policy to midlevel State Department officials.

The Beginning

Like political openings in Egypt and Jordan, Algeria's emerged in the late 1980s, a product of both domestic developments and a changing regional and international context during the twilight of the Cold War. But as is often the case with small, limited openings, they can gain momentum and become something more over time, eclipsing the modest expectations careful autocrats may have originally had.

Today, the late Algerian President Chadli Benjedid, who died unceremoniously in 2012, is mostly remembered for the tragedy he inadvertently helped set in motion. Like King Hussein at around the same time, he was dealing with mounting discontent among a population that was disproportionately young, frustrated, and underemployed. The socialist experiment of predecessors like President Houari Boumédiène had failed, replaced by the international mood music of market allocation and structural adjustment programs. With oil prices declining, the government introduced new austerity measures. Riots, the largest since independence, began on October 5, 1988. For the regime—which included not just Benjedid, but also the military, security services, and other elements of the "deep state"—the riots were a shock. They also turned violent, with security forces resorting to brute force and live ammunition. Around 500 were killed.[47]

Such a violent response provoked divisions within the regime. Benjedid, already impatient with an inflexible old guard, saw his opportunity and seized it. After the riots, he reshuffled the top military brass and fired senior officials in the ruling National Liberation Front (FLN).[48] The FLN was his party, too, and he moved to distance himself from it, resigning as secretary-general. Most importantly, Benjedid made a decision to not merely content himself with cosmetic reforms but to actually initiate a real democratic transition.

It would have been easy for Benjedid to tinker around the margins, to go farther but not far enough, and to strive for democratization but without democracy. Scholars have described this as "defensive" or "controlled" democratization where the goal is *not* for the transition to succeed but to stall somewhere along the way. From the state's perspective, this can be a prudent course of action, where leaders implement modest reforms that give their citizens an outlet to vent and even compete. If there is too much competition, the regime can step back in and reinforce red lines through coercion. What results is an autocracy that appears to be "liberalizing" *ad infinitum*, always engaging in piecemeal reform but never in anything substantive that would alter existing political structures. Regime opponents find themselves ensnared in what Daniel Brumberg calls an "endless transition."[49] This, however, is not what Algeria did, which is why Algeria remains something of an anomaly. There was no endless transition. It ended, after all.

Counterfactual history is a difficult and underdeveloped subgenre, often viewed with scorn and skepticism by practicing historians. As Niall Ferguson puts it in his book *Virtual Alternatives*: "To understand how it actually was, we therefore need to understand *how it actually wasn't*."[50] The whims and idiosyncrasies of unusual rulers play an outsized role in our story, and Benjedid, at least in hindsight, was unusually brave. Or, perhaps he was confident that he could persevere in a battle of wills with the military, leveraging the powers and bully pulpit of the presidency to his favor. Whatever the case may be, he did not proceed particularly carefully. And this lack of caution allowed the transition to proceed extremely quickly. There have been more rapid transitions elsewhere, including in Egypt and Tunisia during the Arab Spring, but those came about after the overthrow of longtime presidents. In this case, it was the president who was driving the process.

Elsewhere in North Africa, Morocco and Tunisia had begun gingerly liberalizing their systems in an attempt to channel growing political and economic discontent. But neither went nearly as far or fast as Algeria. Both stopped before opposition parties had any reason—or opportunity—to grow too confident. To be sure, part of the reason for their caution was their close attention to what was transpiring in Algeria.

It was easy to look at Algeria with awe or alarm, or both. One seemingly historic move followed another. Not long after the October 1988 riots, Benjedid pushed through a new constitution that legalized political parties and multiparty elections. More an umbrella of disparate groups from Algeria's diverse and raucous Islamist scene than a traditional party, the FIS gained legal recognition in September 1989. By then it was routinely gathering crowds in the tens of thousands, and by the following year some rallies would reach as high as half a million.[51] Ever since the early rise of Egypt's Muslim Brotherhood in the 1930s, no Islamist movement had so quickly and convincingly gained such mass support.

As in Jordan, government officials were caught off guard. They expected Islamists to win around 30 percent of the vote at most.[52] They were mistaken. In the June 1990 municipal elections, the FIS won 55 percent of the vote, a margin of victory that has only scarcely been surpassed anywhere in the region. In multiparty systems, it is rare for parties to clear the majority threshold, rarer still to do so by such a clear margin. In what was still an authoritarian, centralized system, the local councils themselves had limited authority, but the result was a harbinger of things to come on the national level. For new parties, it can be difficult to translate popular support into electoral success, but Islamist parties were—as organizers if not necessarily strategists—unusually competent.

For its part, the Algerian regime was increasingly riddled by internal divisions. As the prospect of a FIS victory in parliamentary elections grew ever more likely, hard-liners in the military and security services agitated for more repression, and they got it. They were emboldened by the Western response, or lack thereof, whether it was American indifference or French favor toward the ostensibly secular Algerian military. After the FIS swept the municipal elections, Roger Bambunck, France's youth minister, said: "It is with great sadness that I see the rise of fundamentalism in Algeria," while Michael Vauzelle, chairman of the Foreign Affairs Committee in the French parliament, noted that "fundamentalism's threat can create a zone of instability, insecurity and even hostility at our southern borders."[53]

Not once, but twice, the Algerian government changed the election law to benefit the rural strongholds of the ruling party. Meanwhile, hundreds of FIS activists were arrested in the lead-up to national elections, which were set to be held on December 26, 1991. The party's two leading figures, Abbasi Madani and Ali Belhaj, were detained. Despite this, or perhaps because of it, the FIS opted to run candidates in every district. The message was clear: Islamists were actually trying to *win*. Of course, this is generally what political parties try to do. They want to win, because they want to govern and put their agenda into practice, whatever it may be. After Algeria, however, Islamist parties generally made a habit of losing elections. The odd thing is that they lost them *on purpose*.[54] Algeria stands out for this reason as well. It was one of the few times—with the only notable exceptions occurring during the Arab Spring—that an Islamist party hoped to dominate government by winning with such a commanding margin that no one would doubt it.

Not surprisingly, panic set in. On election day, newspapers arrived with stark headlines "predicting" an army intervention if the Islamists won. In France, the daily *Le Figaro* warned that Algeria was on the verge of "religious dictatorship."[55] Meanwhile, it wasn't an accident that Prime Minister Sid Ahmed Ghozali went on French television informing viewers that all hope was not lost. The fundamentalists could still be denied power. By this, he was not referring to them being beaten at the polls.

In the first round of elections, the FIS won 47.5 percent of the vote and 188 of 232 seats outright, while the ruling party won a dismal 16 seats. Not only did the FIS do well, which was expected; it did *too* well. It was in a strong position to win most of the 200 remaining seats that went to a runoff. In Algeria's first-past-the-post system, similar to that of the United States and the United Kingdom, the party that reached 50 percent of the vote won the district. This meant that the FIS would have very likely won two-thirds of the total seats, putting them in a position to alter the constitution. For the first time but certainly not the last, Islamist leaders seemed caught off guard by their own success. Naturally, after election results this decisive, fears began to mount that the army was preparing to move. In the tense days that followed, FIS leader Abdelkader Hachani addressed a crowd of supporters. "Victory is more dangerous than defeat," he warned, urging them to exercise restraint to avoid giving the army a pretext for intervention.[56] It was too late.

America and the Algerian Precedent

For the remainder of the decade, Algeria was plunged into a bloody civil war that would claim more than 100,000 lives. Well, who exactly was responsible for the plunge?

It is fair to say that the Algerian civil war wouldn't have happened had it not been for the breathtaking rise of the FIS. This does not mean that Islamists "caused" the civil war. In fact, the opposite was true. It was incumbent elites' unwillingness—or perhaps inability—to come to terms with the reality of elections held freely and fairly (although it's worth noting here that the elections weren't even free and fair, yet Islamists won handily regardless).

Somewhat remarkably, there were few international condemnations of the abrupt cancellation of the elections in between rounds (at least if it had happened before the first round, the regime could have conceivably claimed that it wasn't because Islamists were about to win). Coming so soon after the end of the Cold War, Algeria might have been an important demonstration of Western powers' newfound emphasis on democracy and a new world order. Algeria might have been an easier place for the United States to condemn a coup and marshal international pressure to resume the democratic process, precisely because it didn't matter as much. Vital American security interests were not at stake. This, though, was the paradox that would continue to dog American policymakers. Since vital interests weren't under threat, Washington was not about to expend precious political capital trying something new or potentially controversial. At the same time, if Algeria *had* been more important, then the United States wouldn't have had the luxury of boldness. Too much would have been at stake to take risks. Of course, is it really bold if you're not willing to do it when it matters most?

The American response to Algeria was in effect antidemocratic but not straightforwardly so. It was, like American responses to coups tend to be, a microcosm of the broader ambivalence at the heart of U.S. policy in the region. The state of being torn between competing demands, between who we are and who we want to be, is a particularly American one, setting the United States apart from countries like France, which must have found the American indecisiveness on display a bit exhausting.

Initially, the State Department released a statement saying that it "viewed with concern the interruption of the electoral process" and expressed "hope [that] a way can be found to resume progress [toward democracy] as soon as possible."[57] But the Bush administration stopped well short of outright criticism, saying instead that the military intervention did not actually violate the Algerian constitution. A day later, the State Department backtracked from that position, saying it would not take sides on the constitutionality of the intervention. American officials interviewed after the fact gave the impression that Secretary of State James Baker hadn't thought much about the coup and didn't particularly appear to care.[58] Was not caring at least better than the alternative of outright support for the generals? Perhaps. But the effect was similar. Foreign governments closely watched what Washington said, of course, but they also watched what it chose not to say. As Edward Djerejian, who was assistant secretary of state for the Middle East at the time, described it to me, "We basically deferred to the French, who were very hard line and did not want to see the FIS come to power, obviously. And therefore we followed their lead."[59]

Unlike other "normal" countries, the United States didn't have the luxury of neutrality. As one State Department official remarked, by being circum-spect and saying the bare minimum, the Bush administration "supported the Algerian government by default."[60] A study commissioned by the Senate found the U.S. position to be "something of a wink and a nod."[61] One might have expected that after civil war broke out and the killing began, American officials would have considered revising their interpretation of events. However, hindsight provided few benefits. In a 1994 interview, James Baker took a *stronger* position in favor of the coup than he had at the time, describing U.S. policy toward Algeria's Islamists as one of "exclusion":

> When I was at the Department [of State], we pursued a policy of ex-cluding the radical fundamentalists in Algeria, even as we recognized that this was somewhat at odds with our support of democracy. Generally speaking, when you support democracy, you take what democracy gives you. . . . If it gives you a radical Islamic fundamentalist, you're supposed to live with it. We didn't live with it in Algeria because we felt that the radical fundamentalists' views were so adverse to what we believe in and what we support, and to what we understood the national interests of the United States to be.[62]

This level of bluntness is unusual from an official of Baker's stature, and it brings to mind Kissinger's stark if oversimplified juxtapositions of interests and ideals and his disregard for the latter. This was a time when American officials and journalists called Islamists "fundamentalists" (and radical ones to boot), a term that has since gone out of fashion. Baker's remark that Islamists were adverse to both "what we believe in" and "national interests" raises a question that remains challenging to adjudicate: Does Washington object to Islamists in power on the grounds of culture and ideology or on the grounds of interests, and to what extent are those objections intertwined?

The Meridian House Address

It was true, of course, that the FIS wasn't exactly a proponent of American interests in the Middle East. If the United States was intent on fashioning a "liberal order" after the Cold War, then Islamists didn't seem like particu-larly constructive partners. If anything, at the time, they must have seemed a curiosity, at odds with the sentiments of the time even as they happened to be a product of the era's democratic fervor. It would have been forgivable to think that what happened in Algeria was unusual, and in many ways it was. An Algeria-like scenario wouldn't be repeated for some time. In the moment, then, the Islamist dilemma might not have seemed like a dilemma. History was ending. There were no real challengers to liberal democracy. It must have been confusing, then, to see an avowedly illiberal party on the verge of power not in spite of democracy but because of it.

It was to the Bush administration's credit that it felt compelled to offer a statement of purpose on political Islam. The crowds weren't exactly clamoring for such a speech. In June 1992, Assistant Secretary of State Edward Djerejian gave what became known as the Meridian House Address. It was the first and to this day one of the only attempts by an American administration to address the Islamist dilemma with something resembling coherence. Djerejian opened with a tour of American geopolitical concerns in the post–Cold War Middle East, then turned to political Islam.[63] When I asked Djerejian what prompted such an unusual speech, he explained at length:

> So I'm sitting at the State Department, responsible for the Middle East at that point. And the Berlin Wall tumbles down, it's the end of Communism. We won, the West is triumphant, democracy prevails. And I began to note what Samuel Huntington was saying about the clash of civilizations, Fukuyama about the end of history, and then from various academic circles and interest groups that the next enemy after the Cold War would be Islam in its various aspects. And so I thought was very troubling and wrong-headed, but I really did not know how to grapple with it because it was such a huge issue.
>
> So I did something that I wish more policymakers in retrospect would do. I gathered a group of academics, first experts on Islam and then I convened intelligence community experts from the U.S. Intelligence Community. Then I convened policymakers at the Assistant Secretary level and really dug into it. . . . I was able to do it because of my relationship with [Secretary of State James] Baker. He trusted me. It didn't have to go through a tedious bureaucratic process of clearance. It would have been whittled down. It probably wouldn't even have happened.[64]

As for the actual content, there are different ways to interpret Djerejian's remarks. In a 1993 article for the *Los Angeles Times*, Robin Wright wrote that the speech "may rank as the first formal U.S. policy statement on a specific religion."[65] According to Fawaz Gerges, the speech was "a critical attempt" that "inaugurated a subtle but important shift in the Bush administration's stance toward Algeria in particular and political Islam in general."[66] Others like Peter Mandaville remember it less fondly. Djerejian, he writes, "indicated that it was prudent of the Algerian army to have prevented the FIS from coming to power because Islamists reaching power through the ballot box would have been a case of 'one man, one vote, one time.'"[67]

Indeed, Djerejian's "one man, one vote, one time" catchphrase is why the Meridian House Address is remembered in the first place. Speeches by senior diplomats don't usually stand the test of time. This one was notable precisely because it popularized what would become a casual and ultimately misleading assessment of the threat Islamist participation posed to democracy. As Mandaville notes, the worst-case scenario of one man, one vote, one time reflected "the belief—or at least the strong suspicion—that the Islamist embrace of democratic ideals is likely a tactical shift in the service of a longer-term totalitarian vision."[68]

When I spoke to Djerejian about how he remembers the speech three decades later, he was both impressed and irritated by its checkered legacy. That some would use it to disqualify Islamists from participation "is a misinterpretation of my speech":

> It was meant to be a much more general statement. We believe in the alternation of power. And that includes someone like General Sissi. It was addressed also to the secular leaders. It goes across the board. So, I've been misinterpreted. I've not been happy about it, but there's little I can do about it. People will exploit it. . . . This was not brandishing the Islamists, per se, as a lot of the right-wing think tanks and commentators have made it. It wasn't a manifesto against the Islamist parties. I was saying, "We differ with you on these issues. Let's sit down and talk about this and maybe we can find some common ground." I did have an exchange with [Tunisian Islamist leader] Rachid Ghannouchi. One of the major purposes of the speech was to at least lay out the parameters for the beginning of a dialogue. And unfortunately that did not happen on any sustained basis.[69]

In the many years since the speech, one person, one vote, one time has been divorced from its broader context. It has been weaponized to make a particular point—that the onus of respecting democratic outcomes should be put on Islamist parties, the implication being that there is something in-herent to Islamists that makes them particularly worthy of distrust. Despite its popularization, this formulation wasn't merely misleading. It had little basis in reality. At the time of Djerejian's remarks, such a scenario—Islamists coming to power through democratic elections only to cancel elections and govern by fiat—had never happened. Three decades later, it still hasn't. In one study, Tarek Masoud finds that out of fifteen democratic breakdowns in Muslim-majority countries since 1974, zero involved an Islamist party win-ning elections then dismantling democracy. Out of seventy-one "democratic declines" since 1974, Islamists are implicated in only three.[70] Does this mean that the fear of Islamist parties is completely unfounded? No. But it does mean that the fears are too often overstated.

Some of these fears, of course, draw on the experience of watching the Iranian Revolution unfold in 1979, a mistaken analogy but an analogy none-theless.[71] I wasn't alive when the revolution happened, which makes it harder for me to appreciate the extent to which this seminal event shaped a gener-ation of American policymakers. The case of Iran, however, had limited ap-plicability to the question Djerejian was exploring in his address. Ayatollah Khomeini, the leader of the revolution, did not come to power through dem-ocratic means. He assumed control in February 1979 through force—after a series of armed confrontations between rebels and government forces—and began ruling by decree. An Islamist regime had come into being *before* elections.[72]

In Algeria, Islamists would have come to power after elections, if elections hadn't been canceled. But they were, and that fact of history cannot be un-done. In the three decades since, most scholars of the Middle East and many policymakers have come around to the necessity—or at least inevitability—of Islamist participation. That earlier note of skepticism remains, however, if not necessarily in theory then in practice. And that skepticism continues to shape—and distort—America's approach to the Middle East.

5

The American Veto

If you happen to believe in democracy, the intellectual argument against Islamist participation is a difficult one to make. This is why it is made less and less. Arab democracy is simply impossible without the inclusion of Islamist parties. I hesitate to state this as if it might be controversial when it is one of the few notions in Middle East politics that is close to self-evident. It comes down to definitions. At the heart of the democratic idea are various interconnected ideas and principles. A democracy must reflect popular preferences in some fashion. In other words, democracy should be representative and responsive. A democracy must also be competitive. It is possible to imagine a democracy, perhaps on a tiny island, where the people are so in unison—religiously and politically—that they have no reason to compete. And without the need to compete, there is no need for party, clique, or faction. The cheerful, happy denizens of this small island agree on all the big questions and most of the small ones. I have no knowledge of such a democracy, in practice, even if it is conceivable in theory. This is because conflict is inherent to the human condition. Even if there were no reasons to disagree, citizens (or residents of our tiny island) would surely create them.

A democracy without Islamists is certainly possible—but only in those contexts where Islamist parties have little popular support or where ostensibly secular parties uphold Islamic principles to such a degree that Islamist parties lose their raison d'être. To some extent this describes Senegal and the Gambia, both Muslim-majority countries.[1] This does not, however, describe any country in the Middle East (or for that matter in South or Southeast Asia). In the Middle East, a democracy—to be sufficiently reflective of public sentiment—would need to include the largest opposition parties, and those are almost invariably Islamist in orientation. Without allowing for such opposition, it is unclear how a democracy could possibly be democratic.

Some might quibble with aspects of this description. For example, should Islamist parties with militant wings be allowed to participate? Reasonable people may come to different conclusions. In broad terms, however, the premise that nonviolent Islamist parties—and the vast majority *are*

nonviolent—have a right to contest elections and participate in government has grown uncontroversial. There are holdouts of course, particularly
in the Republican Party, but these tend to be individuals who do not believe democracy is appropriate for all peoples, cultures, or religions (ironically, the opposite of President George W. Bush's view). In this sense, today's
Republicans are not quite democrats, so they can't be held to account for
hypocrisy. Having never subscribed to the principles in question in the first
place, they cannot be accused of violating them. Even before Donald Trump
mainstreamed anti-Muslim sentiment among Republicans, this was always
there to some degree. As Jeanne Kirkpatrick, Ronald Reagan's ambassador to
the United Nations, once said: "The Arab world is the only part of the world
where I've been shaken in my conviction that if you let people decide, they
will make fundamentally rational choices."[2] A less offensive (but still somewhat offensive) version of this was Reagan's remark in 1980 that "lately, we
have even seen the possibilities of, literally, a religious war—the Muslims returning to the idea that the way to heaven is to lose your life fighting the
Christians or the Jews."[3]

In a second category of holdouts are realist-minded analysts and
policymakers. They are traditionalist in their preoccupation with stability at
all costs, which in turn makes them risk-averse, weary of "values" talk, and
skeptical of ambition and adventure abroad, especially when it might involve
interfering in another country's domestic politics. They hold to a clear hierarchy of concerns and objectives. Even if they wish to distance themselves
from him, the patron saint of realists is Henry Kissinger, who exemplified
the hard-headed elevation of narrowly defined national security interests. In
Kissinger's view, democracy might be nice, particularly at home, but it was
always a luxury, particularly abroad. In this reading, America should unapol-
ogetically pursue its interests, even if that meant undermining other countries' democracies. Ideals and interests are *not* intertwined.

The power of such a view is that no one can escape it entirely, partly because
it is based on something true. There are, in fact, trade-offs. When George
W. Bush declared that "America's vital interests and our deepest beliefs are
now one," it was what many of us wished to be true.[4] But it is not. There is
always a tension between narrow and broad conceptions of "interests," and
there is always a tension between the short run and the long term, especially
for elected officials who aren't necessarily focused on the broad sweep of history. When I spoke to Congressman Mike Gallagher, a Wisconsin Republican

who wrote his doctoral dissertation on U.S. grand strategy,[5] he summarized the difficulties of keeping faith in the face of bad outcomes:

> It was becoming increasingly clear that our best hopes for the Arab Spring were misplaced, and it was sort of turning into Arab Winter or whatever you want to call it. And I do think there was this sense, particularly as then Syria got worse and worse and eventually, fast forward a year and a half, the bottom falls out of Iraq, ISIS emerges. I think at a practical level it had the effect in both parties of convincing people that we had to almost ruthlessly prioritize our security interests, even if that was at the expense of democracy promotion.[6]

Like many on Capitol Hill, President Obama would come to adopt his own particular brand of ruthlessness.

The Disillusionment of Barack Obama

While President Obama certainly had his realist proclivities, he was still a member in good standing of the liberal foreign policy establishment.[*] This meant that he said he believed that the United States should uphold democratic values in its conduct abroad.

On intellectual grounds, the Obama administration supported Islamist participation in politics. How could it not, particularly during a period as momentous as the Arab Spring, when the tide of history seemed to be turning? As one senior White House official recalled it: "Obama started off very much of the view that we need to accept that Islamists will have a role in government. I think he came in very much believing in that and he wanted to be the president who would have an open mind about Islamists."[7]

---

[*] Obama didn't like labels, which meant that he became a blank slate on which anyone could project their own preferences. An aide to Obama recounted to me a conversation he had with the president: "And, you know, Obama's a smart, intellectual guy. And we eventually stumbled into this kind of debate about realism versus liberalism. And he knew the little bits and pieces. He was kind of talking about realpolitik versus Wilsonian liberalism and the pluses and minuses of both and as we were landing, I remember very vividly, he said, 'Well, you know, you academics, your problem is that you get caught up in one of these paradigms, and your whole career is spent defending the paradigm,' and he said, 'In the real world,' I remember that phrase, 'In the real world of course, it's both. And things change over time'" (interview with author, December 6, 2021).

Even as late as the day of Egypt's July 3, 2013, military coup, President Obama was reiterating the importance of including all parties in Egyptian politics, and he made a note to mention religious parties. "The United States continues to believe firmly," Obama said, "that the best foundation for lasting stability in Egypt is a democratic political order with participation from all sides and all political parties —secular and religious, civilian and military."[8] In the early days of the Arab Spring, administration officials insisted time and time again that they supported democracy, and it would have been odd to sing the praises of democracy while calling for Islamist parties to be marginalized. Considering their own stated commitments, the obvious middle ground was to cautiously support the democratic process and to maintain neutrality over what that process would produce.

Meanwhile, in the Middle East, conspiracy theories abounded. When I was living in Jordan during the 2008 U.S. presidential election, I remember the relief and excitement, sometimes tongue-in-cheek, sometimes serious, that Barack Hussein Obama—vaguely or surreptitiously Muslim—might actually become president. Friends and cab drivers gave me knowing glances, and I generally returned them in kind. In the span of just a few years, however, the bemused curiosity would give way to something darker, particularly among secular elites. The list of theories was long, and it would be hard to do it justice: Obama wanted Islamists to rise to power and would do whatever in his power as the American president to make this dream into a reality; or Israel was secretly propping up the Muslim Brotherhood in the hope that the latter would destroy Egypt, and the Jewish state would be waiting, ready to strike when the largest Arab nation was at its weakest. The logic was often difficult to follow, but it tended to revolve around the notion of Obama as a closet Islamist. The liberal *Wafd*, one of Egypt's leading newspapers, featured a front-page exposé éclaiming Obama was an actual member of the Brotherhood and that his brother Malek was a financier of the Brotherhood *and* a member of al-Qaeda.[9]

Silliness aside, it is certainly true that, during Egypt's 2012 presidential elections, the Obama administration put pressure on the Supreme Council of Armed Forces to respect the result when it looked like the Muslim Brotherhood's Mohamed Morsi was leading by a small margin. This did not mean, however, that President Obama was some sort of Brotherhood booster. It only meant that he was supporting the cornerstone of democracy—holding free elections and accepting the outcome, whatever it may be. This wasn't the most he could have done; it was the least.

Was Mohamed Morsi an Autocrat?

But this intellectual openness to democracy and its outcomes would have its limits against the realities of Middle East politics. During Morsi's brief tenure as president, opposition grew, and Egyptian politics became increasingly polarized. In the months leading up to the coup, it was common to hear some variation of the following: Mohamed Morsi was a new pharaoh, a would-be dictator, or a purveyor of a new, dangerous kind of fascism. He was undoubtedly incompetent and failed to govern inclusively. I spent time with Morsi before he became president, and there is little doubt in my mind that he was the wrong man at the wrong time. But was he really an autocrat? If Morsi was, indeed, a dictator in the making—and if a democratic transition was no longer democratic—then some kind of corrective measure, however painful, could be justified or at least explained away as inevitable. The only way to answer this question is to look not at how Morsi's rule measured up against the hopes of revolutionaries, or our own, but to compare his year in office to other transitional contexts.

With this in mind, a colleague and I scored Morsi's year in office according to the Polity IV index—one of the most widely used empirical measures of autocracy and democracy.[10] We then scored a random stratified sample of thirty-two other countries in the category of "societal transitions," the category under which Egypt fell under Morsi.[11] On a scale from –10 to 10 (with negative values representing more autocratic regimes and positive values representing more democratic regimes), our most charitable reading of Morsi's tenure was a 4. However, we thought the most accurate score—drawing not just on the letter of Polity's coding guidance but also the spirit—was a 2. This was significantly better than the mean value for societal transitions, which was –0.97. In short, Morsi was *more* democratic than other leaders during societal transitions.

None of this changes the fact that the Morsi government, in absolute rather than relative terms, was a failure. Morsi and the Brotherhood did not govern in the spirit of inclusive democracy. The Islamist-dominated constitution drafting process produced a flawed and illiberal framework—though over 60 percent of Egyptians ultimately voted in favor of the document amid low voter turnout. But, as incompetent and divisive a president as Morsi no doubt was, the opposition still had recourse to counter and constrain executive action, as evidenced by the near perpetual anti-Morsi protests in the months leading up to the coup.

Still, perceptions matter in politics. What someone perceives to be real is real to them, regardless of whether it's true. Observers don't have the luxury of carefully considering a political science index and making their judgments accordingly. During Mohamed Morsi's time in office, the Obama administration couldn't help but be affected by the growing alarm over his behavior. Even if Morsi wasn't quite an autocrat, he may have seemed like one at the time. Obama was also in a delicate position, particularly for someone so concerned with his own domestic standing. He may have been more open to Islamism than his predecessors, at least at first, but this perceived openness also proved a liability. "Don't forget, at the beginning, he's accused of being an Islamist sympathizer himself. I think he had to fight that perception. And sometimes he overcompensated in the other direction," one senior White House official told me. This was a time when Obama's very identity was constantly being challenged. Somewhat remarkably, a majority of Republicans came to believe that Obama himself was "deep down" a Muslim.[12] Presumably, a stealth Muslim—and one who had hidden his identity all the way to the presidency—would have unusual loyalties.

The Morsi Government's International Relationships Sour

In my conversations with senior Brotherhood figures as well as Western officials shortly after the coup, what emerged were diametrically opposed narratives about the Obama administration's role in Egypt during the Morsi era. As one former State Department official told me shortly after the 2013 coup, "There was a positive feeling after Morsi's election, not because Islamists came to power but because the fact that they did revealed it was a free election. . . . We were very ready not to prejudge [from an anti-Islamist lens] and keep a much more open mind."[13]

Former advisors to Mohamed Morsi claim that they encountered pressure from the United States and the European Union to appoint prominent liberal Mohamed ElBaradei as prime minister. They recounted to me specific conversations they had with President Morsi himself on the matter. This was a particularly sore point, since ElBaradei was a Western darling—something the Brotherhood was keenly aware it wasn't. Not only was ElBaradei a political liberal (in theory), he was culturally and religiously liberal as well, having lived most of his adult life in the West. EU special envoy Bernardino Leon, who was directly involved in the negotiations, denied the Brotherhood's account of what transpired. "It is not true," he told me. "We suggested that there be a consensus prime minister, not someone from the Brotherhood and its entourage and not from the [opposition] National Salvation Front. We conveyed this to Morsi and Morsi agreed in principle. . . . ElBaradei was a non-starter."[14]

The truth probably lies somewhere in between. Regardless of whether ElBaradei was suggested specifically or explicitly, the Morsi government *perceived* growing pressure from the United States and other international interlocutors to make unwarranted concessions. As one senior Brotherhood figure told me, "This was a very rude interference in our affairs. . . . Why impose a government that is led by an opponent of the government?"[15] Brotherhood members would often point out that ElBaradei and his Dustour party were "not elected" and had no grassroots support. One Brotherhood official, living in exile in Doha at the time, complained to me that "they tried to test the will of the president. If he accepted U.S. interference this time, he would always be indebted to them."[16]

Such tensions came to the fore whenever Western officials called on the Brotherhood to be more inclusive, which they increasingly did as Egypt's political crisis worsened during the first half of 2013. The Brotherhood tended to view "legitimacy" almost entirely through the lens of electoral success. As Brotherhood officials often pointed out, it was the ultraconservative Salafi Nour party, which came in second in the 2011 elections, which was their main rival—not liberals. Brotherhood officials were also suspicious as to why the United States and others were spending significant time meeting with various secular opposition parties, some of whom had little relevance on the ground. In more established democracies, the U.S. government meets regularly with opposition parties. But these are consolidated democracies where no one suspects that American officials are trying to topple the government. In this case, however, Brotherhood leaders suspected just that, at least in their retrospective assessments. In light of what we know now, they weren't entirely incorrect. ElBaradei, for example, wasn't a democrat, even in the minimal sense. Despite his liberalism, or perhaps because of it, he emerged as one of the most outspoken supporters of the military coup, even speaking on behalf of the military in high-profile interviews with the Western press.[17]

Another sticking point was the role of international financial institutions. In the Middle East, the International Monetary Fund (IMF) and the World Bank's decisions are often seen as an extension of U.S. and European policy, which assumes a level of policy coordination that there rarely is. That said, the United States and European nations, as the largest shareholders in both organizations, do have considerable influence and can apply internal pressure if they decide it is worth it.

An IMF deal, which could have unlocked as much as $15 billion for Egypt (including associated grants and commitments), failed to materialize during Morsi's rule. Again, the gap in narratives is striking. As one former State Department official told me: "We were hugely supportive and encouraging of the deal . . . but we can't be more Egyptian than the Egyptians. I cannot overemphasize just how badly everyone wanted the deal to happen."[18] This is not how the Morsi government saw it, but, again, this too is colored by what came after—the bitterness that Morsi's advisors felt in the wake of the coup and subsequent August massacre. Two figures close to Morsi who were privy to or actively involved in the negotiations were more than comfortable blaming the IMF. One told me he was under the impression a deal was very close to done by early June, just weeks before the military coup. "We responded to all the prerequisites of the IMF. The IMF was satisfied, so tell me what's the explanation for it not going forward?" he asked me. It seemed like it was a rhetorical question, but apparently it wasn't. He continued: "If the deal was signed then, it would have been very difficult for the coup to go ahead. The Morsi government would look very successful, having achieved something previous governments couldn't achieve."[19]

From the IMF's standpoint, there were outstanding technical issues, which, of course, were not merely "technical." They were also fundamentally political due to growing concerns about the Morsi government's ability to execute the IMF program in the midst of plummeting public support. As the months went on, the IMF (as well as the United States and EU) increasingly emphasized the importance of buy-in from other political forces, including those like Mohamed ElBaradei that the Brotherhood believed were trying to topple it. The Morsi government felt that it was being held to an unfair and unusual standard. In the IMF's Articles of Agreement, there is nothing about political conditionality.[20] Autocrats and democrats alike are eligible for IMF support. Morsi's aides wondered why, then, the IMF was harping on political consensus.

For the international community, political buy-in mattered not for its own sake, but for what it said about the Morsi government's ability to implement the IMF program. For them, this was always the bottom line. Could the Morsi government deliver? And the doubts would accumulate with each passing month, until the military staged a coup and a rather successful one at that.

Before and After the Coup

The strongest piece of evidence that the Obama administration wasn't as comfortable with the idea of Islamists in power as it initially seemed came relatively late in the Arab Spring, in the lead-up to the Egyptian coup and certainly during it. But there were early signs of concern, and they began to tell a story.

For starters, in the months after Mubarak's ouster, the United States pushed Egypt's transitional authority, the Supreme Council of the Armed Forces, to hold presidential elections before parliamentary elections. As Dennis Ross, a senior advisor to President Obama, recalled: "Part of the reason that we had been pushing for presidential elections first was precisely because it was a given, at least to me, that in parliamentary elections, the Muslim Brotherhood would dominate."[21]

The reasoning was largely but not entirely correct. There was a reason that the Brotherhood itself had initially called for something close to a pure parliamentary system. They had long preferred the presidency to be mostly ceremonial—"completely removed from any executive responsibility for governing" was how they once put it.[22] Some of this was a simple matter of self-interest. Brotherhood leaders knew where their strengths lay. The Brotherhood was a movement, greater than the sum of parts, with no one individual dominating. With its extensive local networks and disciplined cadres, it could out-organize its competitors district by district.[23] A national election for a single individual was an altogether different proposition. Organizational discipline matters less and charisma, money, and media access all matter more.[24] And since Sayyid Qutb's execution in 1966, the Brotherhood in Egypt had lacked charismatic leaders.

For the United States, prioritizing presidential elections must have seemed like the best of both worlds—democracy but without the attendant risks. Moreover, American officials (as well as Egypt's secular parties) preferred a mixed system. Under a framework of divided responsibility, the president would have considerable latitude on national defense, foreign policy, and international coordination with, say, the IMF. In other words, even if the Brotherhood swept parliamentary elections, the world could still rest easy. Democracy's inherent uncertainty and unpredictability would be limited, and Islamist ambitions would be constrained by design. A non-Brotherhood president could keep an unruly parliament in check. "It was clear the Brotherhood was going to do well in any election, but remember our sort of default position was that [secular candidate] Amr Moussa was going to win [the presidency], which was an entirely Western way of looking at things," Ambassador Anne Patterson recalled.[25] Charming and moderately charismatic, Moussa was a known quantity—if not necessarily politically liberal, then at least socially liberal. Respected in Western capitals, he had served ten years as Mubarak's minister of foreign affairs.

It was understandable that the United States would prefer a system in which the Egyptian president maintained significant discretion. There is a considerable academic literature on the dangers of presidential systems in divided societies.[26] But from an American perspective, if "stability" and Israel's security were guiding concerns, then an empowered presidency made sense. In this respect, U.S. officials, regardless of what they themselves might have preferred, were constrained by a longstanding posture toward the Middle East that prioritized certain things rather than others. America's interests were America's interests. And despite the Arab Spring, they hadn't necessarily changed.

Policymakers were also products of a system, and that system had kept groups like the Muslim Brotherhood at a comfortable distance. Not only that, for nearly five years during the Bush administration, direct contacts between the Brotherhood and the United States had been halted entirely.[27] No wonder the topic was fraught. The debate over when and how to initiate a dialogue was, in the words of one Obama administration official, "pretty hot and heavy."[28]

To Engage or Not to Engage?

A policy authorizing initial contacts with the Brotherhood (as well as Salafis) was drafted by the end of February 2011. The State Department signed off, but the issue was perceived as so sensitive that White House approval was sought before any further steps were taken. A senior State Department official, who was involved in the internal debate on whether to authorize contacts, recounted a somewhat labyrinthine process:

[The policy] works its way up to Tom Donilon's desk, who was National Security Advisor at the time. It gets into his inbox, and the way it was described to me by colleagues on the National Security Council staff was that it would work its way up and each time it was at the top of his inbox, he would take it and put it back down because he just didn't want to deal with it [chuckle]. Like, he realized it was something that he was still worried about, like, "Okay, if I sign off on this, I'm gonna be the one who basically signs off on the U.S. jumping into bed with the Islamists."[29]

Even if you *wanted* to be comfortable with Islamists, how you felt about them wasn't necessarily something you could control. In October 2011, nine months into the Arab uprisings, Anne Patterson, the American ambassador in Cairo, made a comment that was as revealing as it was honest. When asked in an interview about meeting with Brotherhood officials, she responded, "I'm not personally comfortable with it enough yet." When pressed for a reason why, she repeated, "Well, I'm just not comfortable."[30]

It was hard to blame her, except perhaps for the misstep of candor in a notoriously tight-lipped administration. As Peter Mandaville, a senior advisor in the State Department at the time, explained: "I think Patterson got a little bit of heat for that, because it seemed to be at odds with our actual posture. I think she literally meant, 'I, the ambassador, am not comfortable meeting with them.' But it came across as the U.S. government doesn't want to meet with them."[31]

The United States had maintained contact with Islamists in remote countries like Morocco or in states like Kuwait where they tended to be more pro-American due to the legacy of the Gulf War. In more strategically vital countries like Egypt and Jordan—incidentally, the only two that had signed peace treaties with Israel—direct contacts with Islamists in general, and the Brotherhood in particular, had been rare, particularly during the 2000s.[32] Anne Patterson was being asked, in effect, to develop a working relationship essentially from scratch with a movement that the United States had long avoided.

The United States was underprepared but not unprepared, at least not completely. Two years before the uprisings began, Quinn Mecham, a leading scholar of Islamist movements who was in government, started an informal State Department working group on political Islam and the question of engagement.[33] Then the Obama administration took another step. As Mandaville writes, "In 2010, the U.S. National Security Council began work on a Presidential Study Directive focused on the question of what a push for genuine political reform in the Middle East would look like—including the normalization of Islamists as political actors."[34] But it was one thing to acknowledge the need to engage with groups like the Brotherhood in Egypt and another thing to actually do it in a serious, sustained way. And for this there could be no real preparation. In 2010, virtually no one thought that popular revolutions would come so quickly, if at all.

Turning a Blind Eye

In some ways, Patterson's offhand remark was a harbinger of things to come. The relationship between the United States and the Muslim Brotherhood would remain an awkward one. It is hard to imagine how it could have been otherwise. The entire edifice of U.S. policy in the region was oriented around security partnerships with pro-American autocrats who could effectively bypass the concerns and objections of their own people. In his appropriately titled book *Democracy Prevention*, Jason Brownlee argues that in the case of Egypt, the United States is "less like an external force and more like a local participant in the ruling coalition."[35] Whatever Obama administration officials might have said or even hoped for, they were constrained by the past. Washington's authoritarian bias was deeply embedded, the product of decades of accumulated policy. One might also call it a status quo bias, since authoritarianism was simply the way things had been for so long. Favoring the status quo meant that the United States would find itself ill equipped for and uncomfortable with the comparative chaos of democracy.

The Egyptian military was seen as a bulwark against such chaos. And so the Obama administration indulged the the Supreme Council of the Armed Forces (SCAF), emboldening it to dominate—and undermine—the democratic transition. This wasn't some accidental outcome, a product of indifference and incompetence. Obama admitted as much. "Our priority has to be stability and supporting the SCAF," he said. "Even if we get criticized. I'm not interested in the crowd in Tahrir Square and [*New York Times* columnist] Nick Kristof."[36]

At critical moments, American officials turned a blind eye to various antidemocratic maneuvers. Just days before the second round of presidential elections between Morsi and Ahmed Shafik, an army man and Mubarak's last prime minister, Egypt's judiciary dissolved the country's first democratically elected parliament on various technicalities. Around 70 percent of its members were Islamists of various stripes. In a moment, an electoral outcome was undone, and millions of votes thrown out.

Can there really be a democratic transition without a parliament? The answer was presumably "no," yet the American response was muted, issuing carefully worded statements of concern but nothing in the way of concrete pressure.[37] And it had been muted just three months prior, when the SCAF launched a wide-ranging crackdown on U.S. democracy assistance organizations. In an odd twist, the regime went so far as to threaten American citizen Sam Lahood with arrest, ultimately forcing him to leave the country. Lahood was the director of the International Republican Institute's branch in Cairo, but he was also the son of Obama's Transportation Secretary, Ray Lahood. Despite these developments, the Obama administration waived congressional conditions on military aid, allowing it to continue flowing. The lesson was clear enough—and one the military appeared to take to heart. It could get away with quite a lot.

On June 16 and 17, tens of millions of Egyptians went to vote in presidential elections. Mohamed Morsi was sworn in on June 30 after a tense two weeks. Morsi was a senior if somewhat obscure functionary in the world's oldest Islamist movement. Now he was president of Egypt. From an American standpoint, this may have been worrying, but it was also tolerable. Morsi would be constrained by the deep state, or what Nathan Brown calls the "wide state."[38] The military had long been the lynchpin of America's relationship with Egypt. It was the devil they knew. Not only that, it was the guardian of the state and had been for decades. As Mandaville notes, "Washington felt confident that its longstanding and trusted ally, the Egyptian military, would serve as an ultimate guarantor of stability regardless of whether Islamists were winning elections."[39] Would an "ultimate guarantor" be quite as necessary if a pro-Western liberal had become president? It may be fair to reply that a pro-Western liberal *wouldn't* have become president in the first place, but this only serves to underscore the point.

Anticipating that Morsi might win the presidency, the military acted preemptively. On June 16, 2012, the first of two days of voting, the SCAF issued a constitutional declaration that stripped any future president of key powers, including the ability to declare war and deploy the army to quell domestic unrest.[40] In addition, the declaration granted full legislative authority to the SCAF in the event of parliament being dissolved (which it already was). This was another critical moment, and yet another moment where the Obama administration did little but issue perfunctory statements of concern.[41] Presumably by then, military leaders understood that they could act with impunity.

This is not to say that the United States longed for the Brotherhood to fail or wished for Egypt to remain authoritarian. There was no conspiracy. In the region, there is often a perception of outright malevolence, as if White House officials wake up in the morning and think of all the ways they can make the lives of Arabs more miserable. Criticism, even harsh criticism, is more than warranted, but criticism is different than attributing malice in the absence of evidence. Most American officials really did want Egypt to be (at least somewhat) more open and democratic. Foreign policy is also difficult, a fact that those on the outside can try to appreciate but still never fully grasp.

In a moment that rings of both tragedy and naivete, one aide to Obama recalled showing Morsi's national security advisor, Essam al-Haddad, around the Situation Room. "We wanted to help them figure out how to run a national security process in Egypt and didn't quite appreciate how out of their element they were," he told me.[42]

In an ideal world, American officials might have preferred democracy, But they also wanted other things. It also depended on which officials one talked to, since they didn't necessarily agree with each other. And so when Egypt's transitional authorities dissolved the country's first democratically elected parliament and then stripped the incoming president of his powers—all in the span of one week—the lack of response to what amounted to a legal coup reflected incoherence rather than something more sinister. Democracy was good, but you could also have too much of a good thing. As a State Department advisor explained:

> We were engaging with the Brotherhood and trying to build our influence over them to achieve our own security interests, but we weren't really standing up for them either in an active way. And so, that was just like, "Oh my God. How could this happen? How could the military do this?" We didn't really react, I think for two reasons. First of all, there was a lingering nervousness and worry about the Brotherhood having unchecked power. So it was thought, "Okay, we're going to try with these guys." They've assured us they're not going to break the peace treaty, but we don't want it to get totally out of control, because it'll be bad for our interests, it'll be bad for Egypt, and then there'll be hell to pay from the Israelis and the Emiratis and the Saudis, who were already in full-on freakout mode.[43]

The military's "legal coup" became just another fact on the ground. But it didn't last. A month and a half into his presidency, Morsi, in a surprise move, sacked the head of SCAF as well as the chiefs of all branches of the armed forces. He also overturned the June 16 constitutional declaration. In some ways, this marked the true beginning of the (brief) Morsi era. Yet, just weeks later, after a mob stormed the U.S. embassy in Cairo, President Obama appeared to revise America's longstanding position on the Egyptian government. "I don't think that we consider them an ally," Obama said in an interview, "but we don't consider them an enemy."[44] This was an odd thing to say just after Egypt had itself, for the first time, a democratically elected head of state. During Mubarak's thirty-year reign, no American president had said anything remotely comparable. Washington had usually gone out of its way to praise Mubarak for his services. Earlier in his first term, Obama had insisted that Mubarak was "a stalwart ally" and "a force for stability and good."[45]

With Morsi now the leader of Egypt, the Obama administration was thrust into an unprecedented position. The broader region was disintegrating into conflict. Concurrent attacks on U.S. embassies in Tunis and Benghazi—the latter claiming the lives of four diplomats, including Ambassador Chris Stevens—eroded what little goodwill was left. "I felt I was watching the Arab Spring turn dark in real time," wrote Ben Rhodes.[46] In Cairo, an anti-American and anti-Israel Islamist had become commander-in-chief of a key ally—and not only a key ally, the most populous Arab state and a bellwether for the region to boot. And it happened because of an ideal that the United States claimed was good for itself as well as being good for the people of the Middle East. This was what democracy brought, or wrought, depending on your perspective.

And what democracy wrought in Egypt was something the United States became increasingly nervous about over the course of Morsi's tenure. It is well known that President Obama refused to call the coup a coup. Memorably and awkwardly, State Department Spokeswoman Jen Psaki was dispatched to tell reporters, "We have determined that we do not have to make a determination about whether or not this was a coup."[47]

That was only the beginning. Weeks later, Secretary of State John Kerry lauded Sissi and the Egyptian army for "restoring democracy."[48] By intimating that Morsi and the Muslim Brotherhood had, in some way, hijacked Egypt's political process, the United States legitimated the logic that the coup was necessary in order to salvage Egyptian democracy. What made Kerry's remark all the more remarkable was that it came after two separate massacres of Brotherhood supporters, which took place on July 8 and July 27. At least

166 were gunned down by police and army units, protesting peacefully against the military takeover.[49]

Chronicle of a Coup Foretold

Less well known are the critical, tense days leading up to the coup, when the disaster—and the subsequent killings—might have been averted. For some time, these were days shrouded in mystery. This offered the United States plausible deniability after the fact. The Obama administration could say that it was caught off guard. The coup happened, it was a fait accompli, and they had to live with the world as it was, not as they wished it to be.

At the time, Ambassador Anne Patterson seemed blissfully unaware of the military's machinations. On June 18, two weeks before the coup, she gave a speech where she took for granted the continuation of the democratic process, discussing forthcoming parliamentary elections at some length. She was skeptical of the utility of street protests. "Some say that street action will produce better results than elections," she said. "To be honest, my government and I are deeply skeptical."[50] She was criticized, including by the likes of Senator Ted Cruz, for "failing to support [the opposition to Morsi] and further the vital interests of the United States without firing a shot." Cruz also faulted Patterson for failing to encourage the opposition "to pursue a true secular democracy in Egypt."[51]

Yet what was less noted about Patterson's speech was that she distanced herself (and the United States) from Egypt's elected government and, in effect, advised dissidents on how to outmaneuver Morsi. She urged Morsi's opponents, many of whom were in the audience, to beat him at the ballot box in the upcoming elections. In other words, for the United States, the Brotherhood losing would have been the preferred outcome.

The Defense Department, due to its own institutional interests and proximity to Egypt's generals, was more skeptical of Morsi, putting it in tension with the State Department and the White House, which were at least paying lip service to democracy. Again, the intellectual premise was important: Obama and his top aides believed that, all other things being equal, it would be better for the United States (and presumably for Egyptians) if Egypt could establish some modicum of democratic practice over the long run. But all things weren't equal. Senior defense officials like James Mattis, who was commander of U.S. Central Command for part of Morsi's tenure, tended to see democracy promotion as a luxury that distracted from hard power and counterterrorism. Mattis once described the Muslim Brotherhood and al-Qaeda as "swimming in the same sea"[52] (despite the fact that al-Qaeda considers the Brotherhood to be outside the fold of Islam[53]). Far from just an offhand remark, Mattis called the question of political Islam's compatibility with American interests a "fundamental" one. The quote is worth citing in full:

> Americans will not ask one fundamental question and that question is, "Is political Islam in the best interest of the United States?" I suggest that the answer is no, but we need to have the discussion. If we won't even ask the question, then how do we ever get to the point of recognizing which is our side in the fight, and if we don't take our own side in this fight, then we are leaving others adrift.[54]

Mattis, himself a military man, found much to like in the military coup that ousted the Brotherhood. "What we basically saw," he said to an audience at the Aspen Security Forum, "was a popular impeachment with the largest crowds in modern world history out in the streets saying I'm done with this guy then we see the military muscle coming in and supporting the popular impeachment".[55]

Interestingly, Michael Flynn, who would rise to fame—and infamy—as Donald Trump's disgraced national security advisor, was the director of the Defense Intelligence Agency during the spring of Morsi's fall. Recounting that period, Flynn recalled that he thought "what we were going to see was a takeover of the country by the Muslim Brotherhood."[56] On the other hand, he liked Sissi in part because he was "very secular."[57] Flynn visited Cairo that April. As the *New York Times*' David Kirkpatrick documents in his brilliant and sometimes chilling account *Into the Hands of the Soldiers*, Egyptian generals organized a "cultural day" for Flynn. Over lunch, Flynn and his Egyptian counterpart "scrawled out a map of the Islamist threats they saw around Egypt."[58]

While the State Department as a whole may have been better, Secretary of State John Kerry—even before his "restoring democracy" remark—was something of an outlier in his own State Department, often provoking consternation among counterparts entrusted with executing U.S. policy in Egypt. As one senior advisor to Kerry told me, "He felt that [the coup] wasn't a bad outcome for us from the standpoint of national security interests. He wasn't a fan of the Muslim Brotherhood, big time not a fan of Morsi."[59] Another State Department official put it more bluntly:

> Kerry hates Islamists. He hates them. I think it's just that he's somebody who is formed and shaped in another era of the world, and I think the way that he gained his knowledge and information about the Middle East was by talking to Arab leaders. And if you're dealing with the leaders for however many decades in the Senate, you get a particular view of the region. My personal opinion is that he likes dictators. Kerry likes dictators. It's kinda like Biden. All these guys. They're all from that generation of 'just deal with strong men.' That's all they ever knew in the Middle East. There never was anybody else.

In a conversation with Kirkpatrick after the fact, Kerry admitted to knowing Morsi was "cooked"—and that the military was readying itself to intervene—as early as March 2013, the first time he met with then Minister of Defense Abdelfattah al-Sissi in Cairo. Rather than push back, Kerry said he found Sissi's remark "reassuring."[60] Remarkably, four years after the coup, after a massacre, and after Egypt had solidified itself as a military dictatorship, Kerry was unrepentant. "I knew [Sissi] was better than Morsi. I still think that. Oh, yeah. Even though he's got problems, he is better than Morsi," he said.[61]

After meeting Sissi alongside Kerry, Ambassador Patterson warned the White House that "a coup was a high likelihood within a few months."[62] She was right. This is important, because it offers little doubt that in the days leading up to the military takeover in July, U.S. officials would have known what was going on—and would have been in a position to try to block Sissi (if they wanted to). And it was during this critical period, when the world was beginning to watch, that the United States gave Sissi what amounted to a green light to proceed with the coup.

It is perhaps here where America's Islamist dilemma became most evident. At the time, Chuck Hagel was secretary of defense. Reflecting on this period, Hagel stated that he agreed with Saudi, Emirati, and Israeli claims that the Brotherhood was "dangerous" and had to be countered.[63] The first inadvertent green light for the military coup also happened to come from Chuck Hagel. Days before the takeover, Hagel said to Sissi: "So I will never tell you how to run your government or run your country. . . . You do have to protect your security, protect your country."[64]

Hagel's ineffectiveness was a source of consternation in the White House. A senior White House official described it in blunt terms:

> Look, between us, Chuck Hagel was a disaster on pretty much every level, literally incompetent. You couldn't make head or tail of what he was saying most of the time in the Situation Room. So relying on him to deliver these kinds of messages to Sissi was a major mistake. Obviously, he didn't really want to do it and he wasn't going to take a hard line. So, there was that element too. I think that's more a reflection of our bureaucratic dysfunction than a reflection of some Machiavellian conspiracy.[65]

Similarly, but less bluntly, a Pentagon official told me, "Hagel spent a lot of time on the phone with Sissi. I was not privy to every conversation, but I was privy to many of them, and I wasn't impressed."

> I never really recalled him being that firm, but I don't think it grew out of some well-thought-through strategy. My view of his calls was that he was kind of a good soldier in the sense that the White House would decide something, and they'd be like, "What message do we need to give the Egyptians, and who's gonna deliver the message?" And it was like, "Alright, here's the message, and Chuck, get Sissi on the line." The talking points were there, he did kind of get through most of them, but—this is always just something funny—I think directors on the National Security Council would be like, "Here is the script I have written for the Secretary of Defense." And I'd be like, "Get the fuck out of here if you think the Secretary of Defense is gonna read your script verbatim." They're not gonna do it. They're gonna have a conversation with someone, and then over the course of that conversation, they're gonna try to hit on these key points, if they believe that your key points really and truly are endorsed by the President.[66]

But then what about the president? What did *he* do (or not do)?

Two days before the coup, on July 1, President Obama called Morsi. On June 30, an estimated 1 million Egyptians had taken to the streets to protest Mohamed Morsi's rule.[67] The military used the popular show of force to give Morsi an ultimatum. But the coup hadn't happened yet, and there was still time for Washington to clarify its intentions and preferences. Instead, Obama seemed to acquiesce, going so far as to rationalize what the army had done and what it was about to do. "We conveyed our interest in avoiding military intervention in the political system," Obama informed Morsi. "The fact is, if the Egyptian military thinks the country's stability is at risk, they are going to make their own decision."[68] In this account, the United States was willed into irrelevance, a prisoner of the very context it had helped to create in the preceding months. Obama sounded more like a political analyst, a powerless bystander from afar, than the president of a superpower that through billions of dollars of aid ensured the comfort of Egypt's generals.

There was, however, an eleventh-hour proposal to Morsi from John Kerry. Later that day, after Obama's call, Kerry urged Morsi to delegate his powers to an unelected prime minister and remain as a figurehead.[69] If Morsi had agreed to this, it would have been only a slight variation on the theme. It would have still been a coup, albeit a softer one: Morsi losing his power and authority at the barrel of a gun and with the threat of tanks in the streets of Cairo. There was no parallel effort to pressure Sissi and the military to compromise and meet Morsi halfway. The military's takeover was assumed as a given, before it had even reached what appeared to be its inevitable conclusion. But none of this was foreordained.

The following day, on July 2, a chaotic situation had only grown more so. To say that the messages were mixed doesn't do it justice. Obama was traveling. His national security advisor Susan Rice was at the White House. Essam al-Haddad, Morsi's national security advisor, called her from the presidential guard house in Cairo (where he and Morsi would be arrested in less than twenty-four hours). Haddad was in a state of panic, alternating between fatalism and defiance:. A senior White House official described the scene to me:

> [Susan] gave an impassioned defense of democracy to this guy who was doing the same thing on the other end, saying that his fathers and forefathers had laid down their lives to try to protect Egyptian freedom and that he and Morsi were prepared to do the same thing. And that the only hope they had left was the United States. And she basically said, "We will not abandon you, we stand for democracy, we have made very clear. . . ." It was an emotional conversation on both ends. And, Obama wasn't part of this conversation, but I assumed that she was reflecting his views. And she said, basically, "We will not let this stand, we will not let it. . . ." It was like over and over again. And I remember saying to her, "Susan, are you sure?" "Are we going to follow through on this?"[70]

On July 3, it was, in fact, too late. By the time Americans would have woken up that day, Morsi would have found himself detained in an undisclosed location. Egypt's democratic experiment—flawed and frightening to those who had to live amidst the uncertainty—had ended.

The following day, President Obama gathered aides in the Situation Room. And something unusual happened. One White House advisor who was part of the meeting walked me through how the conversation unfolded—or, in this case, didn't unfold.

> I came in all hot and bothered, and so did a few others, that there was a clear letter of the law that said, "Declare the coup, cut off military assistance." Actually, we weren't even focused on the first thing, because only somebody who was purposefully obfuscating would say that it wasn't a coup. I didn't even think that that was an issue. So, it was like, "When do we announce this?" That's when I came in, expecting the conversation was going to be about that. And then Obama for the only time that I can recall in the years that I worked for him, the only time, he came in and "cleared the debate." He came in and said, "Well, so, we're not going to declare this a coup, so what should we do?" I was totally taken aback by that, and so were many other people. And so it completely changed the tenor of the conversation. I still argued for it. I think several other people did not, who would have otherwise, but he shut us down pretty quickly, and I still to this day don't really know why that happened.[71]

Others in the room, however, were more enthused. That day, Michael Morell, the deputy director of the CIA, told an Arab ambassador—suspected to be the UAE's Yousef al-Otaiba—that Morsi's overthrow was something to be welcomed and praised. "Morsi was leading the country to ruin, to instability, to extremism," Morell said, which must have been music to Otaiba's ears. Later that night, to commemorate the historic events, Otaiba went to a swanky Washington restaurant, Café Milano in Georgetown, to celebrate with friends.[72]

* * *

Actors have agency. They make choices. President Obama had agency. Abdelfattah al-Sissi certainly did. And what they did—and in this case did not do—shaped the limits of the possible. Sissi, at some point, made a series of calculations that led him to a decision about what he could accomplish and what he could get away with. As it turns out, he deserves some credit. He judged correctly that the United States would not stand in his way if he wished to seize power. What if Kerry, during their first meeting in March 2012, had told Sissi that anything resembling a coup would be unequivocally opposed? That would have just been mere rhetoric, like so much else, but what if Kerry—instead of spending much of his political capital on a thankless Israeli–Palestinian peace effort—had opted to prioritize the Egyptian impasse instead? What if Kerry had warned Obama and other senior officials early and often that Sissi was flirting with a military intervention against the Muslim Brotherhood? What if Mattis, Flynn, and others in uniform *hadn't* joined in the Egyptian military's "bitch sessions" and instead issued their counterparts cautionary notes?

To put it differently, what if there was a policy against a coup before the coup? Transferring blame to the Pentagon and Chuck Hagel is too easy and certainly too convenient. Hagel was not authorized to employ either carrots or sticks. He might have been inarticulate and indulgent of Sissi, but it is unlikely a different secretary of defense would have fared much better without clear guidance from the president on the consequences Sissi would face. Any real effort to avert a coup would have meant communicating to the Egyptian armed forces that a military takeover would trigger a full and immediate suspension of U.S. aid. What if Obama had made a public statement in the week prior to the June 30 protests that the United States supported the right of Egyptians to demonstrate peacefully but that any attempt by the military to use the protests for its own designs would be forcefully opposed, including through punitive measures?

But perhaps that's asking too much from an administration that was overextended in a region that it had always hoped to extricate itself from.[73] I spoke to Anne Patterson about how she remembered some of these critical moments. "The fact is, we probably did have leverage, but we were never going to use maximum leverage to prevent a coup." When I asked her why, she said, "At that point, there were a lot of people that weren't sorry to see Morsi go."[74]

Obama's Middle East policy was biased toward the status quo. Less was more. And "don't do stupid shit," as the president once put it.[75] When Obama brought a group of presidential historians to the White House in 2013, he reflected afterward: "It's interesting: They made the point that the most important thing a president can do on foreign policy is avoid a costly error."[76] It was always better not to act rashly, and of course acting boldly in the Middle East could often prove rash. Wasn't that what we had learned from our many years of missteps and misadventures in the region?

These are all questionable assumptions. But let us imagine for a moment that they were entirely reasonable premises on which to formulate policy. When Obama finally started paying attention to Egypt after the army began moving against Morsi, he could have issued a warning to the generals. He chose not to. We know not the hearts of men, but it seems fair to suggest that by this time Obama had come to terms with the increasing likelihood of a coup. And he was not moved to do anything about it, as evidenced by his phone call on July 1 where he suggested to Morsi, however gently, that he re-sign himself to his fate.[77]

A Failure to Defend Democracy

The original narrative on the Obama administration's role in Egypt was that Obama himself and his top aides were blindsided by the military and didn't have the ability to do much in any case. This narrative, as it turned out, was a convenient fiction.

Once again, the United States had failed a critical democratic test, hear-kening back to the days of Algeria. But it was different this time, because it happened under the watch of a president who had at least rhetorically sig-naled that the prospect of Islamists in power would no longer be the stum-bling block it once was. The dilemma had returned, and it remained just as thorny as it must have seemed two decades before. And instead of contending with the tensions and contradictions of democracy and its outcomes, the United States looked the other way.

Defenders of President Obama's Middle East policy will point to the partial suspension of aid that the administration instituted after the Rabaa massacre, the worst mass killing in modern Egyptian history. On August 14, 2013, over a thousand supporters of Mohamed Morsi were killed in broad daylight by the military and security services. Obama offered solemn remarks the day after the massacre:

> While we do not believe that force is the way to resolve political differences, after the military's intervention several weeks ago, there remained a chance for reconciliation and an opportunity to pursue a democratic path. Instead, we've seen a more dangerous path taken through arbitrary arrests, a broad

crackdown on Mr. Morsi's associations and supporters, and now tragically the violence that's taken the lives of hundreds of people and wounded
thousands more.[78]

It was odd that the United States would condemn something that it had itself, however inadvertently, helped put into motion. The killings were no accident; they were a natural extension of the military's intervention on July
3. This is why coups, no matter how well intentioned or how justified they
may initially seem, are viewed as negatively as they are. Far from resolving
conflicts, they tend to exacerbate them. It is difficult to imagine how a coup
might lead to a constructive outcome, particularly in contexts as ideologically polarized as this. After Morsi was overthrown, millions of Egyptians,
many of whom had voted for him a year before, still saw him as the legitimate president. The millions who opposed Morsi and longed to see him
gone, needless to say, did not. In effect, there were two dueling leaders, one
claiming electoral legitimacy and the other, Sissi, claiming popular legitimacy. This was in a way its own crude form of democracy, with voting booths
replaced by wide boulevards and city squares. The act of counting votes was
replaced by the sheer mass of bodies and inflated crowd counts (according
to state media, 33 million took to the streets on June 30, suggesting that the
absurdity was precisely the point).[79] One senior White House official with
whom I spoke put the number at "something like 13 million," which I found
somewhat baffling.[80]

Egypt wasn't just divided in theory; it was divided in practice. There was
no way to adjudicate who was the rightful head of state. It is unclear what the
American officials advising Morsi to pack up and leave expected. Did they
think that the millions of Brotherhood members and supporters would, after
everything, simply accept the world as it was? With two dueling legitimacies,
one side would have to defeat the other. It was unclear what sort of compromise might be palatable to both sides. And so the new military-backed government decided to wipe out the last remaining outpost of opposition, where
tens of thousands were camped out by Cairo's Rabaa al-Adawiya mosque,
insisting that they would not leave until Morsi was reinstated. A makeshift
city became the site of a killing. If the coup itself was the beginning of the
end, this was the end.

The coda to the story had all the hallmarks of the Obama administration's
bumbling approach to the Middle East—of doing *something* but not
nearly enough, and of projecting a morally conflicted sheen to cold acts of

realpolitik, which only made the sense of betrayal sharper still. This was a president and an administration that could at times seem earnest. You almost sensed that they wanted to do the right thing but that events had conspired against them. They were victims of an unsparing world, and what world was more unsparing than the Arab world, where empires had died off and civil wars raged for years and decades? What could a president do in such circumstances?

President Obama was unwilling to direct an unwieldly bureaucracy, which would have been no easy task. By this time, his heart simply wasn't in it, and the few senior aides remaining who might have prodded him, like Ben Rhodes, had already begun to move on. "Innocent people were going to suffer, some of them were going to be killed, and there didn't seem to be anything I could do about it. Obama had reached that conclusion before I had," Rhodes writes in his memoir.[81] Meanwhile, Kerry, as the face of U.S. policy in Egypt, was indifferent to Obama's preferences, according to several State Department officials I interviewed. One described an illustrative incident:

> There was this unbelievable thing where Kerry goes to Cairo for the first time after the coup. There was some phrase critical of the coup that he was supposed to use in the press conference. So [National Security Advisor] Susan Rice was so certain that he wasn't going to say it that she called him 10 minutes before the press conference to remind him of what the NSC had decided. And he still doesn't do it. . . . He just didn't give a shit. His view of everything was, "I don't care what you say, I'll do what I want. And if the president calls me I might listen. . . ." The president would never call him because the president didn't want to fucking deal with him.[82]

Later that October, despite internal opposition from Hagel and Kerry, President Obama decided to move ahead with a partial aid "cut," which remained in place from October 2013 to April 2015. One might be tempted to argue, then, that the United States did, in fact, try to suspend military aid but that it had little effect on the Egyptian regime's behavior. In reality, though, aid deemed vital for counterterrorism was exempted, and the vast majority of military assistance continued to flow despite the "suspension." During the eighteen-month suspension period, Egypt still received $1.8 billion in assistance, "representing 92 percent of the $1.3 billion per year annual rate during that period," according to a Project on Middle East Democracy budget report by Stephen McInerney and Cole Bockenfeld.[83] Moreover, immediately after the aid suspension was announced, senior officials went out of their way to belittle its importance, emphasizing that business would continue as usual.[84] During a visit to Egypt the following month, Kerry reiterated that message in a more direct fashion, saying that the "aid issue is a very small issue."[85] As if that weren't enough, in the thick of the crackdown with more than 1,000 dead and some 10,000 arrested or detained, Kerry lauded Egypt's progress under Sissi. "The roadmap [is moving] in the direction that everybody has been hoping for," Kerry said.[86]

John Kerry was always moving, and in this case he was moving on. Kerry was focused elsewhere. To be sure, some of it was personal. Among other things, Morsi wouldn't return Kerry's calls, which irritated Kerry to no end. In one instance, Kerry runs into Morsi at an African Union summit and says to him, "Hey, Mr. President, you know I've been calling you a couple of times. You don't return my phone calls." Morsi replies, "I only talk to President Obama."[87]

More of it, though, was about Kerry's priorities. At the time, there were two overriding "legacy" concerns: a quixotic, last-ditch effort to broker a peace deal between Israel and the Palestinians and a much more successful attempt to finalize a nuclear deal with Iran. It is difficult to say which one mattered more. According to one State Department advisor who worked with Kerry, "It was more the Israel–Palestine thing than the Iran thing. He was incredibly focused on Israel–Palestine, and basically his entire Egypt policy or basically every policy he had flowed from his effort to get an Israel–Palestine deal. It was monomania, it was incredible."

According to Martin Indyk, who was Kerry's special envoy for Middle East peace from July 2013 to June 2014, it was ultimately the Iran deal that took precedence, despite Kerry's passions:

> I wanted to try and apply some leverage on the Israelis because their set-tlement activity was causing havoc for the negotiations. But the attitude in Washington was dismissive. "Forget about it," I was told. President Obama wasn't going to fight with the Israelis on two fronts. The President's priority was a nuclear deal with Iran and he needed to conserve his political cap-ital for that. When the negotiations I was involved in subsequently failed in 2014, Kerry, who was irrepressible in his pursuit of Israeli-Palestinian peace, wanted to revive them. He had an elaborate scheme for it. Obama said to him, "John, I need you to focus on the Iran deal. Don't go chasing butterflies."

As far as Kerry was concerned, both were important, but in different ways. For any peace deal, Egypt's support was important (or so the thinking went). And that meant working closely with Sissi, however repressive he may have been. As the Israeli-Palestinian negotiations came to a dead end, however, Kerry threw himself into marathon negotiations with his Iranian counterparts. This had other implications. A troika in the making, Saudi Arabia, the UAE, and Israel were increasingly finding themselves on the same side and sharing similar objections to Obama's policies. They were furious about any impending U.S.–Iranian rapprochement. Obama needed to save his political capital to at least get them to acquiesce to what had become the overriding focus of his Middle East policy.[88] If the United States *also* tried to punish Egypt for the coup, it risked creating an even bigger breach with not just one but three close allies. For them, Iran was an enemy, but so too was the Muslim Brotherhood. They wanted "stability," and stability meant the status quo. And despite their better angels, enough American officials— including the president himself—found such concerns compelling enough to look the other way.

6

Culture versus Interests

America's lack of support for democracy in the Middle East is intimately tied to its Islamist dilemma. To change the former requires addressing the latter. There is no way around it, at least not an obvious one. This is not to say that American officials need to like Islamist parties or think they are good. For many Americans, what Islamists say and believe will be something close to beyond the pale. There is good reason to prefer that they fail or that they lose. But one can think that Islamists are bad and *still* prioritize their participation in the democratic process. This, however, can only be done by recognizing one's discomfort with Islamists and then making the conscious decision to prevent that discomfort from diminishing an otherwise strong commitment to supporting democracy in the Middle East. That would be a start.

But where exactly does this discomfort come from? Is it about culture or interests, or both?

It is certainly possible that the United States would have been uncomfortable with *any* democratically elected government in Egypt, but this is true only up to a point. As we saw in the previous chapter, there was particular concern around the Brotherhood's ideological orientation. Secretary of Defense Chuck Hagel saw the Muslim Brotherhood as "dangerous." General James Mattis believed that the Brotherhood was "swimming in the same sea" as al-Qaeda. CIA Deputy Director Michael Morell believed Mohamed Morsi was leading Egypt to "extremism."[1]

Meanwhile, John Kerry, the country's chief diplomat, had decided early on that Morsi and the Brotherhood were a lost cause. "These guys are wacko," was how Kerry once put it. Perhaps more telling, Kerry also said: "This stinks, these guys aren't doing anything constructive and ultimately they are going to be antidemocratic."[2] The secretary of state assumed that the Brotherhood would—at some unspecified point in the future—become antidemocratic, regardless of what it actually was in the present. Presumably, he wouldn't have thought the same if a secular or liberal party had been in power. This runs the risk of stating the obvious: naturally, Kerry, a liberal in both the classical and political senses, would be better able to relate to a party that seemed proximate to his own ideological inclinations.

And since they already had their doubts, American officials were impressionable. When an Emirati or Saudi counterpart reminded them that the Muslim Brotherhood was backward, extreme, or a threat to regional stability (or all three), they listened. Over time, this couldn't help but sway opinions. As Ben Rhodes observed, the Emirati and Saudi ambassadors "gained this status in Washington where they aren't seen as representatives of foreign governments; they are seen as advisers on Middle East issues."[3] For their part, Israeli leaders also preferred to work with autocrats. In a rough neighborhood, dictators were ideal partners, who, relieved of the need to reflect popular sentiment, could afford to make common cause with Israel.

Still, at least in theory, the Obama administration was the least anti-Islamist administration the United States had had in decades, a contrast that grew more pronounced in light of his successor's intermittent attempts to designate the Muslim Brotherhood as a terrorist organization.[4] As a senior administration official reflected, "I think Obama came in very much believing in that you had to deal with Islamists and accept they would have some role in government. Hhe wanted to be the president who would have an open mind about Islamists."[5] President Obama was trying, in other words. This tells us a few important things that are relevant to this book's broader argument. First, the discomfort with Islamists coming to power and then being in power is sticky and somewhat impervious to rational assessment. Second, this discomfort is not a secondary concern. It can derail a president's stated commitment to respecting democratic outcomes in countries of strategic importance. The Obama administration failed to live up to its own democratic rhetoric in large part because of the dilemma of "bad" democratic outcomes and how to live with them.

What exactly was it, though, about Islamist movements that provoked such reactions? It is understandable that citizens of the countries in question would experience foundational divides over religion as existential threats—and that this feeling would move them to support policies of exclusion and repression against their opponents. For me, even as I recoiled from it, I knew this sentiment intimately, including from my relatives in Egypt. The question of what motivates American officials is a different matter. Was it about ideology or interests? Part of the difficulty in answering this question is that the two areintertwined in complex ways. In theory, it is possible to separate them. In practice, it is not.

As it often does, culture provides the backdrop against which individuals, organizations, and governments make decisions. "Culture"—a big, weighty word—is intangible, which complicates any effort to measure how much it matters. Often, individuals themselves may not be aware that cultural constraints and incentives are shaping their behavior. And they may insist that they are being calculating and coldly rational. But one does not become cold or calculating in a vacuum. As Fawaz Gerges writes: "At the heart of [the] U.S. reservoir of images and ideas on Islam lie not only fear and bewilderment but also deep misgivings about mixing religion and politics."[6] Fair enough. But then there is the question of why this would affect only perceptions of Islamist parties and not others. After all, most governments in the Middle East mix religion and politics. One of America's closest Arab allies is Saudi Arabia—until recently one of the world's last remaining theocracies, featuring a harsh application of sharia that would make the Muslim Brotherhood blush. Interestingly, as Saudi Arabia has become *less* theocratic under the rule of Crown Prince Mohamed bin Salman, its relationship with the United States has come under stress and not the other way around.

Not all "Islamists" are created equal. Saudi Arabia's Islamism at home—if by Islamism we mean the desire to see Islamic law play a central role in public life—has not prevented it from becoming a key partner in and booster of the U.S.-led regional order. But an Islamist regime that does not rely on democratic legitimacy and is insulated from popular anger and protest may have more room for maneuver in this regard. Such a regime would be preoccupied with regime survival above all else. This is why Saudi Arabia is as repressive as it is. It fears even a hint of domestic opposition, since opposition—even if it seems insignificant at any given moment—can always grow stronger. If the United States can credibly ensure regime survival through military assistance and other security guarantees, then this is what matters most to a security-minded regime. To return the favor by acquiescing to American hegemony is a small price to pay.

The Muslim Brotherhood, of course, is not an Islamist regime but rather an Islamist movement, and one that has generally found itself in opposition to existing regimes. Saudi Arabia, on the other hand, has been Saudi Arabia since its founding, which gives it an aura of permanence. The Brotherhood is not only an organization that seeks to challenge and one day replace pro-American regimes; it seeks to do so through elections. This has the effect of making democracy into an instrument for challenging the U.S.-led regional order.

If Islamist parties win elections through democratic means, they will not be interested in regime survival, since they will not be the regime. They would be leading an elected government and would be focused on government and party survival, which largely means trying one's best to avoid getting booted out in the next election. This requires being at least somewhat in line with the popular mood. In a region rife with suspicion and anger over American foreign policy, playing the anti-American card is smart politics.

With Islamist *opposition* parties, however, it isn't just about playing politics or gaining electoral advantage. Since they are opposing pro-American autocracies, they are likely to view the United States as a fundamentally negative force, propping up and protecting the very autocrats that have long suppressed them. If American policy—particularly its role as an autocracy promoter—is the problem, a change in policy could offer a solution. But the distrust of America's role in the region goes considerably deeper than this. If culture matters for American policymakers, it is just as likely to matter for groups like the Muslim Brotherhood. Islamist parties are likely to see the United States not only as a political threat but also a cultural threat, in part because they view the United States—and the West more broadly—as irredeemably secular and secularizing. This is where the ideology of Islamist groups ends up shaping their foreign policy preferences. And, perhaps just as importantly, it shapes how ostensibly secular regimes perceive them.

Regimes can be "secular" only insofar as they are authoritarian and able to resist reflecting the religious conservatism of the population. And regimes are authoritarian insofar as they have external patrons to protect them from their own people. With first the decline and then fall of the Soviet Union, that patron of choice became the United States. Arab regimes assumed, mostly but not entirely correctly, that as long as they remained in the pro-Western orbit, the United States would come to their defense in the event of popular unrest. In practice, signaling deference to American priorities in the region has meant deferring to Israel's regional role. Two of the world's largest recipients of U.S. assistance are, not coincidentally, Egypt and Jordan—the first two countries to sign peace accords with Israel. While most Arab political parties are anti-Israel to one degree or another, Islamist parties are particularly so, due to their religious orientation and emotional attachment to Jerusalem, which looms large in the Islamist imagination. From the Brotherhood's founding, it has viewed Jewish control of the holy land as a powerful symbol of Muslim decline, an imposition from afar and a reminder of what was lost.[7]

Many Muslims, and nearly all Islamists, hold to a stylized story of rise and fall. Muslims had once commanded one of the greatest civilizations the world had ever seen. Military prowess and the vastness of territory were the most obvious manifestations of success. More important, however, was the cultural, intellectual, and religious authority—and the resulting self-confidence—that served as the foundation and driver of worldly gains and seemingly perpetual expansion.

The link that might have once been implicit became more explicit with time, recognized only in its growing absence and when it was too late: adherence to Islam and the one, true God was the guarantor of glory not only in the next life but in this one as well. Without it, and in thrall to Western ideologies, there was only failure and continued decline. This, at least, is how Islamists interpreted defeat at Israel's hands in the appropriately named "Six Day War." Arabs had strayed from the straight path of Islam. God was punishing them for turning away from him and worshiping the false idols of nationalism. The link between commitment to the faith and temporal success—or, in this case, the lack thereof—became explicit.

The predicament Muslims found themselves in over the course of the twentieth century—with one indignity after the other—was one of a growing dissonance. If Islam was the true faith, then why were Muslims suffering under first colonialism and then repression from their own newly independent nations? How had they experienced such a precipitous fall from grace? Unlike Christianity, which was in a relatively weak position in its early centuries, Islam had achieved fairly consistent, impressive earthly success from its founding. Until the modern era, there had never been a period without a great Islamic empire or caliphate. By the end of the nineteenth century, it was hard to avoid the conclusion that "the link between faith and worldly success appeared to have been broken."[8]

That Israel could enjoy so much success so quickly was a reminder of Arab weakness and decline. There was awe as well as envy. Israel had something that Arab societies didn't—the certainty, conviction, and commitment that could only come from believing. Some observers, after the devastation of 1967, saw the triumph of religion in the most unlikely places. One of those was the fiery Islamist preacher Mohamed Galal Kishk. As Fouad Ajami writes, "In Kishk's account there is grudging admiration for the clarity with which the Israelis saw the war, for the fact that young Israeli soldiers prayed behind their rabbis at the Wailing Wall after their capture of Jerusalem."[9]

For groups like the Muslim Brotherhood, the fact of Israel and its military superiority—and the ease with which it could dispatch weak, sclerotic Arab regimes—reflected a deeper truth. The regional architecture that the United States had begun building did not take into account the aspirations of ordinary Arabs. And it was specifically Islamists who began paying the heaviest price during a decade, the 1990s, that seemed heady for much of the rest of the world. Democratic transitions were taking hold across Eastern Europe and in Asia and Africa. Islamist movements had the most to gain from democratic openings. They could have begun translating their rising support into political influence and perhaps even power. And so they saw American dominance in the region—of which Israel became the most tangible, resonant expression—as part of a not particularly secret conspiracy to keep them down.

In this sense, Islamists' perception of U.S. foreign policy is inseparable from their own repression at home, and so domestic and foreign policy are not easily compartmentalized. One appears to flow from the other. Why would Islamists be enthusiastic about supporting America's role in the region, when the resulting order only led to their own marginalization and exclusion?

How Anti-American Is the Muslim Brotherhood?

In the Middle East, Islamists have only assumed power through elections on a few occasions, so the case of Egypt during its brief transition is worth looking at more closely. We can only know so much from two and a half years, but quite a lot happened in the span of those tragic months.

Mohamed Morsi, for example, was distrustful of both American foreign policy *and* American culture. Unlike other more astute Brotherhood leaders, Morsi was rough around the edges when it came to his opinions of the United States, a country that he had once called home. Among the group's senior leaders, Morsi had spent the most time in the United States. He was a graduate of the University of Southern California, where he completed his doctoral degree in material engineering. He was also the father of two American citizens—a reminder that familiarity can sometimes breed contempt.

In one of our conversations before he became president, Morsi volunteered his views on the September 11 attacks without prompting. "When you come and tell me that the plane hit the tower like a knife in butter," he said, shifting to English, "then you are insulting us. How did the plane cut through the steel like this? Something must have happened from the inside. It's impossible."[10] Elsewhere, Morsi had discussed his time living in America, painting a picture of a society in moral decay, replete with crumbling families, young mothers in hospitals who have to "write in the name of the father," and couples living together out of wedlock. We don't have these problems in Egypt, he said during one press conference, his voice rising with a mixture of pride and resentment.[11]

The culture gap was large enough to unsettle any prospective relationship. Morsi was not and would never be a natural partner for a relatively secular country like the United States that happened to have an even more secular elite. Yet, there was only so much Morsi could do to reorient Egyptian foreign policy away from the United States, however much he may have wished to in an ideal world. Egypt depended on the United States, and culture could only matter so much when interests (and survival) were at stake. Under Morsi, Egypt was somewhere in between, and that's where it would have likely remained had the democratic transition continued. Morsi could try to satisfy American concerns and priorities, as he did when he helped broker a cease-fire between Israel and Hamas in November 2012, but there was a limit to how far he could go. He was elected and had a constituency, after all.

If democracy entails *some* responsiveness to the electorate, then elected leaders have little choice but to heed popular sentiment on foreign policy to at least some degree. And in an otherwise divided polity, one of the few real areas of consensus in Egypt was a preference for an independent, assertive foreign policy that reestablished its leading role in the region. This meant that tension and disagreement with the United States would have likely become a normal feature of the bilateral relationship. How far democratically elected leaders, Islamist or otherwise, might go in satisfying—or whipping up—public opinion is another matter, depending on a number of factors. But they certainly couldn't dismiss it, as previous Egyptian presidents had, such as Anwar al-Sadat with the Camp David Accords in 1978 and Hosni Mubarak during the 1990s at the height of the Oslo process.

From an American standpoint, pragmatism is not necessarily a good thing. Pragmatism cuts both ways, and often unexpectedly. Pragmatists will care about what voters think and will look to appease public opinion, when it intensifies. Islamists are no exception. The desire to align themselves with public opinion can lead Islamists to be *more* anti-American than they might otherwise be. Algeria's aborted transition provided an early example of how an organization that was already suspicious of the United States and Western powers could be made more suspicious. As in other countries, Algeria's main Islamist party, the Islamic Salvation Front, orFIS, ended up being swayed by Algerians' enthusiasm for Saddam Hussein and near unanimous opposition to the U.S. invasion of Iraq in 1991. Islamists had little sympathy for Saddam, so they initially found themselves in a difficult spot, torn between being on the right side of popular sentiment in a time of war and their own moral commitments. After all, Saddam Hussein had mercilessly repressed his own Islamist opposition, including the Iraqi branch of the Muslim Brotherhood. When Saddam invaded Kuwait, the Kuwaiti Muslim Brotherhood, along with all the country's political forces, suffered from the invasion itself as well as the interruption of the country's parliamentary process. Kuwait had long featured one of the region's more permissive political environments, and now there was the distinct prospect of having to live under an extended Iraqi occupation, no less from a leader as infamously brutal as Saddam. All of this meant that the FIS originally *opposed* Iraq's invasion of Kuwait. But then it opted to follow public opinion, rather than lead it. Leading wasn't particularly viable once the United States assembled a coalition to invade Iraq. It was one thing to oppose an illegal Iraqi invasion of a fellow Arab country. It was quite another to support an American one.

Since Algeria was relatively remote and less integrated in the regional order, the FIS had thought even less about foreign policy than other Islamist parties. International relations took up "a remarkably small portion" of their 1989 program.[12] This is not to say that they didn't have strong opinions. They certainly did. But their views tended to be instinctive rather than grounded in careful analysis. Whether in Algeria or elsewhere, the prospect of power seemed unfathomable, so there was little incentive to develop a coherent foreign policy. And even if Islamists won, foreign policy would still in large part be constrained by the president, the military, and the security services. The "deep state," after all, was born in the Middle East.

Foreign policy would never be a natural fit for Islamist movements. This was a world of nation-states, with the pursuit of national interests as the overarching concern. When you were poor, weak, and lacking in self-confidence, an ideological foreign policy, hard to implement in the best of circumstances, became even more challenging. Islamists were attuned to thinking about international relations in the transnational terms of the global Muslim *ummah*. In an ideal world, groups like the Muslim Brotherhood (as its name and the presence of similarly named branches suggest) would have hoped to work on a grander scale, with a mind to reducing barriers between Arab states. Although they may have in theory, this didn't mean that they supported the revival of the caliphate in practice, which they were pragmatic enough to know was a non-starter. But that fantasy would always be a part of who they are, and how they felt about politics emotionally and viscerally.

The foreign policy doctrine of Islamist groups, or the lack thereof, is shaped by a series of tensions, where the gap between politics as it is and politics as it might be becomes especially large. "Such contradictions," as Emad Shahin writes, "stem from the classic, yet unresolved, dilemmas of how to define the Islamic state in the world community, the political nature of the *ummah* (community), and the relations between Muslims and non-Muslims."[13]

An Intolerance for Uncertainty

One of the recurring themes of this book is that good things don't necessarily go together—and that there's little reason to think that they can or even that they should. The more quickly the United States disabuses itself of this notion, the better. That Islamist parties might keep winning elections goes against a core, if naïve, belief that democracy should produce people who like us and who are like us. Islamists meet neither of these expectations. Of course, part of the reason they don't like us is because we don't support democracy. But part of the reason we don't support democracy is that they don't like us. Which means that Washington is stuck in a circular loop partly of its own making.

With that in mind, the question turns not to whether Islamist parties are anti-American but to what degree. This, in turn, can help us better assess how much of a problem the presence of Islamists in power actually is for the United States. As we saw earlier, mainstream Islamist movements have a distinctive, albeit vague, conception of an Arab world that is confident, independent, and willing to project influence beyond its borders. On its own, this shouldn't be a major concern for the United States, but unfortunately it is.

I remember when one senior Muslim Brotherhood figure asked me a question I didn't exactly know how to answer:

> I've always had this question in mind: why would the West help Egypt become a powerful country, so that Egypt becomes independent and not needing the U.S.? From a strategic point of view, although we have assured them all the time that we are not planning to break the peace treaty or the

interests of the U.S., they still know that the Muslim Brotherhood, or any other patriotic political party in Egypt, would like to have an independent and strong Egypt. . . . So I believe that the scheme, and I would have done it the same way if I was in their place, is to try to reduce the Brotherhood's influence to something like 20 to 25 percent so the government is not really led by any powerful political player. This way, the parties would be quarreling all the time. So Egypt will remain at a certain level [of weakness] without having a breakthrough.[14]

This does sound awfully close to what many U.S. policymakers would have liked to see in Egypt—a democratic opening but a controlled one where the Brotherhood does well but not well enough to restructure the system or create too much uncertainty. To be fair, such a scenario would be far preferable to what Egypt ended up getting, but the very fact that the bar would be set so low is what led Washington to indulge the Egyptian military as a counterweight to Islamists in the first place.

It is worth acknowledging the obvious. There is little question that democracy will make the region more unpredictable and that some governments will become less amenable to certain U.S. security interests. For many, this might seem like a non-starter. But to counter such concerns, one must simply point out that autocracy has *also* made the region more unpredictable, certainly in the medium to long term. Insofar as the future eventually becomes the present, American policy should prioritize predictability in the long run over predictability in the short term, when the two are in tension.

The first step, then, is that the United States must be better able—and, perhaps more importantly, willing—to tolerate higher levels of uncertainty during democratic transitions. While uncertainty can be institutionalized in due time, the early years of a transition will be chaotic and disorienting. This, after all, is what makes a democratic transition transitional. And to pretend that a country can skip the steps or run through them in the matter of one or two years is contrary to most of what we know about how democratization works, particularly in polarized societies.

The good news is that uncertainty is relative. Islamist parties are unlikely to provoke as much uncertainty in America's bilateral relationships as their harshest critics fear. When their survival has required it, Islamists have proven willing to compromise on their ideological commitments, accepting however reluctantly the realities of an international system that is stacked against them.

If Islamist parties are pragmatic, then the United States should play to those instincts by entering into a strategic dialogue with them as soon as transitions begin—if not well before. Through engagement, Washington can encourage Islamists to at least be cognizant of key Western interests if not necessarily to fully respect them. It is better to develop ties with opposition groups before they come to power, when Washington has the most leverage, rather than afterward. This seems obvious enough if you take the premise that some Islamist groups will reach power at some point in some countries and that some of those countries will be of strategic importance.

Whether it's the Muslim Brotherhood in Egypt or Jordan or even the "progressive" post-Islamists of Tunisia's Ennahda, Islamist parties across the region have not recognized Israel's right to exist and instead call for the liberation of all historic Palestine. They also view Hamas—effectively the Palestinian analog of the Muslim Brotherhood—not as a terrorist group but as a legitimate resistance movement. These positions put most Islamist parties at considerable distance from American preferences. But the bigger issue here isn't so much Islamist attitudes toward Israel as it is Arab attitudes toward Israel more broadly. If democracies reflect public opinion and public opinion is firmly anti-Israel, then any process of democratization will highlight gaps between Arab and American preferences (and certainly Israeli preferences). In this sense, the continued intractability of the Israeli–Palestinian conflict, many decades later, isn't just tragic on its own terms. It also imperils democracy in the region more broadly. And it has already undermined democracy for far too long.

Anti-Israel attitudes can manifest quite differently depending on various factors that have little to do with Israel itself. A country's physical proximity to the Israeli–Palestinian conflict informs how hard-line a party's posture is. Given that a majority of Jordanians are of Palestinian origin, it is little accident that Jordan's Islamists prioritize the struggle against Israel. Unlike many of its counterparts, the Islamic Action Front (IAF), the political arm of the Jordanian Brotherhood, still uses religious language to frame the conflict; in its 2007 electoral platform, the party affirmed that the conflict between the Israelis and the Palestinians is "theological and civilizational," and not one of borders or territory.[15] The IAF's so-called hawks, who tend to be of Palestinian origin, advocate closer ties with Hamas. In Algeria and Tunisia, by contrast, Palestine ranks much lower as a priority for local Islamists. When Ennahda led the government during the Arab Spring, nothing much changed about Tunisia's policies toward Israel beyond rhetorical support.

What after all could Tunisia do? There is a proud history in Tunisia of identifying with the Palestinian cause. After it was expelled from Jordan and then Lebanon, the Palestinian Liberation Organization (PLO) found refuge in Tunis over the course of the 1980s.[16] A strain of left-wing populism remains influential in Tunisia, particularly in the trade unions, which often translates into suspicion of the United States for both its neocolonial and neoliberal adventures abroad. Still, there is little the Tunisian government or civil society can practically do outside expressions of solidarity.

In short, context matters. Most Brotherhood and Brotherhood-inspired movements share similar ideological premises, including a particular way of viewing the Palestinian conflict and Israel's role in it. But this original position is inevitably mediated by political circumstance. It's not enough to assume that all Islamists are the same when it comes to Israel, because they are not.

What any given Islamist party says or does in a particular country is a more complicated product of various local factors. Where the ruling elite is unpopular *and* pro-Western, Islamists will define themselves in opposition to the government's policies to garner support. The cases of Egypt and Jordan fall into this category. Here, the link between the government's perceived closeness to Israel and its authoritarian practices is clear enough—and one that Islamist movements themselves are well aware of. Before Jordan's 2007 parliamentary elections, for example, the IAF released a statement arguing that freedoms in Jordan had diminished after Amman signed its peace treaty with Israel in 1994. The party's attempt to connect pro-Israel policy with a loss of freedom was persuasive, because it happened to be true. Taking a hard line against Israel is an effective way for Islamists in opposition to criticize regimes they see as antidemocratic and beholden to Western interests. Since Islamists, unlike, say, liberals, are already predisposed to a visceral dislike of Israel for religious and historical reasons, intensifying and highlighting that dislike is not a difficult task if the political moment demands it.

If (or when) political systems across the Middle East open up, Islamist parties will have the opportunity to move from the opposition into positions of power, likely as part of coalition or unity governments. During democratic transitions, new political parties will proliferate. As parties fight for votes, the incentives for Islamists to outbid the competition and emphasize anti-American or anti-Israel themes are likely to grow.

Once actually in government, however, the calculus for parties, Islamist or otherwise, changes. For ordinary countries—or even extraordinary ones—the rules of the international system are constraining. While Mohamed Morsi and the Muslim Brotherhood made no secret of their feelings toward Israel, they pledged to honor Egypt's peace treaty with Israel. They didn't accept Israel's *right* to exist, but they accepted Israel's existence. Morsi's tenure lasted only a year, but it is hard to imagine a scenario where Morsi would have attempted to abrogate the peace treaty. Considering his country's dependence on external actors, such a move would have been something close to political suicide. There would be quite a lot to lose—billions of dollars of assistance from the United States, the European Union (EU), and individual EU member states, massive loans from international financial institutions, as well as trade agreements and foreign direct investment. Even "irrational" leaders don't tend to self-destruct in such a manner, particularly when they have been patiently waiting for a democratic opening they doubted would ever come.

Western pressure, when wielded with some degree of seriousness, can be effective. Turkey, wealthier than most of its neighbors and a regional power, is a country that wouldn't normally take kindly to threats. Yet, in the lead-up to the Iraq War, the Bush administration exerted heavy, sustained pressure and dangled billions of dollars of aid in an effort to gain Turkey's support.[17] Although Turkey's staunchly secular Republican People's Party voted overwhelmingly against supporting the U.S.-led war in parliament, most of the Islamist-leaning Justice and Development Party's deputies voted for it.[18] I bring this example up only to suggest that ideological parties are responsive to incentives just as any "normal" party might be. But the resort to such blunt pressure is not necessarily a good thing. It depends on what the pressure is being used for. Too often, as in this particular case, it was wielded to supersede the inconvenience of Turkish democracy and public opinion. The Bush administration was, in effect, demanding that a democratically elected government ignore the preferences of its own electorate, an electorate that firmly opposed the war.

This kind of Western strong-arming—objectionable if understandable—fits within a long arc of American disregard for other countries' internal politics. It runs contrary to the basic impulse at the heart of an alternative Middle East strategy that prioritizes publics over regimes. Even in countries that are overly dependent on the United States, voters have a right to express preferences that have little to do with American priorities. After all, they're not Americans.

Of course, this is why democracy in the Middle East is something of a pain even for otherwise well-intentioned American officials who wish to take it more seriously. In the twilight of the Soviet Union and in the euphoria of the post–Cold War, the presumption was that democracy was good and because it was good it led to good things. No dilemmas had to be resolved, no trade-offs needed to be weighed. But, sometimes, democracy is a problem.

Obama's Lost Opportunity

As is probably clear by now, I am uncomfortable with the realities of what American policy is, what it has been, and what it will likely be for some time to come. There is a temptation to throw up one's hands in exasperation. I remember a friend in the democracy promotion community telling a group of us that, after having spent years meeting with executive branch and congressional staff, he had reached his limit. It is difficult, he said, to escape the conclusion that American policy in the Middle East is "vile"—a series of morally indefensible acts, one after the other.

The notion that the United States might only be persuaded to support democracy if it can be assured that there won't be too much of it is dispiriting. Those of us hoping to persuade policymakers adapt to this reality. So we tell American officials that even if Islamists do come to power, there will still be ways to restrict their room for maneuver *within* the context of democracy. We tell them that Islamist parties are more pragmatic than they may first appear. But what if Islamists were *less* pragmatic and would more aggressively challenge American interests? Would democracy be any less valid? If our belief in an idea is so contingent and provisional, then do we truly believe in it?

With the string of tragedies and after repeated disappointments, many of us have lowered our sights. There are small victories, to be sure. When the United States decides to put a temporary hold on a small portion of aid to a repressive regime, this is a success, but it is a success so minor and insignificant against the backdrop of world historical events.

This is why the Obama years proved devastating—in a way that they weren't with Trump or George W. Bush—for anyone holding out hope for a different approach to the Middle East. Generally, when a particular policy becomes entrenched, it becomes very hard to undo. The Arab uprisings came as an unexpected, exogenous shock, presenting a rare opportunity to shake American policy from its stasis and do something dramatically different. It is difficult to overstate just how unusual the 2011 Arab uprisings were. Mass discontent is a common enough feature of modern Arab societies, but that discontent only rarely translates into anything resembling a revolution. So when revolutions appear to be occurring, those who have the opportunity to shape them should realize that it may, quite literally, be a once-in-a-lifetime event.

This is what was lost. If there was just one time where the United States could have acted differently, this would have been it, a fork in the road for both America and the Arab world. In this sense, we shouldn'tjudge the Obama administration against the Trump administration and ask who was better. There is no doubt that President Obama took democracy much more seriously than his successor. But the more telling juxtaposition is one where we consider the unprecedented circumstances Obama found himself in and the possibilities before him. Something like the Arab Spring hadn't happened before, and it was unclear when (or if) it would happen again. A confident, determined president could have pushed hard for a fairly ambitious reorientation of U.S. foreign policy. Considering the events on the ground, and the nonstop, sympathetic media attention to the protests, senior officials could have more easily dispatched with the traditional caution that had long defined American engagement in the region. As the protests in Egypt gathered strength, "every television in the West Wing showed silent images of protest."[19] At least rhetorically, Obama and some of his closest aides were pulled in this direction, with constant, loose talk of being on the right side of history. Knowing what we know now, there are passages in Ben Rhodes's memoirs that are suitably grandiose but tempered by regret. "History, it seemed, was turning in the direction of young people in the streets, and we had placed the United States of America on their side," he writes.[20]

It is remarkable just how quickly "history" decided to show its face. Perhaps it was both pliable and capable of surprise. Just months before the Arab Spring began in earnest, Western officials—and those on the ground fighting for their freedom—could have been forgiven for thinking it was all hopeless. I was based in Qatar at the time and traveling back and forth to Egypt. Everything appeared to be stuck, a reminder that black swans occasionally do happen and that Western leaders would do well to strengthen their powers of imagination and not assume that things will always be as they were. Arab regimes seemed durable, if not necessarily strong. A whole academic literature emerged around the notion of authoritarian durability. If the Middle East was exceptional in its resistance to democratization, what made it so? In an influential 2007 Brookings Institution paper, Steven Heydemann pointed to what he called "authoritarian upgrading."[21] Arab regimes had

gotten better at outmaneuvering their opponents at home through a sophisticated mix of co-option and coercion.

With the Bush administration's "Freedom Agenda" putting the question of
democracy front and center, dictators nimbly concluded that it was better to
manage and indulge—rather than oppose—the international community's
growing attention to human rights and democratization. They decided, in
other words, to play along. They welcomed and even encouraged civil society initiatives to promote women's rights and youth entrepreneurship.
Good things no doubt, but still things that presented no real threat to existing power structures. By demonstrating an openness to "soft" civil society
activities, autocrats could attract the sympathy or even support of Western
audiences who cared more about liberal values than democracy per se. As
the political scientist Sarah Sunn Bush notes, "Dictators wishing to appear
democratic, for example, increasingly adopt the institutions promoted by democracy promoters, such as quotas for women's representation in politics, in
order to cultivate domestic and international legitimacy."[22] These measures
are attractive to both U.S. officials and authoritarian allies precisely because
they seem immune to criticism. Who, after all, would really argue against
women's participation?

At times, regimes allowed for greater electoral competition, but only up to
a point. Such competition was always controlled, presenting a facade to those
who weren't paying close attention. It *looked* better. And in case anything
got out of hand and the opposition did too well, the regime could always re-
apply targeted repression. When Islamist parties gained dozens of seats in
parliament, as they did in Egypt in 2005, autocrats could say I told you so.
They reminded their Western interlocutors that if democracy was what they
wanted, then that is exactly what they would get.[23] Were they sure this is what
they wanted—untested and unpredictable Islamists, subject to whims of an
angry public, rather than solid if excessively repressive strongmen?

Authoritarian allies also had another tool in their arsenal: their
commitment—sometimes real, sometimes theoretical—to economic liberalization. Political scientists had long assumed that economic growth and the
development of a middle class would pave the way for democratization.[24]
Arab rulers discovered (or perhaps intuited) that this wasn't necessarily true,
as long as they were both clever and careful. Better yet, economic liberalization could be wielded in the service of the regime itself, offering ample
opportunities for patronage and mutual dependence. As Heydemann points
out, regimes exploit regulatory reforms to bind business elites—including

the most powerful and wealthy members of society—to the state. These selective reforms "generate the essential economic resources upon which processes of authoritarian upgrading depend."[25] A better business environment coupled with megaprojects funded by foreign investment and managed by Western contractors and consultants offers international prestige, further legitimizing regimes in the court of international opinion.

For anyone toiling in the opposition, futility and despair must have seemed appropriate. On May 8, 2010, I met with Mohamed Morsi for the first time, when few Egyptians had even heard of him. By then, the brief openings of the Bush era had long since passed. The promise of parliamentary opposition had given way to some of the worst anti-Islamist repression since the so-called inquisition, or *mihna*, of the Nasser era. Like other Brotherhood leaders, Morsi had resigned himself to the grim reality and lowered his ambitions accordingly. In our conversation, he objected to using the word "opposition" to describe the Brotherhood. "The word 'opposition' has the connotation of seeking power," Morsi told me. "But, at this moment, we are not seeking power because that requires preparation, and society is not prepared."[26]

I was back in Egypt a few months later, in November 2010, to observe the parliamentary elections—the most fraudulent in the country's history. The Brotherhood was reduced from eighty-eight seats in parliament to zero. I went from polling station to polling station, talking to Brotherhood activists. The election was being stolen in broad daylight. Brotherhood "whips" ran me through the violations. But they were surprisingly calm. "The regimes won't let us take power," Hamdi Hassan, the head of the Brotherhood's parliamentary bloc, told me. What was the solution then? I asked him. "The solution is in the 'Brotherhood approach.' We focus on the individual, then the family, then society." He was implying that it could take a very long time. "In the lifespan of mankind," he said, "80 years isn't long; it's like eight seconds."[27]

It was this push and pull that defined the 2000s. The sense of drift and decay was hard to ignore, and sometimes this more than anger is predictive of things to come. In the early days of the Obama administration, Dennis Ross, who at the time was special advisor to Secretary of State Hillary Clinton, recalls a visit to Egypt shifted his perception. "I was struck by something," Ross told me. "I was in a motorcade taking me around, and I just felt a kind of solemnness in Cairo that felt different to me. And I was looking at just the gaps, the increasing gaps in terms of wealth and haves and have-nots. And I remember coming back and saying, 'You know, I don't know how long that's sustainable.'"[28]

In part because of internal discussions that Ross led along with Samantha Power and Gayle Smith, both senior directors on the National Security Council, the mood in the State Department and the White House began to shift—up to a point. As Ross recounted at length:

> We had very interesting discussions with people from the Pentagon and the [Central Intelligence] Agency, and they were both more cautious on this than we were. I have to say that what we found in the interagency process was—I think a fair way to put it—a lack of enthusiasm for what we were trying to raise. But to be fair, we had very rich discussions, meaning they didn't pull any punches in terms of their doubts. But they also were willing to concede that probably something had to be done. And so a lot of our discussion was on saying, let's focus on how can we create greater space for civil society. How can we relate what could be some economic reforms and liberalization to at least some limited political reforms?
>
> And we had drafts done by the time that [Tunisian street vendor Mohamed] Bouazizi set himself on fire. So on one hand, we had produced this memo from the President authorizing this interagency discussion. Our whole aim was to then produce a presidential decision memorandum calling on the specific steps that should be taken. The aim was to have a presidential speech, to invest this with even greater political weight by speaking about it publicly and having the President make it part of our agenda. And in a lot of ways, you would think at one level, the fact we'd done all this preparatory work set us up perfectly then to deal with the emergence of the Arab Spring.[29]

On another level, however, what the Obama administration was hoping for and imagining was *limited*—not quite revolution or upheaval. As one senior White House official involved in those early discussions recalled:

> Nobody cared about Tunisia. It was when Egypt started that the principals were involved. For them, I wanna be clear about this, for [National Security Advisor] Tom Donilon, this is a crisis. This is not an opportunity. We're doing our reset to Russia, we're doing our pivot to Asia, and suddenly these Egyptians and Tunisians are screwing everything up. I think that's a really important thing that people on the outside don't forget. It's like you're running your game plan and suddenly there's these other actors that are doing other things that they care about. And so it was just like. . . It was a tragedy, it wasn't seen as an opportunity for most people in the government.[30]

They were surprised. Many were also annoyed. Controlled, gradual, limited reform was the scenario they had considered. And whatever this was, it wasn't that.

As it so happens, reform that is managed and controlled does not necessarily lead to democracy, in part because it's not meant to. And democracy, when it happens, is rarely as manageable and controlled as one might hope. Even at its best, when it was trying to be ahead of the curve, the United States was still behind it. A pessimistic and perhaps harsh spin on this is that the U.S. government—as a system and as a product of any number of competing institutions and interests—does not actually want the Middle East to be democratic. This can lead to a particular kind of schizophrenia. Two weeks before the protests in Egypt began, Hillary Clinton, in a surprisingly frank speech in Doha, said: "In too many places, in too many ways, the region's foundations are sinking into the sand." Yet less than two weeks later, on the first day of what would become a revolution, Clinton insisted: "Our assessment is that the Egyptian regime is stable."[31] She was right the first time around.

Our American schizophrenia has deep roots. One might say it's an essential part of who we are. Because we are small-d democrats and because we are Americans, we think we should want democracy in the Middle East just as we might want it in any other region. We may even persuade ourselves that we *actually* want it. Sometimes we even try. But the institutional context that policymakers find themselves enmeshed in militates against any such desires, however genuine. American policy in the Middle East is fundamentally oriented toward the preservation of a regional order and architecture that was built over decades. It is difficult to promote democracy within an architecture that was designed for its opposite.

What Arab Democrats Want (from the United States)

Considering America's long and checkered history, it would have been both easy and understandable for Arab democracy activists to write the United States off. But the remarkable twist to an otherwise tragic story is that many Arabs still believe—perhaps even more so than Americans—that the United States can be better, living up to the ideals that it claims it holds dear. During the early days of the revolution, even Muslim Brotherhood activists, despite their natural suspicion of the United States, couldn't help believing in a country that most had never been to or fully understood. In Tahrir Square, protesters hung on every major American statement, trying their best to interpret the sometimes impenetrablen language. Like many others in the square, young Brotherhood members—some barely out of college yet risking their lives—broke into applause when, on February 1, President Obama called for an immediate transition to genuine democracy in Egypt.

I still vividly remember the Muslim Brotherhood official who called me in the middle of the night during the uprisings' most violent week. Military aircraft were circling in the sky ominously. "They are going to kill us," he told me, barely holding back tears. What he said next stayed with me. He said that their only hope was the United States. This echoed what I had heard from Islamist activists and leaders time and time again: despite (or perhaps because of) their anti-Americanism, they usually wanted Washington to do more, rather than do less.

During the Egyptian uprising, two leading Brotherhood figures, Esam el-Erian and Abdel Monem Abul Futouh, penned op-eds in the *New York Times* and *Washington Post.* They seemed under the impression that U.S. policymakers could be persuaded to support their democratic aspirations. Futouh's op-ed—simultaneously overestimating America's influence, decrying it, and believing that, somehow, it could be used for Ggood— is representative of the genre: "We want to set the record straight so that any Middle East policy decisions made in Washington are based on facts. . . . [W]ith a little altruism, the United States should not hesitate to reassess its interests in the region, especially if it genuinely champions democracy."[32]

Across the region, activists were scathing in their condemnation of American policy just as they called on President Obama to do *more* to pressure their regimes to democratize. In March 2011, about a thousand Bahrainis protested in front of the U.S. embassy in the capital of Manama. One of the participants, Mohamed Hasan, explained why they were there. "The United States," he said, "has to prove that it is with human rights, and the right for all people to decide [their] destiny." Years before the Arab revolts, an opposition figure named Abdeljalil AlSingace tried to give President George W. Bush a petition signed by 80,000 Bahrainis calling for a new democratic constitution. After Obama was elected, AlSingace wrote in the *New York Times* that "it would be good if Mr. Obama vowed to support democracy and human rights. But he should talk about these ideals only if he is willing to help us fulfill them."[33] AlSingace was no liberal. He was a leader of Al Haqq, a hard-line Shia opposition group with sympathies toward Iran. Yet, he was not asking Iran but rather Iran's enemy, the United States, for assistance in his country's struggle for democracy. They were not worried about a supposed "kiss of death," the notion that the U.S. support would taint indigenous reformers. (This argument is particularly appealing because it subsumes arguments for inaction under the guise of helping reformers on the ground. In effect, it argues for doing nothing at the precise moment that doing something would be most effective.[34])

The "kiss of death" hypothesis first grew popular during the administration of George W. Bush. It is odd, then, that the embrace of an extremely unpopular president didn't appear to hurt the reform movement, and, if anything, the opposite. This is something that regime opponents themselves reluctantly admitted. Referring to the Bush democracy promotion efforts, Abul Futouh told me: "Everyone knows it . . . we benefited, everyone benefited, and the Egyptian people benefited."[35] In 2006, at the tail end of the first Arab Spring, the liberal newspaper publisher and activist Hisham Kassem remarked that "U.S. pressure on the Mubarak regime has been the catalyst for most of the change we have seen."[36] As destructive as Bush's policies may have been in Iraq or Palestine, for many Arab activists, his efforts on democracy were a clear improvement over what came before—as well as after.

An intriguing current of Bush nostalgia became evident in opposition circles. When I spoke to him a year into Obama's first term, Erian, the Brotherhood official, sounded almost wistful of political openings that came under Bush. "Now President Mubarak can do whatever he wants internally. . . . It feels like we've gone backward a little bit," he said.[37] Or, another Brotherhood member complained to me in May 2010: "For Obama, the issue of democracy is the fifteenth on his list of priorities. . . . [T]here's no moment of change like there was under Bush."[38]

During the 2008 U.S. presidential campaign, I was living in Jordan. That summer, Rohile Gharaibeh, a leading figure in Jordan's IAF, seemed optimistic about an Obama presidency. "If I was able to talk to U.S. policymakers," he said to me, "I'd tell them to stop supporting authoritarian regimes and to help people find their voice and move toward real democratic government. The real democratic system is a pillar of stability. . . . And that would be in U.S. interests."[39]

In a roundabout way then, even Islamists seemed to be rooting for the United States. In the same breath, however, Brotherhood leaders could also rail against the United States and the "Zionist entity" as nefarious and somewhat omniscient forces. As it turns out, it was possible to both hate and like America, to hope that it failed while wanting it to succeed. During Egypt's eighteen-day uprising, this form of political schizophrenia was very much on display. In the eyes of many Egyptian activists, the United States was many things at once: the source of its problems but also, potentially, the solution. America's dual role in the Arab revolts is as complex as it is real: the product of decades of contradictory and competing American policies.

American liberals had often told the world—and, perhaps more importantly, themselves—that the Bush administration's destructive policies were a historic anomaly. When a Democrat was elected, America would undo the damage and begin rebuilding its troubled relationship with the Arab and Muslim world. President Obama's claim to the presidency was premised, both implicitly and explicitly, on this assumption. The historic Cairo speech of June 2009 confirmed, for a short while at least, those hopes. Obama promised a "new beginning" with the Middle East. After the honeymoon period, however, the familiar disappointments returned. In a span of just one year, the number of Arabs who said they were "discouraged" about the Obama administration's Middle East policies shot up from 15 percent to 63 percent.[40]

By the time the 2011 uprisings began, attitudes toward the United States had hit rock bottom. In several Arab countries, including Egypt, America's favorability ratings were lower under President Barack Obama than they were at *any point* in President Bush's second term.[41] Remarkably, according to a 2011 Pew Research Center survey, slightly more Egyptians had favorable opinions of Osama Bin Laden than they did of the United States.[42] Of course, this does not mean that many Egyptians actually liked Bin Laden. It means that the bar was so incredibly low that just about anyone could clear it.

Throughout the Obama years, those Islamists who may have said nice things about the United States and its supposed moral authority were being pragmatic and a bit cynical. They favored U.S. democracy promotion, because democratization would benefit them—not because they were Islamists but because they were bound to do well in elections. That said, in my conversations with Brotherhood members, whether on the record or off, whether young or old, I came away with the sense that they actually could imagine a cooperative—but still tense—relationship with the United States. Naturally, Islamists would be at least somewhat less anti-American if a renewed American focus on democratization decreased their own persecution. This is the vicious circle of U.S. democracy promotion policy: Because Islamists are anti-American, we fear what may happen if they win democratic elections, so we suppress democracy. But Islamists are, at least in part, anti-American because we suppress democracy. And so on.

* * *

However regrettable, the inability of U.S. policy in the Middle East to adapt or change is understandable. American policy emerges from a messy, risk-averse infrastructure, and democratization is risky almost by definition, because it creates more uncertainty in the short run even if it ends up stabilizing countries in the long term.

At the same time, there is a danger of overstating the short-term dangers. In any given bilateral relationship in the Middle East, the United States is—by far—the stronger party, so for American officials to fear retaliation from the "junior" partner, or the client state, gets things backward. The leverage runs in the other direction, but of course that depends on the United States behaving as if it actually has that leverage. (In the next chapter, I will discuss *leverage*, its uses and misuses, in much more detail.)

If we are talking about assessing risk, we must return to the question of what Islamist parties would do if they had full or partial control over foreign policy. I hesitate to argue that Islamists wouldn't be *that* bad, even if that may be true. The foreign policy preferences of Islamist parties should have little to do with whether the United States, as a basic moral and strategic commitment, prioritizes democracy promotion in the Middle East. If our commitment to supporting democracy is merely contingent on whether the outcomes are "tolerable," then we will be all too ready to discard democracy if the outcomes prove too frustrating or inconvenient.

That said, we live in a practical world. For policymakers, outcomes can't help but matter quite a lot. But there is little reason to emphasize worst-case scenarios. Islamist parties, in power, are unlikely to be as bad as their harshest critics fear for reasons that I discuss below. Beyond this, the most important thing to stress is that outcomes will vary considerably depending on various factors *other than* the ideological orientation of a particular Islamist party.

I have focused primarily on the Muslim Brotherhood in Egypt and Jordan as well as Algeria's Islamic Salvation Front. In contexts where an authoritarian regime is anti-Western, such as in Syria, there is likely to be greater overlap of interests between a given Islamist party and the United States. This is intuitive: an opposition movement defines itself in opposition to whoever happens to be governing. If the governing party is anti-Israel and anti-American, then the opposition has less to gain by emphasizing those themes. The opposition, in such cases, is more likely to view the United States as a natural ally. I remember a conversation I had with a Syrian Muslim Brotherhood leader in 2012 as the Syrian regime was intensifying its assault on civilians. He was only partly joking when he said that he would be more than happy to go along with an Israeli military intervention if that's what it took to get rid of Assad.

In Syria, the Brotherhood is anti-Assad, anti-Iran, and anti-Hezbollah for reasons specific to the Syrian context. The Syrian Brotherhood, unlike its counterparts elsewhere, does not view Israel as a primary threat and even sometimes seems indifferent to the Jewish state. Instead, fears of a powerful Iran–Syria–Hezbollah axis drive the group's politics. Like the United States, it has often criticized Iran as a dangerous sectarian regime intent on projecting Shiite influence throughout the Arab world. Similarly, the Lebanese Muslim Brotherhood, known as Gamaa al-Islamiyya, has opposed Syria and Hezbollah's role in Lebanon and allied itself with the pro-U.S. March 14 alliance.[43] Elsewhere, mainstream Sunni Islamists, while applauding Iran's support of Palestinian resistance, have been careful to maintain their distance from the Shiite clerical regime, which they see as a deviation from traditional Islamic governance.

In the end, however, this is unlikely to be enough for skeptics. Democratic governments reflect popular sentiment, and in the Middle East, this sentiment is firmly against Israel and U.S. hegemony in the region. If the Arab–Israeli conflict persists or, worse, war breaks out, democratically elected governments—Islamist or otherwise—will come under pressure to take a strong stand in support of Palestinian rights. Such pressure can be difficult to resist.

And so we return to an old problem—the problem of "linkage." If prioritizing Arab democracy and prioritizing Israel's security are at cross purposes, what can the United States do? There are three options. The first is to acknowledge the trade-off and persist with the status quo of elevating Israel's security at the rest of the region's expense. The second is to acknowledge the trade-off but to shift U.S. policy to prioritize Arab democracy at the expense of Israel's security. The third is to prioritize Arab democracy, but to do so while simultaneously providing Israel ironclad guarantees that the United States will come to its defense if attacked.

This last option is the most appealing of the three even if it is also somewhat redundant. The United States has *already* committed itself to Israel's security, and Arab armies, even if you combined them, would be no match for Israel, considering that Arab armies aren't really meant for fighting.[44] The worst-case scenario—of newly empowered Arab democracies becoming more aggressive and deciding to invade Israel—is not merely improbable but something close to unfathomable. There may be a time, however, when this is not the case, and this is where American guarantees become relevant (although it is worth noting that we are talking here about the *very* long term when all of us will likely be dead). The goal would be to "make Israel so strong that Arab democracies still aren't going to attack it no matter how anti-Israel they become."[45] The United States would publicly announce such a guarantee as part of its broader shift in policy. Any resulting discomfort on the part of Arab audiences would be offset by the commitment to replacing a "stability-first" with a "democracy-first" strategy in the region.

Short of such a shift, American policy will remain as it has been, reliant on an authoritarian order of its own making, aligned against the aspirations of tens of millions of Arabs, and dependent on the unlikely premise of permanent autocracy.

7

Anti-Despotism or Democracy Promotion?

America's problem in the Middle East, to the extent that one considers it problematic, is the result of something foundational. That it would come to this wasn't an accident. It was decades in the making. The Obama administration failed, to be sure, but it was deeper than that. The regional order the United States had fashioned in the Middle East for half a century was an authoritarian order that depended on authoritarian allies. And short of questioning and challenging the very foundations of that order—which Barack Obama was not ready to do—the United States would find itself, once again, back where it started. And that is exactly where we are as I write this.

Robert Kagan has argued that the United States "is and always has been a revolutionary power, a sometimes unwitting—but nevertheless persistent—disturber of the status quo."[1] While this may be true in the broader sweep of U.S. foreign policy, it is not true of America's role in the Middle East. In this sense, the region is a useful foil, a way to understand what we have been, or tried to be, almost everywhere else. If Middle East realities happened to be good or at least inoffensive, they might have been worth conserving. Instead, the United States is a status quo power—perhaps *the* status quo power—in a region where the status quo is objectionable on moral terms and unsustainable on strategic ones. This status quo has had a destructive impact on the region's development as well as the basic ability of citizens to live with dignity. The problem is not just bad policy. It is about the most basic assumptions that gave rise to the Middle Eastern order. Rethinking an *order* is an altogether different task than changing a policy.

To the extent that Arabs protest their own regimes, they are protesting an authoritarian order that the United States has been central in propagating. They are fighting on two fronts. The question, then, is whether and how the United States might effectively do two things. The first is to help make repressive regimes less repressive. This is what might be called *anti-despotism*. The second is to proactively promote democracy.

Anti-despotism is a necessary first step, but it is mostly reactive, defensive, and can be done with a mind to decreasing American involvement in the region. As an approach, it often attracts support on the progressive left, because it allows the United States to adopt a moral high ground while still plausibly being "non-interventionist." It does this by punishing autocratic allies and distancing the United States from their bad behavior but without necessarily having a longer-term strategy for improving democratic prospects in the countries in question. In this sense, anti-despotism is often more about "us" than about "them." It seeks to reestablish some semblance of (American) virtue in a fallen world. Extracting America from immoral entanglements becomes its own end. If the Middle East is a nuisance and Americans are better off washing their hands of the whole mess, anti-despotism is an easier way to save face and maintain some self-respect.

As an approach, anti-despotism is probably better than not caring at all. Making the region somewhat less repressive is a worthwhile endeavor, one that can alter lives and livelihoods on the ground. If progressives wish to atone for America's sins in the Middle East, however, this is not how they will find peace. Anti-despotism requires considerable political will, and it would be a major missed opportunity to expend such effort in the absence of broader long-term objectives. If the United States is going to upend its decades-long approach to the Middle East, it should at least make it count.

Perhaps more importantly for our purposes, an anti-despotism strategy without a democracy promotion strategy runs the risk of relegating human rights to a separate category of concerns divorced from American interests. In other words, rights become something that we should support but not necessarily something we must support. When democracy and human rights are perceived this way, they become a luxury to be indulged when they aren't in conflict with "interests" or "stability." As we have seen, however, there is always *some* trade-off, particularly since stability is a "vague and elusive" concept.[2]

Anti-despotism also does not account for how a "moral distancing" approach might leave a vacuum that authoritarian regimes like Russia and China can exploit. If the United States signaled that it was (truly) washing its hands of the Middle East—partly out of a desire to avoid being tainted by the behavior of bad regimes—then autocratic allies would have little incentive to actually alter their behavior. After all, if the United States is intent on disengaging from the region regardless, they might decide they are better off weathering the pressure and plugging gaps with increased Russian or Chinese support until a new American administration reverses course.

There is a reason Washington has never threatened a total suspension of military assistance to any of the countries in question. First, it would be an admittedly radical move—so "radical," in fact, that Arab regimes don't seem to believe it is within the realm of possibility. But radical, here, does not mean unrealistic or extremely costly to implement. It can be done, but it would require that most intangible of political assets—political will, probably from the president, and a determination to see a policy through without flinching in the face of opposition. Considering the difficulty involved as well as the controversy likely to follow, such measures are best presented as part of a methodical reorientation of U.S. strategy in the Middle East, rather than a series of disconnected ad hoc policies. In practice, of course, any such strategy will fall short of the ideal type laid out here, but it is important to think beyond the present set of political constraints. Constraints change, and they can change rather quickly. For example, at the time of writing, democracy promotion seems quaint considering that there is no democracy to promote in much of the region. But so it also must have seemed in the months leading up to the Arab Spring. The sense of what is possible or impossible does not stay constant. One day, inevitably, the region will impose a new set of realities on an international community that will struggle to catch up, just as it struggled in those early days of mass revolt.

Punitive measures, when one must resort to them, are not enough on their own. To punish is a means and not an end. This brings us to the matter of how to create a layered structure of incentives that makes reform more attractive and repression less so. However radical such a course might seem, particularly to bureaucrats and diplomats who spent their careers invested in a stale status quo, policymakers must be willing to use the leverage they have *at some point*. If they don't, they risk losing it altogether. Which raises the question: If not now, when? What conceivably would regimes have to do to trigger real consequences?

I remember a conversation I had with a State Department official in the spring of 2012 that was perhaps too on the nose. It seemed to me that if there was ever a good time to suspend military assistance to Egypt, it was then. As we saw earlier, the Supreme Council of the Armed Forces, which was "managing" the democratic transition, had launched a crackdown on not only Egyptian civil society organizations but also American ones like the National Democratic Institute and the International Republican Institute that were recipients of U.S. government funding. Not only was this a troubling omen for the transition, it was akin to a taunt. The Egyptian military had come to believe that it could continue to act with impunity, because it *had* been acting with impunity. It could receive tens of billions of dollars for decades from the United States while also shutting down U.S.-funded organizations and threatening employees, including American citizens, with criminal charges.

This was, of course, regrettable, the State Department official told me, but the United States needed to save its leverage for when it might matter most, rather than using it—and losing it—prematurely. So I asked when that might be. I will never forget what he said. "In the event of a military coup," he told me.

* * *

The military coup did indeed come, and yet the United States refused to use the leverage that it had. As one Obama administration official put it, "We had no credibility to do anything anyway. We'd been talking for years about withholding the military aid. No one really believed that we would do it."[3] This is true. No one believed we would do it, but presumably this was our fault, and not theirs. After all, they were correct to doubt us, because we had given them ample reason for doubt.

The logic was self-fulfilling and maddeningly circular. If you didn't want to act, you could always find a reason. When the coup was in process but still could have been averted, U.S. officials worried about alienating the Egyptian military. The situation was fluid, they reasoned. Perhaps it was better to save their leverage in the event things got worse. Once the coup had succeeded, however, the reasoning shifted. It was too late. Why threaten an aid cut when the coup itself was a fait accompli? Better to keep it in reserve for the future in case things got even worse. For now, though, perhaps it was better to make the most out of a difficult situation and consider the silver linings of a new military regime. It was during this period that the United States made another controversial decision. President Obama decided not to label the coup a "coup." To call it a coup would legally trigger an immediate cutoff in aid. The running joke among State Department officials was that it was merely a "coup-like event."

In fairness, government officials were right to worry that things might get worse. And they did get worse. I was in Egypt in early August 2013 just weeks after the military seized power. The environment was one of gossip, intrigue, and that potent mixture of fear, anticipation, and the uncertainty that tends to accompany the days leading up to a mass killing. The military had announced that it would "clear" the square where tens of thousands of Brotherhood supporters were camped out.[4] No one doubted it would happen. The only question was how bad it would be and when exactly the military would give the order.

If leverage had been saved and stored, not once and not twice but several times, then perhaps this is where a strategy of strategic patience might have been salvaged. But the United States never made clear what the consequences would be. Even if it had, it is unlikely the Egyptian military would have taken it seriously. When leverage goes unused, it doesn't strengthen; it weakens.

The United States, instead, entered into a flurry of last-minute diplomatic activity, hoping to negotiate an end to the standoff between the Brotherhood and the military.[5] Why threaten consequences that might alienate one side— the more powerful side—in the midst of a negotiation that seemed to bear promise?

This, in short, is the problem of leverage: How much of it do we have? And what are the benefits—or drawbacks—of using it convincingly with our allies?

The Illusion of American Neutrality

When it came to the Arab Spring, American officials and observers alike were fond of saying that it wasn't about us; it was about them.[6] On its face, this seemed like a worthy acknowledgment, allowing us to move away from our own narcissism and appreciate that Arabs were the ones fighting—and dying—for their freedom. However well-intentioned, such sentiments were almost too convenient, offering an excuse for inaction and putting America in the role of the blameless bystander.

From the very start, there was a temptation to discount the importance of external actors. After all, the uprisings were a truly indigenous movement and Arabs themselves did not want others to "interfere" in it—meddling that would, the thinking went, go against the very spirit of the revolution.

The protesters themselves weren't entirely inward-looking, however. How could they be? To be angry at a regime couldn't be disentangled from the anger at an international order that had supported and subsidized that same regime. While those who rose up called for "bread and freedom," a third element—the demand for dignity—was more difficult to characterize. Here,

Egypt's pro-Western policies and perceived subservience to the United States figured prominently, including in the defining chant that echoed throughout Tahrir Square the night Mubarak fell: "You're Egyptian—raise your head up high." During my time in Tahrir, I would hear numerous chants attacking Mubarak for being a lackey of the United States and Israel (one such chant claimed that the Egyptian president only understood one language: Hebrew).

Where exactly is the line between inaction and complicity? The notion of neutrality, for a country as powerful as the United States, is an illusion. To do nothing or to "do no harm" means maintaining or reverting to the status quo, which in the Middle East is never neutral, due to America's longstanding relationships with regional actors. If the status quo is authoritarian, then neutrality looks like the same old support for dictators.

If the Middle East is exceptional in its apparent resistance to democracy, then it may be that external—not internal—factors played a decisive role in making it so, tipping the balance in favor of authoritarian stagnation. Earlier, we saw how this played out in the case of Jordan, which for a moment could claim the region's most promising democratic experiment. In the second half of the twentieth century, American hegemony not only coincided with but also drove the spread of democracy around the globe. Everywhere, it seemed, but here. When it came to the Middle East, American hegemony— after the Soviet Union's demise—made the region safer not for democracy but for authoritarianism. It is easy (and largely correct) to say that, on balance, American unipolarity has been a force for good, if not in absolute terms then at least compared to any counterfactual history where other would-be empires might have been dominant.[7] But it is also easy and largely correct to say that U.S. dominance in the Middle East has been a destructive force, if the inhabitants of the region—their lives and their freedom—are the relevant consideration.

In this sense, as former American diplomat Mieczysław Boduszyński writes, it is the "exceptionalism of U.S. policy toward the region" that helps explain the exceptionalism of the Middle East.[8] Along similar lines, Princeton University's Amaney Jamal argues that "Arab 'exceptionalism' may not be in its Islamic culture but instead may stem from the Arab world's subordinate location in the international system."[9] Centering the United States in the conversation is critical if American policymakers have any interest or hope in restraining the very authoritarianism that they themselves helped nurture.

Over the past decade, coinciding with the rise and fall of the Arab Spring, a growing academic literature has pointed to the role of international actors in bringing down autocrats—or not bringing them down. In Jordan, the United States backed and bankrolled the monarchy when it might have otherwise felt compelled to respond to popular, domestic pressures. In fact, the Clinton administration—because of its prioritization of peace with Israel—significantly increased economic and military assistance just as the Jordanian regime was intensifying its repression. In this sense, America's renewed interest in and attention to Jordan made it possible for the regime to insulate itself from its own population. As Sean Yom and Mohammad Momani write, "International support lowered the cost of domestic repression. . . . By eroding the uncertainty clouding the ruling elite's political choices while also reinforcing its fiscal capacity and security sector, external assistance enabled the regime to constrict opposition mobilization without fear of international repercussions."[10] They conclude: "There is a strong negative correlation between the intensity of Western support for the regime and the trajectory of internal political liberalization."[11]

So the problem isn't Islam, underdevelopment, lack of a middle class, or the absence of a democratic culture. These factors have been present in other parts of the world and have not precluded democratic outcomes. The old arguments about Islam and democracy are also easily discarded. The most populous Muslim-majority nation, Indonesia, is a democracy and various others such as Senegal and the Gambia are democracies to this day, while others like Malaysia and Pakistan have for all their flaws been considerably more democratic than their Arab counterparts. The notion that a democratic culture is a prerequisite for democracy is an odd one. How can a people inculcate democratic habits under an authoritarianism that sees those habits as a threat? A democratic culture, if it comes to be, is a product of democratic practice. It doesn't descend from the sky, an unlikely gift of providence. (As Tocqueville wrote: "It is by charging citizens with the administration of small affairs, much more than by giving them the government of great ones, that you interest them in the public good and make them see the need that they constantly have for each other in order to produce that good."[12])

The failure of the standard explanations to account for Middle Eastern authoritarianism allows us to look elsewhere, and this is where Islamism becomes a problem to grapple with. The presence of Islamist movements as the largest potential beneficiary of democratic openings provokes antidemocratic reactions on the part of domestic actors and, importantly, international actors as well. These international actors, in turn, enable Arab regimes' capacity for repression through security relationships that privilege the coercive arms of the state, including the military. As the political scientist Eva Bellin writes: "The will and capacity of the state's coercive apparatus to suppress democratic initiative have extinguished the possibility of transition. Herein lies the region's true exceptionalism."[13]

If the United States can shore up and strengthen authoritarians' hold on power, then presumably it can weaken their hold just the same. But, obviously, to take something away that has already been given, for years or even decades, is bound to be a more difficult endeavor.

On Leverage: A Conceptual Framework

Leverage is one of those words that is used casually and without much precision. Often it is in the eye of beholder. Some analysts (like myself) criticize the United States for failing to use its leverage in support of democracy abroad, while policymakers impatiently respond that their hands are tied and that American leverage is limited and perhaps even negligible. As the Arab Spring turned dark, Obama appeared to give up, concluding that the Middle East simply wasn't "shapeable."[14] A former State Department official summed up the sentiment well: "We had relatively little influence, we didn't do much good, but we didn't do much bad. So it's hard to feel like there's exactly regret. I don't think we could have. . . Obviously, I don't think the situation turned out that well, but I don't think the U.S. had a lot of agency."[15]

The recent history of democratization in formerly authoritarian regions suggests a different story (although this leaves open the question of whether agency and leverage exist elsewhere but for some reason do not exist in the Middle East). In their book *Competitive Authoritarianism*, Steven Levitsky and Lucan Way provide extensive empirical support to what many suspected was true. They write, "It was an externally driven shift in the cost of suppression, not changes in domestic conditions, that contributed most centrally to the demise of authoritarianism in the 1980s and 1990s." Levitsky and Way find that "states' vulnerability to Western democratization pressure . . . was often decisive."[16]

In various Latin American and Asian autocracies that long took American backing for granted, American protection was withdrawn over the course of the 1980s, including in Peru, Argentina, Chile, the Philippines, and South Korea.[17] With the Cold War coming to a close, right-wing authoritarians lost their raison d'être. They had been a bulwark against the spread of communism, but communism had ceased to spread. With the United States signaling its new priorities, the opposition became emboldened, regimes wavered in their use of force, and powerful elites began to fracture as they contemplated a different future.

Some of this is intuitive. With a large power differential between the United States and "client states" dependent on American backing, the latter had little choice but to give way to the former. Interestingly, though, Levitsky and Way find that, unlike in Latin America, South Korea, or the Philippines in the 1980s, Western leverage has been relatively low in the Middle East.[18] The reason cited is instructive: Middle Eastern states are strategically vital, and strategic interests take precedence over human rights and democracy. Accordingly, Western threats—when they concern democracy—are simply not credible.

Arab leaders know full well the traditional hierarchy of Western priorities, a hierarchy that remained largely intact during the Arab Spring. Newly elected Islamist parties—such as Egypt's Muslim Brotherhood or Tunisia's Ennahda—also knew this, which is why they focused considerable attention on forging stronger relations with the United States (perhaps more so than with their own domestic opposition). Fully aware of American priorities, the Morsi government dialed down anti-Israel rhetoric, maintained the peace treaty, and cooperated with Israel on Sinai security.[19] It is no coincidence that Morsi came out with his infamous November 22, 2012 decree giving himself temporary emergency powers—arguably his most controversial move as president—the day after he had worked hand in hand with the United States to secure a ceasefire between Israel and Hamas.[20]

It is not so much, then, that the United States doesn't have leverage. It's that America's strategic framework in the Middle East—one where it openly telegraphs its disinterest in democracy—renders its leverage null and void. Governments in the region have difficulty imagining any scenario where the United States actually withdraws support in a meaningful sense. They have every reason to be skeptical. As we saw in the previous chapter, for example, the Egyptian military gradually revealed its authoritarian intentions, undermining the democratic transition it was entrusted to oversee. Yet at nearly every key moment from 2011 to 2013, the United States chose to look away.

This is the paradox of leverage. American policymakers are afraid to use the leverage that they have, because then they might lose it. But if you never use your leverage—ostensibly to save it for the future—then it's already lost. Leverage depends on the credible threat of sanction or a persuasive promise of reward, so it atrophies when unused. And the effect is cumulative: leverage either accumulates or diminishes based on past decisions.

In short, American leverage in the Middle East *is* low when it comes to democratization and affecting the internal politics of Arab countries. This is because Arab governments doubt our commitment to those values and think our threats hollow. With this in mind, senior officials, including the president, must make a conscious decision to reconceptualize how we use leverage in the Middle East—and, importantly, *what* we are willing to use it for. The United States would then need to communicate this changed hierarchy of priorities to governments in the region. This will be difficult to do piecemeal, since early on the United States would have to demonstrate that any new policy was, in fact, a policy and not merely a rhetorical gambit. For this reason, it would likely have to be presented as part of a broader reset and reorientation.

In assessing what leverage the United States does or does not have, it is critical to consider the many ingredients of bilateral ties. The Middle East has quite its share of them.[21] In an effort to analyze these relationships more systematically, the political scientists Anne Peters and Sean Yom point to six "provisions of order" that governments receive from the United States, including: economic assistance and food aid; technical assistance and infrastructure enhancements improving their ability to provide public services; access to economic markets; means to augment internal coercion through intelligence sharing; and protection from external threats.[22] To be sure, countries like Egypt are less economically dependent on the United States today than they once were, with American aid representing only a small fraction of overall GDP. If one looks beyond economic assistance, however, it becomes clear that Arab states remain reliant on the United States and would suffer considerably if Washington withdrew its "provisions of order."

The specific provisions that the United States provides countries like Egypt and Saudi Arabia are important enough on their own. Spare parts, which might not sound like a big deal, are critical for keeping military equipment operational. But it goes well beyond this. At the most basic level, the United States provides a security umbrella for various Middle Eastern countries. Saudi Arabia has a close security relationship with the United States, and in the absence of a formal defense treaty, that relationship telegraphs to potential enemies that if it ever came under existential threat, Washington would step in, as it did during the first Gulf War.[23] Without a guarantor, Saudi Arabia would be much more vulnerable than it currently is.

Defensive weapons systems provided to allies include "naval defense, and antimissile, rocket, and drone technologies to protect critical infrastructure."[24] The list, which is long, also includes early warning aircraft and naval surface ships. Big-ticket items like fighter jets and tanks are favorites of Arab allies even if they are not especially useful or in line with what the countries in question actually need for their own security.

The operation of American weapons systems is sophisticated and highly dependent on U.S. maintenance, servicing, and training.[25] For the Egyptian military, maintenance costs alone account for around 15 percent of the $1.3 billion in assistance it receives from the United States.[26] As the world's most powerful and advanced army, there is also an important but less easily quantifiable prestige factor that accompanies security cooperation with Washington. For the foreseeable future, the United States will remain the partner-of-choice for militaries around the world. Joint exercises, war games, and training, including tours at the U.S. Army War College, have provided the United States with deep personal connections at various levels of Arab militaries. As Joshua Stacher notes, "[Egypt's generals] feel like proximity to U.S. generals generates a kind of honor and respectability."[27] These military-to-military relationships have been built over not just years but decades. Letting most of that go and opting for other patrons would be costly, time-consuming, and ultimately damaging for any military that has grown accustomed to the perks and benefits of American backing.

Nations such as Saudi Arabia and the United Arab Emirates might appear insulated from American pressure due to their sheer wealth. This is not quite true, however. For regimes preoccupied with regime security, nothing is more important than existing. Despite (or perhaps because of) their vast wealth, they remain as dependent on American security provisions. To put it simply, they need us more than we need them. "They live under our defense umbrella" is how former U.S. Ambassador to Egypt Anne Patterson put it.[28] Or, as former Deputy Assistant Secretary of Defense Andrew Exum explained it: "Broadly, the Department of Defense is responsible to defend the Arabian Peninsula in the event of some sort of contingency, like if war breaks out in the Persian Gulf or something like that."[29] Which makes it all the more odd that, until now, the leverage has moved in the opposite direction: regimes free-ride on American security guarantees and behave more recklessly as a result. They interpret American bases and troops as both an entitlement and a vote of confidence. Until the United States alters the foundation of these relationships, American backing will be treated as a license to act with impunity.

Saudi Arabia's March 2011 invasion of neighboring Bahrain is a case in point. As Toby Jones notes, "Saudi Arabia would almost certainly not have sent its troops into neighboring Bahrain—a sovereign country—if the Saudi and Bahraini leadership did not assume they were protected by their patrons in the U.S. military."[30] And so the United States becomes hostage to the recklessness of allies who, while benefiting tremendously from U.S. support, increasingly act against American interests and ideals. Recipient regimes see American security provisions as something to which they are entitled, as if they themselves are doing us a favor by allowing us to secure their survival. But the benefit is largely theirs and theirs alone.

For the first time in decades, U.S. imports of Saudi oil fell to zero in 2021, rendering the longstanding bargain of "security for oil" obsolete.[31] While Saudi Arabia can still disrupt energy markets because *other* countries are dependent on Saudi oil, there is relatively little Saudi Arabia can do to punish the United States directly.

Similar arguments can be made about most American allies in the Arab world. As Michael Hanna outlines in detail, the U.S.–Egypt relationship "benefits the Egyptians more than the Americans."[32] The end of the Cold War invited deeper American engagement in the region, largely due to the Clinton administration's focus on Arab–Israeli peace processes, even as Arab countries could no longer claim to be bulwarks against communism. After the September 11 attacks, the Middle East became even more central in the American imagination. Cooperation on counterterrorism became the overriding priority. It is worth remembering, however, that states tend to fight terrorists not because American officials ask them to but because it is in their national interest. They are often the prime targets of terrorists, after all.

To be sure, the risk of retaliatory responses from embattled Arab regimes is not, and could never be, zero. There is a risk. How could there not be? But the risks tend to be overstated. Egyptian officials made similar threats in the 2000s, as President Bush began putting unprecedented pressure on Hosni Mubarak to open up. The threats amounted to little. In fact, Egyptian officials had *more* reason to cooperate with the United States in order to demonstrate their usefulness at a time when it was being doubted. As Michele Dunne, a former State Department official and leading expert on Egypt, wrote at the end of Bush's second term:

What can the next administration learn from the bumpy course of U.S.-Egyptian relations since the inception of Bush's freedom agenda? First, Egypt at no time withheld or even seriously threatened to withhold cooperation on military, counterterrorism, or regional diplomacy due to the freedom agenda. *If anything, Cairo tried harder to please Washington in these areas in 2002–2006 in the hope of relieving pressure for political reform* [emphasis mine].[33]

There is some presumption here of rationality, particularly with regimes that prioritize their own survival. While leaders will not always act "rationally," they are more likely to than not, knowing what we know about what they value above all else. In short, there is little reason to assume that allies benefiting from counterterrorism cooperation with the United States would halt it—the political equivalent of cutting off one's nose to spite one's face.

We again return to the question of credibility, however. If regimes doubt the credibility of the threat, they may be more likely to retaliate in the expectation that the United States will quickly fold. They would, in other words, call our bluff. In the case of the Freedom Agenda, the American threat was credible, because the Bush administration seemed serious and willing to sustain pressure, at least for a time. Mubarak certainly thought so, and so did Islamist and secular opposition figures, who, as we saw earlier, readily credited the Bush administration. While the Iraq War should be separated from the Freedom Agenda since its stated justification was about weapons of mass destruction and not democracy, President Bush's recklessness and enthusiasm for Middle East adventurism made autocratic allies nervous. The man seemed capable of anything, including undoing decades of support in the name of an idiosyncratic crusade for democracy.

Since then, much has changed, including perceptions of American decline and disinterest in the Middle East. Naturally, doubts about American staying power undermine leverage, since regimes wager that they can wait Washington out. It is likely, then, that U.S. threats to withhold aid or suspend weapons sales will not be treated as credible, at least not at first. If tested, policymakers will actually have to follow through on their threats, or risk demonstrating once again the hollowness of American rhetoric. This requires some degree of resolve—and a readiness to absorb the costs of noncooperation if worst-case scenarios actually come to pass. In the unlikely event that the Egyptian government took retaliatory action, for example, the costs would be significant enough to irritate the United States. But, as my Brookings colleague Michael O'Hanlon notes, Egypt's provisions of Suez Canal access and overflight rights, while convenient and helpful, are not needed "in any absolute sense."[34]

The larger issue here is the overall frame of reference for understanding the U.S.–Egypt relationship. The United States, as a superpower and the senior partner in the relationship, can withstand such tensions much more than a regime that is struggling economically, politically, and militarily, and one that is ultimately dependent on U.S. military support.[35] If Egypt withheld Suez Canal access, for example, all Washington would have to do is retaliate in kind to demonstrate that the costs of a breach are higher to the junior partner—or the "client state"—than they are to the senior partner, in this case the United States.

Security relationships, as important as they are, represent just one component of American leverage, albeit the most obvious one. As the importance and price of oil declines over time, Gulf regimes will find themselves even more precariously reliant on a single source of revenue. Economic diversification and building a knowledge economy—and doing so with sufficient Western prestige and using a small army of Western experts and consultants[36]—have long been a priority across the Gulf. In a Quincy Institute report, Annelle Sheline and Steven Simon write that "as [Saudi Crown Prince Mohamed bin Salman] declares his intention to revolutionize the economy and society, the U.S. can reinforce this trajectory with investments, statements of support, and technology sharing. But the U.S. should offer material assistance for economic diversification only if Saudi Arabia ceases to interfere in other countries and begins developing a regional security architecture."[37] Interestingly, they do not advocate for a proactive democracy promotion policy, as I do here, but they still come to a similar conclusion: that leverage can be employed to pursue American objectives. If, from a realist perspective, Saudi Arabia behaves as a destabilizing actor in the region, then the United States should reply with a combination of carrots and sticks, regardless of one's views on democracy. One of those carrots, Sheline and Simon write, is helping the kingdom "achieve the goals established in 'Vision 2030' "—the ambitious and rather expensive and expert-driven project to modernize Saudi society.[38]

Similarly, the political scientists Yasmine Farouk and Andrew Leber write that "opening up Saudi Arabia to the outside world" is critical to Mohamed bin Salman's vision.[39] It's not so much, then, that Saudi Arabia needs the United States more than the United States needs Saudi Arabia. To make such a comparison suggests that the relationships in question are comparable. They are not. The direction and degree of (potential) leverage are unmistakable, and what applies to Saudi Arabia applies just as much or more so to countries that have little or no oil wealth. In sum, whether on economic diversification, foreign investment inflows, or military provisions, the future of rich and poor Arab countries alike hinges on multifaceted relationships with the U.S. government, Western technical expertise, and support from international financial institutions.

Deep States and Divided Government

The term "deep state" gained currency in the United States during the Trump years, wielded by loyalists to claim that the elected president was being undermined by entrenched bureaucracies with their own vested interests.[40] Interestingly, the term itself was imported from the Middle East, in particular Turkey and Egypt. It is generally used to describe the constellation of autonomous and self-perpetuating institutions, namely the judiciary, military, and security services, that operate outside the glare of the public and are immune to the electorate's whims. The deep state, acting as the guardian of national identity, puts limits on what elected politicians can hope to accomplish. It was responsible for four successful coups in Turkey, one of which deposed the country's first-ever democratically elected Islamist prime minister in 1997.

The comparisons have their limits, of course. Unlike in the Middle East, American institutions are inculcated in democratic norms, as one would expect in any long-established democracy. Still, the concept of a deep or "wide state" can be helpful in thinking about how unelected—and at least partly unaccountable—leaders and institutions confront democratically elected ones. As the political theorist Faheem Hussain notes: "Latent in every democracy [is] the permanent bureaucracy's capacity to subvert the elected administration, by virtue of permanence and knowledge."[41]

During the Obama administration's tenure, Pentagon officials were not necessarily against democracy promotion. They just didn't see it as a priority. They often saw it as a distraction, something that would come into conflict with other, more important goals.[42] Where you stand depends on where you sit, and the Department of Defense saw the Middle East primarily through the lens of military-to-military relationships and the need to conserve them.

To take an example, CENTCOM commanders do not only meet with their equivalent in the Egyptian military. They also meet with politicians, including presidents. Their conversations inevitably focus on what American generals know best and are themselves most comfortable with, which include "shared security concerns" and "the strategic nature of the U.S.-Egypt defense relationship."[43]

The dynamic between the United States and Saudi Arabia has been similar in spirit, though anchored somewhat differently in the sale of billions of dollars of weapons (in contrast, Egypt buys American arms with U.S. aid granted to it under the Foreign Military Financing, or FMF, program[44]). It is understandable that Pentagon officials would prioritize defense relationships—that's their job after all—but let us consider for a moment the actual benefits of an American-equipped and -trained Saudi military. As Sheline and Simon write:

> For all the military training the U.S. has provided, Saudi Arabia, in contrast to the UAE, has not demonstrated any high degree of military competence. As a result, the Saudi military has contributed almost nothing of value to U.S.–led coalition operations in Iraq or Syria but has used U.S. weapons systems in Yemen to create a humanitarian catastrophe.[45]

Relationships with other militaries are presumably not ends in and of themselves but rather means to other objectives, but it is unclear what those objectives might be in the case of the Saudi military's prowess, or lack thereof. Regardless of the specific rationales, that things have always been done this way provides its own justification. The problem of leverage, then, is also a problem of different bureaucratic centers of power working at cross purposes.

* * *

The president of the United States is the most powerful person in the world. In reality, though, it's a bit more complicated. In June 2007, George W. Bush was already looking back at his tenure with regret. He was in Prague for a pro-democracy conference, gathering dissidents from around the globe. When he sat down with them, he felt at home. He told the Egyptian activist Saad Eddin Ibrahim, "You're not the only dissident. I too am a dissident in Washington. Bureaucracy in the United States does not help change. It seems that Mubarak succeeded in brainwashing them."[46] The few remaining true believers in the administration had resigned themselves, concluding that it was too late and that there was too much internal resistance anyway. In theory, the president *could* have done something. In practice, he can't do everything he wants to do.

Since the president's time is limited, he must rely on deputies to drive the process—and not all of them will share the same commitments to the same degree. That process, in turn, dilutes the purity of any policy preference. Other agencies will weigh in, reflecting their own institutional priorities.

It is possible for the president to override institutional opposition, but this requires an almost single-minded dedication. And President Bush had already expended much of his time, attention, and political capital on the 2007 Iraq troop surge. Since he had limited support from within the government, Bush ended up drawing considerably on outside experts to formulate a new Iraq strategy.[47] As Elliot Abrams, Bush's deputy national security advisor, recalls, "Basically, Bush had to impose this directly on the generals, and then they did it. You'd need that kind of presidential involvement, and remember the way Bush did it, he did it with Cheney and through the National Security Council. And then the orders were changed. The policy was changed."[48]

A fundamental reorientation of U.S. strategy in the Middle East would require a similar force of will from the president and those around him. Abrams, who oversaw democracy promotion efforts in the Bush administration, laid out what would be required:

> You need to say to [CIA Director] Bill Burns and you need to say to General [Mark] Milley, "This is my opinion, this is my decision. If I hear that your station chief in Riyadh or Abu Dhabi is sending a different message, I will fire him and I will fire you, you put the word out now, it goes right down to every military attaché and station chief. This is the policy. They are to get with it." You can do that. I mean, you absolutely can do that. It's hard because it's a very big bureaucracy, but I think you just got to read people the riot act and say heads are going to roll here.[49]

It is easy to speak of the "U.S. government" as a unitary actor with clear, discernible intent and organizational coherence. But this is not the case in practice, though some administrations are able to present an appearance of coherence even where it does not exist. Occasionally, as with Bush's jarring comment in Prague, the cracks show. Within the Bush administration, there was a clear divide, between the near religious zeal Bush would display and a foreign policy apparatus that was ill-equipped to translate his theory into practice.

During the Arab Spring, the divide within the U.S. government was never as stark. Since Obama himself was conflicted, the resulting incoherence and lack of conceptual clarity reflected itself throughout the bureaucracy. While the White House was more concerned about Egypt's democratic transition, defense officials had a different set of priorities, and the tension was left lingering. We already saw how the CENTCOM commander during Egypt's transition period, Gen. James Mattis, had a particular view of the Muslim Brotherhood that shaped his perspective on whether democracy was appropriate for Egypt in the first place. But it went well beyond Mattis' idiosyncrasies. Senior Pentagon representatives and military brass were doing their part—even if they didn't quite realize it—to undermine the transition, signaling to Egyptian counterparts that they, too, had had enough of the democratically elected government. As *New York Times* journalist David Kirkpatrick writes, "The continual conversations between Egyptian and American military officers were fast becoming mutual 'bitch sessions' about the Morsi government."[50]

It is not quite right to say that Mattis and other military officials were undermining President Obama's policy in Egypt, because it was never clear what the policy actually was. Bureaucratic foot-dragging is real, but at the end of the day the president can override such concerns, assuming he or she has the political will. Subordinates do not need to agree with the policy, but they do need to execute it.

Does the Middle East Matter Enough to Prioritize It?

The reconceptualization of U.S. leverage outlined in this chapter may be intuitive. It may even be *correct*, to the extent that you share some of my starting premises. Actually doing it, however, is another matter.

America's overall trajectory of decreased dependence on Middle East oil and the (for now) diminished centrality of terrorism mean that we need countries like Saudi Arabia less, which, in turn, means that putting pressure on Saudi Arabia becomes more practicable. But declining energy dependence and a diminished terror threat *also* mean that the region is, or appears to be, less important. Why should we expend time and treasure trying to incentivize countries to change their behavior when their behavior affects us less? Operationalizing American leverage in the region would require doing more, rather than doing less. American policymakers would have to stop viewing the region as a nuisance to be avoided, in other words. They would also have to reacquaint themselves with the notion that the United States is capable of being a force for good in a region where it has long been anything but—and that it hasn't been a force for good due to the very decisions made by said policymakers.

By contrast, doing less in the region or "doing no harm" would mean continuing and therefore preserving the authoritarian status quo. The only way to alter this basic orientation is by caring enough to end the entrenched policies that persist on autopilot regardless of whether senior officials are paying attention to the region. To reverse policies as entrenched as these requires reengaging in and with the Middle East. Employing American leverage and designing a program of positive and negative conditionality with Arab autocrats is no easy task. It will entail conscious leadership, resources, attention, time, and patience.

The alternative is to continue in the illusion that the Middle East can be ignored, dismissed, or "pivoted" away from. It can be ignored but only up to a point. Tens of billions of dollars of arms are sold, diplomatic envoys sent, aid delivered, and endless forays into peacemaking insisted upon. Even as politicians try to disentangle us from the Middle East and look the other way, the United States remains implicated by virtue of longstanding security relationships, complex basing operations, and thousands of troops stationed throughout the region. This also means that we remain implicated in what regimes do to their own populations. It is always tempting to *try* to ignore the Middle East. However, if it is authoritarianism itself (and the related misfortune of having bad allies) that provokes instability in the medium to long run, then some president at some point will find him- or herself dragged back in. The only way, in other words, for the region to stop being a "nuisance" is to help Arab citizens build stronger, more sustainable, and legitimate foundations for their societies sooner rather than later. The alternative is to wait for the region to explode in protest and discontent as it inevitably will, if you take my premise that authoritarian regimes—because they lack the consent of the governed—are brittle even when they appear strong.

Prioritizing the long term over the (apparent) necessities of the electoral cycle is something every administration struggles with.[51] They are torn between the urgent and the important. Important things, though, are not necessarily urgent, so addressing them can be postponed indefinitely—with policymakers content in the knowledge that there will always be another day after the crisis of the moment passes. But there are always crises, and there will always be something more urgent. As the historian Michael Doran writes, "The volume of pressing work is so great that officials sometimes fail to answer key strategic questions because they are too busy answering the telephone."[52]

The urgent and the important. The short run and the long term. These are tensions that have hampered American policy for decades.

A Question of Agency

Arabs, of course, have agency. They are not mere bystanders to the passing of their own lives. One potential objection to this book's argument is that in shifting considerable blame onto the United States, I continue in a long tradition of depriving Arabs of that agency and reducing them to passive recipients of what the United States does or doesn't do. For Americans, it is easy to "blame America first,"[53] since it offers a certain clarity and offers up an easy target for our disappointments. For Arabs, though, the temptation to view American power and influence as the decisive factor in their own lives is not exactly healthy. It brings with it a fatalism and fuels a conspiratorial view of politics. Perhaps more perniciously, it undermines a sense of personal responsibility. If external factors are so powerful as to preclude Arab democracy, then why should anyone attend a protest or criticize a government official and risk arrest as a result?

Imagine if you were a citizen of an Arab country, and you were reading this book. You might finish it thinking that democratic change is impossible until the United States changes. And you would be right—but only partly.

What Arabs themselves do shapes how the United States approaches the region. American officials look at the internal dynamics of individual Arab countries and make decisions accordingly. They may misinterpret events on the ground or make the wrong decisions, but they are reacting and responding to what they see. At the start of the Arab uprisings, for example, the Obama administration quickly shifted its posture, from Secretary of State Hillary Clinton saying that the Mubarak regime was "stable" on the first day of protests to President Obama calling on Mubarak to step aside two weeks later.

If American officials wish to repeat Clinton's error by thinking that the Sissi regime is stable, then they may find themselves as disappointed as they were in the early days of Egypt's uprising. It is an open question *when* such disappointment will come, but, short of unexpected developments in combating mortality, the Sissi regime will eventually come to an end. At that point, the problem of succession will make itself apparent. This lies at the heart of why authoritarian regimes are inherently unstable. They have no reliable, institutionalized mechanism for transferring power—a problem further magnified by Sissi's unique charisma and force of personality. Would Sissi's successor be able to command the same degree of loyalty? Would this period of succession—and the resulting doubt and uncertainty—bring with it a growing willingness on the part of Egyptians to take to the streets?

The regime might survive, but, in personalized systems, the character of the regime will, by definition, change when the leader changes. After Gamal Abdel Nasser died, his vice president, Anwar el Sadat, sought to systematically undo his predecessor's economic legacy. At the time, the so-called October Revolution, during which Sadat purged the regime's senior ranks of socialists, caught the country's elites by surprise. Sadat hadn't particularly distinguished himself as a vice president, and so his enemies—incorrectly it turned out—assumed he could be easily manipulated and controlled. When Sadat was assassinated, the uncertainty returned, and this time there was no opportunity to prepare. Sadat's final months had been spent orchestrating an idiosyncratic and elaborate crackdown on a wide array of opposition figures. Perhaps hoping to avoid such a fate, Mubarak—plodding and colorless—looked for a path of less resistance, initiating a real if modest political opening. This opening, in turn, emboldened opposition groups. A decade after its leaders were released from prison under Sadat, the Muslim Brotherhood came into its own under Mubarak. And then, of course, Mubarak's successor was none other than the Muslim Brotherhood's Mohamed Morsi. As long as Egypt's strongmen have stayed alive, they have sustained the perception of stability. The beginning and end of their reigns, however, have been uncertain, chaotic affairs.

At these moments of uncertainty, things that may not have been possible previously become possible. It is difficult, except in hindsight, to know whether one has lived through such a moment. But it shouldn't be controversial to say that individual agency is limited in conditions of dictatorship. This lack of agency is precisely what makes authoritarianism, whatever else its supposed benefits, so pernicious. Ordinary citizens are always at a profound disadvantage when trying to end repressive regimes. Such regimes have the means of considerable violence at their disposal, while dissidents must overcome collective action dilemmas to organize effectively.

One of the sadder lessons of the Arab Spring is that repression "works," at least in the near term. The trajectory of Arab uprisings couldn't have illustrated this more clearly. In the beginning, when Egypt's and Tunisia's strongmen suddenly fell, the power of the people—armed with little more than their smartphones and bravery—was idealized. The new conventional wisdom was that social media would be a thorn in the sides of autocrats. This was naïve. This more promising narrative also allowed the international community to let down its guard. If the people, assuming there were enough of them, could take matters into their own hands and bring down dictators, then the United States had no need to play a central role. The arc of history was bending toward justice, and apparently no one in particular had to help it bend.

But Hosni Mubarak's and Zine al-Abidine Ben Ali's early departures provided a cautionary tale for other autocrats hoping to hold on to power. There were two ways to interpret what happened to the Egyptian and Tunisian presidents. Either they were too stubborn and should have been more willing to compromise and offer concessions to the opposition—or they had conceded *too much* and should have instead taken a hard line, employing more brute force rather than less. This was the interpretation of the most repressive among them—the regimes of the UAE, Saudi Arabia, and Bahrain, and later the Sissi regime in Egypt. Gulf rulers employed a "zero tolerance" approach to impressive effect. On the one hand, they offered up massive social welfare benefits to citizens and subsidies to those employed by the state. This was the carrot. On the other hand, even the mildest hint of dissent would be nipped in the bud, with preemptive arrests and draconian prison sentences.

What could "people power" hope to accomplish in the face of determined autocrats who had no problem employing the vast resources of the state to coerce and silence? Citizens were no match for leaders who were willing to shoot and kill their own people. And one reason they were willing to arrest, torture, and kill is because they knew they could do so with little fear of sanction. And this was the part that was crucial.

Why Nonviolence Doesn't Work in the Middle East

People power—the crowds in the street, the citizens demanding their rights—is the lifeblood of democratic change, and for good reason. Nonviolent action—strikes, demonstrations, and civil disobedience taking place "outside the context of normal political, economic, or social behavior"[54]—has proven much more effective than violent insurrection. But there's a catch. The effectiveness of nonviolent action depends on how other countries, including the United States, react.

In *Why Civil Resistance Works,* Maria Stephan and Erica Chenoweth highlight the central role of external actors in the success or failure of nonviolent campaigns. "Externally, the international community is more likely to denounce and sanction states for repressing nonviolent campaigns than it is violent campaigns," they write.[55] If a regime employs excessive force against peaceful protesters, this is likely to provoke international outrage, particularly when journalists and ordinary citizens are able to share the images in real time. This results in "sympathy and a possible increase in legitimacy" as well as political and financial support from the international community.[56]

For protesters, the question of whether to resort to violence, even in self-defense, is one of tactics as much as principle. One may believe that violence against an oppressive regime is morally or religiously justified while also understanding that it is counterproductive and self-defeating. Once opposition groups choose to take up arms, the narrative is altered irrevocably. What was a story of citizens courageously risking their lives for freedom becomes transformed into a more complicated reality of armed factions and civil war. There is no longer a clear aggressor and a clear victim but a messier moral tale. International sympathy is less forthcoming as a result.

The purity of peaceful protest is compelling—which raises the question of why it hasn't been nearly as compelling in the Middle East. International sympathy came in the early days of the Arab uprisings, but it didn't last, even as regimes employed escalating force. The Rabaa massacre is perhaps the paradigmatic, tragic case. Tens of thousands gathered peacefully in the heart of Cairo, with perhaps unlicensed camping and the blocking of traffic as the extent of their violence. But Rabaa was just the latest in a long line of peaceful protests across the region that were met with repression: countrywide demonstrations in Algeria after the military canceled elections in 1992 or Islamist-led protests throughout the 2000s in countries like Jordan, Bahrain, and Egypt. In the latter case, despite the Bush administration's professed commitment to a "Freedom Agenda," the Mubarak regime spent the last two years of Bush's second term cracking down on an ascendant Muslim Brotherhood. That the victims of repression have tended to be Islamists made—and still makes—the decision easier for the United States and the international community. It is easier to look away when those on the receiving end of repression aren't quite Mandelas or Martin Luther Kings.

Islamists understood this well enough. During the eighteen-day Egyptian uprising from January 25 through February 11, 2011, Islamists were everywhere and nowhere at once.

Two days before Mubarak fell, on February 9, I remember Tahrir Square resembling something like a carnival, with food and beverage carts, music and joy, and an array of speakers' corners—wildly different in their ideological persuasions but managing to respect each other's carved-out spaces. I was interviewing Muslim Brotherhood activists that day, and their discipline was remarkable. Despite victory seeming closer at hand, they insisted on a low profile. Abdel Rahman Ayyash, then only twenty-one years old and already a prominent Brotherhood activist, exuded a nervous excitement. He was worried, particularly when it came to the Brotherhood's role in the uprising. "If it's ever perceived that this revolution is an Islamic one," he told me, "the U.S. and others will be able to justify a crackdown."[57]

The Brotherhood tried to stay out of the news, downplaying its participation. Behind the scenes, however, it provided pivotal support for the protesters. Where other groups tended to embrace the chaos inherent in spontaneous outpourings of mass sentiment, Brotherhood activists worked together to quietly provide food and medical services, offer protection from regime thugs, and generally keep order. Brotherhood officials, generally a cautious bunch who saw themselves as reformers rather than revolutionaries, instructed members to avoid ideological slogans. Why provide the regime with a pretext to crack down? They had waited this long. They also knew that the United States would be less willing to jettison Mubarak if the protests were associated with bearded Islamists and hijab-wearing women rather than young, liberal, English-speaking Twitter users. Those were the people we could be proud of supporting, because it reinforced the notion that good things (uprisings against dictators) led to other good things (youth empowerment and liberalism).

The protesters in Egypt, like protesters anywhere, hoped that if police used excessive force, condemnation would come swiftly—and where else might it come from but abroad? Without the glare of international media attention, regimes would be emboldened to use as much force as they could get away with. That could mean, among other things, firing into large crowds with live ammunition. The early massacres of the Arab Spring, in Syria and Libya, took place in countries that cared little about Western opprobrium. Luckily, in Egypt, much of the world was watching, and this constrained the ability (and willingness) of the army to back Mubarak and shed the blood of innocents on his behalf. If it had been a distinctly Islamist uprising, things might have turned out differently.

Over the last three decades, few if any instances of anti-Islamist repression in the Arab world have elicited significant international outrage or condemnation. This is a striking finding, especially since regimes tend to use more repression against Islamist groups than they do against secular ones. There are more opportunities to condemn anti-Islamist repression because it happens more often and on a larger scale, in part for the simple reason that there are more Islamists than secularists in the Middle East. Despite ample opportunities, however, it rarely happens.

Well before the Arab Spring began, the pattern was clear enough. A telling example—and one that occurred under the U.S. administration *most* willing to condemn regime repression—was the Muslim Brotherhood's campaign in support of judicial independence during 2006 and 2007 during George W. Bush's second term. As far as nonviolent campaigns with specific objectives go, it is largely forgotten, understandably so since quite a lot happened in the intervening years. The crisis started when the Egyptian authorities sent two judges to a disciplinary council after they criticized the government for rigging the vote and other irregularities during the 2005 parliamentary elections. Not only did they criticize, they also listed by name prominent judges allegedly involved in electoral fraud.[58]

The campaign in solidarity with the two judges intensified in April 2006 and continued through June. The Muslim Brotherhood was the largest and most prominent group in the broader effort. In one high-profile event, Brotherhood members of parliament staged a "stand-in", sporting black sashes that read "The People's Representatives with Egypt's Judges."[59] The Brotherhood also paid the highest price. Out of 700 or so people arrested, as many as 85 percent were from the Brotherhood.[60] To make matters worse, the government continued to retaliate even after the protests subsided, with Human Rights Watch reporting the detention of around 800 Brotherhood members in subsequent months.[61]

For an administration that still claimed to support a freedom agenda, the official U.S. response was almost a perfect encapsulation of what happens when Islamists lead protests that would otherwise be lauded if they had a different face. In a May 11, 2006 briefing, at the height of the regime crackdown, State Department spokesman Sean McCormack noted "our serious concern" at the treatment of protesters, but then went out of his way to remind anyone listening that the Brotherhood, as the primary organizer of the protests, remained an illegal organization "that is not allowed to be." In retrospect, this was an odd thing for an American official to focus on while people are being arrested en masse. It was also a misstatement of the Brotherhood's status. While the group was technically illegal, it had long been openly tolerated by Mubarak and was the largest opposition block in parliament. But McCormack, who wasn't exactly an Egypt expert, went further, stating that "the Egyptian Constitution says that . . . there should not be any political parties that are based on religion."[62]

The Tragedy of Islamist Opposition

Revolutions are rare. Mass protests are not. The latter are common features of democratic transitions, and it is difficult to think of a transition that didn't include some form of popular mobilization at a critical moment when the outcome was in doubt. Without such mobilization, autocrats have little reason to cede power. Mass protests signal to Western protectors of a regime—and the international community more broadly—that stability is no longer a given, and that if one protest is quashed, there will likely be another.

Considering the central role that nonviolent protest plays in democratization, the inefficacy of protests in the context of the Middle East is noteworthy. Without effective protests, successful democratic transitions are unlikely. We can take this analysis one or two steps further. Mainstream Islamist organizations like the Muslim Brotherhood have long been the largest opposition groups in most Arab countries. Islamists are well aware of the analysis above—that the United States and other Western powers are unlikely to come to their defense if they stage large-scale protests. This has had the effect of making the Islamist opposition less willing to directly confront authoritarian regimes. It has also made the regimes themselves more willing to repress nonviolent protest, knowing as they do that such repression will elicit minimal international condemnation.

Without international cover, Islamists have little incentive to lead protests or take any kind of bold action to challenge incumbent regimes. In rare instances, such as the uprisings in early 2011 that spread across the region, this is not an insurmountable problem. With spontaneous and leaderless mass mobilization, groups like the Brotherhood do not need to play the central role. And to the extent that they support an uprising, as they did in Tahrir Square over the course of those eighteen days, they can cleverly obscure their role. But Egyptians, or anyone else for that matter, should not have to wait for such unusual moments. In "normal" times, what most democratic transitions require is an opposition that is willing to push, confront, and challenge. In one study on when and how competitive authoritarian regimes lose power in elections, the political scientists Marc Morjé Howard and Philip Roessler identify a strong, unified, and mobilized opposition coalition as the most significant factor.[63] Islamist groups may be strong, but they have generally been unwilling to fully mobilize their institutional networks and massive grassroots support against existing regimes.

To be sure, such failures of mobilization are not solely the fault of Islamists. Arab governments are particularly good at sowing divisions within opposition ranks, and secular and liberal groups have often been hesitant to forge close ties with their Islamist counterparts. As the largest parties in most opposition alliances, however, Islamists do shoulder a significant share of the blame. They all too often retreat into caution, waiting for political openings they can take advantage of after the fact, rather than creating those openings themselves. The guiding principle of Muslim Brotherhood–inspired movements has been "reform over revolution" for a reason.

Islamist parties are not "normal" Western-style parties, and this contributes to their risk aversion. Because their legitimacy and grassroots support come primarily from their social and educational activities and not parliamentary representation as such, Islamists privilege self-preservation over political contestation. Their electoral success is dependent on the success of their charity and social service activities, and not the other way around.

A group like the Brotherhood isn't just interested in winning elections or gaining political power. It is interested in transforming society, and it attempts to do so through a network of parallel institutions that includes mosques, hospitals, clinics, banks, businesses, daycare centers, and even Boy Scout troops. A movement that essentially operates as a mini-state is particularly sensitive to repression. Repression is not just a matter of rigging elections, punishing speech, or arresting dissidents—although all of that is bad enough—but of undermining the vast organizational structure that serves as the engine of the Islamic movement. The costs of a crackdown that would shut down their social, educational, and preaching activities is simply be too high. Whether repressive measures are actually exercised is not the point. The point is that they *can* be. This fear leads Islamist parties to seek accommodation with the state, even as they oppose it. And they know that few things provoke regimes more than mass protests where people say things like "down with the regime."

At the same time, be careful what you wish for. Islamist caution isn't necessarily a good thing, especially when it comes to democracy. In the Arab world, Islamist movements are almost always the largest opposition groups. So if they become neutralized, there aren't obvious alternatives to pick up the slack. An opposition that chooses not to oppose is a godsend for regimes. Morocco is an instructive case. Often considered a model of "moderation," the Justice and Development Party (PJD), the country's main Islamist party, took its nonconfrontational posture to something of an extreme (if such a thing as extremism in the name of nonconfrontation is possible).

The PJD has always, in a sense, been an opposition party, but one so cautious that when it finally won an election and became the lead party in a coalition government, it did little to challenge the country's real power—the king and his royal court.[64] When I started writing this book, the prime minister of Morocco, ostensibly the head of government, was an Islamist and a member of the PJD. It was a fact that was easy to forget, considering how deferential he was, perpetually careful to avoid displeasing the king. The political scientists Holger Albrecht and Eva Wegner use the phrase "anticipatory obedience" to describe the PJD's strategy. "The leadership of the [PJD] has aimed to reassure the palace that it would play by its rules," they write. "Indeed, the party's readiness to help legitimize the regime is remarkable."[65]

The bargain in Morocco has been both clear and constraining. The PJD accepted the confines of a system in which the monarchy has veto power over all major decisions. In return, the PJD is allowed to legally exist, participate, and even enjoy a bit of power—but only a bit. In practice, this means that the PJD cannot meaningfully alter or transform the country's politics.[66] But this may be a feature rather than a bug. Compared to Islamist parties elsewhere, the PJD has it rather good. Its members aren't in prison. It can, and did, serve in government. They don't have to hide who they are. Their affiliated religious movement, Tawhid wal Islah, can operate mosques, hospitals, and charity organizations without fearing that bank accounts might be frozen or assets seized. This, in turn, allows them to do the slow and quiet work of organizing and preaching in the broader society. The one thing they cannot do is challenge the political and religious authority of the king.

All of this might be fine for the PJD and its abiding interest in self-preservation. It is not, however, fine for Morocco's democratic prospects.

Because of its bargain with the monarchy, the PJD—which might have otherwise been a powerful pro-democracy force and opposition party—has been neutralized. So if democracy ever comes to be in Morocco, it will need to happen not through the PJD but in spite of it.

This basic bargain—access, survival, and legalization in exchange for "obedience"—has been replicated to various degrees across the region. And, in the process, Islamist parties have all too often become obstacles to the very thing that they ostensibly seek. They have become obstacles to democracy.

The Role of the International Community

Mainstream Islamist movements have failed to play the role that true opposition parties must play for democracy to emerge. In this respect, Islamist exceptionalism helps to account for the Arab world's exceptional resistance to democratization. And Western democracies, including the United States, have contributed to this state of affairs, often unwittingly. It probably hasn't occurred to most American policymakers that *their* calculations have shaped Islamist calculations of whether holding mass protests is even worth it.

Of course, Islamists themselves have an interest in overdramatizing and overestimating the extent to which they are powerless in the face of nefarious forces beyond their control, while at the same time loudly raising the specter of American decline. They are wrong that these forces are "nefarious." The truth is only slightly more encouraging: U.S. officials don't hate Islamist parties or want to destroy them. They don't mutter to themselves in the morning that "democracy in the Middle East must be stopped." Individual policymakers may even be well intentioned, but they are often uncomfortable with the idea of Islamists and Islamism. Prosaic and unremarkable, this is what it often comes down to.

But Islamist leaders *are* correct about the basic premise, even if they exaggerate it and use it as an excuse to elide responsibility for their own mistakes and missteps. They call it the "American veto," and it means exactly what it says. I remember what the Brotherhood's Esam al-Erian, now deceased after a long prison stint after the 2013 coup, told me in 2008 just as Obama was about to become president. "Even if you come to power through democratic means," he said, "you are facing an international community that doesn't accept the existence of Islamist representation. . . . I think this will continue to present an obstacle for us."[67]

Over the last few decades, particularly since the Algerian coup of 1992, Islamist leaders have internalized the notion that the United States will not support them if they call for democracy; the United States will not stand up for their rights when they are arrested; and the United States will offer, at best, only light condemnations when their protests are quashed through force. This only exacerbates Islamists' longstanding preoccupation with survival above all else. In such a survival mode, democracy is a luxury they can't afford to advocate for too strongly. And what's the point of believing democracy is possible, considering that even the millions who took to the streets during the Arab Spring weren't enough to make it happen? When you're facing extreme repression, merely being allowed to live must seem rather wonderful.

How External Actors Can Influence Islamist Behavior

The United States is powerful but not all-powerful. It cannot change the way Islamists think, nor should it try. But Washington *can* begin to reshape the overall context that finds Islamist movements unwilling to mobilize against regimes out of fear of repression. External actors can address this fear in a number of ways, first by encouraging cross-ideological coalitions. Islamists are more vulnerable to repression when they are isolated from other political forces. Forming coalitions with more liberal and "respected" groups gives Islamist parties political cover and makes it more difficult for governments to crack down on them with impunity.

While the United States cannot compel cooperation between groups with divergent ideologies, it can certainly encourage it. The United States, the European Union, and individual member states, either directly or indirectly through organizations working on the ground, can encourage otherwise disparate parties to make common cause. One example of this was the formation of Yemen's Joint Meeting Parties (JMP)—an alliance between the Muslim Brotherhood–linked Islah Party and the Yemeni Socialist Party to back a compromise presidential candidate in the 2006 elections—which resulted from discussions mediated by the U.S.-funded National Democratic Institute (NDI).[68] While NDI's budget comes from congressionally appropriated funding, it is insulated from direct executive branch interference and can set its own agenda and priorities. It does, however, take its cues from what American officials say and do. Leaders set the tone.

Then there is the role of rhetoric in encouraging Islamists to be or become "normal," as in other regions where opposition parties actually oppose. Let's imagine a future American president announcing a new democracy promotion strategy in the Middle East. Ultimately, the sort of hard policy shifts discussed earlier—such as suspending weapons sales or military aid—are essential. But rhetoric is important, too, as long as it goes beyond the standard, vague professions of support for democracy that were common enough during the Bush and Obama administrations. We know the United States says it wants to support democracy; the question is whether it actually can and will. And whether it will depends on addressing the Islamist dilemma. It would be a significant step in the right direction for a top U.S. official to state unequivocally, for the first time, that Washington would oppose repression against Islamist-led protests just as it would protests organized by secular or seemingly pro-American groups.

Knowing that the international community will back their right to participate and protest would empower the nonliberal opposition, particularly Islamists, to take greater risks and push more aggressively for democratic change. More consistent Western support for the rights of pro-democracy activists, regardless of ideological orientation, would alter the way opposition groups weigh the costs and benefits of mass mobilization. And, apart from the unexpected implosion of a regime, mass mobilization is one of the few paths to real and lasting democratic change.

* * *

The Arab Spring was supposed to be the inflection point where the wall of fear, built assiduously over decades, came crashing down. After they saw a succession of seemingly invincible autocrats falling, ordinary Arabs, the thinking went, would change and be changed, perhaps permanently. They would find themselves armed with the knowledge that they, too, had power, even if it wasn't a power based on the use of force. But the wall of fear was rebuilt rather quickly, and even if its foundations weren't necessarily stronger, the wall was now harder to scale. It was propped up by regimes' determined use of coercion not just against their own citizens but also against the citizens of *other* Arab countries.

Repression went transnational in a way that it hadn't before, led by two rising powers: Saudi Arabia and the UEmirates. Saudi Arabia had always been one of the most influential Arab countries by virtue of its oil wealth and custodianship of the two holy mosques. Ruled by a conglomerate of royals in a largely consensual manner, the country had avoided the impulsive and sometimes unpredictable tendencies of its republican neighbors. Not all dictatorships were created equal. There was the rule of one, and then the rule of the few. And then that changed.

Like so many, Saudi officials were caught off guard by the Arab revolutions. It dawned on them that their hold on power wasn't as secure as they thought. The American security umbrella was still there, of course, but Obama's apparent sidelining of a close ally, Mubarak, made them nervous. And then there was the Obama administration's prioritization of the Iran deal, which Gulf allies perceived as a means to the end of removing the possibility of an American or Israeli war with a nuclear Iran. To clip Iran's nuclear ambitions would offer its own kind of freedom. If Iran could be tamed, the United States would more easily be able to justify its pivot away from the Middle East and toward more important things (and regions).

The Gulf Factor

The overall geopolitical context produced by the Iran deal, then, was one of greater insecurity—at least from the perspective of allies in the region. That perceived insecurity, in turn, emboldened Saudi Arabia and the UAEUAE to play a stronger and ultimately more destabilizing role in the region. The most obvious example was the Saudi-led intervention in Yemen, which, despite being associated with the Trump administration in the popular imagination, began under an Obama administration that, despite its various moral qualms, provided critical military and logistical support to the Saudi war effort. Hal Brands points to the "panicked behavior by an exposed Saudi Arabia, whose effort to push back unilaterally against Tehran in early 2015 led it into a war in Yemen that further destabilized the region."[69]

The rise of Crown Prince Mohamed bin Salman, architect of the Yemen war, coincided with the adoption of a new "Saudi nationalism"[70] that was at once less Islamist and more confrontational. Domestic instability, or in this case the *fear* of domestic instability, can easily fuel regional conflict. Insecurity at home fuels insecurity abroad. For Saudi Arabia and the UAE, the Muslim Brotherhood, perhaps even more so than Iran, was an existential threat. After all, there was no plausible way Iran could destroy their regimes. Neither country had a large enough Shia population whose sympathy Iran could exploit. And Iran obviously wouldn't try to directly wage war against Saudi Arabia, since that would trigger U.S. retaliation.

The Brotherhood, on the other hand, was a challenger from within in more ways than one. The world's oldest Islamist movement was unusual in that it captured the dual nature of domestic and regional fears; it was a local as well as a regional threat, and it was difficult to disentangle the two. This didn't mean that the Brotherhood was some shadowy international force pulling the strings of local branches. If anything, the opposite was closer to the truth. The Brotherhood's "international organization" was almost entirely toothless and served mostly as a coordinating and advisory body. Individual branches in the Gulf have increasingly gone their own way. The most well-known example of the prioritization of the local over the transnational came during the Gulf War when Kuwait's Muslim Brotherhood, diverging from other branches, backed the U.S. invasion of Iraq. Even referring to them as "branches" is misleading. To the extent that branches remain formally affiliated with the international organization, they are branches in name only.

All of this might suggest an ebbing of regime fears. If there was no Islamist "Comintern,"[71] then why all the paranoia? Part of the answer is that, as the international Brotherhood weakened or became irrelevant, individual Brotherhood affiliates increasingly focused the bulk of their attention on local concerns and domestic grievances. And many of those grievances had to do with mounting repression and the near total lack of democracy at home. Unlike, say, Kuwait, Saudi Arabia and the UAE remain resolutely opposed to any political opening. As Courtney Freer, a leading scholar of Islamism in the Gulf, notes:

> The more the Brotherhood is seen as a viable domestic political actor, either by working with secular opposition or by holding political sway through ministerial positions in government, the more dangerous it is considered, and thus likelier a crackdown will result.[72]

Ironically, however, such crackdowns are "justified by the use of rhetoric about the threatening nature of the transnational Muslim Brotherhood, despite the fact that the organization's involvement in local political life often violates some of the transnational movement's initial goals."[73]

For these Gulf regimes, the Brotherhood is the worst of both worlds. It's not *that* much of a transnational threat in an organizational sense, but Brotherhood affiliates do pay attention to their counterparts elsewhere in the region. Ideas and strategies travel organically and sometimes un-expectedly. Lessons are learned about what works and what does not. If a Brotherhood branch succeeds in one country and gains power, it can't help but embolden other like-minded groups. As the political scientists Donatella Della Porta and Sidney Tarrow point out, this kind of diffusion "does not in-volve connections across borders, but only that challengers in one country or region adopt or adapt organizational forms, collective action frames, or targets of those in other countries or regions."[74] The Muslim Brotherhood is a remarkably flexible movement. The Brotherhood believes in implementing sharia. By design, however, its founder Hassan al-Banna imprinted a pur-poseful vagueness when it came to *how* sharia might be implemented in any particular context. It was easy to become an Islamist. All you had to do was believe in the basic premise of Islamism—that Islam should play a central role in public life and politics and that individuals should organize politi-cally around that goal. This was a powerful idea, and one that was, at least in theory, accessible to most Muslims. It was also an idea that could travel across borders and adapt itself to any particular national context, in part be-cause it was pleasantly vague.

The (brief) rise of Islamist movements from 2011 to 2013 fueled the re-gionalization of Arab politics. But this regionalization had the counterintu-itive effect of highlighting local specificity. It became clear, for instance, that the Syrian Muslim Brotherhood's challenges and priorities were completely different than those of Tunisian Islamists in the Ennahda party. The former was dealing with a civil war and debating whether to engage in armed resist-ance,[75] while the latter was trying to govern in the context of a democratic transition in a relatively secular society. It was this local specificity—under a broader umbrella of shared Islamist ideas that could travel easily—that rat-tled authoritarian regimes and pushed them to crack down on the Islamist opposition.

Repression goes hand in hand with the nation-state. And no one does it "better" than strong, bureaucratized, and centralized states. In different ways and to differing degrees, Arab regimes have wielded the authority and ma-chinery inherent in the nation-state to reify it, giving it an almost religious character. The mantra might as well be something like "the State above all."[76] It might accept the nation-state, however grudgingly, but the Brotherhood diverges considerably from the narrow national consensus that regimes have hoped to impose on the larger public. It also presents an alternative source of religious legitimacy, and few things are more threatening than this, particularly for countries like Saudi Arabia that have long relied on a particular kind of religious legitimacy. Because Islam is resonant in the public sphere, religion becomes not merely a private matter but also a question of national security.

This puts international observers in something of a bind: stronger, more effective states are better at implementing economic reforms, combating terrorist networks, and claiming a monopoly over the use of force. Yet improving state effectiveness, at least in the context of the Middle East, tends to strengthen and entrench the repressive capabilities of those same states. Weak states, of course, are a problem, but so, too, are strong states. And, for decades, the United States has been invested in keeping these states strong and, where possible, "stronger." Stronger might not be exactly the right word, since there is a brittleness there. Leaders themselves are aware of this brittleness. It's what fuels their insecurity, paranoia, and the perception that escalating levels of repression are needed for survival.

To have such an unconducive regional environment for democratization is a marked shift from previous eras. It was always bad, but now, with three of the most influential Arab countries—Saudi Arabia, the UAE, and Egypt—promoting extreme repression both at home and abroad, it is worse. This less conducive environment is often used by American policymakers as a justification for deprioritizing democracy promotion.* This is an odd argument to make, since U.S. policy is one of the *causes* of such an environment. In effect, then, American officials are arguing that we can't promote democracy because of the things we did in the past to make democracy harder to promote.

Transforming the Regional Context

The regionalization of repression means that any democracy promotion strategy must be similarly regional in both conception and implementation. Before anything else, the United States would need to dissuade its own allies

---

* In my interviews with current and former U.S. officials, the role of Saudi Arabia and the UAE came up repeatedly, with or without prompting. I expected this to *some* extent, but the degree to which it figured prominently was still surprising. This led me to revise parts of the book, in the hope of better reflecting what might be called the misfortune of having bad allies. This remark from a former assistant secretary of state captures it well: "I don't think Egypt's that important for us anymore but I'm not ready to go through the entire disengagement with all the Gulf friends, which would happen if we suddenly disengage with Egypt because the Gulf can be such a nuisance elsewhere. This question of Egypt becomes part of our discussion with the Gulf."

from undermining its efforts. If an administration is trying to avert a coup, then it can't have UAE officials simultaneously telling the Egyptian military, "If the U.S. cuts your aid, we will make it up."[77] This should go without saying. If the United States prioritizes a diplomatic initiative, then it shouldn't be too much to ask a close ally to stand back and not undermine said initiative— even more so when the ally in question depends on the United States for its own security. As Elliot Abrams, one of George W. Bush's top national security aides, told me:

> If any president makes the decision, "we're going to go all in and stop this coup," then you have to say to [the UAE and Saudi Arabia], "I don't want to see you there next week bailing Sissi out and announcing a deposit of a billion dollars, don't do it." Now, that requires leadership. At certain points, I think Bush and Obama could have done that. Could Biden do it today? I don't think so. So you need a president who is strong and committed to this.[78]

This first step removes obstacles, but it doesn't necessarily provide an affirmative vision that others can get behind. A regional vision requires an offering of carrots and not just sticks. One way of doing this is through a signature initiative that elicits attention and controversy and sets broad, even sweeping objectives but also has some practical effect. During the Arab Spring, former State Department advisor Peter Mandaville and I proposed a "Multilateral Endowment for Reform" (MER) with an initial funding stream of $5 billion and a goal to reach $20 billion in ten years, with contributions from the EUnion, individual EU member states, Norway, Japan, South Korea, and others. Rather than relying solely on ad hoc, country-specific initiatives, a regional reform endowment would provide an overarching framework to reground American policy in the Middle East.

Unlike other funds or endowments, the MER would focus exclusively on *democracy* and not any of the other things that pass as democracy but are more about liberalism, religious pluralism, or minority rights. These may be important things, in theory, but in practice they all too often redound to the benefit of autocrats. Regimes are happy to weaponize gender equality and minority rights to curry favor with secular elites and legitimize themselves in the court of international opinion. Increasing women's representation in parliament with gender quotas, for example, gives the appearance of progress without the substance. A weak parliament with more women is still a weak parliament. It might even be *weaker*. According to a 2012 survey experiment conducted by Sarah Sunn Bush and Amaney Jamal, gender quotas can end up depressing popular support for women's representation.[79]

Much of what falls under U.S. "democracy assistance" programming isn't actually about promoting democracy, since it doesn't—and isn't necessarily even intended to—weaken the hold of authoritarian regimes. The MER, then, would prioritize structural and explicitly political reforms. The "multilateral" part is also key. At the start of the Arab Spring, various initiatives were announced with little follow-up and limited coordination, which meant that the whole ended up being far less than the sum of its parts. (The contents of the much hyped Deauville Partnership, announced by the G8 in the spring of 2011, remain a mystery to this very day.) As Mandaville and I wrote at the time, what is needed is a "single, dedicated mechanism for aggregating, programming, and disbursing large-scale assistance focused on democratic reform in the Middle East."[80]

Briefly, the MER would be constructed as follows. Conceptually, it would take its lead from innovations in large-scale development assistance such as the Bush administration's Millennium Challenge Corporation, which established a firm linkage between governance quality and economic aid. Based on reform goals agreed to jointly by the Endowment, partner governments, and civil society, the MER would disburse funds against reform commitments by partner governments. Mechanisms of accountability would be built into all partnerships, with clear and enforceable benchmarks, ongoing monitoring, and transparent criteria for suspension or termination of funding if reform commitments are not met.

With the rising tide of nationalism, the idea of external "interference" isn't exactly in vogue, and many leaders will no doubt interpret it as such. That's fine. They can decide to reject it. However, due to the endowment structure, unused funds would be reinvested and accumulate over time. In such circumstances, politicians in cash-strapped countries might be hard-pressed to justify rejecting billions in international support. In the event of democratic transitions, such support can give political cover to democratically elected leaders—Islamist and secular alike—in their efforts to restructure corrupt government bureaucracies and institutions.

The temptation to dilute "reform" will always be there. Certain reform commitments, particularly those focused on technical and regulatory issues, will always be easier to stomach for autocratic allies. Such initiatives are sometimes grouped under the framework of "good governance," a convenient substitute for democracy, since even a dictator can (at least in theory) be good at governing. To avoid these pitfalls, the MER would need to be insulated from political considerations. It would maintain this distance by operating according to a mechanism that holds both parties—the MER and the partner government—accountable to a set of publicly agreed upon benchmarks. If the benchmarks are not met, then funds don't flow, no matter how strategically important the country might be to the United States or other international donors.

Partial democracies like Iraq and Lebanon and "soft" authoritarian regimes like Morocco and Jordan would be eligible. For a country like Morocco, potential benchmarks could include expanding parliament's authority and introducing checks and balances on the king's prerogatives. The goal would be substantive, measurable progress toward constitutional monarchy. For Jordan, difficult but plausible benchmarks could include having the prime minister drawn from the ranks of parliament rather than appointed by royal decree.

Yes, this might all sound a bit technical and wonky. But there is a broader purpose beyond the details: For the first time, a major and enduring commitment to Arab democracy—wholly separate from the short-term obsession with "stability"—would be institutionalized as a permanent part of U.S. foreign policy. The pomp of policy is often superficial, but the unveiling of a signature initiative can help set the tone for the whole of government and put skeptics and competitors in the region on notice. The pomp is better off coming after the policy and not before, though. Grand rhetoric, no matter how impeccably communicated, is no substitute for action, as quickly became evident after the Deauville Partnership was launched (or for that matter after Obama's 2009 Cairo speech).

It is difficult for me to imagine an American president championing an initiative like the one outlined above. But it becomes easier to imagine if two or three Arab countries experience mass uprisings, surprise coups, or succession crises in the coming decade. Then, the United States will be compelled once again to think more strategically about a region it might have otherwise hoped to ignore.

* * *

In writing this book, I am reminded of the tension—one might call it a dilemma—that anyone writing about policy with a hope of changing it must contend with. There are two general ways of thinking about writing on

U.S. foreign policy. One is to take the contours of existing policy as a given and to work within those constraints, to accept the world as it is without necessarily resigning yourself to it. Any given policy recommendation must be something that current officials could conceivably implement in this world, rather than the counterfactual world of our imaginations. Under this first tendency, large chunks of this book might seem intriguing if fantastical.

The problem with the "realistic" approach is that it, in effect, narrows the debate and casts those offering alternative frameworks as naive dreamers unschooled in the ways of the world. It also presumes that things will always be as they were (or are). This mindset is distorting for obvious reasons. It cannot account for dramatic changes that occur within short spans of time. To be oblivious to such dramatic possibilities is understandable and quite rational, since dramatic change *is* rare. On any given day an uprising is improbable, at best. But a president's term in office consists of 365 days, and there are more than twenty countries in the Middle East and North Africa.

The second approach, which is the one I adopt here, is to write with a mind to the unpredictability of international affairs. Here, the guiding principle is to *not* accept "reality" as a given and to instead write about what can and should happen. I'm someone who believes that authoritarian regimes are unpredictable in predictable ways. But even I have to remind myself that things that seem beyond the realm of possibility can become possible sooner than we might expect. I know any number of friends and colleagues in the democracy promotion community who have basically given up out of a sense of futility. They do what they can, but they know that their life's work is something like a Sisyphean struggle. And so they trudge along in disillusionment. Sometimes this is how I feel, too. I found these chapters hard to write since they are so at odds with U.S. foreign policy as we conceive it today.

If prior experience is any guide, every presidential term in my adult life has featured its share of surprises and outright black swans. Some of those surprises happened organically and came from within the region, while some were a product of the decisions of external actors. Most, however, were a mix of both (since what individuals or governments do in a given Middle Eastern country is shaped partly by their perceptions of what the United States has and hasn't done in the past).

Until these accidents of fate come to pass, the second approach aims to appeal to a wider audience and influence the public debate, in the hope of shifting the contours of what is considered "possible" or "realistic." It bides its time, waiting for the moment when the important overtakes the urgent.

It assumes that this moment will come (eventually) and plans accordingly. In this sense, the relative scarcity of world historical moments like the Arab uprisings is both a blessing and a curse. The rarity of such moments is good insofar as it allows time to build, plan, and anticipate. But their rarity along with their unpredictability means that the incentives to build, plan, and anticipate are fairly limited, particularly for politicians and officials with short time horizons and shorter attention spans.

What counts as realistic or unrealistic, then, is a matter of perspective. Is one thinking about what matters most now or what might matter more later? What I believe we can say with some degree of confidence is that the realistic approach, however realistic it may have been, did not help produce a more "stable" region in any meaningful sense of the word. If *this* is what stability looks like, then we might be better off doing away with the term since it can claim upon us no shared meaning.

Short of the wholesale reorientation in American policy that I propose, however, perhaps it is better—and more realistic—to tinker around the margins, search for small wins, and make U.S. policy in the region at least a little bit better than it has been. I would certainly hope that those operating within the constraints in question—namely American policymakers—do the best they can under whatever circumstances they find themselves in. But if outside analysts confine themselves to this approach, then it entrenches the status quo and distracts from addressing foundational questions. If the foundation is in fact weak, outdated, and corrupt, then insisting on building on top of it will only offer a succession of pyrrhic victories.

8

Islamists in Government

At times, in his memoir *A Promised Land*, Barack Obama sounds a little bit like me—or any other critic of Arab dictatorships. He recalls telling an aide after his first trip to the region that "sometime, somewhere things are going to blow."[1]

But he is conflicted. In the few pages Obama devotes to the Arab Spring, his concerns that the Muslim Brotherhood would rise to power through elections and undermine the U.S.–Egypt relationship figure prominently, perhaps too prominently. If Obama was a closet Brotherhood member, he was doing an awfully good job of hiding it. It might be asking too much of a president to think carefully about something as complicated as Islamism. But all he musters is that the Brotherhood's central goal was to see "the entire Arab world governed by sharia law."[2] What did President Obama mean by this exactly?

The question of what Islamists would *really* do in power is an important one. It is also one of those questions that both can and cannot be answered. No answer is satisfying, in part because the question is so speculative about something that is already quite vague. Which Islamists and in what country and what kind of power would they actually have? This is a question about the future. We can also ask about the past. What would have become of Algeria if Islamists had been allowed to win in 1992? What would Egypt have become if Mohamed Morsi and the Muslim Brotherhood weren't deposed in the summer of 2013?

These histories of what might have been aren't mere intellectual indulgences for idle minds. As Niall Ferguson writes in *Virtual History*: "The business of imagining such counterfactuals is a vital part of the way in which we learn. Because decisions about the future are—usually—based on weighing up the potential consequences of alternative courses of action, it makes sense to compare the actual outcomes of what we did in the past with the conceivable outcomes of what we might have done."[3] What might the United States have done differently during key moments? Based on this assessment of the past, what can or should the United States do differently in the future?

How one answers these questions depends on how they view the alternative history, a history where Islamist parties remained in power for some unspecified—and perhaps long—period of time. In Egypt, Morsi was increasingly unpopular, but the Brotherhood would have still likely won a plurality in the next parliamentary elections for the simple reason that there was no obvious party to take its place. Non-Islamist parties were fragmented, having little in common with one another beyond their dislike of Islamists. Meanwhile, the second-largest party was the ultraconservative Salafi Nour party, outflanking the Brotherhood from the right, so that wasn't necessarily encouraging either.

The question of what Islamists want is difficult to answer in part because they themselves don't quite know what they want, a problem that simultaneously reflects and fuels their ambivalence toward power, particularly after the debacle of Mohamed Morsi's year as president. Moreover, since Islamist parties have so rarely held executive authority, any blunders tend to taint the broader Islamist endeavor. So Morsi's failures end up being an albatross for Islamist parties thousands of miles away, however much they try to distance themselves from his failures. As Rachid Ghannouchi, the leader of Tunisia's Ennahda party, once put it: "The most dangerous thing for the Islamists is to be loved by the people before they get to power and then hated afterward."[4]

When he founded the Brotherhood in 1928, Hassan al-Banna had no precise governance model, but this was a feature rather than a bug, allowing the movement to appeal to a diverse group of Muslims, who might have been spooked had Banna outlined specific—and presumably controversial—positions on thorny topics. Some things were better left to the imagination, particularly as different national contexts would require different approaches. This allowed each Brotherhood affiliate, whether in Jordan, Kuwait, or Syria, to adapt Banna's core principles to their local environments.

Hovering within generality and abstraction is the task of any big-tent movement, and this is what Banna wanted most for the Brotherhood. This was not meant to be a small vanguard of elites. It was meant to be a *movement*, and a movement required numbers, the larger the better. Banna's recruitment strategy reflected this. He traveled across the country, visiting coffeehouses and talking to ordinary Egyptians about Islam and what Islam could do for them. As Banna recounts in his memoirs:

I selected three main coffeehouses which were always overcrowded with people. I made a program to deliver two sermons in every coffeehouse every week. And I delivered my sermons in these coffeehouses regularly. My way of preaching proved to be a matter of astonishment for the people in the beginning. But soon they got used to it and took great interest.[5]

In theory, every single Muslim was a potential recruit. Islamists believed that Islamism—although, for them, this was merely Islam—was the natural disposition of Muslims. If Muslims were practicing, as most were, and if they believed that Islam should play some role in politics, as most did, then there was no reason to think they couldn't be won over. But the key to success would be a certain kind of strategic ambiguity. This is the same ambiguity that would dog Islamists for decades to come. Their purposeful vagueness led would-be friends and enemies to fear that they were dissembling, attempting to lull domestic critics and Western audiences alike into complacency.

This vagueness, however, is not something they can necessarily resolve, at least not easily. Islam, in its scripture as well as an accumulating corpus of law over the centuries, has had quite a lot to say about politics and public life. But modern politics, and especially the modern state, imposes its own constraints on what is possible. Islam was revealed—and then its legal structures developed—in a pre-modern context where nation-states did not exist, where the state was inherently limited in its ability to control and coerce, and where the idea of citizenship hadn't yet been fashioned. Islam, in other words, was not designed for the modern nation-state, and short of an act of God, the modern state is all we have for the foreseeable future.

Naturally, if God is revealing scripture, he will tailor that scripture to those receiving it—and the audience in this case was Prophet Mohamed and his companions. The task of Islamists, then, was to take pre-modern Islamic law and reconcile it with the demands of modern life and politics—as part of a broader political program that could appeal to disillusioned masses, who were suffering a crisis of confidence in the face of Western dominance. No one had attempted this before. In this respect, Islamism is best understood as an attempt to square an impossible circle.

Ideologies aim for coherence but inevitably fail. There were principles at the heart of Islamism that made it susceptible to being distorted by "Western" ideas, despite the ostensible anti-Westernism at its core. Because of their emphasis on practicality and rationality, Islamists had little recourse but to see the state as an engine for transforming society. Under Nasser and Sadat, the

Egyptian state centralized and promoted public education and hired millions of Egyptians to preside over a rapidly expanding bureaucracy. It became ever more intrusive in the lives of others. Egyptian humor featured the faceless, petty bureaucrat as one of its enduring archetypes. Low-level officials, lacking power in their own right, were able to crush the aspirations of even more lowly citizens with (or by withholding) the stroke of a pen.

Islamists, like everyone else, were products of this burgeoning bureaucratic state. Even as it failed to meet basic expectations, the state was everywhere. Even when it was absent, which was often enough, its absence was felt. And so Islamists came to see the state as both the source of and solution to their problems. They could bide their time, and then one day when the opportunity was ripe, they could acquire the levers of the state through democratic means. But to see the nation-state as the engine of Islamization was never the original premise of Islamism, in part because such a state did not exist when Hassan al-Banna founded the Brotherhood.

Over time, the Muslim Brotherhood came to believe in the state, not necessarily because it wanted to but because a mix of inertia, socialization, and a lack of alternatives made it difficult to resist. It might be dispiriting for anyone to see salvation in a state, but it must have been particularly dispiriting for groups like the Brotherhood that had been founded with a mind to Islamization from the bottom up rather than the top down.

This bottom-up gradualism was another reason why Hassan al-Banna and other early Brotherhood leaders could afford to be vague in their policy prescriptions. Islamic governance was not an immediate goal; instead, Islam would come to play a role in politics and government *naturally*, as a byproduct of more Muslims returning to their faith. Religious renewal would start with individuals. They would become Brotherhood members, and they would have wives and children. Islamic families would, over time, multiply and become Islamic communities. In this organic fashion, broader society would follow suit, slowly, gradually, and unmistakably. Norms and values would change. In turn, an Islamic society at the local level would naturally produce a more Islamic government on the national level. Of course, in retrospect, there were a number of steps missing in the process. What exactly was the concrete causal mechanism by which the Islamization of society would translate into Islamic governance, particularly when no one knew exactly what Islamic governance was meant to look like?

Upholding Islamic law had traditionally been more of a question of what *not* to do. As the legal scholar Mohamed Fadel writes, "Even the most diligent, fair-minded, and sincere ruler is incapable of knowing the public interest independently; and, second, the ruler is not permitted to legislate in a manner that contradicts Islamic law, but it is not possible for the ruler, by himself, to know whether his proposals are in conformity with the law without relying on the input of legal specialists."[6] Legal specialists, though, were hard to come by. The religious establishment, being an establishment, had been subsumed under an increasingly powerful state. An oddity in Western nations, almost every Arab country, no matter how "secular," ended up having a ministry of religious affairs, entrusted to regulate and oversee religious production and knowledge. Mosques would be registered and surveilled, their resident imams approved and appointed. Friday sermon guidance—or scripts to the letter—would be distributed ahead of time. Religious curriculums would be devised with the state's interests and security in mind.

As a result, Islamist movements like the Muslim Brotherhood in Egypt or Ennahda in Tunisia were—and still are—generally nonclerical or even anticlerical. They have few clerics in their senior ranks and fewer still who specialize in Islamic legal theory. Islamists were products of the modern world, and the nature of modern politics rendered the old arrangements null and void. In the great caliphates, the caliph was not a religious scholar and didn't need to be. The clerical class, in an inversion of what it would later become, maintained a significant degree of autonomy and local authority. And so Islamists, operating within the constrained canvas of modernity, found themselves fashioning "projects" and "programs" that were politically powerful but intellectually weak and philosophically unmoored. There was also no guarantee that they would ever come to power, at least not in anyone's actual lifetime, so there was rarely a sense of urgency. There would always be more time—until there was none.

A Question of Virtue

The Islamist theory of change relied on a questionable premise—that good individuals would lead to good governance, that an individual with virtue would emanate that virtue outward, somehow. As the French scholar Olivier Roy put it, in an observation that would grow only more prescient with time: "For the Islamists, Islamic society exists only through politics, but the political institutions function only as a result of the virtue of those who run them, a virtue that can become widespread only if the society is Islamic beforehand. It is a vicious circle."[7]

This preoccupation with virtue has proved a blind spot, leading Islamists to fall for fair-weather friends, including General Abdel Fattah al-Sissi, whom Morsi had appointed minister of defense under the impression that Sissi wasn't as bad as others in the military brass. Brotherhood leaders saw Sissi as devout (which was true). His wife and daughter wore the headscarf, which was unusual for Egyptian leaders, even though by the 1990s a large majority of Egyptian women were covering their hair. Until Mohamed Morsi, there had never been an Egyptian first lady who wore the hijab. But the Brotherhood made the error of assuming that someone who was religiously conservative would naturally incline toward Islamism more than someone who wasn't. This was true on average, for obvious reasons, but it was still a risky assumption to base one's political future on.

This preoccupation with individual virtue and moral conduct cuts across otherwise disparate Islamist groups. Tunisia's Ennahda party is an interesting case, because it opted to dilute its Islamism over time, presenting instead as a "Muslim democratic" party.[8] Having largely given up on articulating a distinctive ideological vision, it was easy for Ennahda to fall back on a simpler and more straightforward argument. As Ennahda leaders would sometimes describe it, their party was different not because of anything they might do; they were different because of who they were. I remember an odd but instructive conversation with Noureddin Erbaoui, a close associate of Rachid Ghannouchi and enthusiastic supporter of the party's new, gentler image.

I asked Erbaoui: When you talk about employment and putting people to work, why should voters think Ennahda would do a better job than secular parties that have more economists in their ranks and more experience in government? "The program of Ennahda, the program of [secular party] Nidaa Tounes, the programs of the others, they're similar," he admitted. "So, then, what makes me as a citizen vote for Ennahda? It's like what Erdogan said, 'we don't steal.'" To underscore the point, he offered an example of why people voted for Hamas over Fatah in the 2006 Palestinian elections:

> When Hamas gets funding for job-creation programs, out of 100 dinars, you know that 90 will go to people who deserve it, 10 dinars might get lost in some corruption. If you give the same 100 dinars to Fatah, 90 dinars will go to corruption, even though it's roughly the same program.[9]

I could tell that Erbaoui thought this sounded appealing to Western audiences. In this account, Islamists were just like secularists, but better because they were less corrupt. Erbaoui's comment, however innocuous it sounded, betrayed a belief that the religious commitments of Islamists made them not just better people but better politicians, too. This was still the traditional Islamist premise, but taken to a new extreme, ostensibly in the service of modernity and moderation. As Roy writes: "For Islamists, a discussion about institutions quickly turns into a discussion about determining the virtues and personal qualities of those qualified to fulfill the various functions."[10]

The institutional setup of the state is treated as a given. Instead of changing the foundations of the state in a way that centers Islam, the Islamist project is reduced to accepting existing structures, as if they always were and always will be, and then "Islamizing" them. This lends itself not to deep critiques but to superficial adaptations, and it is telling that "progressive" Islamist movements like Ennahda and conservative ones like the Egyptian Brotherhood have fallen into the same trap, but in different ways. This problem is in many ways inherent to Islamism, which was the successor ideology to the ascendant "Islamic modernism" of the late nineteenth and early twentieth centuries. The modernists—most prominent among them the pan-Islamic ideologue Jamal al-Din al-Afghani (d. 1897), the Egyptian theologian Mohamed Abduh (d. 1905), and the Levantine theorist Rashid Rida (d. 1935)—wished to regain God's pleasure by returning to the unblemished purity of Islam's founding. This itself was a very modern impulse. They believed that Islam had become ossified, buried under layer after layer of highly technical Qur'anic and legal commentaries. Scholars wrote commentaries about other commentaries. In this sense, they were skeptics of the pre-modern Islamic tradition and believed, perhaps counterintuitively, that Islam could be modernized by putting more emphasis on Islam's founding moment fourteen centuries ago. This would liberate Islam similar to how the Reformation intended to liberate Christians from the clerical despotism of medieval Catholicism.

Animated by a sense that something—and perhaps quite a lot—had gone wrong, the modernists wanted to close the gap between the Muslim world and the West. And it was this "overwhelming awareness of Muslim weakness relative to non-Muslim strength" that drove first Islamic modernism and then Islamism.[11] It wasn't just a reaction to modernity but a product of it. This preoccupation with modern things unmoored Islamism from Islam's "discursive tradition,"[12] and without a discursive tradition to animate it, Islamist movements could become surprisingly flexible for what were otherwise perceived to be rigid ideological organizations. But they were not rigid, and to think so is to misunderstand what Islamists hoped to accomplish.

Islam never experienced something resembling the Protestant Reformation—in part because it didn't need one. Within Christianity, the Reformation came about as a direct reply and challenge to the clerical despotism of the Catholic Church. In stark contrast, clerical domination was not the problem in the great Islamic empires. To be sure, the Islamic modernists were not impressed by clerics and their obscure passions, but by then the clerical class had been weakened considerably. Co-opted by the state, they fell into disrepute.[13]

Still, for both better and worse, the rise of Islamic modernism and Islamists was the closest analog to a reformation, even if they happened to be responding to secular rather than religious despotism. Like the Islamists after them, early Protestants may have been dogmatic and evangelical, but they were also theologically heterodox. The fact that there were Lutherans and Calvinists—but also Anglicans, Anabaptists, Mennonites, and so forth—suggested the scale of difficulty in fashioning coherent alternatives to Catholicism. Because of their desire to return to the pure, untainted sources of scripture, and their need to do away with the intervening Catholic legacy, they were surprisingly nimble in terms of doctrine, with each new sect going its own way.[14] This doctrinal chaos suggested an uncertainty and openness that was very much in line with modernity—the privileging of the individual and his or her relationship to God coupled with a deprioritizing of tradition. Likewise, Islamists were innovators. But innovators without a strong foundation could find themselves aimless.

The Brotherhood's most distinguishing characteristics bore various markers of the modern. These were not mystical movements concerned with the inner life; they were preoccupied with the outward manifestations of inner faith. No one could be a Muslim Brother in private. Brotherhood branches were preoccupied with inherently public and political questions of dignity and justice and how the nation-state undermined both. While they could, at times, fall back into the fatalism of movements that see humans humbled before God's majesty, they believed that societies could be changed through the collective power of individual acts. They were activists, above all, and activism did not lend itself to self-criticism or self-awareness. For a body as large as the Brotherhood became, looking inward would have presented an obstacle to concerted action. Activism, on the mass level, required loyalty and discipline, neither of which were necessarily the best means to deep intellectual exploration.

In the beginning, Banna's program was one of action and organization. He was not a theorist or thinker. He was a teacher, and he taught followers a relatively simple and straightforward way to re-engage with Islam and make it relevant to their daily lives. He spoke in broad strokes and was suspicious of theoretical digressions. Such digressions would only confuse and confound. As Ovamir Anjum writes, the Brotherhood's founder was a "master of synthesis and compromise."[15] In his epistles, Banna explains his approach: "I decided to write as I speak and to discuss my topic . . . without any false pretense or complexity. I simply wish people to understand me as I am, allowing my message to reach their minds devoid of any fancy ornament and decoration."[16]

In practice, the desire to synthesize a program of action for millions of supporters produced an ambivalence toward a classical Islamic tradition that was rich and dense—and often quite complex. Instead, because politics (and survival) required flexibility and pragmatism, groups like the Brotherhood often found themselves prioritizing good outcomes over good methodology. They did so by using sweeping *maslaha* (public interest) and *maqasid* arguments. Again, we return to the legacy of the modernists, who in their attempt to rationalize Islam and make it practical scoured the Islamic tradition for useful tools. They saw a need, and then they found what they were looking for. According to the principle of *maslaha*, the collective welfare of the *ummah* became an overarching consideration. Anything that was not explicitly discussed in a revealed text could be subject to an assessment of whether it would serve the general interest. This lent itself not to the question of whether something was right, but whether something would *work* in the sense of serving the interests of the larger Muslim community. Of course, since Islamic law was designed for individual salvation as much as worldly success, it was easy to get carried away by a results-oriented discourse.

To operationalize *maslaha*, one had to be aware of the *maqasid*, or the objectives of the sharia, since this would determine what constituted the public interest. In the classical tradition, jurists had identified five primary purposes of the law—the preservation of life, mind, religion, property, and offspring. After studying and searching, these were conclusions that scholars came to over time. Islamists took them as starting points and re-engineered the process of deduction backward, although not necessarily consciously. If a rule in the sharia—however Islamically sound—undermined life or property, then it could in effect be suspended out of *darura*, or necessity, if not necessarily discarded outright. For example, a man is normally forbidden from seeing a woman whom he is not married to unclothed, but if the only doctor available to treat a life-threatening injury is male, then treating the woman becomes permissible by necessity.[17] This might be an obvious case, but what if Islamists (or anyone else) insisted on applying the principle to less clear-cut examples? Necessity was the mother of invention, but it was also in the eye of the beholder.

Along similar lines, there was the interpretive backdoor of *'illa*, roughly translated as the legal "rationale" or "reasoning." Islamic injunctions—such as the prohibition on interest-bearing loans—contained within them a *'illa*. Once the reasoning was extracted from the rule, it could be used to generalize for a broader set of cases. Used liberally, this prioritization of the reason behind the injunction over the injunction itself offered a convenient workaround even for rules with an explicit basis in revealed text. The point of the rule was not the rule itself but the reasoning that led to the rule. In effect, the human (and fallible) endeavor of finding the *'illa* took precedence over revelation.[18]

Let us return, then, to the question of interest. If the original reason behind the prohibition of interest is that it leads to the unfair and unreasonable exploitation of the borrower, then the permissibility of modern, better regulated loan instruments could be judged according to whether they were "unfairly" exploitative. Perhaps they weren't. But who, exactly, decided what was unfair or exploitative? The emphasis on circumstantial reasoning is what would allow Islamists to lend their support to IMF loans, which, however unfair their terms, ultimately served the common good and the public interest. Of course, whether or not an IMF loan served the common good was not necessarily something everyone could agree on.

There was another modernist move that helped liberate Islamists from the letter of the law. Islamic theorists such as Rashid Rida sharpened the distinction between two categories of jurisprudence: *ibadat* and *mu'amalat*. The former covered acts of worship and one's individual relationship with God and could not be altered by circumstance or necessity. In other words, there could be no justification for praying three times instead of five or of changing the fast to entail refraining from only food and not drink. *Mu'amalat*, on the other hand, concerned the individual's relations with society, most of which wouldn't have been covered by revealed text. In the absence of any explicit textual injunction to the contrary, *mu'amalat* was a category of constant change and flexibility, subject to considerable interpretative latitude based on the needs of place and time.

All of these premises and principles existed in the classical Islamic tradition, but the modern innovation was assembling them together, in somewhat haphazard fashion, and synthesizing them as part of a whole that was larger—and more radical—than the sum of its parts.

Preoccupied with reviving Islam in the face of a Western cultural onslaught, Islamists inadvertently managed to liberate themselves from the traditional constraints of Islamic jurisprudence. As the legal theorist Wael Hallaq writes of Rashid Rida, "[His] anchoring of all law (i.e., of *mu'amalat*, defined by Western legal standards as law proper) in the otherwise limited concept of necessity, which in turn is validated by the principle of *maslaha*, amounts, in the final analysis, to a total negation of traditional legal theory."[19]

In arguing that necessity and the common good were not just overarching principles but *overriding* principles, reason and rationality filled the gap where the constraints of law once were. Islamists, in other words, weren't what most Westerners thought they were—superstitious, backward, or fundamentalist; they were rationalists par excellence. This was fine as far as it went—it was probably better than being irrational, after all—but there was a final step, and it was this step that magnified the perils of relying on rationalist tools of reinterpretation: the matter not of what but of who. The tools were there, but who would implement them? In the pre-modern era, law was decentralized. The state mattered, but it wasn't all that mattered. The clerical class retained significant autonomy. In the twentieth century, however, the nation-state became the central actor and increasingly the only actor of note when it came to legislating and executing law. There was another tool at the behest of authorities, and it was known as *siyasa shar'iya*, or discretionary law. Here, the caliph would execute public law based on the state's needs as long as the laws in question did not obviously contradict the sharia as understood by the clerical establishment. In effect, this was legislation that agreed with the spirit of the sharia "without being bound by its text."[20]

In the context of the modern state, the problem—or solution, depending on your perspective—was that the state was no longer bound by a religious establishment. The religious establishment was now *within* the state, co-opted and subsumed. Now, it was the state that used its discretion as it wished, with its newly centralized power. What was necessary for the state was necessary for Islam, or vice versa. Try as they might, there was no real way for Islamists to escape this sort of thinking. After all, they had spoken of necessity and the public interest, which could easily be transmuted to the "national interest." And the national interest was the state's interest, and so on. These state-centric implications became obvious with Islamists' emphasis on *tatbiq al-sharia*, or the application of sharia. It was perhaps Islamists' most uttered mantra after "Islam is the solution." But who would apply the sharia? Again, there was a clear answer, if not necessarily an encouraging one.

For Islamists, sharia wasn't something that arose organically as a natural outcome of jurisprudential efforts on the local level. It was to be consciously applied, and this meant that they had little choice but to fall back on the state as the means of Islamic transformation. If the Islamist project was about applying Islamic law, then it meant the state would have to apply it, because it was only the state that could. This role for the state was justified by necessity, and the state justified its policies by necessity.

The problem for Islamists, though, was that the wrong people were in charge of the state, and this is what prevented the implementation of sharia. In many Arab states, even ostensibly secular ones, the constitution included a clause on the sharia as a, or *the*, principal source of legislation. The state's machinery was satisfactory, and constitutions, however vague, made Islam's cause legitimate. It was just a matter, then, of doing what the constitution allowed and what the people wanted. This, perhaps, was and still is the most innovative—and controversial—of Islamist contributions. If it was no longer clerics who determined laws and channeled God's will, then someone else would have to, and it would be "the people," as represented not by scholars but by their own elected representatives. In his book *The Caliphate of Man*, the political theorist Andrew March argues that this was "a genuine intellectual revolution."[21] The people would be elevated as the "ultimate arbiters of God's law."[22]

Indeed, Brotherhood-inspired parties and movements have undergone one of the more remarkable ideological shifts of the past several decades. While embracing the democratic process and the idea of popular sovereignty may not seem groundbreaking, for Islamists it was. There was no particular reason why Islamic government should be democratic, and for much of the twentieth century, most works of Islamic political theory had little use for political pluralism and free elections. In 1969's *Preachers Not Judges*, one of the key works expounding on the Brotherhood's understanding of the Islamic state, General Guide[23] Hassan al-Houdaiby stays well within the bounds of orthodoxy. Drawing on the writing of medieval scholars, he calls for the revival of the caliphate. As Houdaiby sees it, the job of the executive is simply to implement the preexisting corpus of Islamic law. The leader, *imam al-haqq*, rather than being elected through open, popular vote, must meet the prerequisites of Islamic education and fitness of character. As Barbara Zollner notes, "[Houdaiby] does not even consider the possibility of an Islamic state without the leadership of the *imam al-haqq*."[24] What Islamists, in time, would become reflects a striking departure from Houdaiby's thinking.

With the end of the Cold War, the democratic idea was in vogue. Islamists, like nearly everyone else, understood that the United States was ascendant. As Washington redoubled support for autocrats, using America's own rhetoric against its actions was an easy and obvious gambit. Importantly, Islamists came to the realization that democracy was useful, since they were the ones most likely to win—a stark reversal from the 1960s, when they would have been more than happy with a handful of parliamentary seats. Central to democracy was the notion that legitimacy came from the people rather than God. Before the Islamic awakening, the "people" were still dangerous since they were more likely to vote for socialists than Islamists. The will of the majority would easily come into conflict with that of God.

It was, in this sense, the very fact of an Islamic revival in the 1970s and 80s—and not any real ideological reappraisal—that produced a growing acceptance of democracy. In other words, Muslims' growing religiosity and Islam's rising stature are what caused, if indirectly, democracy to become normalized in public discourse. Once Islamist groups saw that Muslims wanted more religion in politics, it became safe to want more democracy in politics. Democratic politics became the best way to secure Islamist objectives, and so it remains today. As Muslim Brotherhood branches and affiliates emerged as the largest and most influential sociopolitical movements across the Middle East, they set the tone for broader public debates. And if supposed defenders of the faith had come to terms with democracy's compatibility with Islam, then it was all the more difficult for millions of sympathizers and supporters to condemn democracy as some Western secular scheme.

In the end, Islamists went considerably further than mere acceptance of the democratic process as a system of selecting leaders, as important as that first step was. What began as a tactical, self-interested move became something deeper. The language of "divine sovereignty"—a mainstay of Islamist discourse for decades—no longer figured prominently.[25] Today, it is relatively rare to hear the Brotherhood use the term in either Arabic or English. The people (*shaab*) were now the "source of authority," a phrase that began to pepper Muslim Brotherhood programs and platforms during the 2000s, solidifying as a core concept during and after the Bush administration's "Freedom Agenda." March calls this apparent embrace of popular sovereignty Islamism's "grand idea."[26] In my book *Temptations of Power*, I go into more detail on how and why this shift occurred.[27] Popular sovereignty, in some sense, was the bridge between the seemingly opposed realities of wanting to apply sharia and acknowledging that the state was the only party that could apply it. If the people were sovereign, it helped resolve the tension. An "Islamic state" could actually come into being—and it could be legitimatized and perhaps even accepted internationally because of its democratic premise.

But where does this leave us, and what does all this really mean in practice? For three decades now, mainstream Islamist movements have been focused on survival, resisting repression, and calling for popular sovereignty and alternation of power—two of the foundational elements of modern democratic politics. I will touch on the perpetual question of sincerity later in the chapter, but in terms of what these groups actually say in English and Arabic, there is no doubt that they have made considerable strides on key questions of political pluralism, respect for minority rights, and the role of women. And they have done so at the cost of alienating their own cadres, who intermittently grumbled and complained while their leaders attempted to do something they had never done before—synchronize their positions and even their beliefs with modern human rights norms, not all the way perhaps but farther than might have been expected.

* * *

In 1994 and 1995, the Egyptian Muslim Brotherhood released a series of position papers. Despite receiving little attention from Western observers, these were "the first glimmers of the Ikhwan's ideological revisions."[28] Published as pamphlets, they laid out in detail the organization's position on democracy, pluralism, the role of women, and the rights of Christian minorities. As Khaled Hamza, a Brotherhood official, described it to me, these statements represented a "reassessment of the ideas of Hassan al-Banna."[29]

The document "Shura in Islam and Party Pluralism in Muslim Society" outlines the Brotherhood's understanding of intellectual and political pluralism and affirms that the concept of *shura*, or consultation, guarantees that the "umma is the source of authority," an earlier iteration of today's more common "the people are the source of authority."[30] The Brotherhood also explains its support for political pluralism: "Difference of opinion deepens and diversifies one's outlook, something which is necessary to discern the truth and to reach that which is most beneficial, particularly if it is coupled with tolerance and a multitude of avenues [for expression]."[31]

In 2004, when the Bush administration put forward its Freedom Agenda, the Brotherhood released its landmark "Reform Initiative," where the group affirms its "commitment to a republican, constitutional, democratic system of government within a framework of Islamic principles," a new formulation it had not used before.[32] The Brotherhood then calls on political forces in Egypt to support the reform initiative as a basis for a national charter anchored around a set of democratic and even liberal ideas, including "full recognition that the people are the source of authority" and "freedom of personal belief." Just as important is what the Brotherhood chooses not to say— there isn't a single reference to *tatbiq al-sharia*. The references to "Islamist" content are minimal and, when they do appear, seem to fulfill a largely rhetorical purpose on the margins. This is not to say that the Brotherhood does not employ liberal doses of religious language. It does. But there is a discernible move away from past preoccupations with Islamic law and toward a more general, and presumably less controversial, promotion of religious values in society.

The 2004 initiative cannot easily be dismissed as a mere publicity stunt. Despite internal dissent around its contents, including from within the group's Guidance Bureau, there was a strong, coordinated effort to build support for the initiative at all levels of the Brotherhood organization. According to Khaled Hamza, each Brother with full membership privileges was given a copy of the initiative and was expected to study and familiarize himself with the contents. Members of each *shu'ba*[33] (consisting of forty to fifty individuals) engaged in formal discussion on the initiative upon its release.[34] Hamza himself spoke to local *shu'bas* regarding the reform program and its contents, leading discussions and answering any questions from members.

In its 2005 electoral program, the Brotherhood's democratic vocabulary is further updated. The program is "based on a reference from which our method of change stems, and that is the Islamic reference (*marji'iya islamiya*) and the democratic mechanisms of the modern civil state (*dawla madaniya*)."[35] As for the sharia, it "represents a way for establishing progress, development and reform, and defines the lawful and unlawful in legislation, and social interactions. All of this connects politics with morals and makes our means noble and, consequently, our ends noble too."[36]

The two terms—*marji'iya islamiya* (Islamic reference) and *dawla madaniya* (civil state)—were new additions to the Brotherhood's discourse,

suggesting a newfound willingness to concede an implicit separation between the sacred and the political:

> Since Islam rejects clerical rule, the state in Islam is a civil one, in which
> the people, being the source of authority, determine its systems and
> institutions. This is a human judgment, among others, which changes and
> improves within the fixed principles of sharia. . . . Concerning the authority
> of the ruler, it is according to the social contract between the governor and
> the governed. [The social contract] is established by the people, thereby
> improving the civic institutions [of the state]. . . . So the nation has the right
> to appoint the ruler, control him, and depose him if necessary, for he is a
> civil governor in all aspects.

It sounded good, but was it too good to be true?

Should the Brotherhood Be Trusted?

All of this was just rhetoric. The Brotherhood was often obsessed with survival, even if it came at the expense of principle, so was it wise to trust them?
Indeed, after the release of their 2005 electoral program, Rifaat al-Said,
the longtime leader of the socialist Tagammu party, raised the criticism of
"double discourse" that had dogged the Brotherhood for decades. "I wonder,"
he asked, "what suddenly prompted them to scrap their strict and rigid interpretation of Islam—exemplified by their long-time slogan 'Islam is the solution'—in favor of this new liberal image?" As these things often are, it was a
rhetorical question, and one that he quickly answered; the reform initiative
was evidence of "the Brotherhood's old opportunistic style, which aims at
usurping power at all costs."[37]

The question of double discourse, while often posed in bad faith, remains
a legitimate one. It is one that American policymakers worry about—and
they have every right to worry about it, since the answer isn't self-evident,
perhaps not even to Islamists themselves. Charges of double discourse aren't
unique to Islamists. To different degrees, every ideological party must contend with it, particularly those that have had to weather decades of repression due to their ideology. If you want to survive, and you know that your
ideas are perceived as dangerous, it only makes sense to temper them. This
isn't dissembling, or *taqiya*, as anti-Islam advocates are eager to claim. (In any

case, *taqiya*, as a concept, is scarce in the Sunni tradition, since Sunnis, who were usually numerically and politically dominant, were rarely suppressed for being Sunni.)

In Western democracies, Marxist and socialist parties suppressed their ultimate aims, for obvious reasons. They had to pledge loyalty to constitutions and democratic processes (and outcomes) even if this ran counter to some idealized and impractical understanding of a workers' dictatorship. In polarized societies, accusations of dissembling will tend toward the commonplace. Even in established democracies, such doubts have become increasingly normal. In the United States, the Republican Party is routinely criticized for its disregard of procedural democracy, to say nothing of liberal democracy. In Western Europe, similar concerns around the role of far-right parties are used to maintain *cordon sanitaires*, where mainstream center-left and center-right parties try to exclude their more radical counterparts from government (and polite society). When the stakes are sufficiently high, it becomes easier to view your opponent as someone to be not just defeated but destroyed.

There is little doubt that Islamist parties have occasionally been too clever by half and become overly preoccupied with persuading skeptical Western audiences that they have nothing to fear from Islamists. Sometimes, the messaging is rather explicit. There was that time when Brotherhood leader Khairat al-Shater wrote a *Guardian* op-ed titled "No Need to Be Afraid of Us."[38] In some ways, this was good. It showed that Islamists were attuned and sensitive to what the international community wanted. This was part of their pragmatism, after all. In other ways, it was concerning, suggesting an over-eagerness to please, perform, and present themselves as normal and unobjectionable. For liberals and secularists, there were reasons to be afraid. For those who prioritized the U.S. relationship with Israel, there were reasons to be afraid, too. This, though, is what Islamist leaders believed they had to do, and they were right to think that presenting themselves as amenable to Western values and goals might help erode Western opposition to their participation in politics.

This doesn't make it any less unfortunate. Over time, the broader dynamic at the heart of Islamist behavior and self-presentation has been an unhealthy one. It has encouraged Islamist groups to make a virtue out of the vague, particularly when it comes to the outlines of their preferred end state. Threatened with repression at home and fearful of provoking Western opprobrium abroad, there were simply some things Islamists could not say. When they did decide to say them, however mild, the penalties could be considerable.

When he was mayor of Istanbul, Recep Tayyip Erdogan was imprisoned for reciting an overtly Islamic poem. He apparently learned his lesson, biding his time and "suppressing" his Islamism for years to come, presenting himself instead as a new kind of Muslim democrat. He, and many others, were waiting for revenge, for a time when they could punish their opponents just as they had been punished.

In effect, they were being asked to cease being who they were. If they were "Islamists," then they would have to stop or stay quiet. Or, they would have to learn to delicately straddle a blurry line, testing the limits, sometime falling afoul of them, and then learning how to hover on the right side the next time. They learned how to couch their Islamic demands in secular language. They did not talk about sharia, to say nothing of "implementing" it.

I remember one official from Erdogan's Justice and Development Party (AKP), Mazhar Bagli, describing the enveloping nature of the experience. "There was a lot of pressure in Turkey coming from the military, on how to behave in society and within the family," he told me. "You had to speak a certain way, behave a certain way. The main aim of the Turkish state is to design our life, at all times."[39] Governments were in the position to "design" the lives of their citizens. Which made it at least somewhat ironic that Bagli could so quickly move from castigating the state for what it had done to him and his family to seeing the state as the solution, now that his own party was in power. "Policies came from the deep state," he said, without skipping a beat. "Now the state, government, and society are hand-in-hand, walking in the same direction."

In hindsight, one could look at Turkey today and say that the AKP should have been banned, just as previous parties had been banned by judicial fiat by institutions that saw themselves as guardians of both secularism and the state. Islamists were given a chance and look what happened, the argument goes. Such bans, of course, would be preemptive, raising a whole host of questions about the limits of tolerance and participation and whether democracies should act vigilantly and aggressively against "antidemocratic" actors—at the risk of considerable overreach. To ban a party *before* it violates democracy in the name of democracy is obviously a risky proposition, even if we put aside normative concerns.

In polarized contexts, there is unlikely to be a neutral arbiter of who is a threat to democracy and who is not. One would have to have faith in the state to do the job—another risky proposition. We have already seen how the premise of seeing the state as the solution is precisely part of the problem that this book seeks to address. Taking the path of state-imposed restrictions on party participation would raise the already high stakes of electoral competition higher, since whoever gains control of state institutions would then be in a position to regulate participation based on changing criteria. For example, in a staunchly secular democracy, the constitution might enshrine secularism, requiring all parties to work within those confines, even if they are Islamists. This is what happened in Turkey, where successive Islamist parties de-Islamized their entire political platforms to make themselves appear sufficiently secular.

The preamble of the Turkish constitution states that "there shall be no interference whatsoever by sacred feelings in state affairs and politics," while Article 2 enshrines a secular order "based on the fundamental tenets set forth in the Preamble." Article 2, moreover, is one of the so-called irrevocable provisions that cannot be amended. Those provisions are still there, in other words. The only difference today is that an Islamist party is in power and finally has enough control of the state, after a long tug of war with the judiciary. Eventually, after winning consecutive elections, the AKP was able to reshape the judicial branch through its appointment powers.

In theory, an Islamist party could seek to use party bans against its opponents, applying a different set of criteria. So while Western observers might be comfortable with the notion of an established democracy (like Germany) putting far-right parties under constitutional surveillance or a secular democracy barring religious parties, they might be less comfortable with a religious party doing something similar—but in reverse. In a hypothetical democracy that substituted a staunchly secular constitution for an "Islamic" one, secular parties would still be able to participate, provided they respected Islamic values and didn't invite the ire of the courts. But, without sufficient safeguards, this could (and probably would) be abused. This is why the principle of state noninterference in the formation and participation of political parties is essential.

There is no such thing as "neutral" criteria. Liberalism is only neutral to those who are already liberal.[40] As the political theorist Stanley Fish argues, "It cannot be a criticism of a political theory or of the regime it entails that it is unfair. Of course it is. The only real question is whether the unfairness is the one we want."[41] Some criteria might be better than others, but there is no ultimate authority, at least in this life, that can arbitrate between conflicting conceptions of the Good. In the place of such an authority, there is only coercion. That tendency to coerce, in the absence of consensus, should be avoided wherever possible.

If party bans and other preemptive restrictions are either counterproductive or undemocratic, then it leaves open the question of what Islamist parties would become over time, if they had enough time. Over the course of this chapter, I have tried to lay out the intellectual foundations—and contradictions—inherent in the Islamist idea, as expressed by the largest and most influential Islamist movements. Islamists are rationalists who seem to be anti-rationalist. They are modernists who can appear anti-modern. They are skeptical of the nation-state, but willing to indulge in its power when given the opportunity. By default, Islamist parties improvise, which makes it difficult for outside observers to assess their intentions and aims. In all their diversity and internal contradictions, they have struggled to define what it is exactly that they want. They have no models to emulate. Mainstream Islamists of the Brotherhood ilk do not consider Saudi Arabia, Afghanistan, Sudan, or Iran to be anything close to models. In hundreds of hours of conversations, on and off the record over nearly two decades, I do not believe I have ever heard a Brotherhood member mention any of these examples in positive terms. I have only heard them as cautionary tales to be avoided.

Keeping these caveats in mind, it is still possible to outline what Islamist movements might do if they came to power through democratic elections and if they managed to stay in power long enough. Because Brotherhood-inspired parties have "secularized" insofar as they have little idea of how to alter the basic structure of the nation-state, they are likely to overcompensate through gestures and policies that are both superficial and attention grabbing. This is the low-hanging fruit of the Islamist project. If they could cobble together a parliamentary majority, including other social conservatives and ultraconservative Salafis, instituting restrictions on alcohol consumption is both easy and obvious. It is useful as a signal that a given Islamist party, which may not have many interesting or original ideas for "Islamic" governance, is still somehow taking Islam seriously.

Alcohol consumption, one of the traditional Islamist-secular flashpoints, can often become a sort of Rorschach test. In Turkey, a fascinating if misunderstood case of Islamists in government, the AKP increased taxes on alcohol. It also banned sales in the vicinity of mosques or schools and prohibited late-night sales after 10 p.m. When I asked Ibrahim Kalin, Erdogan's chief advisor at the time, about the controversy, he was irritated. Kalin, a scholar of Islamic philosophy and former Georgetown professor, asked me: "Have you ever seen a government in the world that encourages people to use alcohol?

Of course we encourage people not to use alcohol."[42] The question seemed rhetorical, so I didn't say anything and just nodded.

He complained about a double standard: "When Britain introduces a law like that, it is considered protecting the public interest. When we introduce it, it is Islamization." This was an understandable objection, but it is also true that actions are made more or less meaningful by the reasoning behind them. The "reasoning" here becomes more complicated by the fact that alcohol is prohibited in Islam not just because God said so, but because of how its intoxicating effects can impact both individuals and communities—in part a secular rational for an Islamic prohibition. As we saw earlier, Islamic injunctions dealing with social relations often have a *illa*, or rationale, built into them—and the rationale is often "secular" insofar as it is intelligible to believers and non-believers alike.

In addition, the AKP provided financial stipends to young couples who married early (an effort to increase birth rates but also presumably to discourage premarital sex). This "soft" Islamization attempted to increase piety without coercing it. When Erdogan remarked that "there is no difference in killing the fetus in a mother's womb or killing a person after birth,"[43] it was clear that, in his ideal world, he would have liked to ban abortion. But he didn't even try. This was Erdogan sharing his own views about the virtuous life, acting in his "spiritual leader" mode, a role more appropriate for a powerless cleric than a powerful president. As one senior AKP official put it to me: "Erdogan at times behaves like a father. Not everything that he says is a law. It is a suggestion. It is also to protect young people from bad things."[44]

"Soft" Islamization is the more likely outcome in relatively secularized countries like Turkey, where there is no longstanding tradition of any parties, Islamist or otherwise, calling for the actual implementation of sharia (in part because it would have been illegal, due to the constitution's irrevocable provisions). In religiously conservative countries like Egypt or Jordan, where popular support for sharia is more widespread and uncontroversial, Islamists are likely to go further. In addition to levying taxes and restricting hours of sale, they might introduce restrictions on alcohol production or consumption. These would likely fall short of full bans, due to backlash from secular parties and media, dependence on tourism, and the presence of significant Christian minorities and expatriate communities. On the municipal level, local governments could carve out "dry counties" by blocking or suspending the renewal of alcohol licenses for restaurants and bars.

There is a long precedent for these ideas, although Brotherhood movements never cared to go into detail on how such restrictions would actually be implemented (in part because they wouldn't be the ones implementing them). Restricting alcohol was usually one among various moves Islamists would call for in their litanies. In Egypt during the 1980s, Muslim Brotherhood members of parliament called for banning interest, closing nightclubs, keeping businesses closed on Fridays, objecting to immoral television programs, ensuring that government workers could leave work for prayer, and increasing religious programming on television as well as in the educational curriculum.[45]

Meanwhile, also in the mid-1980s, twenty-two of the sixty members in Jordan's parliament backed a bid to prohibit the manufacture and sale of alcohol, while a majority of thirty-three deputies called on the government to implement a mandatory *zakat* tax.[46] The catch, here, was that there were only three Islamists in parliament at the time, which offers a useful reminder that Islamists aren't the only ones who support Islamist initiatives.

At this point, Jordan's Islamists were more akin to a sharia lobby than a political party. Later, from 1989 to 1992, the Jordanian Brotherhood had a significant plurality in parliament, so it's worth looking at what they tried to do with their newfound influence. They proposed three pieces of legislation that focused on the application of sharia: a law banning co-education in all primary and secondary schools, community colleges, and universities;[47] a law banning production and consumption of alcohol; and a law prohibiting interest.[48] All failed to pass. They had one legislative success, albeit short-lived. The Brotherhood parliamentary bloc proposed legislation to prohibit male hairdressers from working in women's beauty salons. Even though the law did not pass, Islamists were able to successfully lobby the Ministry of Interior to issue the ban as an executive order. However, a backlash ensued, forcing the government to rescind the decision just four weeks later.[49]

What about when the Brotherhood joined a coalition government for the first (and last) time in 1991? The organization, not without internal dissent, decided to join the government after Prime Minister Mudar Badran accepted a fourteen-point plan that would "bring Jordan closer towards implementing Islamic sharia."[50] The "demands" were largely symbolic, and only one marked a tangible concession on Badran's part. For a brief period, Jordan prohibited the serving of alcohol at official government functions and on Royal Jordanian flights to Muslim countries. That this was the most the Brotherhood could coax out of the prime minister is suggestive: it had no effect on the state and it had no measurable effect on the lives of citizens (unless one was prone to bouts of drunkenness on airplanes).

Still, there were five Brotherhood cabinet ministers during the first half of 1991. They must have done something worthy of attention, one assumes. Six months wasn't a lot of time, but it can still offer interesting indications of what the Brotherhood wanted *before* it became overly concerned with its international image. For starters, Minister of Education Abdullah al-Akaileh and Minister of Social Development Youssef al-Azm instituted a policy of sex segregation within their respective ministries. In response to media criticism, Islamist deputy Daoud Kojak argued that "if the majority of people were against coeducation and coeducation was allowed for a minority, then dictatorship of a minority over the majority would take place."[51] This suggested that Islamists were becoming more comfortable with the language of democracy, even as they used it for illiberal ends.

Now that religious conservatism was gaining throughout society, the Brotherhood would increasingly couch its appeals in populist terms. It was no longer just that Islamist ideas were right; now they reflected the will of the people. Gradually, the popular will and the Islamist will would become inextricably intertwined, at least in the minds of Islamists themselves. Was democracy good because it worked? Or, was democracy useful because it worked?

Another controversial decree from Akaileh barred fathers from attending their daughter's sporting events. (One disgruntled father asked, "Does he think that looking at legs can possibly be on our minds?"[52]) The measure provoked outrage as thousands of parents organized meetings, distributed petitions, and lobbied the prime minister to intervene. Akaileh was also active on foreign policy, which for Jordan was also a matter of domestic policy. Under Akaileh's directives, every morning schoolchildren were made to recite a "victory prayer," which condemned Western influences and called on God to "bring the destruction [of the Zionists] through their own doing; may God encircle them, may God shame them and bring us victory over them."[53]

The Education Ministry also issued directives to schools warning of "Zionist" influence and calling on teachers to focus greater attention on the value of jihad.[54] Other measures included "banning male sports coaches from teaching sports to girls, limiting schools' freedom to close on Christian holidays, setting mid-term examinations in the week of the Christmas holidays and attempting to ban certain books deemed incompatible with the kingdom's 'religious and moral ethics.'"[55]

This might sound alarming to the casual reader, but much of it was concerned with appearances, rhetoric, and symbols. Moreover, unilateral policies from one education minister could easily be undone by the next education minister. Akaileh's efforts reflected an attempt at virtue-signaling without much in the way of virtue. It was an attempt to superimpose Islamic trappings on a secular status quo. This suggested a failure of imagination, to be sure, but it also reflected the fact that few had a clear idea of how to make a state Islamic or what would make it so—beyond, perhaps, having Islamists in government. Viewed this way, Islamists being in government was not a means to an Islamist re-rendering of the state; to have virtuous personnel became its own end.

That was Jordan. Egypt, as it turns out, experienced a much more far-reaching attempt at Islamization—a formal effort over several years to synchronize Egyptian law, an odd patchwork of French and British codes, with sharia. Announced in December 1978, this synchronization project was serious and wide-ranging, which makes it all the more surprising that it has largely been forgotten. I have discussed the details of what exactly happened elsewhere, so I will only mention some brief highlights here.[56] Similar to the twenty-two deputies in Jordan's parliament who called for an alcohol ban, the effort in Egypt was led by ostensibly secular politicians—or, more precisely, they were "secular" only insofar as they weren't Islamists.

The architect of the Islamization effort was one of Egypt's most powerful men, Speaker of Parliament Sufi Abu Talib, who was a close associate of President Sadat. Sadat had fashioned himself "the believing president." In his earlier years, he had briefly been a Muslim Brotherhood member, some of which perhaps hadn't rubbed off entirely.[57] Abu Talib announced the formation of five committees—on litigation, criminal codes, social affairs, civil and trade regulations, and monetary and economic affairs—entrusted to "[study] all legislative proposals relating to the application of Islamic law."[58] After several years of work, Abu Talib addressed parliament in July 1982, speaking of the need to close the gap between "what the Egyptian believed and the laws that governed him" and explicitly mentioned the examples of alcohol, adultery, and usury.[59] The five committees had painstakingly produced hundreds of pages of detailed legislation. A draft law on civil transactions was more than 1,000 articles long, one on tort reform included 513 articles, while legislation revising criminal punishments had 635. Draft legislation on the maritime code included 443 articles, while commercial code legislation included 776.[60] None of it was ultimately implemented. Abu Talib lost his primary patron after Sadat's assassination, and he was soon replaced as speaker of parliament. Mubarak showed little interest in the initiative, and no one—this being a dictatorship—was really in a position to push the matter.

* * *

These are all examples of what Islamists would have or might have done. Surprisingly, they are also examples of what "secularists" have actually done, under pressure from an electorate that was growing more conservative. This is the phenomenon of *Islamism without Islamists*; in devout societies where a large majority of citizens say they support a larger role for Islam in public life, one can sympathize with or support Islamist policies without being an Islamist.

At the time of Abu Talib's sharia synchronization project, the Muslim Brotherhood, whose leaders had only recently emerged from prison, was not yet large, influential, or even particularly well known. The organization had effectively disappeared from public life over the course of the 1950s and 60s. To lack influence and visibility had its benefits. It meant that the Brotherhood's project of "Islamization" wasn't perceived as a partisan preoccupation or the province of one faction. Islamization was a cross-cutting priority that attracted support across the political spectrum, even among liberals.

The Wafd party, for example, was one of the few historic relics from Egypt's short-lived "liberal age" in the first half of the twentieth century.[61] Yet, even the country's closest approximation of what a liberal party might be appeared enthusiastic about bringing Egyptian legal codes in line with sharia. Mumtaz Nasar, a member of the litigation committee who would later serve as the head of the Wafd's parliamentary bloc, congratulated Abu Talib on the progress being made. Speaking of his own committee's work, Nasar explained:

> The committee ensured that the project [to revise the law] had two sources, the first of them the Quran, the prophetic traditions, and the consensus of the scholars . . . and secondly [the authority of the president] in accordance with sharia law as it relates to the organization of the affairs of state. . . . And the objective of this second source is the realization of the public interest on matters that do not have a specific textual injunction [in the Quran or prophetic traditions].[62]

This conservative consensus—encompassing Islamist and non-Islamist parties alike—has frayed, but not because support for Islamic law has dwindled. If anything, markers of religious conservativism and support for sharia, either in general or regarding specific prohibitions, are more widespread today than in the late 1970s and early 1980s when the Islamic revival was still in its infancy. What changed instead was the partisan and ideological rancor that would begin to consume Egypt and the broader region. As the Muslim Brotherhood grew in strength and popularity, it could no longer hover in relative obscurity. Due to its history, checkered and secretive, the Brotherhood was viewed with alarm by elites, who were beginning to grasp that the organization might threaten their political and economic privileges. In a country where mass politics didn't much exist, a mass movement was probably something worth worrying about.

As the Brotherhood became more visible and vocal with their trademarks of "Islam is the solution" and *tatbiq al-sharia*, the more they cornered the market. How could a liberal party compete with Islamists when it came to Islam and Islamic law? The more prominent the Brotherhood became, the more incentives secular parties had to draw clear differences. After all, if someone really cared about restricting alcohol and gender segregation at school, they would vote for the real thing, not a pale and not entirely convincing imitation. As late as 1984, the Brotherhood and the Wafd found enough agreement on Islam to form an electoral alliance, which performed admirably. But it couldn't last, and it didn't. Where Islam had, up to a point, been a unifying force, now it would present itself as a source of disunity and division.

Sharia in Democratic Contexts

There are other places where Islamism has flourished without Islamists, but we have to go somewhat further afield to find them, namely in South and Southeast Asia. Here, too, Islam plays an outsized role in public life. According to Pew, 93 percent of both Malaysian and Indonesian Muslims say religion is "very important" in their lives, easily surpassing the percentage who say so in Egypt, Turkey, or Tunisia, while 86 percent of Malaysian Muslims and 72 percent of Indonesian Muslims favor making Islamic law the official law of the land in their countries.[63] Figures such as these suggest an unusually conducive environment for Islamist parties. Yet, it hasn't been. In Malaysia and Indonesia, Islamist parties receive the backing of a small if significant percentage of the population. Similar to the Egyptian example above, we have a situation of Islamism without Islamists. Or, to put it differently, a nation doesn't need Islamist parties in government to actually implement Islamist policies.

In South and Southeast Asia, demands for sharia legislation have spread well beyond the usual suspects, enjoying the sanction and support of secular ruling parties. As Joseph Liow, a leading scholar of Islamism in Malaysia and Indonesia, notes, most Malaysian states have laws on the books regarding sharia criminal offenses, backed by government-sanctioned religious bodies. "A large segment of the incumbent UMNO party," he writes, "has also been either sympathetic to this push or, in some cases, actively involved in agitating for implementation of sharia."[64]

Indonesia, meanwhile, has featured the implementation of more sharia ordinances than Egypt, Jordan, Tunisia, Turkey, Algeria, or Morocco have at any point in recent decades, despite the fact that all six of these countries have had Islamist parties in power on either the local or national level. In Indonesia, democratization has gone hand-in-hand with decentralization, which has allowed more conservative provinces to experiment with religiously inspired legislation. In one study, Robin Bush, a scholar of Indonesian politics, documents the implementation of sharia by-laws in South Sulawesi, West Java, and other regions. They include: requiring civil servants and students to wear "Muslim clothing," requiring women to wear the headscarf to receive local government services, and requiring demonstrations of Qur'anic reading ability to be admitted to university or to receive a marriage license.[65] But there's a catch. According to a study by the Jakarta-based Wahid Institute, most of these regulations have been overseen or executed by officials of *secular* parties like Golkar.[66]

How is this possible? In Indonesia, the implementation of sharia is part of a mainstream discourse that cuts across ideological and party lines, again suggesting that Islamism is not necessarily about Islamists but is about a broader electorate that is supportive of Islam playing a central role in politics. As Liow writes, "The piecemeal implementation of sharia by-laws across Indonesia has not elicited widespread opposition from local populations."[67] This offers a reminder that democratization is conducive to either the rise of Islamist parties or Islamism (although not necessarily both together). If we return to the Arab world, there have only recently been three exceptions to the authoritarian rule—Tunisia, Lebanon, and Iraq. And each of these countries has seen Islamist parties in positions of power. (At the time of writing, a seemingly successful coup attempt in July 2021 has put Tunisia back on an authoritarian path. Still, Tunisia experienced ten years of democratic opening, and we can assess this period for lessons learned even if it is in the past tense.)

For almost the entire duration of Tunisia's democratic transition, the Islamist party Ennahda was either been the ruling party in a coalition, the junior partner in a coalition, or the single largest party in parliament. The case of Iraq, meanwhile, tends to be accompanied by an asterisk, due to the U.S. invasion in 2003, which means that it is often omitted. This would be a mistake. In 2014, after the military ousted the Brotherhood in Egypt, a leader of Morocco's Justice and Development Party (PJD) observed: "We're the one last Islamist party remaining in government in the region."[68] The PJD leader's remark is telling, since he seems to have forgotten about Iraq's existence. As David Patel writes, "By almost any measure, the most successful mainstream Islamists in the Arab world are in Baghdad, where Islamists have governed Iraq since 2005. . . . Yet, Iraq and its participatory Islamist movements remain pariahs for comparative scholars."[69] Iraq's landmark 2005 elections marked the rise of the Dawa party's Ibrahim al-Jaafari to the position of prime minister, after a mostly Islamist coalition won 48 percent of the vote. Dawa was a Shia Islamist party. Iraqi Muslim Brotherhood members also served in various cabinet positions in subsequent years, including as ministers of higher education and planning. While their fortunes in Iraq have dimmed somewhat more recently, Islamist parties have been part of coalition governments for the near entirety of the post-Saddam era. Finally, in Lebanon, Hezbollah—however much the United States and Saudi Arabia oppose it—has become a fixture of coalition governments. The point here isn't that these groups are good (Hezbollah is a U.S.-designated terrorist organization as well as an active participant in the Syrian regime's mass killing of civilians), but rather that the more democracy there is in a given country, the more likely it is that Islamists will have significant political representation.

What is striking about these cases is the extent to which Islamist participation simply became uncontroversial. Few major politicians argue for banning the parties in question. This participation "norm" gains a certain momentum over time: the longer Islamist parties participate, the more difficult it becomes for political actors to argue for placing legal or constitutional restrictions on them. In turn, the less political actors argue for proscribing Islamist parties, the more the participation norm is strengthened.

What Does It Mean for Democracy to Be Illiberal?

As we saw in the first chapter, the idea of "illiberal democracy" was popularized only relatively recently, which is surprising since liberalism (as constitutionally guaranteed rights and liberties) and democracy (as expressed through the results of elections) have historically been in tension, in theory if not necessarily always in practice. In modern times, though, the two seemed to go together quite well. Liberalism preceded democracy, allowing the latter to flourish.

In the early twentieth century, there weren't many democracies, but they were all liberal to various degrees—certainly more liberal than their non-democratic counterparts. But this was because of a particular sequencing that would prove difficult to replicate. As Richard Rose and Doh Chull Shin note:

> Countries in the first wave [of democracy], such as Britain and Sweden, initially became modern states, establishing the rule of law, institutions of civil society and horizontal accountability to aristocratic parliaments. Democratization followed in Britain as the government became accountable to MPs elected by a franchise that gradually broadened until universal suffrage was achieved.[70]

Reversing this sequence—or getting "democratization backwards"[71]—is what produces illiberal democracies. In his book *The Future of Freedom: Illiberal Democracy at Home and Abroad*, Fareed Zakaria doesn't merely argue that liberalism and democracy are in tension, but rather that democratization is "directly related" to illiberalism.[72]

Knowing what we know about Islamism, what can we now reasonably say about the potential clash between liberalism and democracy in the Middle East? Just how illiberal would Islamists be, and what should we make of their illiberalism? To answer this question requires rethinking how we assess and measure certain concepts. Like everything else in life and politics, liberalism and illiberalism are a spectrum. There are also different kinds of illiberalism—social illiberalism and political illiberalism. They sometimes go together, but not always. For example, we discussed scenarios where Islamists and non-Islamists restricted alcohol or mandated sex segregation in public schools. While these are illiberal in a general sense insofar as they reduce rather than expand individual freedom, they fall primarily under cultural or *social illiberalism*. However problematic they may be, they do not affect basic questions of political equality or political freedom.

In contrast, freedom of association and assembly and, say, protection from arbitrary arrest would figure prominently under the category of *political liberalism*. They affect political participation and shape the nature of political competition. For example, if you fear that the government will arrest you if you criticize it, then this will make you less likely to participate in politics. Not being able to freely criticize a government would also make it difficult to challenge that government in an election, presumably.

Arab authoritarian regimes reflect and accent these contrasting liberalisms. However liberal they may be on social issues, gender equality, or minority rights, they routinely deny the freedoms of association, assembly, and expression. They use their cultural liberalism on the former to deflect from fundamental violations on the latter. A democratically elected Islamist government, meanwhile, would likely be less socially liberal but more politically liberal than most authoritarian regimes we might be able to imagine. It is difficult to argue that a secular or "liberal" dictator—something of an oxymoron—would be better on liberal grounds, unless one is using the word in a fairly narrow sense.

Of course, most people aren't doing side-by-side comparisons and distinguishing carefully between different kinds of illiberalism. They may also calculate, not without reason, that liberal authoritarianism today may lead to liberal democracy tomorrow (or in several decades). Some of the sharia ordinances discussed above in Indonesian regions go well beyond alcohol restrictions and put forward religious tests that intrude into the most personal realms of life, including what one chooses to wear. To tie clothing requirements to the receipt of government services adds another layer of intrusion, where the state is not merely asking, but requiring, you to act like a certain kind of Muslim. The "conservative consensus" in Indonesian localities makes these ordinances less controversial than one might expect. In the Middle East, however, these are likely to be non-starters, particularly in countries with powerful and entrenched secular elites. And to my knowledge, these types of very specific, performative sharia ordinances are no longer proposed by any mainstream Islamist party in the Arab world. There is also the fact of Western attention and criticism. Because of the region's strategic importance, what Islamists do in the Middle East tends to attract international controversy. What happens in Indonesia or Malaysia doesn't.

Still, there remains an open question of whether an "illiberal democracy" would stay democratic over time—and how the United States should respond to the blurry line of majority excess. Contrary to how it is often described, illiberal democracy does not entail elections and nothing else. If it did, it wouldn't be an illiberal democracy but something closer to an electoral authoritarian regime or competitive authoritarian regime. While this might appear to some as splitting hairs, the differences are fundamental. For even a minimalistic conception of democracy to be democratic, there needs to be sufficient freedom of association and expression for elections to be both competitive and meaningful. This, after all, is at the heart of the democratic idea. No matter what voters choose in one election, they should never lose recourse to change their minds or try something different, even quite different, in the future. This is why democracy, however majoritarian, requires some basic protections of political rights. If an opposition party cannot organize meetings, hold protests, or communicate its ideas and policy preferences through the media, then democratic competition is not fair. If individuals or groups are denied speech protections, then that limits their ability to speak out against the excesses of the governing party, and so on.

Similarly, if disrespect for minority rights reaches a certain level whereby, for example, minorities are barred from voting (although I am not aware of any such cases), then the word "democracy" would no longer apply. Needless to say, if a democratically elected government launches a genocide against a particular minority group, then this would no longer be a democracy. After all, if you're dead, you can't really vote. As for whether citizens can hypothetically vote for an alternative political regime, such as a monarchy or aristocracy, they can, but only so long as they don't violate or otherwise end the democratic process. Citizens should always have recourse to change their minds in subsequent elections, and the opposition should always have an opportunity to oppose and organize. Otherwise, outcomes can no longer be trusted to reflect popular preferences. Not anything goes, but most anything should go *within* the context of a fairly minimalist democratic process and constitutional framework that protects the right to recourse and the right to oppose, which would need to include various basic protections on freedom of association and expression. Without that, opposition parties would not be able to make their case in subsequent elections.

Under democratic minimalism, rights would be reconceptualized. Instead of the predominant liberal view that democracy leads to liberalism, liberal rights would be derived from the democracy. These liberties are vital to democracy insofar as they facilitate democratic competition. Considered this way, political liberalism is a means to an end, instrumentalized in the service of more fundamental values of individual self-determination: the ability to make your own choices and to have a say in the laws and decisions that shape your own life. Rights are not freestanding, self-evident, or morally transcendent. They have a more specific purpose. This is not too dissimilar from Robert Dahl's view, described as follows:

> Rights are at root procedural, not sacred political attributes, not ontological features of persons. Free speech, for instance, is necessary to challenge government and to provide citizens not only with information but also with choices about their destiny.[73]

This different foundation allows us to more carefully delineate between illiberalism that undermines democracy and illiberalism that doesn't. Of course, this can be abused. Social or religious illiberalism, even if it's not coercive or infringing upon political rights, can alter a citizen's relationship to their nation and state. Few things are perceived more personally than an individual's understanding of God. If the government tries to alter such a religious understanding, this can elevate religious cleavages to the realm of the politically existential. This in part is what plagued the Arab Spring, particularly in a country like Egypt that was otherwise relatively homogenous. During its brief stint in power, the Muslim Brotherhood did not impose sharia, nor did it try. In fact, despite dominating both the legislative and executive branches, the Brotherhood did not attempt to pass any "Islamic" legislation, except for a law on Islamic bonds, or *sukuk*, which angered ultra-conservative Salafis more than it did liberals (for not being Islamic enough, of course).[74]

The lack of Islamist legislation, though, misses the point somewhat. Ideological divides aren't about specific policies; they are about identity—the identity of citizens as well as the identity of the state. There is a certain kind of psychic harm in looking at your country anew and failing to recognize it. In the case of Egypt, secular opponents of the Brotherhood feared that their country would change irrevocably if the Brotherhood remained in power. This fear was exacerbated by a lopsided power imbalance. There were too many Islamists and too few liberals. This might have been democracy, but it was new and frightening in its uncertainty. To have lived your whole life under authoritarianism is to have acquiesced to its predictable, almost comforting arbitrariness, particularly if you were wealthy and could weather the storms.

A few days after Egypt's first ever free parliamentary elections in January 2012, I remember visiting my great-aunt in her extravagant flat, tucked off to the side of the presidential palace on a tree-lined street in a Cairo suburb. She was in a state of a shock. More than that, she was confused. It was one thing for the Brotherhood to win 40 percent, but how could 28 percent of her countrymen vote for ultraconservative Salafi parties? She might as well have been in mourning. It raised the following question: Was democracy worth it if this is what it brought? For my great-aunt, it apparently wasn't.

To be alienated from your own state is not an easy thing to ask someone else to accept. This, moreover, was a state that had demanded loyalty and subservience of its citizens since independence in 1952. I was an outsider, an American waltzing in with my ideas and ideals. I believed I was right. But they were the ones who would have to live with the consequences. And there was no doubt—this brief era, running from February 2011 to June 2013, was an odd one in Egypt's modern history. It was a time of unprecedented polarization, fear, and uncertainty. Egyptians were shouting, protesting, striking, and hoping—both for and against the Muslim Brotherhood. This is also what made those two and a half years frightening: the freewheeling intellectual combat, the seemingly endless sparring of ideas and individuals, and a sheer sense of openness.

The Authoritarian Impulse

Over the course of democratic transitions, that sense of openness and angst is, for both better and worse, unavoidable even in the best of circumstances. In ideologically polarized contexts, elections will be fraught regardless of who wins, and even more so in a country with institutions as corrupt and partisan as Egypt's.

There is no way to predict whether Islamist parties will govern democratically if they assume power through democratic means. There is, of course, a chance that they will renege on their democratic commitments. At the same time, there is little reason to think that any prospective authoritarianism would be a *product* of their Islamism rather than a product of more prosaic temptations of power. The case of Turkey's Recep Tayyip Erdogan is a Rorschach test for opposing positions in an unresolved debate. For some, Erdogan's regression from Muslim democrat to Islamist autocrat is proof positive that there is something inherently wrong with Islamists. It is who they are, and it is only a matter of time before the authoritarian impulse makes itself apparent. The other view is that Erdogan is the product of a distinctively Turkish political culture and tradition that cuts across ideological lines. A leading scholar of modern Turkey, Jenny White, places Erdogan in a long line of Turkish "bigmen." A bigman, she writes, "achieves status by being particularly good at provisioning and protecting his increasing numbers of followers."[75] In a polarized society, being the bigman requires the steady accumulation of power and the will to subvert potential competitors. But the bigman can be of any ideology, Islamist or otherwise, and Turkey's modern history is a testament to this, with its long line of secular bigmen prior to Erdogan.

Whichever interpretation you follow, the Turkish case stands out as a cautionary note. If we look at a broader universe of cases, however, there is no evidence that Islamist parties are less likely to accept democratic outcomes than their non-Islamist counterparts. The truth may be closer to the opposite, in fact. If we look at the empirical record of the post-independence period, secular and "liberal" forces have played critical roles in forestalling democratization across the region, including in the two major antidemocratic coups of recent decades in Egypt and Algeria and in several of Turkey's coups to boot. Of course, one might argue that Islamists haven't had enough chances to be as autocratic as their secular counterparts. However, this only underscores the broader point: autocrats have been blocking democratization for many decades now—with the backing of ostensibly liberal elites.

Without exception, all major *liberal* (and not merely non-Islamist) parties in Egypt backed the 2013 coup that ended the country's democratic experiment. In Tunisia, a similar story unfolded. After the coup, the Tunisian opposition organized mass protests demanding a repeat of the "Egyptian scenario."[76] During that summer of 2013, most of the secular opposition called for dissolving either the democratically elected constituent assembly or the democratically elected government, or both. The constituent assembly and the government were led by Ennahda, the country's Brotherhood analog. The echoes of Egypt were hard to miss wherever one looked. Tunisia's own "Tamarrod" (Rebellion) modeled itself after Egypt's Tamarrod movement, which was instrumental in toppling Mohamed Morsi. Tunisia's "Salvation Front," drawing inspiration from Egypt's National Salvation Front, announced a campaign to remove local and national officials appointed by Ennahda.[77]

What is one to make of this? Just as we might say that Islamists become authoritarian because of their Islamism, perhaps liberals become authoritarian because of their liberalism? Or, perhaps it means that secularists, by virtue of being secular, are inherently opposed to democracy? But this would be silly as a general rule, unless we could identify something intrinsic and unique to liberalism or secularism that inevitably leads to authoritarian outcomes. Of course, there are reasons that liberals have supported coups in the Middle East. They may judge (correctly) that they have a built-in electoral disadvantage in religiously conservative societies. They may believe that liberalism should precede democracy even at the high cost of decades of authoritarian rule. But these are contextual factors having to do with liberals' and liberalism's relative weakness in particular places at particular times. If they were stronger and better organized, then they would have less to fear from mass politics, just as Islamists would have more to fear if they were the ones outmatched in democratic contests.

The international factors explored in previous chapters help to shape an overall context where liberals regularly ally with autocrats. Liberals are less likely to suffer less reputational costs for embracing autocrats than Islamists are. This is not speculative. They did, in fact, suffer minimal reputational costs in the eyes of Western policymakers during and after Egypt's 2013 coup. Western observers and officials routinely question Islamists' commitment to democracy but rarely do the same for liberals' commitments. It's not so much a purposeful omission. It simply wouldn't occur to them to pose the question in the first place.

Even if Islamists *were* more likely to give in to authoritarian impulses— for whatever reason—this would not be cause enough to oppose democratization. Similarly, if you accept my opposite contention that liberals are more likely to succumb to authoritarianism in the particular context of the Middle East, that is not reason enough to ban them from participating in the democratic process. If anything, such a suggestion would be dismissed as absurd on its face, and rightly so. In any polarized society, especially one in which a democratic transition hasn't even begun, one side will always be perceived as—and will actually be—more prone to authoritarianism than the other.

In the end, the question of authoritarian impulses, while important, must be treated as separate from the question of illiberal ones. Islamist parties, by definition, are meant to be illiberal. Islamists are Islamists for a reason. To state the obvious, if they weren't illiberal, they would presumably be liberal, and then they wouldn't be Islamists. Conflating illiberalism with authoritarianism muddies the waters, since it suggests that Islamists are inherently unfit for democracy. And if the largest opposition parties are a threat to democracy, then it offers a permanent rationale for delaying democratization in the Middle East as long as possible—perhaps forever.

9

On Hypocrisy

Known for his witty maxims, the French moralist François de La Rochefoucauld once quipped that "hypocrisy is the homage that vice pays to virtue." The hypocrite has always been a subject of fascination, not merely because he is bad. Mere badness is pedestrian. He also tends to be transparent, which has the benefit of providing a certain clarity (what one wishes to do with this clarity is another question). The hypocrite is different because of his ostentatious morality, which is meant to obscure and deceive. The pretense of morality, in other words, is just that: a pretense. But that pretense is weaponized for self-interested ends. This compounds the crime and the sense of being wronged. As the political theorist Ruth Grant writes, "[The] victims are the more to be pitied because of the painful betrayal of trust involved in their victimization."[1]

In the Qur'an, the hypocrites, or *munafiqoon*, are worse in the eyes of God than idolaters and other enemies of Islam. They are condemned to the lowest depths of hell.[2] What makes them dangerous is that ordinary Muslims may put their trust in them, because they have the outward appearances of faith. This puts them in a position to undermine the Muslim community from within, without being detected. Similar to secular accounts, then, the betrayal of trust after it has been granted figures prominently.[3]

From a perspective of survival and self-preservation, it makes sense that religions would reserve special condemnation for hypocrites and hypocrisy. A prophetic hadith points to one of the reasons: "He who dies without having gone or thought of going out for jihad in the cause of Allah will die while being guilty of having one of the qualities of hypocrisy."[4] The hypocrite cannot be trusted to fight when a community's survival is in question, as it was in the early days of Islam. Moreover, hypocrites may defect to the opposing side with little warning.

In the Islamic account, the hypocrisy of hypocrites isn't a product of sin or brokenness, or of trying to be good but failing. This would merely make one a sinner. The question of intent is critical when moving from discussing individuals to entire nations in the aggregate. Can a nation that professes to be moral also be malevolent? What would it mean for a nation to be at once hypocritical and malevolent?

Of course, the nation most often accused of hypocrisy is the United States—and for good reason. This book has been, in part, a story of the gap between words and deeds. No other country can claim a gap as large. For better and worse, the United States is, in fact, one of a kind. Most other nations are merely "normal." They pursue their self-interest, narrowly defined. They do not pretend that they are moral or just in their conduct abroad. Countries, particularly weaker ones, do not generally have the luxury of high-minded idealism. In the United States, there is instead "the popular belief in the happy marriage of power and virtue—existentially experienced by Americans as a combination of national pride and innocence."[5]

To pretend, in other words, is a privilege, and it is a privilege that America has rightly earned. Its unrivaled power allows it two things: the ability to have ideals but also the ability to ignore them. After all, it is difficult to betray one's ideals if one doesn't have any to begin with. For the United States, the charge of hypocrisy is effective precisely because it speaks to something true. Consider America's adversaries, such as China or Russia. To accuse China of hypocrisy because it backs friendly autocrats would make little sense. No one expects China to promote democracy abroad, so there is no way to judge it wanting, at least not in this regard.

There is something endearingly naive about a country that would declare in a presidential directive, as the Clinton administration did in 1995, that it would "act unilaterally to restrain the flow of arms . . . where the transfer of weapons raises issues involving human rights."[6] In what context would the transfer of weapons *not* raise issues involving human rights?

Where the gap between rhetoric and policy is large, there are two options for closing the gap and therefore reducing the perception of hypocrisy—to shift rhetoric to align with policy or to shift policy to align with rhetoric. But the gap can never be closed entirely, so a country like the United States will always be hypocritical. It is only a question of to what degree and in what direction. This is where La Rochefoucauld's maxim invites a more positive reading. For a nation, if not necessarily an individual, to be seen as hypocritical is one of the costs of trying to be moral. Or, to put it differently, insofar as hypocrisy points to an aspiration not met, the aspiration remains. This is better than the alternative.

In *Ordinary Vices*, the philosopher Judith Shklar argues that hypocrisy is a by-product of becoming liberal and democratic.[7] As the role of religion and traditional hierarchies declines, societies require other means to legitimate themselves. The sometimes overblown rhetoric of liberal aspiration, replete with references to fairness, justice, and equality, fills the vacuum. In believing themselves to be morally superior, liberal democracies "present themselves as better than they are" and "inflate the expectations of citizens."[8]

When it comes to individuals, the gap between presentation and reality is rightly perceived as a character flaw. It is theoretically possible for individuals to eliminate hypocrisy or at least come close to synchronizing words and deeds. They do not *need* to present as better than they actually are; after all, they are not trying to legitimate a state or conduct foreign affairs. States, however, do not have consciences. They do not have a clear will. The policies of states are the aggregate outcome of various institutions and individuals vying for control. Bureaucracies have vested interests, independent of the particular preferences of individuals in those bureaucracies. In short, what Stephen Krasner calls "organized hypocrisy" is qualitatively different than personal hypocrisy.[9]

The problem with promoting democracy is that whoever promotes it will face the charge of hypocrisy. There is no way to be entirely consistent, and it is unclear what such consistency would look like in practice. And, in any case, consistency isn't always a virtue. The United States is not a human rights organization. It will, at times, treat allies differently than adversaries. Even as it puts pressure on autocrats, it will still need to cooperate with them, however brutal, on short-term mutual interests. In their defense of hypocrisy, Henry Farrell and Martha Finnemore remind us: "A world where words and deeds always and transparently matched each other—one where the United States refused to work with foreign leaders whose countries did bad things—would be unworkable and probably dangerous."[10]

While state hypocrisy may not be as objectionable, in part because states are not people, it still creates some of the same problems. It encourages cynicism and distrust. If hypocrisy is the norm, then professions of virtue and idealism are devalued. They are more easily dismissed as empty talk and posturing. If the gap between rhetoric and action is especially large, as it was during the Egyptian coup and massacre of 2013, it is less about mere disappointment and more about whether it is wise for the United States to make a mockery of its own ideals in full public view.

For some, the inevitable incongruence between ideals and interests is reason enough for more closely aligning rhetoric with policy, rather than the other way around. If American policy is in thrall to autocrats, we might as well stop pretending and be more forthright about our lack of virtue. Insofar as such an approach would reduce the gap between what we say and what we do, it would reduce hypocrisy. But would this necessarily be good?

Fortunately, at least for the purposes of analysis, the presidency of Donald Trump provided a sort of natural experiment. It was unlikely Americans would ever have a president quite like him again. There was something refreshing, for instance, about Trump's complete disinterest in American support for human rights and democracy abroad. It was not so much that he couldn't be bothered but more that it didn't seem to occur to him to be bothered in the first place. The standard lofty rhetoric about values in the Middle East (or anywhere) was close to nonexistent. If anything, Trump seemed to prefer the predictability of friendly autocrats. At least he could do business with them without the complications of transparency or accountability.

For perhaps the first time in decades, the gap between words and deeds had been closed considerably. The United States, under Donald Trump, was *less* hypocritical than it was under previous administrations. But was this necessarily better for pro-democracy activists and dissidents in the region? On the one hand, those dissidents no longer had to wonder if the United States would come to their aid. They could be relatively certain that it wouldn't. Under no illusions about American interest in their plight, they could adapt their activism accordingly and focus exclusively on their own local, domestic context. They wouldn't have to worry about being betrayed. In his honest and frank disregard, Trump simply did not have the power to betray them.

If Donald Trump couldn't raise expectations, then it also meant he couldn't shatter them. This was most striking in the case of Syria. Because Trump didn't appear to care one way or the other about the Syrian opposition's struggle against the regime of Bashar al-Assad, it meant that when he did act—with limited airstrikes against regime military assets in 2017 and 2018—it was met with jubilation, even though it did little to address Assad's momentum, as he steadily recaptured territory and claimed victory in the years-long civil war. By contrast, Barack Obama, in the early days of the Arab Spring, declared that "Assad must go," fueling hopes that the United States would not turn a blind eye to the Syrian regime's atrocities. Obama, like other presidents before him, seemed to possess a basic humanity. He couldn't possibly allow Syrians to die by the hundreds of thousands, the thinking went. And the Syrian opposition based its own strategy on the presumption that the United States might not do everything it wanted, but that it would do something. Meanwhile, tens of thousands of ordinary Syrians put themselves at risk by speaking out against the Assad regime, because they, too, assumed some level of international backing for the right not to be killed.

Perhaps if they had known from the beginning that the Obama administration would not directly intervene militarily against Assad, then they would have made different calculations about their own lives. In Obama's defense, he said that Assad *must* go, not that he actually would. In any case, even though Trump didn't ultimately do much more for Syrians than Obama did, there was less anger and disappointment with Trump. Trump hadn't betrayed them, whereas Obama clearly had. Policy matters, but policies are not assessed in a vacuum or with perfect objectivity. The success or failure of a particular policy is judged against what it might have otherwise been. Trump never gave anyone reason to think that he would try to remove Assad from power, and so it would be unreasonable to attack Trump for "failing" to remove Assad.

Policymakers might wish it were otherwise, but policies cannot be separated from their justifications. The rhetoric is the context, and context will always matter, because observers are simply unable to perceive the platonic ideal of a policy divorced from the context in which it came to be. In practice, this means that, despite a similar desire to avoid entanglements in the region, Obama's Syria policy was judged more harshly than Trump's. The Syrian civil war might be dismissed as an example anomalous in both its degree of difficulty and the destruction that it invited, but the harshness of judgment applies to other cases as well. The Obama administration liberally employed the language of rights, freedom, and dignity but, as we saw, did little in response to a friendly autocrat's mass killing of more than a thousand Egyptians in August 2013. Among pro-democracy activists (and the friends and relatives of the dead), there was once again a sense of betrayal.

On one level, this might cast Trumpian "anti-hypocrisy" in a more favorable light. On another level, anti-hypocrisy in foreign policy, if applied as consistently as the Trump administration (inadvertently) attempted, does not necessarily produce better outcomes. All it offers is the "virtue" of a misbegotten consistency. Under the Trump administration, authoritarian regimes became more authoritarian, while pro-democracy activists had less success in promoting democracy. To be sure, democracy advocates had the benefit of not having to wonder whether the United States might be by their side, but it is unclear how beneficial this was in practice, except perhaps in offering a certain peace in resignation.

In foreign affairs, to oppose hypocrisy to an extreme, then, is to give up hope that the United States can become better—even if, in being better, it still falls well short of what we might wish it to be. Extreme anti-hypocrisy invites American officials to indulge their worst instincts. As Shklar writes, this is the danger of being not just good, but too good: "The more [conscience] rails against hypocrisy, the more it encourages the vice."[11]

On the other hand, to accept hypocrisy as an inevitable fact of living imperfectly is to hold on to our sense of morality in the breach. Hypocrisy does something that anti-hypocrisy cannot; it "accepts the sanctity of societal standards, even while violating them. It says: What I'm doing is wrong; therefore I must not be found out."[12] What applies to social affairs appears to apply in global politics—precisely the realm where morality and moralism are more casually dismissed because of the presumed anarchy of the international system.

It is good—at least for what remains of democratic prospects in the Middle East—that the charge of hypocrisy can be leveraged against U.S. officials. Such criticisms, including the ones I have leveled in this book, would not be effective if it wasn't for the sense that the United States has failed to meet the most minimal standards of conduct in the Middle East. For their part, many American officials, to their credit, maintain some conviction that the United States should not unquestioningly support the region's most brutal regimes. They know it is wrong; some realize, and say so publicly, that doing so is not in America's long-term interests.

In theory, the alternative of anti-hypocrisy was available to Barack Obama and those before him, but it was far from plausible in practice. It is difficult to imagine a scenario where past presidents might have followed through and completely done away with pretenses—for the simple reason that each of them, Trump excepted, was a product of a bipartisan tradition that understands America's moral aspirations as intertwined with its power.

The United States is one of the world's few ideological states, ideological insofar as it relies on ideas and ideals rather than traditional modes of belonging to forge its sense of nationhood. This is what makes America exceptional—an antiquated cliché perhaps but not a normative judgment as much as it is a descriptive reality. As Seymour Martin Lipset reminds us, to be exceptional is to be "qualitatively different," not "better."[13] America, like a faith community, may be shaped by but does not depend on ethnicity or inherited culture, a fact reflected in the country's very name. The United

States of America is not the "land of a particular people," the political theorist Samuel Goldman notes.[14]

The entrenched nature of American ideals, even if honored in the breach, complicates any effort to reimagine U.S. foreign policy as merely ordinary. If America, in the most foundational sense, isn't normal, then it is unclear why it would (or should) have a normal foreign policy. To do so, it would have to defy its own history. While this is possible, it is highly unlikely.

The idea of democracy—and democratic ideas—have guided American foreign policy for decades, but primarily in regions other than the Middle East. To argue against supporting democracy in the Middle East, then, is to insist that the United States apply a different set of standards to one region, as opposed to others.

10

On Power

After marching from Selma to Montgomery, Alabama, in the spring of 1965, Martin Luther King Jr. famously declared that "the arc of the moral universe is long, but it bends towards justice."[1]

In the broader sweep of historical time, this sentiment may have run contrary to the eschatology of the monotheistic faiths, but it was certainly true in the moment, and one could argue that it has continued being true in the decades since. But when President Barack Obama appropriated the remark, it took on a more expansive meaning, applied not just to America's own civil rights struggles but to America more generally, including its role in the world.

On that night of November 5, 2008, after his first electoral victory was assured, Obama lost little time in emphasizing the rhetorical themes that would define his presidency: "It's the answer that led those who have been told for so long by so many to be cynical, and fearful, and doubtful of what we can achieve to put their hands on the arc of history and bend it once more toward the hope of a better day," the then president-elect declared to an audience of millions that hoped, beyond hope, that it was true.[2]

It was a slight but telling innovation. Obama had modified King's phrase and come up with the more succinct (and less distinctly Christian) "arc of history." It was catchy and memorable from the standpoint of oratory, and it provided a certain pat summation of how one might look at the world without cynicism. Over the course of his presidency, as *The Atlantic*'s David Graham noted, Obama also popularized the phrase "the right side of history," but it wasn't entirely new. Bill Clinton, when he was president, had used the phrase around twenty times.[3]

What was new was President Obama's emphasis on the "wrong side of history" and the danger of being on that wrong side. To the extent that one ends up disappointed in Obama's foreign policy, particularly his approach to the Middle East, it is due to the suspicion, largely correct, that he was animated by a sense of moral mission. Or at least, by so often insisting on the existence of this moral historical arc, he made it seem so. This is what opened Obama to so much criticism during and after the Arab Spring. If the "right side" was to hope that the young, seemingly liberal protesters in countries like Egypt and Tunisia would find their voice and demand their freedom, then it was clear enough who was on the wrong side. (And not just the wrong side, but the wrong side *of history*.)

What was interesting about these various "sides" was that they were supposed to be self-evident. When Russia invaded Ukraine in 2014, Secretary of State John Kerry gently explained that such invasions weren't allowed. "You just don't in the 21st century behave in 19th-century fashion by invading another country on completely trumped-up pretext," is how Kerry put it. When Russia launched its military intervention in Syria in the fall of 2015, Obama seemed almost nonplussed. Russia had made a mistake, and it would soon come to see the error of its ways. "I think Mr. Putin understands that . . . with Afghanistan fresh in the memory, for him to simply get bogged down in an inconclusive and paralyzing civil conflict is not the outcome that he's looking for," is how Obama put it.

Evil, then, was something outside of history, a violation of the arc that Obama believed bent toward justice. Not surprisingly, then, Obama often seemed annoyed with other people's resistance to history's inexorable march. He wanted others, friends and enemies alike, to act rationally in what he thought was their own best interest. And rationality would lead others to understand what he already understood.

Because history had a direction and because this should have been apparent to any reasonable individual, it was easy to become frustrated. As Graham writes, "The problem with this kind of thinking is that it imputes an agency to history that doesn't exist."[4] History wasn't a person or a country or a machine. To insist on history as an engine or a mechanism was to anthropomorphize something that could only be told after it had happened.

If history is to bend, someone needs to do the bending. As it turned out, President Obama—during the Arab Spring when it would have mattered most—wasn't willing to back his own premise with the hard power it demanded. And without power, the moralism on display revealed itself as both empty and presumptuous. The much heralded "liberal world order" existed, intellectually, but authoritarian leaders around the globe did not seem to believe in it. And if they believed in it, they did not pay it much heed. With this in mind, there were, and still are, two options. The first is to separate questions of order from those of morality, as Machiavelli might have advised. There is a danger of expecting too much of the world—and too much from politics where the disappointments are almost built in. Machiavelli, as the author Damir Marusic reminds us, "is best read as warning of the perils that come if we take morality as our starting point for the creation of any kind of order."[5]

A somewhat different conclusion to draw is that if we care about promoting our values, we must back them up with something beyond rhetoric. To "back them up" doesn't necessitate stupid wars of aggression, but it does require power and the willingness to use it. Our values are not freestanding facts; they must be guaranteed, and in international politics, nothing can be guaranteed without a credible threat of punitive action. This can run the gamut of suspending economic aid, halting arms sales, diplomatic isolation, or sanctions. To move beyond the temptations of the passive voice, who, exactly, provides this guarantee? In most cases, for better or worse, there is only one obvious candidate. The United States, however, will not remain powerful forever—or at least not as powerful as it is today or once was. The longer we wait, then, the higher the cost.

In this sense, contra Machiavelli, power and morality are inextricably intertwined. The legitimacy of a U.S.-led order depends on the notion that it is better than the alternative, and it is better because morality plays some role in American foreign policy in a way that it doesn't for revisionist powers like China or Russia. Or to put it somewhat differently, it is in our national interest to be moral. And morality is impossible without power. This doesn't make American power intrinsically good; it means that power is a means to another, different end.

Notes

Introduction

1. Roger Scruton, "Limits to Democracy," *The New Criterion*, January 2006, https://newcriterion.com/issues/2006/1/limits-to-democracy.
2. Michael Brendan Dougherty, *My Father Left Me Ireland* (New York: Sentinel, 2019), p. 63.

Chapter 1

1. Anthony Lewis, "The Kissinger Doctrine," *New York Times*, February 27, 1975, https://www.nytimes.com/1975/02/27/archives/the-kissinger-doctrine.html.
2. For a fascinating and somewhat revisionist account of Kissinger's attitudes toward Chile (and democracy more generally), see Barry Gewen's new book *The Inevitability of Tragedy: Henry Kissinger and His World* (New York: W.W. Norton, 2020).
3. Gewen, *The Inevitability of Tragedy*, p. 27.
4. Henry Kissinger, *World Order* (New York: Penguin 2014), p. 125.
5. As the editors of an overview of U.S. democracy promotion note: "Honed in the first instance as a means of countering European imperialism and later given even sharper definition in the struggle against fascism and communism, it was no mere talisman but the cutting edge of the United States' rise to world-power status" (Michael Cox, G. John Ikenberry, and Takashi Inoguchi, *American Democracy Promotion: Impulses, Strategies, and Impacts*, eds. Michael Cox, G. John Ikenberry, and Takashi Inoguchi [New York: Oxford University Press, 2000],) p. 10).
6. Robert Kagan, *The Jungle Grows Back: America and Our Imperiled World* (New York: Knopf, 2018), p. 9.
7. David Van Reybrouk, *Against Elections* (New York: Seven Stories Press, 2016), p. 1.
8. James Traub's *The Freedom Agenda: Why America Must Spread Democracy (Just Not the Way George Bush Did)* is one of the best and most comprehensive accounts of the Bush administration's efforts (New York: Farrar, Straus and Giroux, 2008).
9. One version of this—the so-called pothole theory of democracy—made its way into the statements of George W. Bush. Responding to a question about Hezbollah in 2005, Bush had this to say: "I like the idea of people running for office. There's a positive effect. . . . Maybe some will run for office and say, vote for me, I look forward to blowing up America. . . . I don't think so. I think people who generally run for office say, vote for me, I'm looking forward to fixing your potholes" ("Transcript: Bush

News Conference," *Washington Post*, March 16, 2005, http://www.washingtonpost. com/wp-dyn/articles/A40191-2005Mar16_4.html).

10. Condoleezza Rice, *Democracy: Stories from the Long Road to Freedom* (New York: Twelve, 2017), pp. 368–369.

11. Interview with author, Elliot Abrams, November 2, 2021.

12. John J. Mearsheimer, *The Great Delusion: Liberal Dreams and International Realities*; Stephen Walt, *The Hell of Good Intentions: America's Foreign Policy Elite and the Decline of U.S. Primacy* (New York: Farrar, Straus and Giroux, 2018).

13. Stephen Wertheim, *Tomorrow, The World: The Birth of U.S. Global Supremacy* (Cambridge, MA: Belknap Press, 2021).

14. Mearsheimer, *The Great Delusion*, p. 123.

15. Yascha Mounk, *The People vs. Democracy: Why Our Freedom Is in Danger & How to Save It* (Cambridge, MA: Harvard University Press, 2018), p. 13.

16. For a version of this argument, see Damir Marusic, "How Not to Bend the Arc of History," *Wisdom of Crowds*, January 24, 2022, https://wisdomofcrowds.live/how-not-to-bend-the-arc-of-history/.

17. See, for example, Max Fisher, "Obama's Cringe-Worthy Line Claiming Middle East Conflicts 'Date Back Millennia,'" *Vox*, January 12, 2016, https://www.vox.com/2016/1/12/10759008/state-union-address-obama-middle-east-millennia.

18. Donald J. Trump, "Remarks by President Trump to the 73rd Session of the United Nations General Assembly," The White House, September 25, 2018, https://www.whitehouse.gov/briefings-statements/remarks-president-trump-73rd-session-united-nations-general-assembly-new-york-ny/.

19. Interview with author, special assistant to President Barack Obama, October 21, 2021.

20. Jeffrey Goldberg, "The Obama Doctrine," *The Atlantic*, March 10, 2016, https://www.theatlantic.com/press-releases/archive/2016/03/the-obama-doctrine-the-atlantics-exclusive-report-on-presidents-hardest-foreign-policy-decisions/473151/.

21. Ibid.

22. Barack Obama, "Remarks of President Barack Obama—State of the Union Address as Delivered," The White House, January 13, 2016, https://obamawhitehouse.archives.gov/the-press-office/2016/01/12/remarks-president-barack-obama-%E2%80%93-prepared-delivery-state-union-address.

23. Goldberg, "The Obama Doctrine."

24. Ibid.

25. Barack Obama, "Address to the Nation by the President," The White House, December 6, 2015, https://obamawhitehouse.archives.gov/the-press-office/2015/12/06/address-nation-president.

26. Goldberg, "The Obama Doctrine."

27. John Rawls, *Political Liberalism* (New York: Columbia University Press, 2005), p. 6.

28. Francis Fukuyama, "Liberalism and Its Discontents," *American Purpose*, October 5, 2020, https://www.americanpurpose.com/articles/liberalism-and-its-discontent/.

29. In his discussion of "reasonable pluralism," Rawls risks trapping himself in his own tautology. The very fact of pluralism, in the first place, means that there is limited shared understanding of what meets the standard of "reasonable." To say that

pluralism is fine but that it must be reasonable might even be considered an anti-pluralist move. Similarly, when Rawls insists on the importance of respecting the "comprehensive doctrines" of others, he caveats it, again using "reason" as the self-limiting principle. For example, "Central to the idea of public reason is that it nei-ther criticizes nor attacks any comprehensive doctrine, religious or nonreligious, except insofar as that doctrine is incompatible with the essentials of public reasons and a democratic polity." See Rawls, "The Idea of Public Reason Revisited," in *Political Liberalism*, p. 441.

30. Richard Youngs, *The Puzzle of Non-Western Democracy* (Washington, DC: Carnegie Endowment for International Peace, 2015), p. 89.

31. "From John Adams to John Taylor, 17 December 1814," *Founders Online*, National Archives, https://founders.archives.gov/documents/Adams/99-02-02-6371.

32. James Madison, "Federalist No. 10," in *Federalist Papers: Primary Documents in American History* 10; "The Same Subject Continued: The Union as a Safeguard against Domestic Faction and Insurrection," *New York Packet*, November 23, 1787, https://guides.loc.gov/federalist-papers/text-1-10#s-lg-box-wrapper-25493273.

33. Van Reybrouk, *Against Elections* , p. 89.

34. Alexander Hamilton or James Madison, "Federalist No. 57: The Alleged Tendency of the New Plan to Elevate the Few at the Expense of the Many Considered in Connection with Representation," *New York Packet*, February 19, 1788, https://guides.loc.gov/federalist-papers/text-51-60#s-lg-box-wrapper-25493433.

35. Katerina Dalacoura, *Islamist Terrorism and Democracy in the Middle East* (Cambridge: Cambridge University Press, 2011), p. 17.

36. Fareed Zakaria, *The Future of Freedom: Illiberal Democracy at Home and Abroad* (New York: W.W Norton, 2003), p. 124.

37. Richard Rose and Doh Chull Shin, "Democratization Backwards: The Problem of Third-Wave Democracies," *British Journal of Political Science* 31 (April 2011), p. 332.

38. Joseph S. Nye, Jr., *Do Morals Matter? Presidents and Foreign Policy from FDR to Trump* (New York: Oxford University Press, 2020), p. 2.

39. Patricia O'Toole, *When Trumpets Call: Theodore Roosevelt after the White House* (New York: Simon and Schuster, 2006), p. 131.

40. For a realist critique of Kennedy's quote as repurposed by the Bush administration's Freedom Agenda, see Jonathan Rauch, "'Real Is Not a Four-Letter Word," *The Atlantic*, June 2006, https://www.theatlantic.com/magazine/archive/2006/06/real-is-not-a-four-letter-word/305008/.

41. Traub, *The Freedom Agenda*, p. 31.

42. Joseph Kaminski, *Islam, Liberalism, and Ontology* (New York: Routledge, 2021), p. 3.

43. I thank Eliora Katz for highlighting this point.

44. John Rawls, *A Theory of Justice* (Cambridge, MA: Harvard University Press, 1971).

45. Lenn Goodman, "The Road to Kazanistan," *American Philosophical Quarterly* 45 (April 2008), 85.

46. Mustafa Akyol, *Reopening Muslim Minds: A Return to Reason, Freedom, and Tolerance* (New York: St. Martin's Press, 2021).

47. Rice, *Democracy*, pp. 364–365.

48. For example, "only 16 percent of Iraqis indicate they are generally satisfied with the overall government performance," from "Arab Barometer V: Iraq Country Report," 2019, p. 2, https://www.arabbarometer.org/wp-content/uploads/ABV_Iraq_Report_Public-Opinion_2019.pdf.

49. David Runciman, *The Confidence Trap: A History of Democracy in Crisis from World War I to the Present* (Princeton, NJ: Princeton University Press, 2015).

50. Mohammad Fadel, "Modernist Islamic Political Thought and the Egyptian and Tunisian Revolutions of 2011," *Middle East Law and Governance* 3 (2011), https://doi.org/10.1163/187633711X591459.

51. For how U.S. assistance can reinvigorate corrupt bureaucracies, see Jennifer Brick Murtazashvili, "Afghanistan: A Vicious Cycle of State Failure," *Governance* 29, no. 2 (2016), and Murtazashvili, "Pathologies of Centralized State-Building." *PRISM* 8, no. 2 (2019), 14.

52. Sheri Berman, "The Promise of the Arab Spring," *Foreign Affairs*, January/February 2013, https://www.foreignaffairs.com/articles/syria/2012-12-03/promise-arab-spring.

53. Mara Karlin and Tamara Cofman Wittes, "America's Middle East Purgatory," *Foreign Affairs*, January/February 2019, https://www.foreignaffairs.com/articles/middle-east/2018-12-11/americas-middle-east-purgatory. See also Martin Indyk, "The Middle East Isn't Worth It Anymore," *Wall Street Journal*, January 17, 2020, https://www.wsj.com/articles/the-middle-east-isnt-worth-it-anymore-11579277317.

54. Karlin and Cofman Wittes, "America's Middle East Purgatory."

55. According to polling by my colleague Shibley Telhami, favorable views of Islam actually *increased* during the 2016 presidential campaign, but this increase came entirely from Democrats and independents. See Shibley Telhami, "American Attitudes toward Muslims and Islam," Brookings Institution, July 2016, https://www.brookings.edu/research/american-attitudes-toward-muslims-and-islam/.

56. Vali Nasr, *The Dispensable Nation: American Foreign Policy in Retreat* (New York: Doubleday, 2013), p. 4.

57. Ben Hubbard and Amy Qin, "As the U.S. Pulls Back from the Mideast, China Leans In," *New York Times*, February 1, 2022, https://www.nytimes.com/2022/02/01/world/middleeast/china-middle-east.html.

58. Ibid.

59. Joe Biden, "Remarks by President Biden in Press Conference," The White House, March 25, 2021, https://www.whitehouse.gov/briefing-room/speeches-remarks/2021/03/25/remarks-by-president-biden-in-press-conference/.

60. Dalibor Rohac, "We Need to Talk about Liberalism and Foreign Policy," American Enterprise Institute, July 27, 2020, https://www.aei.org/foreign-and-defense-policy/we-need-to-talk-about-liberalism-and-foreign-policy/.

61. Elections are central to the democratic idea, but they must be meaningful. And they can only be meaningful if incumbents have a plausible chance of losing. As Michael McFaul notes, "A competitive and meaningful election is the pivotal feature of a democratic political system—the one attribute that distinguishes democracy

from autocracy" (*Advancing Democracy Abroad: Why We Should and Why We Can* [Lanham, MD: Rowman & Littlefield, 2010], p. 29)..

62. On Hugo Chavez's illiberalism, see, for example, Gregory Wilpert, "Venezuela: Participatory Democracy or Government as Usual?," *Socialism and Democracy* 19 (2005).

63. Sarah Sunn Bush and Amaney A. Jamal, "Anti-Americanism, Authoritarian Politics, and Attitudes about Women's Representation: Evidence from a Survey Experiment in Jordan," *International Studies Quarterly* 59, no. 1 (March 2015), p. 34. See also Marina Ottaway, "The Limits of Women's Rights," in eds. Thomas Carothers and Marina Ottaway, *Uncharted Journey: Promoting Democracy in the Middle East* (Washington, DC: Carnegie Endowment for International Peace, 2005).

64. See, for example, Martha Nussbaum, *Cultivating Humanity: A Classical Defense of Reform in Liberal Education* (Cambridge: Cambridge University Press, 1997); Susan Moller Okin, "'Mistresses of Their Own Destiny': Group Rights, Gender, and Realistic Rights of Exit," *Ethics* 112, no. 2 (January 2002); and Amy Baehr, "Towards a New Feminist Liberalism: Okin, Rawls, and Habermas," *Hypatia* 11, no. 1 (Winter 1996).

65. Mark Landler, "Obama Seeks Reset in Arab World," *New York Times*, May 11, 2011, https://www.nytimes.com/2011/05/12/us/politics/12prexy.html.

66. See, for example, David Smith, "After Trump: Biden Set to Outline US Policy to Johnson, Putin and More," *The Guardian*, June 6, 2021, https://www.theguardian.com/us-news/2021/jun/06/trump-biden-us-policy-johnson-putin-queen-erdogan-eu; Jordyn Phelps, "Biden's Most Important Message Overseas: He's Not Trump," *ABC News*, June 12, 2021, https://abcnews.go.com/Politics/bidens-important-message-overseas-hes-trump/story?id=78220169.

67. Phil Gordon was White House coordinator for the Middle East from 2013 to 2015. In his book *Losing the Long Game: The False Promise of Regime Change* (New York: St. Martin's Press, 2020), one of his chapter subheadings is "Americans don't know enough about the Middle East." He has a point, but presumably this weakness can be corrected by knowing more about the Middle East, rather than accepting that we are doomed by our lack of understanding.

68. "US Urges Restraint in Egypt, Says Government Stable," *Reuters*, January 25, 2011, https://www.reuters.com/article/ozatp-egypt-protest-clinton-20110125-idAFJO E70O0KF20110125.

69. McFaul, *Advancing Democracy Abroad*, p. 57.

70. Economist Intelligence Unit, "Democracy Index 2020: In Sickness and in Health?," https://www.eiu.com/n/campaigns/democracy-index-2020-download-success.

71. Laurence Whitehead, *The International Dimensions of Democratization: Europe and the Americas* (Oxford: Oxford University Press, 1996), p. 9.

72. See David Kirkpatrick, "How American Hopes for a Deal in Egypt Were Undercut," *New York Times*, August 17, 2013; interview with author, Anne Patterson, former U.S. ambassador to Egypt, November 5, 2021.

73. Derek Chollet, *The Long Game: How Obama Defied Washington and Redefined America's Role in the World* (New York: Public Affairs, 2016), p. 196.

74. Sean Yom, *From Resilience to Revolution: How Foreign Interventions Destabilize the Middle East* (New York: Columbia University Press, 2016), p. 167.

75. Ibid., pp. 172–173.

76. For more on how external support undermines incentives to compromise with opponents, see Yom, pp. 2, 6.

77. Jeffrey Goldberg, "Sleepy Chuck Hagel Has Some Bigger Questions to Answer," *Bloomberg*, January 31, 2013, https://www.bloomberg.com/opinion/articles/2013-01-31/sleepy-chuck-hagel-has-some-bigger-questions-to-answer.

78. Ibid.

79. Interview with author, former senior White House official, October 12, 2021.

80. As former Deputy Assistant Secretary of Defense Andrew Exum put it: "The two interests that have guided U.S. Middle East policy for the past 60 years have been the security of the State of Israel and preserving access to hydrocarbon resources in and around the Arabian Peninsula" (interview with author, October 28, 2021). See also Chollet, *The Long Game*, p. 95.

81. Interview with author, Martin Indyk, November 2, 2021.

82. Interview with author, Elliot Abrams, former deputy national security advisor, November 2, 2021.

83. Interview with author, former senior White House official, October 12, 2021.

84. On the sources of Americans' support for Israel, see Walter Russell Mead's brilliant and comprehensive account *The Arc of a Covenant: The United States, Israel, and the Fate of the Jewish People* (New York: Knopf, 2022).

85. Interview with author, former foreign policy advisor to a U.S. senator, October 25, 2021.

86. ABC News, "Jordan's King Abdullah Open to Constitutional Monarchy," October 18, 2017, https://abcnews.go.com/WNT/story?id=583538.

87. How the seeming impossibility of change under conditions of dictatorship can quickly give way to its possibility and even its inevitability (in retrospect) is a recurring theme in the literature on revolution. See, for example, Hannah Arendt's *On Revolution*. Or as Sean Yom pithily notes, a revolution "only becomes apparent after it has ended" (*From Resilience to Revolution*, p. 147).

88. Edmund S. Morgan, *Inventing the People: The Rise of Popular Sovereignty in England and America* (New York: W.W. Norton, 1989).

89. Joint survey commissioned by Freedom House, the Penn Biden Center, and the George W. Bush Institute, "The Democracy Project," 2018, https://freedomhouse.org/report/special-report/2018/democracy-project.

Chapter 2

1. Joseph A. Schumpeter, *Capitalism, Socialism and Democracy* (London: Routledge, 2010).

2. Gerry Mackie, "Schumpeter's Leadership Democracy," *Political Theory* 37 (February 2009), p. 129.

3. On how socialist parties decided to pursue their aims through the democratic process, see Adam Przeworski and John Sprague, *Paper Stones: A History of Electoral Socialism* (Chicago: University of Chicago Press, 1988).

4. Schumpeter, *Capitalism, Socialism and Democracy*, pp. 250–251.

5. Ibid., p. 266.

6. Larry Diamond, "Elections without Democracy: Thinking about Hybrid Regimes," *Journal of Democracy* 13, no. 2 (2002); Steven Levitsky and Lucan A. Way, *Competitive Authoritarianism: Hybrid Regimes after the Cold War* (New York: Cambridge University Press, 2010); Terry Lynn Karl, "The Hybrid Regimes of Central America," *Journal of Democracy* 6 (1995); Jason Brownlee, "Portents of Pluralism: How Hybrid Regimes Affect Democratic Transitions," *American Journal of Political Science* 53, no. 3 (July 1, 2009), pp. 515–532.

7. *Democradura* is directly translated as "hard democracy," wherein the foundational democratic procedures such as elections still take place but are not accompanied by traditional civil freedoms. See David Collier and Steven Levitsky, "Democracy with Adjectives: Conceptual Innovation in Comparative Research," *World Politics* 49 (1997).

8. Viktor Orbán, "Viktor Orbán's Speech at Bálványos Free Summer University and Youth Camp," July 26, 2014, https://budapestbeacon.com/full-text-of-viktor-orbans-speech-at-baile-tusnad-tusnadfurdo-of-26-july-2014/.

9. Yascha Mounk, *The People vs. Democracy: Why Our Freedom Is in Danger & How to Save It* (Cambridge, MA: Harvard University Press, 2018).

10. Ibid., pp. 64, 77.

11. On Catholic integralism, see Adrian Vermeule, "Integration from Within," *American Affairs*, Spring 2018, https://americanaffairsjournal.org/2018/02/integration-from-within/; and Kevin Vallier, "Political Liberals vs. Integralists: Where the Conflict Really Lies," *Reconciled*, October 30, 2020, https://www.kevinvallier.com/reconciled/political-liberals-vs-integralists-where-the-conflict-really-lies/.

12. Isaiah Berlin, *Liberty: Four Essays on Liberty*, ed. Henry Hardy (Oxford: Oxford University Press, 2002), p. 175.

13. Robert Inglehart et al., "World Values Survey: Round Six (2010–2014)" (Madrid, 2014), https://www.worldvaluessurvey.org/WVSDocumentationWV6.jsp.

14. Roberto Stefan Foa and Yascha Mounk, "The Danger of Deconsolidation: The Democratic Disconnect," *Journal of Democracy* 27, no. 3 (2016), p. 13.

15. See, for example, Yuchao Zhu, "'Performance Legitimacy' and China's Political Adaptation Strategy," *Journal of Chinese Political Science* 16 (June 2011).

16. Gary Lawson, "The Rise and Rise of the Administrative State," *Harvard Law Review* 107, no. 6 (April 1994).

17. As of November 2021, Belgium had counted over 27,000 COVID-related deaths. Belgium's high death rate can be partially explained by the government's decision to overcount deaths. While most countries include only confirmed COVID cases in their official statistics, Belgium also includes suspected COVID cases. This led to the

perception that Belgium was harder hit by the pandemic than other countries. Teri Schultz, "Why Belgium's Death Rate Is So High: It Counts Lots of Suspected COVID-19 Cases," *NPR*, April 22, 2020, https://www.npr.org/sections/coronavirus-live-upda tes/2020/04/22/841005901/why-belgiums-death-rate-is-so-high-it-counts-lots-of-suspected-covid-19-cases.

18. See, for example, Associated Press, "China Didn't Warn Public of Likely Pandemic for 6 Key Days," *AP News*, April 15, 2020, https://apnews.com/article/virus-outbreak-hea lth-ap-top-news-international-news-china-clamps-down-68a9e1b91de4ffc166acd 6012d82c2f9.

19. Evelyn Cheng, "Biden Calls for U.S. to Become More Competitive against a 'Deadly Earnest' China," *CNBC*, April 29, 2021, https://www.cnbc.com/2021/04/29/biden-calls-for-us-to-become-more-competitive-against-china.html?__source=share bar%7Ctwitter&par=sharebar.

20. Alex Ward, "Joe Biden Wants to Prove Democracy Works—before It's Too Late," *Vox*, April 28, 2021, https://www.vox.com/2021/4/28/22408735/joe-biden-congress-spe ech-democracy-autocracy.

21. Joseph R. Biden, "Remarks by President Biden in Press Conference," The White House, March 25, 2021, https://www.whitehouse.gov/briefing-room/speeches-rema rks/2021/03/25/remarks-by-president-biden-in-press-conference/.

22. I thank Samuel Kimbriel for emphasizing this point when reviewing this section.

23. Sheri Berman, "Democracy, Authoritarianism and Crises," *Social Europe*, March 30, 2020, https://www.socialeurope.eu/democracy-authoritarianism-and-crises.

24. On the superiority of parliamentary systems, Juan Linz's work has been particularly influential. See, for example, Juan J. Linz and Arturo Valenzuela, eds., *The Failure of Presidential Democracy: Comparative Perspectives* (Baltimore: Johns Hopkins University Press, 1994); Juan J Linz, "The Virtues of Parliamentarism," *Journal of Democracy* 1, no. 4 (1990). See also Scott Mainwaring and Matthew S. Shugart, "Juan Linz, Presidentialism, and Democracy: A Critical Appraisal," *Comparative Politics* 29 (1997).

25. Ian Shapiro, Introduction, in Robert Dahl, *On Democracy*, 2nd ed. (New Haven, CT: Yale University Press, 2020), p. xviii.

26. "Why Does Italy Go Through So Many Governments?," *The Economist*, January 31, 2021, https://www.economist.com/the-economist-explains/2021/01/31/why-does-italy-go-through-so-many-governments.

27. Foa and Mounk, "The Danger of Deconsolidation," p. 16.

28. Christopher H. Achen and Larry M. Bartels, *Democracy for Realists: Why Elections Do Not Produce Responsive Government* (Princeton, NJ: Princeton University Press, 2017).

29. Dahl, *On Democracy*, p. 46.

30. I thank Tom Barson for this rendering of my position, in response to an article I had written.

31. Josiah Ober, "Natural Capacities and Democracy as a Good-in-Itself," *Philosophical Studies* 132 (2007), p. 66.

32. Josiah Ober, "Political Animals Revisited," *The Good Society* 22 (2013), p. 205.

33. Ober, "Natural Capacities and Democracy as a Good-in-Itself," p. 59.

34. Aristotle, "Politics," *Internet Encyclopedia of Philosophy* (Book 6, Part 2), https://iep. utm.edu/aris-pol/#H11.

Chapter 3

1. On the question of why the Egyptian left failed to gain traction, see also Tarek Masoud, *Counting Islam: Religion, Class, and Elections in Egypt* (Cambridge: Cambridge University Press, 2014).

2. See Sharan Grewal and Shadi Hamid, "The Dark Side of Consensus in Tunisia," Brookings Institution, February 2020, https://www.brookings.edu/research/the-dark-side-of-consensus-in-tunisia-lessons-from-2015-2019/.

3. Interview with author, Mustafa al-Naggar, October 15, 2011.

4. "The Arab World in Seven Charts: Are Arabs Turning Their Backs on Religion," Arab Barometer, June 23, 2019, https://www.arabbarometer.org/2019/06/the-arab-world-in-seven-charts-are-arabs-turning-their-backs-on-religion/. See also Kate Hodal, "Arab World Turns Its Back on Religion—and Its Ire on the US," *The Guardian*, June 24, 2019, https://www.theguardian.com/global-development/2019/jun/24/arab-world-turns-its-back-on-religion-and-its-ire-on-the-us; "Arabs Are Losing Faith in Religious Parties and Leaders," *The Economist*, December 5, 2019, https://www.economist.com/graphic-detail/2019/12/05/arabs-are-losing-faith-in-religious-parties-and-leaders.

5. Tareq Y. Ismael, *The Middle East in World Politics* (Syracuse, NY: Syracuse University Press, 1974), p. 204.

6. See, for example, Kristin Kobes Du Mez, *Jesus and John Wayne: How White Evangelicals Corrupted a Faith and Fractured a Nation* (New York: Liveright, 2020); and Richard Kyle, *Evangelicalism: An Americanized Christianity* (New York: Routledge, 2017).

7. On how gaps in religious observance shape perceptions of Muslim minorities in Europe, see Shadi Hamid, "The Role of Islam in European Populism: How Refugee Flows and Fear of Muslims Drive Right-Wing Support," Brookings Institution, February 2019, https://www.brookings.edu/research/the-role-of-islam-in-european-populism-how-refugee-flows-and-fear-of-muslims-drive-right-wing-support.

8. The United States had long been a holdout among Western democracies, uniquely and perhaps even suspiciously devout. This is changing. From 1937 through 1998, church membership remained constant, hovering at around 70 percent. Over the last two decades, however, that number has dropped below 50 percent, the sharpest recorded decline in American history. See Jeffrey M. Jones, "U.S. Church Membership Falls below Majority for First Time," Gallup, March 29, 2021, https://news.gallup.com/poll/341963/church-membership-falls-below-majority-first-time.aspx.

9. Christine Tamir, Aidan Connaughton, and Ariana Monique Salazar, "The Global God Divide," Pew Research Center, July 20, 2020, https://www.pewresearch.org/global/2020/07/20/the-global-god-divide/.

10. Luna Simms, "Iran's Revolution Reconsidered," *Law & Liberty*, February 20, 2019, https://lawliberty.org/forum/irans-revolution-reconsidered/.

11. For a discussion of the broader meanings and expressions of sharia, see Wael B. Hallaq, *Shari'a: Theory, Practice, Transformation* (Cambridge, UK: Cambridge University Press, 2009), pp. 1–3.

12. See, for example, Mustafa Akyol, *Reopening Muslim Minds* (New York: St Martins, 2021), pp. 136–142.

13. Wael B. Hallaq, *The Impossible State: Islam, Politics, and Modernity's Moral Predicament* (New York: Columbia University Press, 2013), p. 11.

14. Michael Cook, "The Appeal of Islamic Fundamentalism," *Journal of the British Academy* 2 (2014), p. 28.

15. Thomas Hegghammer's definition—"activism justified with primary reference to Islam"—also helpfully captures the conscious, and even self-conscious, nature of Islamism ("Should I Stay or Should I Go: Explaining Variation in Western Jihadists' Choice between Domestic and Foreign Fighting," *American Political Science Review* [2013], p. 1).

16. As Mustafa Akyol, a Muslim liberal thinker and author of *Reopening Muslim Minds*, notes: "Since liberalism is largely associated with 'the West,' and the West itself with colonialism, anti-colonial reactions in Muslim societies have condemned liberalism as well. Had liberalism rather came from a non-threatening non-Muslim power—such as, say, Japan—it could have found more interest and have made more progress" (email correspondence with author, June 15, 2021).

17. On the millet system as "a successful example of non-territorial autonomy," see Karen Barkey and George Gavrilis, "The Ottoman Millet System: Non-Territorial Autonomy and Its Contemporary Legacy," *Ethnopolitics* 15 (2016), p. 24.

18. Jonathan A. C. Brown, *Misquoting Muhammad: The Challenge and Choices of Interpreting the Prophet's Legacy* (London: Oneworld, 2014), p. 186.

19. On the Qur'an as "God's actual speech" rather than merely "the word of God," see Shadi Hamid, *Islamic Exceptionalism: How the Struggle over Islam Is Reshaping the World* (New York: St. Martin's Press, 2016), pp. 49–51.

20. Knut Vikør, *Between God and the Sultan: A History of Islamic Law* (Oxford: Oxford University Press, 2005), p. 185.

21. On the relative autonomy of the clerical class during Islam's classical period, see also Noah Feldman, *The Fall and Rise of the Islamic State* (Princeton, NJ: Princeton University Press, 2008), pp. 6–7; and Ahmet Kuru, *Islam, Authoritarianism, and Underdevelopment: A Global and Historical Comparison* (Cambridge, UK: Cambridge University Press), pp. 3–4.

22. *Jordan Times*, March 7, 1990.

23. Hasanayn Tawfiq Ibrahim and Hoda Raghib Awad, *al-Ikhwan al-Muslimun wa al-Siyasa fi Misr* [The Political Role of the Muslim Brotherhood under Limited Political Pluralism in Egypt] (Cairo: Markaz al-Mahrusa, 1996), p. 328.

24. In the more religiously conservative societies of the Middle East, the word "secular" can be confusing, since parties and politicians would never use a word in Arabic—'almani—that has the negative connotation of irreligiousness and moral laxity.

25. During Islam's classical period, religious scholars, or *ulama*, had close ties to industry and business, and many were involved in commerce themselves (Kuru, *Islam, Authoritarianism, and Underdevelopment*, pp. 3, 5–6).

26. For more on different approaches to secularism, see Ahmet Kuru, *Secularism and State Policies toward Religion: The United States, France, and Turkey* (Cambridge, UK: Cambridge University Press, 2009).

27. Abraham Kuyper, *Our Program: A Christian Political Manifesto* (Bellingham, WA: Lexham Press, 2015).

28. Dankwart A. Rustow, "Transitions to Democracy: Toward a Dynamic Model," *Comparative Politics* 2 (April 1970), 359.

29. Chantal Mouffe, *The Democratic Paradox* (London: Verso, 2009), p. 93.

30. Pew Research Center, "In 2018, Government Restrictions on Religion Reach Highest Level Globally in More Than a Decade," November 10, 2020, https://www.pewforum.org/2020/11/10/in-2018-government-restrictions-on-religion-reach-highest-level-globally-in-more-than-a-decade/.

31. Sarah Alaoui, "Morocco, Commander of the (African) Faithful?," Brookings Institution, April 8, 2019, https://www.brookings.edu/blog/order-from-chaos/2019/04/08/morocco-commander-of-the-african-faithful/.

32. Vali Nasr, *Islamic Leviathan: Islam and the Making of State Power* (Oxford: Oxford University Press, 2001), p. 8.

33. Pew Research Center, "Government Restrictions."

34. Faheem Hussain, "Egypt's Liberal Coup," *Faheem Hussain—Some Thoughts*, August 13, 2014, https://faheemabdmominhussain.wordpress.com/2014/08/13/egypts-liberal-coup/. A shorter version was published on the website *Open Democracy*: https://www.opendemocracy.net/arab-awakening/faheem-hussain/egypt%27s-liberal-coup.

35. Jean-Jacques Rousseau, "Discourse on the Arts and Sciences," in *The Basic Political Writings*, 2nd ed., trans. and ed. Donald A. Cress (Indianapolis, IN: Hackett, 2012).

36. Larisa Epatko, "Mubarak in 1993: Egypt 'Keen' on Democracy, but It Takes Time," *PBS NewsHour*, February 4, 2011, https://www.pbs.org/newshour/world/mubarak-on-democracy.

37. John Gray, *Two Faces of Liberalism* (Cambridge, UK: Polity Press, 2000), p. 2.

38. Ibid., p. 4.

39. Lenn Goodman, *Religious Pluralism and Values in the Public Sphere* (Cambridge, UK: Cambridge University Press, 2014), p. 1.

40. For my argument on when and how an "Islamic reformation" already happened, see *Islamic Exceptionalism*, pp. 25–26, 68–79.

41. Mustafa Akyol, "The Islamic World Doesn't Need a Reformation," *The Atlantic*, October 31, 2017, https://www.theatlantic.com/international/archive/2017/10/muslim-reformation/544343/.

42. Nader Hashemi, "A Clash of the Sacred and the Secular," *Law & Liberty*, February 13, 2019, https://lawliberty.org/forum/a-clash-of-the-sacred-and-the-secular/.

43. Oriana Fallaci, "Henry Kissinger," *Interview with History* (Universe Publishing, 2016), p. 42, 44.

44. See Hamid, *Temptations of Power*, pp. 45–47.

45. For example, David Pollack of the Washington Institute wrote in 2017 that "a reliable survey conducted in Jordan last month shows that many Jordanians now hold *unexpectedly moderate views* [emphasis mine] on all these topics, and more, including Islamic reform, relations with the United States, and even cooperation with Israel." David Pollack, "New Jordan Poll Reveals Surprisingly Moderate Public Opinion," Washington Institute for Near East Policy, September 20, 2017, https://www.washingtoninstitute.org/policy-analysis/new-jordan-poll-reveals-surprisingly-moderate-public-opinion.

46. Interview with author, former senior Pentagon official, October 28, 2021.

47. According to a 2019 poll, 72.5 percent of Jordanians favor limiting military and security relations with Israel; only 4.9 percent favor strengthening relations; 17.4 percent favor maintaining current levels ("Survey on Jordanians' Perceptions on Foreign Relations," Amman: Konrad Adenauer Stiftung Jordan Office and NAMA Strategic Intelligence Solutions, 2019), https://www.kas.de/en/web/jordanien/single-title/-/content/survey-jordanians-perceptions-on-foreign-relations.

48. Martha Nussbaum, *Cultivating Humanity: A Classical Defense of Reform in Liberal Education* (Cambridge, UK: Cambridge University Press, 1997), p. 211.

49. Philip Gordon, *Losing the Long Game: The False Promise of Regime Change in the Middle East* (New York: St. Martin's Press, 2020), p. 20.

50. Interview with author, Stephen Krasner, former director of policy planning at the State Department, October 21, 2021.

51. Interview with author, Jeffrey Feltman, former assistant secretary of state for Near Eastern affairs, October 13, 2021.

52. Jack Knight and James Johnson, *The Priority of Democracy: Political Consequences of Pragmatism* (Princeton, NJ: Princeton University Press, 2011), p. 20.

Chapter 4

1. Freedom House ratings are the most widely used measures of human rights and democracy. Each country receives two scores on an annual basis. As the organization explains in the methodology section of its annual world report, *Freedom in the World*, the "political rights" score includes measures on "electoral process," "political pluralism and participation," and "functioning of government." The "civil liberties" score includes measures of "freedom of expression and belief," "associational and organizational rights," and "rule of law." For more on the methodology used, see Raymond D. Gastil, "The Comparative Survey of Freedom: Experiences and Suggestions," in Alex Inkeles, ed., *On Measuring Democracy: Its Consequences and Concomitants* (New Brunswick, NJ: Transaction, 1991), pp. 21–46.

2. Freedom House, "Country and Territory Ratings and Statuses, 1973–2021," https://freedomhouse.org/sites/default/files/2021-02/Country_and_Territory_Ratings_and_Statuses_FIW1973-2021.xlsx.

3. William E. Farrell, "Sadat Assassinated at Army Parade as Men amid Ranks Fire into Stands; Vice President Affirms 'All Treaties,'" *New York Times*, October 7, 1981, https://www.nytimes.com/1981/10/07/world/sadat-assassinated-army-parade-men-amid-ranks-fire-into-stands-vice-president-041355.html; David B. Ottaway, "Sadat Assassinated at Military Show," *Washington Post*, October 7, 1981, https://www.washingtonpost.com/archive/politics/1981/10/07/sadat-assassinated-at-military-show/604a2b32-408f-4e99-972d-ad6379c880c2/.

4. Anthony McDermott, *From Nasser to Mubarak: A Flawed Revolution* (New York: Croom Helm, 1988), p. 76.

5. Robert Springborg, *Mubarak's Egypt: Fragmentation of the Political Order* (Boulder, CO: Westview Press, 1989).

6. Eberhard Kienle, *A Grand Delusion: Democracy and Economic Reform in Egypt* (London: IB Tauris, 2001), p. 14.

7. Najwa Najjar, "Shift towards Democratization Crucial to Arabs' Progress," *Jordan Times*, March 27, 1989.

8. Caspar Weinberger, *Fighting for Peace: Seven Critical Years at the Pentagon* (New York: Grand Central, 1990); Raymond Tanter, *Who's at the Helm?: Lessons of Lebanon* (Boulder, CO: Westview Press, 1990); George Shultz, *Turmoil and Triumph: My Years as Secretary of State* (New York: Scribner, 2010); Robert Gates, *From the Shadows: The Ultimate Insider's Story of Five Presidents and How They Won the Cold War* (New York: Simon and Schuster, 2007).

9. Larry Diamond, "Is the Third Wave of Democratization Over? The Imperative of Consolidation," Helen Kellogg Institute for International Studies, Working Paper 237, 1997, pp. 23–24.

10. Hesham al-Awadi, *In Pursuit of Legitimacy: The Muslim Brothers and Mubarak, 1982–2000* (London: IB Tauris, 2004), p. 193.

11. Mona el-Ghobashy, "The Metamorphosis of the Egyptian Muslim Brothers," *International Journal of Middle East Studies* 37 (August 2005), p. 381.

12. Eberhard Kienle, "More Than a Response to Islamism: The Political Deliberalization of Egypt in the 1990s," *Middle East Journal* 52 (Spring 1998), p. 287.

13. Carrie Rosefsky Wickham, *Mobilizing Islam: Religion, Activism and Political Change in Egypt* (New York: Columbia University Press, 2002), p. 178.

14. Arab Center Washington DC, "The 2019–2020 Arab Opinion Index: Main Results in Brief," Doha, November 16, 2020, http://arabcenterdc.org/survey/the-2019-2020-arab-opinion-index-main-results-in-brief/#section9.

15. On Jordan's position during the Gulf War, see Jamil E. Jreisat and Hanna Y. Freij, "Jordan, the United States, and the Gulf Crisis," *Arab Studies Quarterly* 13, no. 1/2 (1991), 101–116.

16. King Hussein, *Uneasy Lies the Head* (New York: Bernard Geis Associates, 1962), p. 210.

17. Curtis R. Ryan, "Peace, Bread and Riots: Jordan and the International Monetary Fund," *Middle East Policy* 6, no. 2 (1998), 54–66.

18. Interview with author, Mudar Badran, February 23, 2005.

19. Ibid.

20. Ali Abdul Kazem, "The Muslim Brotherhood: The Historic Background and the Ideological Origins," inJillian Schwedler, ed., *The Islamic Movement in Jordan* (Amman: Al-Urdun Al-Jadid Research Center, 1997), p. 20.

21. See, for example, "Democracy in Jordan 2003," Center for Strategic Studies, June 2003, https://jcss.org/en/2488/democracy-in-jordan-2003/; and "National Priorities, Governance and Political Reform in Jordan: National Public Opinion Poll #7," International Republic Institute, October 2009, https://www.iri.org/sites/default/files/2009-October-27-Survey-of-Jordanian-Public-Opinion, August-8-11,2009.pdf.

22. See, for example, Edward D. Mansfield and Jack Snyder, *Electing to Fight: Why Emerging Democracies Go to War* (Cambridge, MA: MIT Press, 2007).

23. *Jordan Times*, August 20, 1990.

24. King Hussein, "Address to the Nation," February 6, 1991, https://www.jstor.org/stable/pdf/2537562.pdf?refreqid=excelsior%3Ac4ddea17cc2c53f09e7b30c4c5aa7828.

25. Markus Bouillon, "Walking the Tightrope: Jordanian Foreign Policy from the Gulf Crisis to the Peace Process and Beyond," in George Joffe, ed., *Jordan in Transition: 1990–2000* (New York: Palgrave, 2002), p. 6.

26. For more on the Jordanian Brotherhood's relationship with Hamas, see Nael Masalha and Shadi Hamid, "More Than Just the Muslim Brotherhood: The Problem of Hamas and Jordan's Islamic Movement," Brookings Institution, Washington, DC, February 6, 2017, https://www.brookings.edu/research/more-than-just-the-muslim-brotherhood-the-problem-of-hamas-and-jordans-islamic-movement/. See also Joas Wagemakers, *The Muslim Brotherhood in Jordan* (Cambridge, UK: Cambridge University Press, 2020), pp. 101–103, 118.

27. Bouillon, "Walking the Tightrope," p. 10.

28. World Bank, "Developing the Occupied Territories: An Investment in Peace: Overview," World Bank, Washington, DC, September 1993, https://documents.worldbank.org/en/publication/documents-reports/documentdetail/869901468780572753/overview.

29. Jillian Schwedler, *Faith in Moderation: Islamist Parties in Jordan and Yemen* (Cambridge, UK: Cambridge University Press, 2006), p. 56.

30. Renate Dietrich, "The Weakness of the Rule Is the Strength of the Ruler," in George Joffe, ed., *Jordan in Transition: 1990–2000* (New York: Palgrave, 2002), p. 134.

31. For example, a Brotherhood supporter could vote for the two Brotherhood candidates running in his or her district, vote for one Christian, one leftist, and still have one vote to spare. Similarly, a Christian, with a vote to spare, could vote for two Christian candidates as well as the two Brotherhood candidates. By being selective about which districts to contest and by forming alliances with a variety of groups and individuals, the Brotherhood could effectively guarantee the victory of nearly all its candidates.

32. Previously, Japan had used SNTV in national elections (but switched to a two-tier proportional representation and first-pass-the-post system in 1996). In their study of the Japanese case, Arend Ljiphart and Bernard Grofman note that the "unusual property" of SNTV is that its voter threshold is almost zero: "If all but two of the voters in a three-member SNTV district concentrate their votes on one candidate,

two other candidates can be elected with one vote each. This example shows that SNTV entails special problems for the larger parties" (Arend Ljiphart and Bernard Grofman, *Choosing an Electoral System: Issues and Alternatives* [New York: Praeger, 1984],) p. 210).]

33. "Assessment of the Electoral Framework: The Hashemite Kingdom of Jordan," Democracy Reporting International and New Jordan Research Center, 2007, p. 16.

34. Ibid., pp. 16–17.

35. Ibid., p. 18.

36. Ibid., p. 19.

37. Glenn E. Robinson, "Can Islamists Be Democrats? The Case of Jordan," *Middle East Journal* 51 (Summer 1997), p. 398.

38. *Jordan Times*, November 9, 1989.

39. Ibrahim Gharaibeh writes that the Brotherhood's percentage of the vote went from 12 percent in 1989 to 17 percent in 1993. It is difficult to compare results because the electoral systems were extremely different (plurality bloc voting vs. SNTV). In addition, the number of candidates the Brotherhood ran increased from twenty-six in 1989 to thirty-five in 1993. So even if the Islamist share of the vote increased, it may be attributable not to increased popularity but to increased coverage of districts (Ibrahim al-Gharaibeh, *Jama'a Al-Ikhwan Al-Muslimin Fi Al-Urdun, 1946–1996* [The Society of Muslim Brothers in Jordan], Amman: Al-Urdun Al-Jadid Research Center, 1997).

40. *Freedom in the World 1994–1995: The Annual Survey of Political Rights and Civil Liberties* (Washington, DC: Freedom House, 1995), p. 329.

41. Amaney Jamal, *Of Empires and Citizens: Pro-American Democracy or No Democracy at All?* (Princeton, NJ: Princeton University Press), p. 20.

42. Gharaibeh, *Jama'a Al-Ikhwan Al-Muslimin Fi Al-Urdun*, p. 129.

43. Malik Mufti, "Elite Bargains and the Onset of Political Liberalization in Jordan," *Comparative Political Studies* 32, no. 1 (February 1999), 116.

44. *Jordan Times*, May 11, 1991.

45. Interview with Azmi Mansour, Amman, May 29, 2005.

46. *Na'am, al-Islam hoa al-hal: Al-Barnamaj al-Intakhabi li-Murashahi Hizb al-Jabha al-Amal al-Islami, 1993–1997* [Yes, Islam is the solution: The electoral program of the Islamic Action Front candidates], Amman, Jordan, 1993, p. 12.

47. Emad Eldin Shahin, *Political Ascent: Contemporary Islamic Movements in North Africa* (Boulder, CO: Westview Press, 1997), p. 128.

48. Ibid.

49. Daniel Brumberg, "Liberalization vs. Democracy: Understanding Arab Political Reform," *Carnegie Endowment for International Peace*, no. 37 (May 2003), 13.

50. Niall Ferguson, ed., *Virtual History: Alternatives and Counterfactuals* (London: Picador, 1997), p. 87, original emphasis.

51. Michael Willis, *Politics and Power in the Maghreb: Algeria, Tunisia and Morocco from Independence to the Arab Spring Brothers* (Oxford: Oxford University Press, 2014), p. 169.

52. Youssef M. Ibrahim, "Islamic Party in Algeria Defeats Ruling Group in Local Elections," *New York Times*, June 14, 1990, https://www.nytimes.com/1990/06/14/world/islamic-party-in-algeria-defeats-ruling-group-in-local-elections.html.

53. Emad Eldin Shahin, "The Foreign Policy of the Islamic Salvation Front in Algeria," *Islam and Christian-Muslim Relations* 14 (2003), p. 121.

54. For more on the phenomenon of "losing on purpose," see Shadi Hamid, "Arab Islamist Parties: Losing on Purpose?," *Journal of Democracy* 22 (January 2011).

55. Ibid.

56. Willis, *Power and Politics in the Maghreb*, p. 172.

57. George A. Pickart, *The Battle Looms: Islam and Politics in the Middle East: A Report to the Committee on Foreign Relations* (Washington, DC: United States Senate, 1993), p. 2.

58. Fawaz Gerges, *America and Political Islam: Clash of Cultures or Clash of Interests?* (New York: Cambridge University Press, 1999), p. 78.

59. Interview with author, Edward Djerejian, former assistant secretary of state for Near Eastern affairs, October 22, 2021.

60. Ibid., p. 75.

61. Pickart, *The Battle Looms*, p. 6.

62. "James Baker Looks Back at the Middle East," *Middle East Quarterly* 1, no. 3 (September 1994).

63. Edward P. Djerejian, "The U.S. and the Middle East in a Changing World," Address at Meridian House International, June 2, 1992.

64. Interview with author, Edward Djerejian, October 22, 2021.

65. Robin Wright, "Security Fears, Political Ties Cloud U.S. View of Islam's Rise," *Los Angeles Times*, March 7, 1993, https://www.latimes.com/archives/la-xpm-1993-03-07-mn-8322-story.html.

66. Gerges, *America and Political Islam*, p. 78.

67. Peter Mandaville, "Islamism and U.S. Foreign Policy," in Shadi Hamid and Will McCants, eds., *Rethinking Political Islam* (New York: Oxford University Press, 2017), p. 205.

68. Ibid.

69. Interview with author, Edward Djerejian, October 22, 2021.

70. Tarek Masoud, "Contemporary Islamic Politics," Islamic World Today Conference, Brigham Young University, October 19, 2021, https://islamconf.byu.edu/page-5.

71. For a discussion of how Iran analogies influenced Obama's national security team during the Egyptian uprising in 2011, see Michael McFaul, *From Cold War to Hot Peace: An American Ambassador in Putin's Russia* (New York: Mariner Books, 2018).

72. The Islamic Republic of Iran's experience has limited applicability in the rest of the Middle East for another reason. Its theological orientation—one based on the innovative and relatively new Shiite doctrine of "guardianship of the clerics"—has not seriously been attempted anywhere else and is anathema to Sunni Islamist movements. For more on the Muslim Brotherhood's views of the revolution and its aftermath, see Shadi Hamid, "The Lesser Threat: How the Muslim Brotherhood Views Shias and Shiism," *Mediterranean Politics* 25 (2020).

Chapter 5

1. On the weakness of Islamism in West Africa, see Andrew Lebovich and Shadi Hamid, "Why Are There So Few Islamists in West Africa? A Dialogue," Brookings Institution, April 20, 2017, https://www.brookings.edu/on-the-record/why-are-there-so-few-islamists-in-west-africa-a-dialogue-between-shadi-hamid-and-andrew-lebovich/.

2. Gerges, *America and Political Islam*, p. 27.

3. "An Interview with Ronald Reagan," *Time*, November 17, 1980, http://content.time.com/time/subscriber/article/0,33009,950485-3,00.html.

4. George W. Bush, "President Bush's Second Inaugural Address," *NPR*, January 20, 2005, https://www.npr.org/templates/story/story.php?storyId=4460172.

5. Michael Gallagher, "Changing Course: The Sources of Strategic Adjustment," unpublished PhD dissertation, Georgetown University, December 2015, https://repository.library.georgetown.edu/bitstream/handle/10822/1029877/Gallagher_georgetown_0076D_13140.pdf?sequence=1.

6. Interview with author, Rep. Mike Gallagher, November 4, 2021.

7. Interview with author, October 12, 2021.

8. Barack Obama, "Statement by President Barack Obama on Egypt," The White House Office of the Press Secretary, July 3, 2013, https://obamawhitehouse.archives.gov/the-press-office/2013/07/03/statement-president-barack-obama-egypt.

9. "The American President Is a Member of the International Organization of the Brotherhood . . . and His Brother 'Malek' Is Active in Al-Qaeda: 'Barack' Embraced the Brotherhood Ideology in Indonesia . . . and Al-Shater's Son Threatened to Reveal Documents," *Al-Wafd*, August 28, 2013, https://asrararabiya.com/?p=1246.

10. The Polity IV index measures three key indicators of democracy: executive recruitment (whether a leader is elected or appointed), constraints on the executive, and the openness of political participation. See "Polity IV Project: Political Regime Characteristics and Transitions, 1800–2013," http://www.systemicpeace.org/polity/polity4.htm.

11. Shadi Hamid and Meredith Wheeler, "Was Mohamed Morsi Really an Autocrat?," *The Atlantic*, March 31, 2014, https://www.theatlantic.com/international/archive/2014/03/was-mohamed-morsi-really-an-autocrat/359797/.

12. Max Fisher, "Poll: 54% of Republicans Say That, 'Deep Down,' Obama Is a Muslim," *Vox*, February 25, 2015, https://www.vox.com/2015/2/25/8108005/obama-muslim-poll.

13. Interview with author, former State Department official, March 2014.

14. Interview with author, EU special envoy Bernardino Leon, March 26, 2014.

15. Interview with author, senior Muslim Brotherhood official, December 2013.

16. Interview with author, Muslim Brotherhood official, November 2013.

17. See, for example, David Kirkpatrick, "Prominent Egyptian Liberal Says He Sought West's Support for Uprising," *New York Times*, July 4, 2013, https://www.nytimes.com/2013/07/05/world/middleeast/elbaradei-seeks-to-justify-ouster-of-egypts-president.html.

18. Interview with author, former State Department official, January 2014.

19. Interview with author, senior advisor to President Mohamed Morsi, December 2013.

20. "Articles of Agreement of the International Monetary Fund," International Monetary Fund, March 2020, https://www.imf.org/external/pubs/ft/aa/index.htm.

21. Interview with author, Dennis Ross, special assistant to President Barack Obama, October 21, 2021.

22. *Mubadira al-Ikhwan al-Muslimin houl Mabadi al-Islah fi Misr* [The Initiative of the Muslim Brotherhood regarding Principles of Reform in Egypt], Cairo, Egypt, March 2004.

23. Tarek Masoud identifies mosque density as a key predictor of Islamist success on the local level. See Masoud, *Counting Islam: Religion, Class, and Elections in Egypt* (Cambridge, UK: Cambridge University Press, 2014), p. 198.

24. Ibid., p. 206.

25. Interview with author, Anne Patterson, former U.S. ambassador to Egypt, November 5, 2021.

26. For more on the advantages of parliamentary systems, see Juan J. Linz, "The Perils of Presidentialism," *Journal of Democracy* 1 (1990); Juan J. Linz and Arturo Valenzuela, *The Failure of Presidential Democracy: Comparative Perspectives*, Vol. 1 (Baltimore: Johns Hopkins University Press, 1994). For more on the advantages of consensual parliamentary systems, see Arend Lijphart, *Thinking about Democracy: Power Sharing and Majority Rule in Theory and Practice* (New York: Routledge, 2008). For other perspectives, including on different kinds of presidential regimes, see Scott Mainwaring and Matthew Soberg Shugart, *Presidentialism and Democracy in Latin America* (Cambridge, UK: Cambridge University Press, 1997).

27. Martyn Frampton, *The Muslim Brotherhood and the West: A History of Enmity and Engagement* (Cambridge, MA: Belknap Press, 2018), p. 413.

28. Interview with author, former senior State Department official, October 15, 2001.

29. Interview with author, former State Department official, October 21, 2001.

30. Matt Negrin and Reem Abdellatif, "US Ambassador to Egypt Won't Sit Down with Muslim Brotherhood . . . Yet," *PRI*, October 18, 2011, https://www.pri.org/stories/2011-10-18/us-ambassador-egypt-won-t-sit-down-muslim-brotherhoodyet.

31. Interview with author, Peter Mandaville, former member of policy planning staff, State Department, October 12, 2001.

32. Frampton, *The Muslim Brotherhood and the West*, p. 413.

33. Quinn Mecham is the author of *Institutional Origins of Islamist Political Mobilization* (Cambridge, UK: Cambridge University Press, 2017).

34. Peter Mandaville, "Islamism and U.S. Foreign Policy," in Shadi Hamid and Will McCants, eds., *Rethinking Political Islam* (New York: Oxford University Press, 2017), p. 208.

35. Jason Brownlee, *Democracy Prevention: The Politics of the U.S.-Egyptian Alliance* (Cambridge, UK: Cambridge University Press, 2012), p. 10.

36. Ben Rhodes, *The World as It Is: A Memoir of the Obama White House* (New York: Random House, 2018), p. 175.

37. "Daily Press Briefing," U.S. Department of State, June 14, 2012, https://2009-2017.state.gov/r/pa/prs/dpb/2012/06/192346.htm.

38. Nathan Brown, "Egypt's Wide State Reassembles Itself," *Foreign Policy*, July 17, 2013, http://mideast.foreignpolicy.com/posts/2013/07/17/egypt_s_wide_state_reassembles_itself.

39. Mandaville, "Islamism and U.S. Foreign Policy," p. 210.

40. Von Ulrike Putz, "Egypt's Military Secures Far-Reaching Powers," *Der Spiegel*, June 18, 2012, https://www.spiegel.de/international/world/egypt-s-quiet-putsch-could-lead-to-new-unrest-a-839586.html.

41. "Daily Press Briefing," U.S. Department of State, June 18, 2012, https://2009-2017.state.gov/r/pa/prs/dpb/2012/06/193204.htm.

42. Interview with author, White House official, December 1, 2021.

43. Interview with author, former State Department official, October 13, 2021.

44. Margaret Chadbourn, "Obama: Egypt Neither Enemy nor Ally," *Reuters*, September 13, 2012, https://www.reuters.com/article/us-usa-obama-egypt/obama-egypt-neither-enemy-nor-ally-idUSBRE88C0S820120913.

45. Obama, Interview with BBC, "Obama: Mubarak Is a "Stalwart Ally . . . Force for Stability & Good," June 2, 2009, https://www.youtube.com/watch?v=tmLX37f4ZgQ.

46. Rhodes, *The World as It Is*, p. 183.

47. "State Department Briefing on U.S. Aid to Egypt," C-SPAN, July 26, 2013, https://www.c-span.org/video/?314224-2/state-department-briefing-us-aid-egypt.

48. "All According to Plan: The Rab'a Massacre and Mass Killings of Protesters in Egypt," Human Rights Watch, August 2014, http://www.hrw.org/sites/default/files/reports/egypt0814web_0.pdf.

49. Paul Owen and Tom McCarthy, "Egypt: 51 Morsi Supporters Killed in Shooting at Republican Guard Compound—as It Happened," *The Guardian*, July 8, 2013, https://www.theguardian.com/world/middle-east-live/2013/jul/08/egypt-34-killed-in-shooting-at-compound-where-morsi-is-being-held-live-coverage.

50. John Hudson, "Knives Come out for U.S. Ambassador to Egypt Anne Patterson," *Foreign Policy*, July 3, 2013, https://foreignpolicy.com/2013/07/03/knives-come-out-for-u-s-ambassador-to-egypt-anne-patterson/.

51. Ted Cruz, "Our Friend in Cairo," *Foreign Policy*, July 3, 2013, https://foreignpolicy.com/2013/07/03/our-friend-in-cairo/.

52. James Mattis, "The State of the World," Heritage Foundation, May 14, 2015, https://www.youtube.com/watch?app=desktop&v=SCD5zHBNWG8.

53. Al-Qaeda leader Ayman al-Zawahiri wrote an entire tract called *The Bitter Harvest: The Muslim Brotherhood after 60 Years*, published in 1991.

54. Mattis, "The State of the World."

55. James Mattis, "CENTCOM Review: Turmoil in the Mideast and Southwest Asia," Aspen Institute, July 20, 2013, https://www.youtube.com/watch?v=l5Un0NUmGRk.

56. David Kirkpatrick, *Into the Hands of the Soldiers: Freedom and Chaos in Egypt and the Middle East* (New York: Penguin Books, 2018), p. 210.

57. Ibid.

58. Ibid.

59. Interview with author, senior advisor to John Kerry, October 29, 2021.

60. Kirkpatrick, *Into the Hands of the Soldiers*, p. 212.

61. Interview with David Kirkpatrick, John Kerry, March 23, 2017.

62. Kirkpatrick, *Into the Hands of the Soldiers*, p. 212.

63. Ibid., p. 226.

64. Ibid., p. 227.

65. Interview with author, former senior White House official, December 1, 2021.

66. Interview with author, former senior Pentagon official, October 28, 2021.

67. Neil Ketchley, "How Egypt's Generals Used Street Protests to Stage a Coup," *Washington Post*, July 3, 2017, https://www.washingtonpost.com/news/monkey-cage/wp/2017/07/03/how-egypts-generals-used-street-protests-to-stage-a-coup/.

68. Ibid., p. 234.

69. Ibid.

70. Interview with author, former senior White House official, December 1, 2021.

71. Ibid.

72. Kirkpatrick, *Into the Hands of the Soldiers*, p. 242.

73. The Middle East scholar Vali Nasr, who served in the Obama administration from 2009 to 2011, writes that "as the extraordinary events were unfolding, there was a certitude of sort in the White House. Obama remained intent upon leaving the Middle East, and he was not going to let himself be distracted from that mission by sudden eruptions of pro-democracy protests, teetering dictators, and looming civil wars (*The Dispensable Nation: American Foreign Policy in Retreat* [New York, Random House, 2013], p. 164).

74. Interview with author, Anne Patterson, former U.S. ambassador to Egypt, November 5, 2021.

75. David Rothkopf, "Obama's 'Don't Do Stupid Shit' Foreign Policy," *Foreign Policy*, June 4, 2014, https://foreignpolicy.com/2014/06/04/obamas-dont-do-stupid-shit-foreign-policy/.

76. Rhodes, *The World as It Is*, p. 277.

77. Kirkpatrick, *Into the Hands of the Soldiers*, p. 234.

78. Barack Obama, "Remarks by the President on the Situation in Egypt," The White House Office of the Press Secretary, August 15, 2013, https://obamawhitehouse.archives.gov/the-press-office/2013/08/15/remarks-president-situation-egypt.

79. Ruth Alexander, "Counting Crowds: Was Egypt's Uprising the Biggest Ever?," *BBC News*, July 16, 2013, https://www.bbc.com/news/magazine-23312656.

80. Interview with author, senior advisor to President Barack Obama, October 20, 2021.

81. Rhodes, *The World as It Is*, p. 206.

82. Interview with author, former State Department official, October 14, 2021. For the full transcript of what Kerry actually said, see John Kerry, "Remarks with Egyptian Foreign Minister Nabil Fahmy," Department of State, November 3, 2013, https://2009-2017.state.gov/secretary/remarks/2013/11/216220.htm.

83. Stephen McInerney and Cole Bockenfeld, "The Federal Budget and Appropriations for Fiscal Year 2016: Democracy, Governance, and Human Rights in the Middle East and North Africa," Project on Middle East Democracy, May 2015, http://pomed.org/wp-content/uploads/2015/05/FY2016-Budget-Report.pdf.

84. Jen Psaki, "U.S. Assistance to Egypt," Department of State, October 9, 2013, https://2009-2017.state.gov/r/pa/prs/ps/2013/10/215258.htm; Michael R. Gordon and Mark Landler, "In Crackdown Response, U.S. Temporarily Freezes Some Military Aid to Egypt," *New York Times*, October 9, 2013, https://www.nytimes.com/2013/10/10/world/middleeast/obama-military-aid-to-egypt.html.

85. Kerry and Fahmy, "Remarks With Egyptian Foreign Minister Nabil Fahmy," Department of State, November 3, 2013.

86. Ibid.

87. Interview with author, former senior State Department official, November 4, 2021.

88. As one White House official described it: "There were already so many disagreements and nobody wanted a break with Saudi Arabia at the time in particular because we wanted them to be more reassured because they fear a pivot to Iran" (interview with author, October 12, 2021).

Chapter 6

1. See pp. 128–132.

2. David Kirkpatrick, *Into the Hands of the Soldiers: Freedom and Chaos in Egypt and the Middle East.*

3. Ibid., 207.

4. At various points, the Trump administration considered designating the Muslim Brotherhood as a terrorist organization but ran into bureaucratic resistance. The designation process requires a threshold of evidence to be met, and one that would have been very difficult, if not impossible, to meet in this instance, for the simple reason that the Egyptian Muslim Brotherhood hadn't committed anything that could be construed as a terrorist act in decades (one would likely have to go back to the 1960s). On assessing claims that the Brotherhood is a terrorist organization, see William McCants and Benjamin Wittes, "Should the Muslim Brotherhood Be Designated a Terrorist Organization?," *Markaz*, January 20, 2017, https://www.brookings.edu/blog/markaz/2017/01/30/should-the-muslim-brotherhood-be-designated-a-terrorist-organization/; and Lawrence Pintak, "The Trump Administration's Islamophobic Holy Grail," *Foreign Policy*, February 22, 2017, https://foreignpolicy.com/2017/02/22/the-trump-administrations-islamophobic-holy-grail/.

5. Interview with author, former senior White House official, October 12, 2021.

6. Fawaz A. Gerges, *America and Political Islam: Clash of Cultures or Clash of Interests?* (New York: Cambridge University Press, 1999), p. 9.

7. See, for example, Richard P. Mitchell, *The Society of the Muslim Brothers* (London: Oxford University Press, 1969), pp. 56–58, 227; and Lia Brynjar, *The Society of the Muslim Brothers in Egypt: The Rise of an Islamic Mass Movement, 1928–1942* (Reading, UK: 1998), pp. 235–236.

8. John O. Voll, *Islam, Continuity and Change in the Modern World* (Boulder, CO: Westview Press), p. 351.

9. Fouad Ajami, *The Arab Predicament: Arab Political Thought and Practice since 1967* (Cambridge: Cambridge University Press, 1981), p. 55..

10. Interview with author, Mohamed Morsi, May 8, 2011.

11. "Munaqashat Mu'tamar Al-Aryani Ya'qabahu Ijtimaa Mohamed Morsi" [Discussion of Al-Aryani's Conference Followed by Mohamed Morsi's Meeting], Al-Jazeera, June 5, 2012, https://www.youtube.com/watch?v=zkSmIKhq_6U.

12. Emad Eldin Shahin, "The Foreign Policy of the Islamic Salvation Front in Algeria," *Islam and Christian-Muslim Relations* 14, no. 2 (2003), 121.

13. Ibid.

14. Interview with author, Muslim Brotherhood official, Doha, Qatar, November 2013.

15. *Al-Barnamaj al-Intakhabi li Murashi Hizb Jabha al-'Amal al-Islami, 2007–2011* [The electoral [rogram of the Islamic Action Front candidates], Islamic Action Front, Amman, October 2007.

16. On the relationship between the PLO and their Tunisian hosts, see, for example, Alan Cowell, "PLO, in Tunis, Is Shadow of Former Power," *New York Times*, June 24, 1987, https://www.nytimes.com/1987/06/24/world/plo-in-tunis-is-shadow-of-former-power.html.

17. Richard Boudreaux and Amberin Zaman, "Turkey Rejects U.S. Troop Deployment," *Los Angeles Times*, March 2, 2003, https://www.latimes.com/archives/la-xpm-2003-mar-02-fg-iraq2-story.html.

18. "Iraq: Turkey, the Deployment of U.S. Forces, and Related Issues," Congressional Research Service, May 2, 2003, p. 2, https://www.everycrsreport.com/files/20030502_RL31794_e7988e5adca54b642493ff4f3e7652ab376819d5.pdf.

19. Ben Rhodes, *The World As It Is: A Memoir of the Obama White House* (New York: Random House, 2018), p. 100.

20. Ibid., p. 121.

21. Steven Heydemann, "Upgrading Authoritarianism in the Arab World," Washington, DC: Brookings Institution, October 2007, https://www.brookings.edu/wp-content/uploads/2016/06/10arabworld.pdf.

22. Ibid., p. 5.

23. On what Mubarak said to President Bush during their last meeting, see Elliot Abrams, *Realism and Democracy: American Foreign Policy after the Arab Spring* (Cambridge, UK: Cambridge University Press, 2017), p. 85. On what Mubarak said to President Obama, see Philip Gordon, *Losing the Long Game: The False Promise of Regime Change in the Middle East* (New York: St. Martin's Press, 2020), p. 154.

24. See, for example, James A. Robinson, "Economic Development and Democracy," *Annual Review of Political Science* 9 (2006); Bruce Bueno de Mesquita and George W. Downs, "Development and Democracy," *Foreign Affairs*, September/October 2005, https://www-foreignaffairs-com.brookings.idm.oclc.org/articles/2005-09-01/development-and-democracy.

25. Heydemann, "Upgrading Authoritarianism in the Arab World," p. 15.

26. Interview with author, Mohamed Morsi, May 8, 2010.

27. Interview with author, Hamdi Hassan, November 26, 2010.

28. Interview with author, Dennis Ross, special assistant to President Obama, October 21, 2021.

29. Ibid.

30. Interview with author, former senior White House official, December 6, 2021.

31. "US Urges Restraint in Egypt, Says Government Stable," *Reuters*, January 25, 2011, https://www.reuters.com/article/ozatp-egypt-protest-clinton-20110125-idAFJO E70O0KF20110125.

32. Essam El-Erian, "What the Muslim Brothers Want," *New York Times*, February 9, 2011, https://www.nytimes.com/2011/02/10/opinion/10erian.html; Abdel Moneim Abou el-Fotouh, "Democracy Supporters Should Not Fear the Muslim Brotherhood," *Washington Post*, February 10, 2011, https://www.washingtonpost.com/wp-dyn/cont ent/article/2011/02/09/AR2011020906334.html.

33. Abduljalil Alsingace, "Promises Kept," *New York Times*, June 2, 2009, https://www. nytimes.com/2009/06/03/opinion/03Alsingace.html.

34. See, for example, Lee Smith, "The Kiss of Death," *Slate*, November 24, 2004, https:// slate.com/news-and-politics/2004/11/why-do-arab-reformers-claim-u-s-support-is-hurting-them.html.

35. Interview with author, Abdel Moneim Abul Futouh, August 4, 2006.

36. Jackson Diehl, "The Freedom to Describe Dictatorship," *Washington Post*, March 27, 2006, https://www.washingtonpost.com/archive/opinions/2006/03/27/the-freedom-to-describe-dictatorship/f2bbb4c2-5f6a-441b-b129-c2ac384c5a42/.

37. Interview with author, Esam al-Erian, May 12, 2010.

38. Interview with author, Muslim Brotherhood activist, May 14, 2010.

39. Interview with author, Ruheil al-Gharaibeh, June 8, 2008.

40. Mohamed Elshinnawi, "aArabs Have Negative View of the United States," Voice of America, August 8, 2010, https://www.voanews.com/a/arabs-have-negative-view-of-united-states--100279354/172232.html .

41. "Arab Spring Fails to Improve U.S. Image," Pew Research Center, May 2011, p. 37, https://www.pewresearch.org/global/wp-content/uploads/sites/2/2011/05/Pew-Glo bal-Attitudes-Arab-Spring-Topline.pdf.

42. Ibid., pp. 37, 45.

43. Raphaël Lefèvre, "A New Direction for Lebanon's Muslim Brothers," *Diwan*, February 11, 2016, Carnegie Middle East Center, https://carnegie-mec.org/diwan/62740.

44. On the somewhat embarrassing weakness of Arab armies and their basic fighting ability, see Kenneth Pollack, *Armies of Sand: The Past, Present, and Future of Arab Military Effectiveness* (New York: Oxford University Press, 2019).

45. Interview with author, Stephen Krasner, former director of policy planning at the State Department, October 21, 2021. I thank Krasner for pushing me to think through this scenario in more detail.

Chapter 7

1. Robert Kagan, "America's Crisis of Legitimacy," *Foreign Affairs*, March/April 2004; see also Kagan, "Cowboy Nation," *New Republic*, October 23, 2006.

2. Meczysław P. Boduszyński, *U.S. Democracy Promotion in the Arab World: Beyond Interests vs. Ideals* (Boulder, CO: Lynne Rienner, 2019), p. 3.

3. Interview with author, November 28, 2021.

4. The word for "dispersal" or "clearing" in Arabic, *fadd*, is onomatopoetic, evoking the sound of an unexpected thud or the staccato of a shotgun.

5. For a detailed account of diplomatic efforts to avert what became the Rabaa massacre, see David Kirkpatrick, "How American Hopes for a Deal in Egypt Were Undercut," *New York Times*, August 17, 2013, https://www.nytimes.com/2013/08/18/world/mid dleeast/pressure-by-us-failed-to-sway-egypts-leaders.html.

6. Speaking at the 2012 Manama Dialogue, then Deputy Secretary of State William Burns made a version of this point, saying, "It's important for Americans, self-absorbed as we sometimes are, to understand that the Middle East is not all about us" (William Burns, "Remarks at the Manama Dialogue," U.S. State Department, December 8, 2012, https://2009-2017.state.gov/s/d/former/burns/remarks/2012/201 701.htm).

7. Regarding would-be empires in the Middle East, the United States seems to meet David Lake's definition of an "informal" one. "When both security and economic hierarchies exist between two polities," he writes, "the relationship becomes what is commonly known as either an informal empire or, at an extreme, empire" ("Escape from the State of Nature: Authority and Hierarchy in World Politics," *International Security* 32 [Summer 2007],) 61).

8. Mieczysław Boduszyński, *US Democracy Promotion in the Arab World*, p. 4.

9. Amaney Jamal, *Of Empires and Citizens: Pro-American Democracy or No Democracy at All?* (Princeton, NJ: Princeton University Press), p. 28.

10. Sean L. Yom and Mohammad H. Al-Momani, "The International Dimensions of Authoritarian Regime Stability: Jordan in the Post–Cold War Era," *Arab Studies Quarterly* 30, no. 1 (Winter 2008), 40.

11. Ibid., 43.

12. Alexis de Tocqueville, *Democracy in America: Historical-Critical Edition of De la démocratie en Amérique*, ed. Eduardo Nolla, trans. James T. Schleifer (Indianapolis, IN: Liberty Fund, 2010), p. 97, https://www.scribd.com/document/159371658/ DeTocqueville-a-Democracy-in-America-03-En#download.

13. Eva Bellin, "The Robustness of Authoritarianism in the Middle East Exceptionalism in Comparative Perspective," *Comparative Politics* 36, no. 2 (January 2004), 143.

14. Ben Rhodes, *The World As It Is: A Memoir of the Obama White House* (New York: Random House, 2018), p. 158.

15. Interview with author, former State Department official, October 14, 2021.

16. Steven Levitsky and Lucan A. Way, *Competitive Authoritarianism: Hybrid Regimes after the Cold War* (New York: Cambridge University Press, 2010), p. 24.

17. On how the Reagan administration shifted against authoritarian allies, see Elliot Abrams, *Realism and Democracy: American Foreign Policy after the Arab Spring* (Cambridge, UK: Cambridge University Press, 2017), pp. 53–57.

18. Levitsky and Way, *Competitive Authoritarianism*, p. 24.

19. Zack Gold, "Why Israel Will Miss Morsi," *Foreign Affairs*, August 20, 2013, https://www.foreignaffairs.com/articles/egypt/2013-08-20/why-israel-will-miss-morsi.

20. See, for example, "The United States' Reaction to Egypt's November 22 Decisions," U.S. Department of State, November 23, 2012, http://www.state.gov/r/pa/prs/ps/2012/11/200983.htm; "Daily Press Briefing," U.S. Department of State, November 26, 2012, http://www.state.gov/r/pa/prs/dpb/2012/11/201015.htm.

21. As Amaney Jamal notes in *Of Empires and Citizens*: "No other region in the world shows the remarkable levels of hierarchy between the Arab world and the U.S. in terms of its security and economic needs." What does hierarchy look like in the Middle East?

22. Anne Mariel Peters and Sean L. Yom, "US Hierarchy in the Middle East," APSA 2011 Annual Meeting, August 2011, https://papers.ssrn.com/sol3/papers.cfm?abstract_id=1900426.

23. The United States does not have a formal security commitment with Saudi Arabia, but the provision of advanced weaponry, training, and technical assistances communicates to adversaries that an attack or invasion on Saudi territory would be met with American retaliation.

24. Daniel Benaim, "A Progressive Course Correction for U.S.–Saudi Relations," The Century Foundation, June 25, 2020, https://tcf.org/content/report/progressive-course-correction-u-s-saudi-relations/?agreed=1.

25. Elliot Abrams, who served as George W. Bush's deputy national security advisor, estimates that it would take Egypt ten to twenty years "to get away from American weaponry" and there would be no obvious candidate for a true shift, rather than a hypothetical one: "They could do things that tweak us but to really switch, I think, is extremely hard. The Russians don't give away things. They may give away symbolic things for free, but when it comes to $10 billion worth? No." (interview with author, November 2, 2021).

26. Eric Schmitt, "Cairo Military Firmly Hooked to U.S. Lifeline," *New York Times*, August 20, 2013, https://www.nytimes.com/2013/08/21/world/middleeast/cairo-military-firmly-hooked-to-us-lifeline.html?smid=tw-nytimesglobal&seid=auto&_r=0&pagewanted=all.

27. Joshua Hersh, "Egypt Military Sees U.S. Aid Package as Key Part of Honor-Bound Relationship," *Huffington Post*, August 21, 2013, http://www.huffingtonpost.com/2013/08/21/egypt-military-aid_n_3789668.html?utm_hp_ref=tw.

28. Interview with author, Anne Patterson, former U.S. ambassador to Egypt, November 5, 2021.

29. Interview with author, Andrew Exum, former deputy assistant secretary of defense, October 28, 2021.

30. Toby C. Jones, "Time to Disband the Bahrain-Based U.S. Fifth Fleet," *The Atlantic*, June 10, 2011, https://www.theatlantic.com/international/archive/2011/06/time-to-disband-the-bahrain-based-us-fifth-fleet/240243/.

31. Sheela Tobben and Julian Lee, "U.S. Imports No Saudi Crude Oil for First Time in 35 Years," *Bloomberg*, January 6, 2021, https://www.bloomberg.com/news/articles/2021-01-06/saudi-oil-exports-to-u-s-at-zero-for-first-time-in-35-years.

32. Michael Wahid Hanna, "Downgrading U.S.-Egyptian Relations," *Foreign Affairs*, November 2015, https://www.foreignaffairs.com/articles/egypt/2015-11-01/getting-over-egypt.

33. Michele Dunne, "The Baby, the Bathwater, and the Freedom Agenda in the Middle East," *Washington Quarterly*, January 2009, http://carnegieendowment.org/files/09jan_Dunne.pdf.

34. Michael O'Hanlon, "The U.S. Can Afford to Rethink Aid to Egypt," *Washington Post*, August 23, 2013, http://www.washingtonpost.com/opinions/access-to-suez-is-convenient-but-not-essential-for-us/2013/08/22/224a001c-09d9-11e3-9941-6711ed662e71_story.html.

35. For more on the question of U.S. leverage with Egypt, see Shadi Hamid and Peter Mandaville, "A Coup Too Far: The Case for Reordering U.S. Priorities in Egypt," Brookings Doha Center, September 2013, http://www.brookings.edu/~/media/research/files/papers/2013/09/05-us-priorities-egypt-hamid-mandaville/us_egypt-relations_english.pdf.

36. Michael Forsythe et al., "Consulting Firms Keep Lucrative Saudi Alliance, Shaping Crown Prince's Vision," *New York Times*, November 4, 2018, https://www.nytimes.com/2018/11/04/world/middleeast/mckinsey-bcg-booz-allen-saudi-khashoggi.html.

37. Annelle Sheline and Steven Simon, "Reset Overdue: Remaking U.S.-Saudi Relations," Quincy Institute for Responsible Statecraft, Washington, DC, October 2020, p. 8.

38. Ibid., p. 2.

39. Yasmine Farouk and Andrew Leber, "What's Missing in the Recalibration of the U.S.-Saudi Relationship?," Carnegie Endowment for International Peace, March 4, 2021, https://carnegieendowment.org/2021/03/04/what-s-missing-in-recalibration-of-u.s.-saudi-relationship-people-pub-84015.

40. See, for example, Amanda Taub and Max Fisher, "As Leaks Multiply, Fears of a 'Deep State' in America," *New York Times*, February 16, 2017, https://www.nytimes.com/2017/02/16/world/americas/deep-state-leaks-trump.html.

41. Faheem Hussain as quoted in Shadi Hamid, "Donald Trump vs. the 'Deep State,'" *The Atlantic*, March 7, 2017, https://www.theatlantic.com/international/archive/2017/03/deep-state-democracy/518817/.

42. Andrew Exum, former deputy assistant secretary of defense, helpfully outlines the mindset: "The things the Department of Defense is going to be on the hook for are all the security-related equities, so do we feel security in the Sinai is compromised? Are we worried about the security of the State of Israel, from its southern flank? Are we worried about our ability to have priority access to the Suez Canal? Or, are we worried about overflight rights in Egypt?" (interview with author, October 28, 2021).

43. See, for example, USCENTCOM, "Readout from Gen. Frank McKenzie's Visit with Egyptian President Abdul Fattah Al-Sisi & Chief of Staff of the Egyptian Armed Forces Lieutenant Gen. Mohamed Farid Hegazy," U.S. Central Command, February

22, 2021, https://www.centcom.mil/MEDIA/STATEMENTS/Statements-View/Arti cle/2511107/readout-from-gen-frank-mckenzies-visit-with-egyptian-president-abdul-fattah-al/.

44. Joseph A. Christoff, "Security Assistance: State and DOD Need to Assess How the Foreign Military Financing Program for Egypt Achieves U.S. Foreign Policy and Security Goals," Washington, DC, April 11, 2006, https://www.gao.gov/products/gao-06-437.

45. Sheline and Simon, "Reset Overdue," p. 10.

46. Peter Baker, "As Democracy Push Falters, Bush Feels Like a 'Dissident,'" *Washington Post*, August 20, 2007.

47. See, for example, Michael R. Gordon, "Troop 'Surge' Took Place amid Doubt and Debate," *New York Times*, August 30, 2008, https://www.nytimes.com/2008/08/31/washington/31military.html ; and Michael Fletcher and Thomas Ricks, "Experts Advise Bush Not to Reduce Troops," *Washington Post*, December 12, 2006, https://www.washingtonpost.com/archive/politics/2006/12/12/experts-advise-bush-not-to-reduce-troops-span-classbankheadpresident-looking-beyond-study-groups-planspan/8522a4f0-35cb-4fb0-a1f9-83137335cccd/.

48. Interview with author, Elliot Abrams, November 2, 2021.

49. Ibid.

50. David Kirkpatrick, *Into the Hands of the Soldiers: Freedom and Chaos in Egypt and the Middle East* (New York: Penguin Books, 2018), p. 209.

51. For an Obama administration perspective on the urgent versus the important, see Derek Chollet, *The Long Game: How Obama Defied Washington and Redefined America's Role in the World* (New York: Public Affairs, 2016), pp. xv–xvi.

52. Michael Doran, "The Nexus and the Olive Tree," *Foreign Policy*, August 22, 2011, https://foreignpolicy.com/2011/08/22/the-nexus-and-the-olive-tree-2/.

53. The phrase originates from Reagan's U.N. Ambassador Jeanne Kirkpatrick's criticism of the left at the 1984 Republican Convention. "They always blame America first," she said, insinuating that Democrats and leftists view the United States, rather than the Soviet Union and other communist regimes, as the primary source of evil in global affairs. For a transcript of Kirkpatrick's speech, see "1984, Jeanne Kirkpatrick," *CNN. com*, August 20, 1984, https://www.cnn.com/ALLPOLITICS/1996/conventions/san. diego/facts/GOP.speeches.past/84.kirkpatrick.shtml.

54. Hardy Merriman, "Theory and Dynamics of Nonviolent Action," in ed. Maria J. Stephan, *Civilian Jihad: Nonviolent Struggle, Democratization, and Governance in the Middle East* (New York: Palgrave, 2009), p. 17.

55. Erica Chenoweth and Maria J. Stephan, *Why Civil Resistance Works: The Strategic Logic of Nonviolent Conflict* (New York: Columbia University Press, 2011), p. 12.

56. Ibid., p. 15.

57. Interview with author, Abdel Rahman Ayyash, February 9, 2011.

58. Tarek Osman, "Egypt's Phantom Messiah," *OpenDemocracy*, November 7, 2006, www.opendemocracy.net/democracy-protest/egypt_massiah_3729.jsp.

59. Samer Shehata and Joshua Stacher, "The Brotherhood Goes to Parliament," Middle East Research and Information Project, Fall 2006, https://merip.org/2006/09/the-brotherhood-goes-to-parliament/.

60. Ibid.

61. "Egypt: Muslim Brotherhood Detainees Face Military Tribunals," Human Rights Watch, February 14, 2007, https://www.hrw.org/news/2007/02/14/egypt-muslim-brotherhood-detainees-face-military-tribunals.

62. Sean McCormack, "Daily Press Briefing," U.S. Department of State, May 11, 2006, https://2001-2009.state.gov/r/pa/prs/dpb/2006/66163.htm.

63. Marc Morjé Howard and Philip G. Roessler, "Liberalizing Electoral Outcomes in Competitive Authoritarian Regimes," *American Journal of Political Science* 50 (2006).

64. On the relationship between the PJD and the Moroccan monarchy, see Avi Spiegel, *Young Islam: The New Politics of Religion in Morocco and the Arab World* (Princeton, NJ: Princeton University Press, 2015).

65. Holger Albrecht and Eva Wegner, "Autocrats and Islamists: Contenders and Containment in Egypt and Morocco," *Journal of North African Studies* 11 (June 2006), pp. 132–133.

66. On the PJD's limited influence on the country's politics despite being the ruling party for an extended period, see Avi Spiegel, "Reaction Essay—Morocco," Brookings Institution, Rethinking Political Islam series, December 2015, p. 2, https://www.brookings.edu/wp-content/uploads/2016/07/Morocco_Spiegel-2.pdf.

67. Interview with Esam al-Erian, Cairo, July 16, 2008.

68. Michaelle Browers, "Origins and Architect of Yemen's Joint Meeting Parties," *International Journal of Middle East Studies* 39 (November 2007), pp. 565–586.

69. Hal Brands, *American Grand Strategy in the Age of Trump* (Washington, DC: Brookings Institution Press, 2017), p. 63.

70. Kristin Diwan, "Saudi Nationalism Raises Hopes of Greater Shia Inclusion," Arab Gulf States Institute, May 3, 2018, https://agsiw.org/saudi-nationalism-raises-hopes-greater-inclusion-shias/.

71. Robert Leiken and Steven Brooke, "The Moderate Muslim Brotherhood," *Foreign Affairs* 86 (2007).

72. Courtney Freer, ."Kedourie, nationalism, Islamism, and the *umma*," *Middle Eastern Studies*, 58:3 (March 2022).

73. Ibid.

74. Donatella Della Porta and Sidney Tarrow, "Transnational Processes and Social Activism: An Introduction," in eds. Donatella Della Porta and Sidney Tarrow, *Transnational Protest and Global Activism* (Lanham, MD: Rowman & Littlefield, 2005), p. 3.

75. See, for example, Raphael Lefevre, "Militias for the Syrian Muslim Brotherhood," *Sada*, October 29, 2013, https://carnegieendowment.org/sada/53452.

76. Abbas Kelidar, "States with Foundations: The Political Evolution of State and Society in the Arab East," *Journal of Contemporary History* 28 (April 1993).

77. Interview with author, former senior White House official, December 1, 2021.

78. Interview with author, Elliot Abrams, former deputy national security advisor, November 2, 2021.

79. Sarah Sunn Bush and Amaney A. Jamal, "Anti-Americanism, Authoritarian Politics, and Attitudes about Women's Representation: Evidence from a Survey Experiment in Jordan," *International Studies Quarterly* 59, no. 1 (March 2015).

80. Shadi Hamid and Peter Mandaville, "Bringing the United States Back into the Middle East," *Washington Quarterly*, Fall 2013, https://www.tandfonline.com/doi/abs/10.1080/0163660X.2013.861716.

Chapter 8

1. Barack Obama, *A Promised Land* (New York: Crown, 2020), p. 637.

2. Ibid., pp. 643–644.

3. Niall Ferguson, ed., *Virtual History: Alternatives and Counterfactuals* (London: Picador, 1997), p. 2.

4. Rachid Ghannouchi, "Tunisia's Democratic Future: An Address by Rached Ghannouchi," Brookings Institution, May 31, 2013, https://www.brookings.edu/events/tunisias-democratic-future-an-address-by-rached-ghannouchi/.

5. Hassan al-Banna, *Memoirs of Hasan al-Banna Shaheed* (Karachi: International Islamic, 1981), p. 127.

6. Mohammad Fadel, "Modernist Islamic Political Thought and the Egyptian and Tunisian Revolutions of 2011," *Middle East Law and Governance* 3, no. 1–2 (March 25, 2011), 9–10.

7. Olivier Roy, *The Failure of Political Islam*, trans. Carol Volk (Cambridge, MA: Harvard University Press, 1994), p. 60.

8. See Saida Ounisi, "Ennahda from Within: Islamists or 'Muslim Democrats'?," in Shadi Hamid and Will McCants, eds., *Rethinking Political Islam* (New York: Oxford University, 2017), pp. 230–238.

9. Interview with author, Noureddin Erbaoui, February 11, 2015.

10. Roy, *The Failure of Political Islam*, p. 62.

11. Simon A. Wood, *Christian Criticisms, Islamic Proofs: Rashid Rida's Modernist Defense of Islam* (Oxford: Oneworld, 2008), p. 17.

12. For a discussion of the discursive tradition in Islam, see Talal Asad, "Thinking about Tradition, Religion, and Politics in Egypt Today," *Critical Inquiry* 42, no. 1 (Autumn 2015).

13. That the scholars fell into disrepute was not necessarily a positive development, since it was an autonomous and confident clerical class that might have provided a meaningful check on an ever encroaching, centralized state. Scholars of Islam such as Noah Feldman, Wael Hallaq, and Mohammad Fadel have documented how a self-regulating clerical class provided a crucial check on the Sultan's executive power and authority. As keepers of God-given law, the clerics ensured that the caliph was bound by something beyond himself. As Feldman notes in *The Fall and Rise of the Islamic*

State: "To see the [sharia-based system] as containing the balance of powers so necessary for a functioning, sustainable legal state is to emphasize not why it failed but why it succeeded so spectacularly for as long as it did" (*The Fall and Rise of the Islamic State* [Princeton, NJ: Princeton University Press, 2008], pp. 6–7).

14. As the historian of Christianity Brad Gregory writes: "Protestants didn't just disagree on some things. They disagreed about *a lot* of things, including fundamental matters of doctrine: They disagreed about the meaning and prioritization of biblical texts, and the relationship of those texts to doctrines regarding the sacraments, worship, grace, the church, and so forth. They disagreed about the broad interpretative principles that ought to guide the understanding of scripture, such as the relationship between the Old and New Testaments or the permissibility of religious practices not explicitly prohibited or enjoined in the Bible. They disagreed about the relationship among the interpolation of scripture, the exercise of reason, and God's influence in the hearts of individual Christians. And they disagreed about whether (and if so, to what extent) explicit, substantive truth claims were even *important* to being a Christian" (*The Unintended Reformation: How a Religious Revolution Secularized Society* [Cambridge, MA: Belknap Press of Harvard University Press, 2012], p. 109).]

15. Ovamir Anjum, "Do Islamists Have an Intellectual Deficit?," in Shadi Hamid and Will McCants, eds., *Rethinking Political Islam* (New York: Oxford University Press, 2017), pp. 300–307.

16. Hassan al-Banna, "Our Message," *Collection of Epistles*, p. 5, available at http://www.masmn.org/Books/Hasan_Al_Banna/Rasail/index.htm.

17. Knut Vikør, *Between God and the Sultan: A History of Islamic Law* (Oxford: Oxford University Press, 2005), p. 66.

18. Ibid., pp. 71–72.

19. Wael B. Hallaq, *Sharīʿa: Theory, Practice, Transformations* (New York: Cambridge University Press, 2009), p. 508.

20. Vikør, *Between God and the Sultan*, p. 69.

21. Andrew March, *The Caliphate of Man: Popular Sovereignty in Modern Islamic Thought* (Cambridge, MA: Belknap Press of Harvard University Press, 2019), p. x.

22. Ibid., p. xi.

23. The General Guide is the highest-ranking official in the Egyptian Muslim Brotherhood.

24. Barbara Zollner, *The Muslim Brotherhood: Hasan al-Hudaybi and Ideology* (New York: Routledge, 2008), p. 117.

25. On divine sovereignty, see Muhammad Qasim Zaman, "Islamism and the Sovereignty of God," in *Islam in Pakistan: A History* (Princeton, NJ: Princeton University Press, 2018).

26. Andrew March, "The Problem of Popular Sovereignty in Modern Islamic Thought," *Maydan*, December 16, 2020, https://themaydan.com/2020/12/maydan-book-forum-the-caliphate-of-man/.

27. See, for example, Shadi Hamid, *Temptations of Power* (New York: Oxford University Press, 2014), pp. 92–101, 131–137.

28. Mona El-Ghobashy, "The Metamorphosis of the Egyptian Muslim Brothers," *International Journal of Middle East Studies* 37, no. 3 (August 2005), 382.

29. Interview with author, Khaled Hamza, September 7, 2009.

30. Muslim Brotherhood, "Moujiz min al-Shura fi al-Islam wa Ta'adud al-Ahzab fi al-Mujtama' al-Muslim" [Summary on Shura in Islam and Political Party Pluralism in Muslim Society], pamphlet (Cairo: Al-Markaz al-Islami li al-Darasat wa al-Buhuth, March 1994), pp. 37–38.

31. Ibid., p. 39.

32. *Mubadira al-Ikhwan al-Muslimin houl Mabadi al-Islah fi Misr* [The Initiative of the Muslim Brotherhood regarding Principles of Reform in Egypt], Cairo, March 2004.

33. Each *shu'ba*, or branch, is made of four or five *usras*, or families.

34. Interview with Khaled Hamza, October 4, 2009.

35. *Al-Barnamaj al-Intikhabi li al-Ikhwan al-Muslimin fi al-Intakhabat al-Tashri'iya* [The Electoral Program of the Muslim Brotherhood in the Legislative Elections], Cairo, November 2005.

36. Ibid.

37. Gamal Essam el-Din, "Brotherhood Steps into the Fray," *Al-Ahram Weekly*, March 11–17, 2004.

38. Khairat El-Shatir, "No Need to Be Afraid of Us," *The Guardian*, November 22, 2005, https://www.theguardian.com/world/2005/nov/23/comment.mainsection.

39. Interview with author, Mazhar Bagli, February 20, 2015.

40. For a discussion of liberalism's non-neutrality, see Stanley Fish, "Mission Impossible: Settling the Just Bounds between Church and State," *Columbia Law Review* 97 (1997), p. 2266; and Lenn Goodman, "The Road to Kazanistan," *American Philosophical Quarterly* 45 (April 2008), 85.

41. Fish, "Mission Impossible," p. 2256.

42. Interview with author, Ibrahim Kalin, February 20, 2015.

43. Sebnem Arsu, "Premier of Turkey Seeks Limits on Abortions," *New York Times*, May 29, 2012, http://www.nytimes.com/2012/05/30/world/europe/turkish-premier-calls-for-more-abortion-restrictions.html.

44. Interview with author, senior AKP official, February 20, 2015.

45. Hasanayn Tawfiq Ibrahim and Hoda Raghib Awad, *al-Dawr al-Siyasi li Jama'a al-Ikhwan al-Muslimin fi Dhil al-Ta'adudiya al-Siyasiya al-Muqayada fi Misr* [The Political Role of the Muslim Brotherhood under Limited Political Pluralism in Egypt] (Cairo: Markaz al-Mahrusa, 1996), p. 364.

46. Marion Boulby, *The Muslim Brotherhood and the Kings of Jordan, 1945–1993* (Atlanta: Scholars Press, 1999).

47. *Jordan Times*, April 2, 1991.

48. *Jordan Times*, March 23, 1991.

49. *Jordan Times*, May 19, 1990.

50. *Jordan Times*, September 14, 1996.

51. *Jordan Times*, May 23–24, 1991.

52. Ibid.

53. Ibid.

54. *Jordan Times*, May 11, 1991.

55. *Jordan Times*, May 23–24, 1991.

56. For more on the sharia synchronization project, see Hamid, *Temptations of Power*, pp. 65–66.

57. It was in 1940 that Sadat met Hassan al-Banna for the first time. Sadat recounts the sense of mystery that enveloped Banna. Sadat left their meeting overwhelmed, his admiration for Banna "unbounded." The man was "like a saint," Sadat recalled. "It seemed strange to me but here was a theologian with a sense of reality, a man of religion who recognized the facts." The two men—Banna was thirty-four and Sadat only twenty-two—met regularly for two years and developed a close friendship (Anwar el-Sadat, *In Search of Identity* [New York: Harper & Row, 1977],) p. 22; and Anwar el-Sadat, *Revolt on the Nile* [New York: John Day, 1957], p. 29).]

58. Mohammad al-Taweel, *Al-Ikhwan fi al-Parliman* [The Muslim Brotherhood in Parliament], (Cairo: al-Maktab al-Masri al-Hadith, 1992), p. 66. Translations of excerpts from this book are my own.

59. Ibid., p. 77.

60. Ibid., p. 72.

61. Joel Gordon, "The False Hopes of 1950: The Wafd's Last Hurrah and the Demise of Egypt's Old Order," *International Journal of Middle East Studies* 21 (May 1989): 194, https://www.jstor.org/stable/pdf/163074.pdf?refreqid=excelsior%3A47d59bc4f849f5004f398fe0b175f75d.

62. Al-Taweel, *Al-Ikhwan fi al-Parliman*, p. 74.

63. Pew Research Center, "The World's Muslims: Unity and Diversity," August 9, 2012, pp. 131, 201, http://www.pewforum.org/Muslim/the-worlds-muslims-unity-and-diversity.aspx.

64. Joseph Liow, "Southeast Asia," in Shadi Hamid and Will McCant, eds., *Rethinking Political Islam* (New York: Oxford University Press, 2017), p. 186.

65. Robin Bush, "Regional Syari'ah Regulations: Anomaly or Symptom?," in Greg Fealy and Sally White, eds., *Expressing Islam: Religious Life and Politics in Indonesia* (Singapore: Institute of Southeast Asian Studies, 2008), pp. 3–4, 11, https://asiafoundation.org/resources/pdfs/ShariaRegulations08RobinBush.pdf.

66. Ibid., p. 7.

67. Liow, "Southeast Asia," *Rethinking Political Islam*, p. 185.

68. Avi Spiegel, "Morocco," in Shadi Hamid and Will McCants, eds., *Rethinking Political Islam* (New York: Oxford University Press, 2017), p. 69.

69. David Patel, "Reaction Essay—Jordan," Brookings Institution, Rethinking Political Islam series, December 2015, https://www.brookings.edu/wp-content/uploads/2016/07/Jordan_Patel.pdf.

70. Richard Rose and Doh Chull Shin, "Democratization Backwards: The Problem of Third-Wave Democracies," *British Journal of Political Science* 31 (April 2011), 332.

71. Ibid.

72. Fareed Zakaria, *The Future of Freedom: Illiberal Democracy at Home and Abroad* (New York: W.W Norton, 2003), p. 124.

73. Michael Bailey and David Braybrooke, "Robert A. Dahl's Philosophy of Democracy, Exhibited in His Essays," *Annual Review of Political Science* 6 (2003), 99–118.

74. "Sukuk It and See," *The Economist*, April 19, 2013, http://www.economist.com/blogs/pomegranate/2013/04/egypt-finance.

75. Jenny B. White, "The Turkish Complex," *American Interest*, February 2, 2015, http://www.the-american-interest.com/2015/02/02/the-turkish-complex/.

76. Tarek Amara and Erika Solomon, "Analysis: Tunisia Eyes 'Egypt Scenario' after Assembly Freeze," *Reuters*, August 7, 2013, https://www.reuters.com/article/us-tunisia-crisis-government-analysis/analysis-tunisia-eyes-egypt-scenario-after-assembly-freeze-idUSBRE9760XK20130807.

77. Nissaf Slama, "'Irhal' Campaign Attempts to Oust Ennahda Officials," *Tunisia Live*, August 14, 2013. .

Chapter 9

1. Ruth Grant, *Hypocrisy and Integrity: Machiavelli, Rousseau, and the Ethics of Politics* (Chicago: University of Chicago Press, 1997), p. 1.

2. The Qur'an, Al-Nisaa' 4:145.

3. As one prophetic hadith states: "If you trust him, he proves to be dishonest."

4. "11: Jihad," *Sunnah*. Retrieved from https://sunnah.com/bulugh/11.

5. John Kane, "American Values or Human Rights? U.S. Foreign Policy and the Fractured Myth of Virtuous Power," *Presidential Studies Quarterly* 33 (December 2003), 780.

6. The White House, "Fact Sheet Conventional Arms Transfer Policy," February 17, 1995, https://fas.org/asmp/atwg/clinton/pdd-34.html.

7. Judith Shklar, *Ordinary Vices* (Cambridge, MA: Belknap Press, 1985).

8. Suzanne Dovi, "Making the World Safe for Hypocrisy?," *Polity* 34 (Autumn 2001), 5–6.

9. Stephen Krasner, *Sovereignty: Organized Hypocrisy* (Princeton, NJ: Princeton University Press, 1999).

10. Henry Farrell and Martha Finnemore, "Hypocrisy Is a Useful Tool in Foreign Affairs. Trump Is Too Crude to Play the Game," *Washington Post*, November 5, 2018, https://www.washingtonpost.com/outlook/2018/11/05/hypocrisy-is-useful-tool-foreign-affairs-trump-is-too-crude-play-game/.

11. Judith N. Shklar, "The Phenomenology: Beyond Morality," *Western Political Quarterly* 27 (December 1974), 611.

12. William Raspberry, "In Praise of Hypocrisy," *Washington Post*, October 5, 1984, https://www.washingtonpost.com/archive/politics/1984/10/05/in-praise-of-hypocrisy/20e75377-9d6e-4e6f-a08d-efa1b3aeb055/.

13. Seymour Martin Lipset, *American Exceptionalism: A Double-Edged Sword* (New York: W.W. Norton, 1996), p. 18.

14. Samuel Goldman, *After Nationalism: Being American in an Age of Division* (Philadelphia: University of Pennsylvania Press, 2021).

Chapter 10

1. Martin Luther King Jr., "Our God Is Marching On!," March 25, 1965, Martin Luther King, Jr. Research and Education Institute, https://kinginstitute.stanford.edu/our-god-marching.

2. "Transcript of Barack Obama's Victory Speech," *NPR*, November 5, 2008, https://www.npr.org/templates/story/story.php?storyId=96624326.

3. David A. Graham, "The Wrong Side of 'The Right Side of History,'" *The Atlantic*, December 21, 2015, https://www.theatlantic.com/politics/archive/2015/12/obama-right-side-of-history/420462/.

4. Ibid.

5. Damir Marusic, "How Liberal Triumphalism Breeds Passivity," *Wisdom of Crowds*, June 4, 2021, https://wisdomofcrowds.live/how-liberal-triumphalism-breeds-passivity/.

Index

For the benefit of digital users, indexed terms that span two pages (e.g., 52–53) may, on occasion, appear on only one of those pages.